W9-BWM-125

Morgan's Raiders

Morgan's Raiders

by

DEE ALEXANDER BROWN

KONECKY&KONECKY

Konecky & Konecky
156 Fifth Avenue
New York, NY 10010

Copyright © 1959 by Dee Alexander Brown

Reprinted by special arrangement by William S. Konecky
Associates, Inc.

ISBN 0-914427-79-2

All rights reserved

Printed in the United States of America

For
TWO GRANDFATHERS

ACKNOWLEDGMENTS

The writing of this book was made possible only through the co-operation of a number of archivists, librarians and students of the Civil War, who generously offered their resources and knowledge for my use. Among those I am most indebted to are Dr. Lawrence Thompson and Miss Jacqueline Bull of the University of Kentucky Library, Lexington; Miss Frances Coleman, Librarian of the Kentucky State Historical Society, Frankfort; Mrs. Dorothy Thomas Cullen and Miss Mabel C. Weeks, Filson Club, Louisville; J. Winston Coleman, Winburn Farm, Lexington, amiable historian of the Bluegrass; Mrs. Julian Elliott, hostess at Hopemont, Lexington; the peripatetic Richard B. Harwell, who patiently unknotted some problems from his encyclopedic store of Confederate history; A. H. Packe, Burnham, Bucks, England, who supplied a photograph and useful information concerning George St. Leger Grenfell; John Rogers, who assisted in searching out many obscure facts; Icko Iben, archivist and guardian of old newspapers, University of Illinois, Urbana; and Mrs. Gertrude Morton Parsley, reference librarian, Tennessee State Library and Archives, Nashville.

Contents

Morgan's Raiders

1

Kentucky Boys Are
Alligator Horses

I

AT DUSK the town of Lexington was quiet, the gas lamps not yet lighted, and only an occasional horseman was moving along tree-shaded Main Street. From the Lexington Rifles' armory at the corner of Main and Upper streets, passers-by could hear the tramp of marching feet and the hoarse calls of a drillmaster, but the sounds were familiar ones. For the past two or three years the Rifles had been drilling regularly twice a week. Although a month had passed since the pro-Union state government ordered this militia company's members to pack their rifles and ship them to Frankfort, the men continued their semi-weekly meetings, drilling without arms.

The day was September 20, 1861, the soft air of the dying Blue-grass summer deceptive of the time. After months of indecision, of uneasy neutrality, Kentucky was about to enter the Civil War.

During the past eighteen hours events had moved swiftly in Lexington. At midnight of the nineteenth, a regiment marched in from the Federal recruiting post at Camp Dick Robinson, twenty-five miles away, and occupied the Lexington fairgrounds. All day of the twentieth, rumors ran through the town that the Federal commander had issued orders to arrest certain members of the Lexington Rifles, including the company's commander, Captain John Hunt Morgan.

Morgan had been flying a Confederate flag over his hemp and wool factory since the fall of Fort Sumter in April, and most of his military subordinates made no effort to conceal their preference for the Confederate cause.

Sometime that afternoon, Captain Morgan dispatched notes to the most trusted members of the Rifles, and in a hurried meeting revealed to those not in the secret that he had not shipped the company's arms to Frankfort after all. The packing cases which some of them had helped to make ready for shipment actually had been filled with stones. The rifles were concealed in the armory and in the homes of the members.

The time had come, Captain Morgan informed them, to leave Lexington and join the Confederate forces. He had information that Kentucky's own Confederate leader, General Simon Bolivar Buckner, had marched up from Tennessee, occupying Bowling Green with five thousand soldiers. From Bowling Green an advance force was moving north to form a Confederate line along Green River, and that was where Captain Morgan would march his Lexington Rifles, a little more than a hundred miles to the southwest.

"We then and there took an oath," one of the Riflemen recalled afterward, "to stand by our arms till death."

And so at dusk they gathered at the armory on Main Street, a dozen or so going through the drills in which they were so proficient, stamping boots firmly on the hard flooring, the drillmaster's voice more strident than usual. At the same time, others were busy in the alley entranceway where two farm wagons piled high with hay were drawn up, the drivers dressed in country jeans. At each end of the alley, guards loitered with a pretended indifference belying the alertness in their eyes, ready to signal any hint of danger—the approach of a stranger, a known Union sympathizer, or a blue-clad soldier from the camp at the fairgrounds.

The men in the armory slipped rifles outside to the wagons where they were buried deep in the hay. When the last weapon was safely packed aboard, the alley guards signaled all clear and the wagons moved out into Main Street. The gas lamps had been lit now against the darkness which bore a hint of autumn chill, a faint scent of autumn smoke. They passed a few Federal soldiers, in town from the fairgrounds to see the sights before taps sounded. After weeks of drilling in the back country at Camp Dick Robinson, the blue-coated soldiers strolling on the brick sidewalks were not interested in a pair of hay wagons rumbling along the hard-packed earth of Main Street.

Entrusted with this first dangerous mission of a militia company which later would form the nucleus of the 2nd Kentucky Cavalry Regiment, Confederate States Army, were Sergeants Henry Elder and William R. Jones, Corporal Tom Logwood, and Privates Tom Howe and Bowlin Roberts. They turned south on the turnpike, heading west for Versailles.

Somewhere along the way they were overtaken by Captain Morgan and about a dozen Riflemen who had remained behind in the armory for a while to continue the deception of drilling. These men were all mounted. Being from the horse country of Kentucky they had already made up their minds they would serve the Confederacy as cavalrymen. They had cartridge boxes belted on their backs and when they reached the wagons they armed themselves with rifles. Already they considered themselves soldiers of the Confederate States of America.

Around midnight the party crossed the Kentucky River at Shryock's Ferry, and as dawn began breaking over the misted, rolling hills they reached their first prearranged stop, pulling the wagons into the barn of one of Captain Morgan's trusted friends.

After making certain that all was secure, Morgan turned back to Lexington to round up other men he was certain would be eager to join his expedition.

Throughout the day, Logwood, Elder, Howe, Jones, Roberts and the others remained concealed in the barn with their wagons and horses, eating good food brought them by their host, resting in the hay and trying to sleep against the excitement of the past night's ride. They talked, joked, and in lapses of silence, they thought and wondered on what was happening to them.

They were all young, most of them a full decade or more younger than their captain, John Morgan, who was thirty-six, a veteran of the War with Mexico. Few were interested in politics, as Morgan was. To his young followers the Civil War was a part of the natural fabric of their lives; it had come upon them as slowly and inevitably as summer turning to winter, gradual as time.

When John Morgan organized the Rifles back in 1857, about fifty young men joined up for fun, excitement, and perhaps the prestige of the company's gay green uniforms. Almost immediately, the Rifles were much in demand for parties and picnics. In August, 1858, the *Kentucky Statesman* reported a visit of the company to Crab Orchard Springs, a fashionable watering place of the day, noting particularly "their bright and shining uniforms, tail coats, braided trousers, cross-belts and fancy headgear."

The following summer, with John Brown's abolitionist raid only a few weeks away in the future, the *Lexington Observer & Reporter* took note of the Rifles' presence at Blue Lick Springs. "We are certain that a finer body of men never shouldered a musket—a beautiful uniform, well drilled, and being composed of young and handsome gentlemen, we should advise all beautiful 'young sixteens' at the Springs to guard well their hearts, or perchance some of them will become attached to the 'Rifles' and be persuaded to learn the 'infantry tactics.' "

After John Brown's raid at Harpers Ferry in 1859, Kentucky organized a state guard, composed of local militia companies, and the Lexington Rifles had the honor of being named Company A of the 1st Regiment. Captain Morgan reported to Governor Beriah Magoffin that he had fifty guns and sixty men ready for duty. But there was to be no immediate call for their services. Radical abolitionist sentiment being scarce in Kentucky, local controversies centered mainly on fine points of states' rights questions, and as 1860 moved into 1861, the Bluegrass remained a comparatively calm center in the raging national storm. Kentucky's leaders generally agreed on the aim of preserving peace.

Then came Fort Sumter, a cold shock of reality, startling the many Kentucky families with close blood ties in the deep South. When President Lincoln called for volunteers, Governor Magoffin replied: "Kentucky will furnish no troops for the wicked purpose of subduing her sister Southern States." The legislature, eager to preserve neutrality, approved the Governor's decision 89 to 4, and a sudden quietness fell over the state.

Neutrality became the popular standard. The word "secession" had not yet become a malediction, Kentuckians recalling that New England radicals had proposed secession for that section as recently as 1857. Peace advocates from both parties seriously proposed a separate confederacy of border states—Kentucky, Virginia, and Missouri—to secede and form a buffer nation between North and South to keep the peace.

In the early summer, General Buckner, then still commanding Kentucky's state guard, met with General George B. McClellan and received a promise that Kentucky's neutrality would be observed by the United States military authorities. For a time, all but a few hotbloods relaxed in Kentucky; the state lived under the illusion of neutrality.

Too much was happening, however, everywhere around them, portentous events involving relatives and friends beyond their peaceful borders. Late in July they heard the news from Bull Run; the Confederacy had won the first round.

Almost immediately, hundreds of young men began enlisting for service outside the state. Kentucky might remain neutral, but they would organize local companies and offer their services to Virginia and Tennessee. So many volunteered that Richmond sent word the Confederacy would accept no more from Kentucky—unless the men could furnish their own arms.

As a counter to this wave of Confederate volunteering, Union sympathizers established the recruiting camp for Federal enlistments at Camp Dick Robinson. Union representatives carefully pointed out that the volunteers at Dick Robinson were not an invading force, merely recruits, but Confederate sympathizers claimed the camp's presence was a violation of the state's neutrality.

Events moved swiftly. The first week in September, General Leonidas Polk led a Confederate force from Tennessee to Columbus, Kentucky. "A military necessity," Polk telegraphed Governor Magoffin, "for the defense of Tennessee." As a countermove, a Federal General few had heard of at that time occupied Paducah. The General's name was Ulysses S. Grant.

On September 10, the Confederate War Department ordered Albert Sidney Johnston—a Kentuckian—to command of all forces in the western theater, and by mid-September General Felix Zollicoffer had advanced from Tennessee into the Cumberland Mountain passes of Kentucky. Meanwhile, the state's guard commander, Simon Buckner, had gone over to the Confederate Army, organizing a division of Kentuckians in Tennessee.

One of Sidney Johnston's first orders sent Buckner's Kentuckians marching up to Bowling Green. And thus the Confederates established their first western defense line in neutral Kentucky, a three-hundred-mile front running from the Mississippi River east to the Cumberland Mountains. It was a line thinly held by twenty-five thousand amateur soldiers, but it was a military line, and not only was Kentucky now in the war, it had become a battleground.

2

As soon as darkness fell on their first day out of Lexington, the members of the Rifles hidden in the barn near the Kentucky River resumed their journey westward. Somewhere between Bloomfield and Bardstown, they halted at another prearranged camp in the woods.

This was a neighborhood largely pro-Confederate, and the residents welcomed the young men as heroes. Because these friendly people refused pay for food and supplies brought into camp, some wag in the company named the place "Camp Charity."

Captain Morgan, after narrowly escaping arrest in Lexington, soon joined them, bringing in additional recruits. For five days Camp Charity was a busy place, new recruits coming in almost hourly, the "veterans" making secret journeys by night to obtain additional ammunition, weapons, horses, and whatever gear they felt a man would require for a short war. There was practically no organization, no commander other than Captain Morgan—who was away much of the time on various missions—to enforce discipline, and life at Camp Charity resembled a summer outing much more than a recruiting station.

Most of these young men came from leading Kentucky families, and by the time the 2nd Cavalry Regiment—of which they were the cadre—was formed, many familiar names of the South would be represented on its muster rolls. Undoubtedly they considered themselves cavaliers in the old meaning of the word, certain of their invincibility, overconfident by nature, rash, impetuous, romantic, poetic, sentimental, imbued with the spirit of clanship. They were certain their homeland was "the best place outside of heaven the Good Lord ever made," but they were no more provincial than other Americans of that day, no more so than their opponents who felt the same way about their particular states or regions.

James Lane Allen, who was later to write of the Bluegrass of that time, was too young to join the cavalry, but his older brother was in the 2nd Kentucky, and the younger Allen knew these men well. They were possessed, he said, "of that old invincible race ideal of personal liberty, and that old, unreckoning, truculent, animal rage at whatever infringes on it . . . the old sense of personal privacy and reserve which has for centuries entrenched the Englishman in the heart of his estate." For they were of English blood, most of them, "usually of the blond type, robust, well-formed, with clear, fair complexion."

If any one of them had asked himself, or been asked, why he was at Camp Charity, he would likely have replied in the romantic language of the time and place, speaking of duty, home, honor and family. They had inherited a traditional distrust of the North, too, running back to the time of the War of 1812, as Timothy Flint noticed in 1816, "a jealousy, almost a hatred of Yankees, prevailed among the mass of this people, during the late war . . . much of this feeling still existing . . . the manner in which the slave question is agitated, keeps the embers glowing under the ashes." The observant Yankee, Flint, was generous enough to admit that Kentuckians were "a high-minded people, and possess the stamina of a noble character . . . scions from a noble stock—descendants of planters of Virginia and North Carolina . . . they seem to feel that they have an hereditary claim to command, place, and observance."

Even Timothy Flint might have been surprised at how long and deep this distrust of Northerners was to run among Kentucky cavaliers. One of Morgan's young followers, a devout Presbyterian, described New England as "the land of intolerant Puritans, the home of witchcraft, the cradle of isms from abolitionism to free-love-isms." Whether they were interested in politics or not, they were aware of the Supreme Court's decision in the Dred Scott case, and as the Civil War approached they generally considered radical Northerners as flouters of the law of the land because they refused to accept the court's decision that slaves were property. And it was not unusual in Kentucky to hear a pro-Southern man refer to Lincoln's call for troops as a "rebellion" that probably would have to be put down.

One may grasp the wide gulf that lay between these young cavaliers and the men they were preparing to fight from a letter written by General William T. Sherman in the midst of the struggle. Sherman was writing to Major General H. W. Halleck about the varying types of Southerners: "The young bloods of the South, sons of planters, lawyers about towns, good billiard players, and sportsmen—men who never did work nor never will. War suits them, and the rascals are brave; fine riders, bold to rashness, and dangerous subjects in every sense. They care not a *sou* for niggers, land, or anything. They hate Yankees *per se*, and don't bother their brains about the past, present, or future. As long as they have good horses, plenty of forage, and an open country, they are happy. This is a larger class than most men supposed, and are the most dangerous set of men which this war has turned loose upon the world. They are splendid riders, shots, and utterly reckless. Stuart, John Morgan, Forrest, and Jackson are the types and leaders of this class. This class of men must all be killed or employed by us before we can hope for peace. They have no property or future, and therefore cannot be influenced by anything except personal considerations."

Sherman's views may or may not have been representative of other Federal generals' opinions. Certainly Kentuckians could not be typed, no more so than any other Americans. Since they thought of themselves as being different from others, as cavaliers, more likely the image took the form of the frontiersman ideal—a Daniel Boone-Davy Crockett type, the trusty rifleman hero of the Dark and Bloody Ground.

After the Battle of New Orleans in 1814, Samuel Woodworth, author of "The Old Oaken Bucket," wrote a song for the heroes, "The Hunters of Kentucky":

> We are a hardy freeborn race,
>   Each man to fear a stranger,
> Whate'er the game, we join in chase,
>   Despising toil and danger;
> And if a daring foe annoys,
>   Whate'er his strength and forces,
> We'll show him that Kentucky boys
>   Are "Alligator horses."

These verses hold the key to Camp Charity's reason for existence. Each man there believed himself to be a member of a special free-born race, with an inbred disregard for personal danger, a readiness to join in a hard chase against any annoying foe, and a sureness they would endure to victory because "Kentucky boys are Alligator horses."

Any attempt to consider these men as Cavaliers engaged against Roundhead Puritans fails at the outset. Almost every "Cavalier" family in Kentucky was divided by the war; there were knights, squires, and yeomen on both sides. "My parents are opposed to my going into the army and opposed to my politics," wrote James B. McCreary, one of Morgan's officers who in later life became a Governor of Kentucky. "God knows I love them dearly and as their only son I would have remained at home their comforter and the solace of their declining years, but I cannot stay in peace and I believe it my solemn duty to assist in hurling back oppression and ruin from people of whom I am a part."

Three of Henry Clay's grandsons went to the Union, four to the Confederacy. The Crittenden family was likewise split. Robert Breckinridge had two sons in the Union Army, two in the Confederate. George D. Prentice went through the war a staunch Union editor of the *Louisville Journal* while his two sons were fighting for the cause he hated, one of them in the 2nd Kentucky Cavalry Regiment. Mary Todd Lincoln, late of Lexington, had a brother who was in the Confederate Army. The list is long.

If the Lexington Rifles were bluebloods, so were their rivals, the Lexington Chasseurs, a militia company commanded by Sanders Bruce, who was John Morgan's brother-in-law. Bruce and Morgan were good friends during the prewar years. They owned race horses in partnership, and each visited regularly in the other's home. But when the war came, Sanders Bruce joined the Union Army, taking many of the Chasseurs with him.

The Morgan brothers were exceptions—John, Calvin, Richard, Charlton, Tom, and Key—clinging together as a feudal clan. (And there were Morgan cousins and nephews who would fight and die with the 2nd Kentucky.) The oldest, John, was the complex personality of the clan, outwardly easygoing, soft-voiced, more courteous to his inferiors than to equals or superiors, a lax disciplinarian, subject to alternate moods of despondency and elation.

When John was twenty-one in 1846, he and nineteen-year-old Calvin enlisted for the Mexican War. John returned with the rank of captain, and if his friends thought his war experiences had destroyed his taste for civil pursuits they were soon reassured. He established a hemp factory and a woolen mill, importing thousands of pounds of raw wool all the way from New Mexico to be processed in the plant.

In 1848, he married Sanders Bruce's sister, Rebecca, but their life was marred by tragedy, the death of their young son. His friends believed that the reason why Morgan waited five months to offer his services to the Confederacy was the illness of his wife, whose brother's sympathies were with the Union. After Rebecca's death in July, 1861, Morgan immediately began arranging his affairs so that he would be free for Confederate military service.

Six feet tall, weighted at about 185 pounds, bearded with a Van Dyke—when he was seated in his saddle with his keen gray-blue eyes flashing fire, Captain Morgan was the very model of a cavalier. It is doubtful, however, if even his most devoted followers would have described John Morgan as an alligator horse. He was too fond of luxurious living; he preferred feather beds to blankets on the ground. Besides, he had been born in Alabama, and only Kentucky boys are alligator horses.

3

On their foraging expeditions out of Camp Charity in search of requirements for their short war, a few of the Lexington Riflemen who owned slaves made arrangements for their body servants to join them at the secret rendezvous. Not many of Morgan's men, however, were to keep their servants with them throughout the war. While it was not too difficult for an infantryman to retain a servant in camp, raiding cavalrymen with temporary bases, at best, found it almost impossible to do so.

To keep a servant close at hand, a cavalryman had to support two horses, and as the war wore on it became increasingly difficult to keep one serviceable mount, virtually impossible to ration two men and two horses. A few officers, however, managed to retain their personal servants to the end, and it was typical of the Morgan clan that its surviving members were still encumbered with their faithful Negro attendants—dressed in captured blue Yankee uniforms—on the very day they surrendered.

In 1861, slavery was a dying institution in Kentucky, and probably would have been outlawed long before but for the continual pressures of abolitionists from outside the state. As early as 1833, the legislature enacted a law prohibiting further importation of slaves into Kentucky, and another law forbade the separation of slave families by selling them singly. As James Lane Allen explained it: "the general conscience of Kentuckians was always troubled" over the question of human bondage, but they were implacable enemies of "the agitators of forcible and immediate emancipation . . . they resented any interference with their own affairs, and believed the abolitionists' measures inexpedient for the peace of society."

They particularly resented Northern attempts to make the South a scapegoat for the national sin of slavery, and were quick to reply to abolitionists from New England that it was their own people who had established the diabolical institution—the Yankee slave traders who had made their fortunes trading Africans to Southerners after it was discovered that slavery was unprofitable in New England.

In the Bluegrass, the average slaveholder owned no more than six or eight slaves. The plantation system of the deep South did not exist here, the farms being small with much of the land in meadows and woodland. Life was slow and leisurely, the slaves usually being considered a part of the owner's family, oftentimes given opportunities to earn money with which to buy their freedom.

Even the critical Harriet Beecher Stowe, author of *Uncle Tom's*

Cabin, was aware of the Kentuckians' light attitude toward the institution. "The mildest form of the system of slavery," she said, "is to be seen in the State of Kentucky."

And so it was that a Kentucky Confederate could leave his farm, his home, his wife and children, with all the confidence in the world, knowing that crops would be planted and harvested, livestock tended, buildings kept in order. If he worried at all, it was not about the loyalty of his slaves, it was what the marauding abolitionist Yankees might do to them.

4

By September 26, the Lexington Rifles and the other recruits who had slipped away from Lexington and neighboring towns numbered almost two hundred men. Only about twenty of the Riflemen were mounted, most of them on blooded Bluegrass horses, but they had acquired several additional wagons to transport their assembled supplies, and the additional volunteers were prepared to march on foot.

Midafternoon of that day, Captain Morgan gave the order to march out, and they turned southwest toward Green River and the Confederate outposts. "We threw out scouts," said Tom Berry, one of the Riflemen, "with videttes in front and on each flank, with a rear guard, so as not to be surprised by any enemy." Few other Confederate units of that early period of the war in the West had the experience brought by these Riflemen, with their four years of drilling and of studying military evolutions and tactics. Their knowledge lent polish to the march column.

They moved on into the night, into the darkness of the wooded hills below Bardstown. When the alert forward scouts saw fires burning ahead, they sent back a warning of enemy campfires. The column halted, forming in line of battle, but closer investigation revealed the flames as only autumn forest fires burning in the underbrush.

At daybreak the main body entered the turnpike running south to Munfordville. A few minutes later gunfire sounded from the advance scouts' position. Immediately, Captain Morgan ordered the column's pace quickened. A small force of home guards, loyal to the Union, had fired on the scouts, but the unexpected Confederate squad galloping down upon them sent the guards scattering into the woods.

This was the only incident of the march. No blood was shed, but it was a memorable occasion. The Lexington Rifles had exchanged their first shots of the war.

5

While Captain Morgan was marching his column south toward Munfordville, a former officer of the Lexington Rifles was riding north into Kentucky from Tennessee, on the Louisville & Nashville Railroad. The officer was Lieutenant Basil Duke, and his future association with the organization—as it developed into the 2nd Kentucky Cavalry—was to be so close and of such duration that the regiment was often referred to in official reports as Duke's Cavalry rather than by its numbered designation.

A slightly-built young man of only twenty-three, Basil Duke had been engaged in the war almost from its beginning in Missouri, where he had gone to practice law after his graduation from Transylvania College in Lexington. He was in the vanguard of a number of Kentuckians who had left home to make their fortunes, and who were now returning to offer their services against what they considered an invasion of their native state. They were coming from as far away as California and Texas, hundreds of alligator horses who had followed the frontier star as naturally as their fathers had followed it long ago into Kentucky.

As Duke's train rattled northward into Kentucky, he must have reflected on the swift changes that had come over his homeland since his last visit there early in the summer. When he was in Lexington in June—to marry Henrietta Morgan, John Morgan's sister—the talk had been of neutrality. Life in the Bluegrass had seemed the same as always, the old congeniality and hospitality— soft-voiced males talking of horse trades and fox hunts, of shooting matches and cockfights—beautiful women living graciously in their spacious lofty-ceilinged houses with spiral staircases and rich mahogany woods, candelabras and great fireplaces with imposing carved mantels, drawing rooms and well-stocked libraries.

He loved it all, this land where every child old enough to ride had his horse and dog, every boy his gun. He loved the long vistas before the country houses, each with a winding drive approaching, and the trees—great oaks, hickories, walnuts, ash, and sugar maple. The air seemed always soft in the Bluegrass, the lines of the country soft and curving as a woman's, the pastures in certain lights and seasons a dusty bluish-green.

Perhaps more than any of the young men whom he was to lead through four years of war, Basil Duke came closest to being a true Cavalier. One of his relatives described him as "essentially a man of the Seventeenth Century, that century in half-armor, torn between chivalry and realism." Gravely remote, with deep-set eyes and a square jaw covered with a rich black beard, he attracted respect without raising his resonant voice. Duke once described a cavalier as a man who was "not only absolutely true to principle and conviction, but a strong strain of romantic sentiment pervaded his character, making him sensitive to everything he regarded as an obligation, either of honor or friendship," adding almost as an afterthought: "He liked the hazard and excitement of battle."

This might very well have been a description of John Morgan or of Basil Duke himself, though no two men could scarcely have been more different in temperament. Perhaps the essential difference was that Morgan could not qualify as an alligator horse, while Duke for all his gentility and chivalry was to prove himself to be tougher and more enduring than the hardiest of that legendary breed.

At Munfordville, the brothers-in-law met for the first time since Basil Duke's marriage to Henrietta Morgan. "Captain Morgan," Duke recorded, "was riding Black Bess when I met him at Munfordville in the early part of October."

2

Green River Cavaliers

I

WHEN CAPTAIN JOHN MORGAN marched his column into a Confederate outpost at Green River on the last day of September, the new arrivals were greeted with rousing cheers. Colonel Roger Hanson, in command of the small force already there, was an old friend, having served with Morgan in the Mexican War, and the two men quickly reached an understanding. Hanson's soldiers were infantrymen; the only horses in camp were a few heavy animals attached to a battery of artillery pieces. So it was agreed that those of Morgan's "cavalrymen" who were dismounted for lack of horses would serve with Hanson's infantry companies until such time as they might procure mounts for cavalry service.

Within a few days, Morgan's small unit of mounted men was acting as Hanson's advance picket force. Learning that a company of Federals had pushed down from Elizabethtown, they scouted up to Nolin Creek one day and had their first brush with some well-armed Federal infantrymen.

Morgan's men saw the enemy's bayonets glistening above a little rise in the road before they saw the troops, and with smooth precision immediately dismounted and posted themselves in thickets on either side the road, sending horse-holders to the rear, as prescribed in their military manuals. Everything went according to the books until the Federals came within firing range.

29

From that moment on, said one of the scouts, "every man acted as his own commander." At the first fire, the Federals deployed to the flanks and opened a volley upon the Confederate ambush. Basil Duke described the encounter as being "much like a camp-meeting or an election row. After it had lasted ten or twelve minutes, an intelligent horse-holder came up from the rear, breathless, and announced the enemy was flanking us. . . . Every man withdrew after his own fashion and in his own time."

Three Morgan men were slightly wounded in the decidedly unmilitary withdrawal, but even they agreed afterward that the fiasco was a useful lesson in military science. They had all learned that their prideful mastery of smart militia turns and drills was about as useful as a knowledge of Latin or Greek when applied to cavalry skirmishing.

A few days later, Morgan and Duke took the boys south of Green River to Woodsonville, where a number of other companies were establishing training camps. For several days the forests echoed with shouts and commands—as they practiced from D. H. Maury's *Skirmish Drill for Mounted Troops,* with evolutions modified to suit the wooded countryside. To discourage a general inclination to open fire without command, Captain Morgan also drilled them in the infantry manual of arms.

Most of these rituals would be abandoned later in combat situations, but the leaders knew that something had to be done to establish habits of discipline and to develop a sense of mutual dependence among these freeborn youngsters. "Handle cartridge!" the sergeants would yell, and every man would take a cartridge from his cartridge box with thumb and first two fingers and carry it to his mouth. "Tear cartridge!" meant to bite off the paper end to the powder and carry it to the chamber of the weapon. At "Charge cartridge!" they emptied the powder into the chamber, pressing the ball in with the forefinger. Next came "Ram cartridge!" and "Prime!" Not until they accomplished all these movements were they prepared for "Commence firing!"

They endured this training without complaint only because the men in neighboring companies around Woodsonville were suffering the same treatment. None of them actually was officially a soldier of the Confederate States Army as yet, the various camps operating under such individualistic organization names as Deadshots, Hell-roarers, and Yellow Jackets. The Lexington Rifles were generally known by that name, or simply as Morgan's Company.

By October 27, Morgan had eighty-four men mounted and ready for service, and on that day Major William Preston Johnston, son of the commanding general, arrived to administer the oath which would muster them into Confederate service. The ceremony was held in front of an old Woodsonville church which Morgan was using as his headquarters. After the custom of the day, they elected their own officers. John Morgan of course was captain; Basil Duke, first lieutenant; James West, second lieutenant; and Van Buren Sellers, third lieutenant. Among the men were many who would later become officers when other companies were formed. The names have the ring of Robin Hood's band: Tom Ballard, Ben Biggstaff, Ben Drake, David Llewellyn, William Leathers, Winder Monroe, Tom Quirk, Greenberry Roberts, Jeff Sisson. One of them, Winder Monroe, would meet William Preston Johnston again under rather strange circumstances in the last days of the war. These eighty men and their four officers would make much of the history of the yet-unformed 2nd Kentucky Cavalry.

They considered it quite an honor to have the commanding general's son come up to Woodsonville to administer the oath, and were delighted to learn on the very next day that General Johnston himself was moving his headquarters from Nashville to Bowling Green. Some real action would follow, they were certain now, and few were surprised when on November 4, General Johnston sent them a special order: "Captain J. H. Morgan's company will proceed without delay to Bowling Green and report for duty."

Meanwhile three other cavalry companies which had been training along with Morgan's men had been so impressed by the Lexington Rifles' verve and *esprit de corps* that they requested permission to join them. One was under the command of Captain Thomas Allen; the other two being understrength were combined into one under Captain James Bowles. Thus "Morgan's Company" became "Morgan's Squadron," his own company lettered A, the others B and C.

The manner in which Company A mounted all its troopers in order to meet cavalry company strength was unorthodox, to say the least. Noticing thirty or so artillery horses standing idle most

of the time around Colonel Hanson's camp, Captain Morgan persuaded the Colonel to "condemn" them for artillery service. The
animals' actual unfitness was doubtful; Company A's first use of
them was on a sixty-eight-mile scout lasting twenty hours, and the
big mounts came through in fine shape.

When his squadron was ordered to Bowling Green, Morgan felt
obligated to return these borrowed steeds, but before doing so he
secured from General Buckner an authorization on the Confederate
quartermaster to buy horses for all his men. There was one hitch
in the arrangement, however; the Kentucky quartermaster had no
funds. With his usual persistence, Morgan extracted a promise from
the quartermaster to pay later. He and his men would advance their
own money to buy the horses.

It is unlikely that the promised money was ever received, as it became Confederate Army policy shortly afterward to require all
cavalrymen to furnish their own mounts. The army could do this
with equanimity because practically every Southern soldier wanted
to be a cavalryman, and most of them were willing to buy, beg, or
borrow a horse to get into the service.

Being Kentuckians, the troopers of Morgan's squadron knew exactly what kind of horses they wanted. Those without funds
borrowed from friends, relatives, or from the Captain himself, and
went out through the countryside searching for mounts for sale.
Good saddle horses cost around one hundred dollars (equal to five
or six hundred dollars a century later) and the horse deals around
Bowling Green in late 1861 must have been carefully considered
transactions indeed.

One thing they were sure of—if the animal had Bluegrass blood
in its line, it must be a good horse. The muscular fiber of the Bluegrass horse, they believed, when compared to that of any other
area, "was as silk to cotton; the texture of the bone as ivory beside
pumice stone." Basil Duke was convinced that the American Saddle
Horse breed, with its Thoroughbred blood, was the best for cavalry
service. "The American Saddle Horse," he said, "is very valuable for
cavalry service because of other reasons than merely his superior
powers of endurance. His smoother action and easier gaits render
the march less fatiguing to the rider; he succumbs less readily to
privations and exposures, and responds more cheerfully to kind

and careful treatment. He acquires more promptly and perfectly the drill and habits of the camp and march, and his intelligence and courage make him more reliable on the field."

Captain Morgan's mare, Black Bess, was such an animal: "as nimble as a cat, agile as an antelope." A touch of the ear would bring Black Bess "from a run to a lope, from a lope to a single-foot, from that to a fox-walk."

In war matériel, the South was short of everything except fast cavalry horses. Because of this unique supremacy, Confederate cavalry troops would far outclass their Northern opponents during the first two years of war. Long before the war began, Southern planters had turned to using mules as work animals, devoting their tastes in horses to fine blooded stock for riding and sport. The breeding of blooded Thoroughbreds was so far advanced, for example, that some Southern states had laws on their books permitting owners of brood mares to geld any mature unblooded stallion caught running at large; the offended owner could collect damages from the stallion's owner as well as the fee for castration.

Northern horse breeders, on the other hand, had been raising horses intensively for plow and wagon—draft horses in the cities, plow horses in the country—big, lumbering, slow-moving animals. In 1851, a Middlewestern breeder imported the great Percheron, Louis Napoleon, and "Norman" horses became a Northern fad during the following decade. These Yankee Percherons might pull ten tons, but they were "as wide as a barn door and slow as molasses," and a Southern cavalryman would have laughed himself into stitches at the very thought of a man riding one off to war. A time would come, however, when some of Morgan's men would gladly ride Percherons—under a hot July sun in flight across southern Ohio.

During those first months of war, therefore, it was not surprising that the South was able to put a superior cavalry force into the field from its rich supply of runners, trotters and hunters—horses accustomed to the saddle rather than traces, trained to the pressure of a knee or the drop of a rein. What could plowmen on plow horses expect to accomplish against such mounts as these?

2

In early December, Federal forces began threatening the Green
River outposts, occupying Woodsonville and moving more men and
supplies down from Louisville on the L. & N. Railroad. To strike
a blow at this concentration of enemy strength, the Confederate
command ordered Morgan's squadron out on a special mission. With
105 picked men on fast horses, Captain Morgan left camp late on
December 4, crossing Green River after dark and marching steadily
on to the objective, a railroad bridge at Bacon Creek Station. They
set the wooden bridge supports to blazing and stayed around long
enough to see that it was completely destroyed, blocking railroad
passage. Then they turned back south.

The Bacon Creek bridge was a minor incident in the war, but it
was important for the squadron because it brought them their first
national press notices. Newspaper correspondents from Nashville
and Memphis had been waiting around Bowling Green for days,
eager for news, and when the squadron rode in with a report of
the bridge-burning, the correspondents made a big story of it. Other
papers in the South reprinted the Bacon Creek bridge incident, and
in time some Northern papers picked it up—the first of many stories
to come from the exploits of Morgan's raiders.

As autumn turned to winter along the Green River front, the
Federal soldiers kept close to their camps, leaving Morgan's squadron
and the other cavalry commands at Bell's Tavern, twenty-five miles
east of Bowling Green, with little to do other than ride out on
uneventful patrols. Yet there were other diversions. After the end-
less duties of saddling, bitting, packing, feeding, and shoeing mounts,
they found time now for sitting around campfires. They learned to
enjoy the smell of woodsmoke from crackling logs, the luxury of
inaction after the weariness of long rides, the comradeship of men
who have faced danger together. In a way this forest life was like
living the pages from books of knighthood and romantic legendry
which most of them had read—*Ivanhoe, The Scottish Chiefs, La
Morte d'Arthur, Robin Hood*. Three months of outdoor living had
leathered their skins and hardened their muscles so that they could
stay in the saddle for twenty-four hours and come galloping back

down the turnpikes to camp, singing at the top of their voices.

But with the coming of the new year of 1862, January rains and sleet set in, and camp life turned dreary indeed. A dozen diseases seemed to strike all at once. Measles, typhoid, pneumonia and dysentery were the most deadly, but even minor illnesses were often fatal to a man lying in a leaky brush shelter. As winter deepened, mortality ran high in the Army of Kentucky.

Morgan's cavalrymen continued their patrol missions, however, bringing in more prisoners and more information until there was no longer any doubt that the Federal command was preparing a massive attack somewhere along the Kentucky front.

The big blow was dealt a hundred miles to the west by General Grant, who had moved south along the Tennessee and Cumberland rivers, his forces smashing Fort Henry into surrender February 6. Fort Donelson held out a few days longer, but Sidney Johnston did not dare risk leaving his main army at Bowling Green, with both its flanks being rolled up.

On February 14, Johnston issued orders for Bowling Green to be evacuated. It was a bleak Valentine's Day for the men of Morgan's squadron. Kentuckians all, they had endured the winter's hardships thus far secure in their minds that with the coming of springtime the Confederate forces would smite the Federal Army a mighty blow and send it reeling back out of their home state and across the Ohio River. But now, suddenly in mid-February, here they were, instead, retreating south to Tennessee.

As they marched out on the road to Nashville, sleet was falling from a cold gray sky, and the only comfort John Morgan could give them was a vague promise that they might have an opportunity to do battle with enemy forces reported to be hellbent to head the Confederate Army off from its line of escape south—the suspension bridge at Nashville over the Cumberland River.

3

"It seemed to us like a march to our graves," one of Morgan's troopers wrote of the retreat from Bowling Green. Although they encountered no human enemy along the frozen pike to Nashville, they were continually harassed by sleet, flurries of snow, and a wind that pierced "like needles of ice." Many infantry companies, unable to obtain transport on railroad cars, were strung out along the roads.

The cavalry units covered the rear, and it was not until late on Sunday, February 16, that Morgan's squadron crossed the strategic bridge over the Cumberland. Along the Nashville wharf a disorganized rabble of civilians had boarded some commissary boats loaded with supplies for the Confederate Army of Kentucky. Men were pitching slabs of bacon from the boats to the shore where others were loading carts and hauling the meat away. So hurried was the work of plundering these boats, many slabs of bacon splashed into the river waters. The squadron moved into Nashville through streets filled with panicked citizens, on to the public square where mobs were ransacking buildings.

By nightfall of the sixteenth, rumors spread that General Sidney Johnston would not attempt to make a stand in Nashville, and a long line of soldiers marching through the city all evening in a southeasterly direction was silent confirmation. The local government could not handle the roving mobs. Doors of the army's commissary and quartermaster depots were thrown open to soldiers and civilians, and like a swarm of locusts they took what they wanted, strewing foodstuffs and bales of clothing and shoes out into the streets.

For the next seven days Morgan's men joined forces with Nathan B. Forrest's cavalry units to patrol the streets and restore order in the city. Then on the afternoon of the twenty-third, they helped to spike forty pieces of artillery which could not be moved, and as the raw February day waned, they fell into line, formed fours, and turned their mounts southeastward.

Morgan's squadron served as rear guard, and when the men looked back for the last time into the desolate, darkening city, they could see the enemy marching in.

Although the military situation of the Confederate forces in the West was grave, Johnston in Murfreesboro, Tennessee, maintained a calm front and kept the telegraph wires humming to Richmond until he secured authorization to bring up General Braxton Bragg's troops from Pensacola, and the forces of Van Dorn and Price from Arkansas. His objective was to weld all available forces in the West into one powerful army, and then strike a massive blow at the Federals wherever they might concentrate. He knew he would have to make further withdrawals below the Cumberland ridges before he could achieve his aims, and had already selected Corinth, Mississippi, just south of the great bend of the Tennessee River as rallying point for the new army.

During the two weeks the Army of Kentucky camped around Murfreesboro, Johnston organized it into a more tightly knit force than had been possible along the loosely held line across Kentucky. His eleven thousand effectives became three divisions, with an additional reserve division under Kentuckian John C. Breckinridge, the entire force being renamed Western Department, Central Army.

Although Morgan's squadron was attached to General Breckinridge's reserves, the Bluegrass boys along with other cavalry units took up screening positions between Nashville and Murfreesboro. Headquarters for the squadron was La Vergne, a village fifteen miles below Nashville, built upon an elevation from which it was possible to survey the whole of a wide valley formed by the confluence of Stone's River and the Cumberland.

Morgan's camp was so close to the 4th Ohio Cavalry, which was guarding Nashville, that the night pickets could fire upon each other when they chose to do so. Headquarters of the 4th Ohio was a lunatic asylum seven miles north of La Vergne, a location which led to a considerable amount of pointed bantering on the part of the Kentuckians when they rode close enough in the dark to call out insults to the opposing pickets.

Securing authorization for a night raid on Nashville, Morgan and fifteen volunteers rode out of La Vergne late on February 26. It was dark when they reached the outskirts of Nashville. "We proceeded into the city on Front street as far as the waterworks," Morgan later reported, "and there saw a steamboat, the *Minnetonka*." He decided to fire the boat, cut it loose, and let it float down the stream to where the Federal gunboats were tied up, hoping the blaze would spread to them. Dismounting, the men fumbled about in the darkness until they discovered the vessel was too securely moored with chain cables to be cut loose with what tools they had.

One of the boys noticed a skiff tied to the landing, and Privates Buckner, Warfield and Garrett volunteered to row out, board the steamboat, set it on fire, and try to loosen the other end of the mooring. The skiff's owner had concealed the oars, but they ripped palings off a nearby fence and paddled merrily away. They boarded without challenge, surprising a skeleton crew which was firing up the boilers, and ordered them to take a boat and row ashore to where Captain Morgan was waiting. Unable to cut the steamer loose, Sam Buckner and his comrades set fires blazing in several places on the vessel, and departed.

As they stepped ashore, Morgan ordered them to mount in haste; they could hear the hoofbeats of Federal cavalry clattering up Front Street. They rode off at a gallop into the night, almost colliding with another Federal cavalry patrol. Turning off the road, Morgan ordered them to silence; they could hear the clink of enemy sabers; then a challenge. Gunfire crackled, and they sprang away, escaping in the intense darkness. But there was an empty saddle when they rode back into La Vergne. Peter Atherton was the first of the alligator horses to die in military action.

After a few hours' rest, Captain Morgan and several of the boys rode down to Murfreesboro on the twenty-eighth to watch Johnston's army march away in a cold rain, heading for the rendezvous at Corinth.

It was probably on this day that John Morgan first met the young girl who was to become his wife before the year's end, Martha Ready. At the invitation of General Hardee, Morgan went to the home of Colonel Charles Ready for a discussion of the Kentucky squadron's future duties, and while the March rain drummed on the windows of the Ready parlor the two men talked leisurely. Part of their conversation was recorded by Martha Ready's sister, Alice. Hardee warned Morgan to be more careful, to avoid such personal risks as he had taken in Nashville. "You'll be killed or captured," Hardee said.

"Sir," replied Morgan with a confident smile, "it would be impossible for them to catch me."

With the departure of Johnston's army, Morgan's squadron moved down from La Vergne and set up headquarters in Murfreesboro. The three companies maintained alert patrols along both the Shelbyville and Nashville roads. "We lived in the saddle most of the time," said one of the men, "and our clothing was continually wet."

Three weeks of patrolling this middle-Tennessee country gave the squadron an intimate acquaintance with its topography, a knowledge which would prove useful later. And the gradual approach of springtime gave the men an added buoyancy, a renewed confidence in the future. Each day at dawn when they saddled up, their horses' flanks steamed against the frosty air, but by midday the March sun raised musty aromas of spring from the manured fields. Sunlight, bird song, and greening grass—all brought nostalgic memories of Kentucky, and they were sure they would see their homes again by full summer.

John Morgan also was feeling the tug of springtime, especially when in the company of Miss Martha Ready. Whenever he rode into Murfreesboro from various scouting missions, he was usually invited to dinner by Colonel Ready. Martha, only twenty-one and fifteen years younger than Morgan, was gay, pretty, and flirtatious. Alice Ready recorded in her diary that Martha sometimes sang in the parlor for the dashing Kentucky Captain, and when the weather was good John Morgan and Miss Martha went for horseback rides together.

On March 19, the squadron received orders to withdraw from Murfreesboro. Companies formed in front of the red-brick courthouse on the square, and with most of the townsfolk there to bid them farewell, they wheeled off in fours and faced once again toward the south to join Sidney Johnston's assembling army at Corinth. As hoofs beat on the hard-packed street, the crowd cheered, shouting encouragements after the column. Above the clatter of cavalry in motion, one of the boys broke into a song. They rode out of Murfreesboro singing "Cheer, Boys, Cheer."

On April 3, they were in Burnsville, Mississippi. Captain Morgan reported to General Breckinridge, and learned that he had been promoted to a full colonelcy, effective April 4.

From Burnsville to Corinth, pastures and woodland glades were covered with the tents of a vast army. General Polk had brought his forces down intact from Columbus, Kentucky; General Pierre Gustave Toutant Beauregard had collected thousands of fiery Louisianans in vari-colored militia uniforms; from Pensacola, General

Bragg had marched ten thousand men, all nattily uniformed in Confederate gray. The weather-stained, travel-worn veterans of the old Army of Kentucky may have felt superior to these polished additions to their ranks, but they were also impressed by this brilliant multitude of forty thousand fighting men.

As for the invaders, one prong began driving down toward northern Alabama as soon as Morgan's rear-guard squadron withdrew from there. But the main body of Federals, the massed force that Sidney Johnston aimed to destroy, was only twenty miles northeast of Corinth. All during March, General Grant had been moving troops south along the Tennessee River, and now they were camped around Pittsburg Landing, fifty thousand soldiers in blue.

General Breckinridge received his orders from Johnston, and relayed the substance to Colonel Morgan: The Confederate forces would launch a surprise attack Saturday, April 5. "Hold troops in readiness to move out at a moment's notice, with five days' provisions and one hundred rounds of ammunition."

3

Shiloh

By THREE O'CLOCK Friday morning, April 4, Morgan's squadron was moving northward out of Burnsville, Mississippi, with General John C. Breckinridge's reserve corps. A few hours before departure, "some Enfield rifles, with accoutrements and ammunition, just received," were distributed among the men. As they moved toward Pittsburg Landing, an order went out: "All persons, black and white on the line of march to be seized and sent to the rear." Sidney Johnston was taking no chances on informers reporting the presence of his approaching columns to the unsuspecting Federals camped on the banks of the Tennessee River.

With the dawn, a spring rain began falling, gentle yet persistent, and those who possessed ponchos or oilcloths considered themselves fortunate.

The road they were following through red clay hills was narrow and rough; heavy wagons and artillery batteries quickly cut it into a slippery mire. All day, showers sprayed upon the column. Horses were struggling against caissons stuck in the ruts, artillerymen were pushing, straining, and cursing. The infantrymen's shoes became mud-clogged; they hurled good-natured insults at Morgan's cavalrymen filing past, the mounts' hoofs spattering red mud.

From every slogging platoon, the wits would jeer: "Come out of that hat!—you can't hide in there!" "Come out of that coat, come

41

out—why, there's a man in it!" "Come out of them boots!" Or enviously: "If you want to have a good time, jine the cavalree!" To which an echo usually came back from the ranks: "If you want to catch hell, jine the webfoots!"

Morgan's men would hear such quips from foot soldiers until the end of the war. "Buttermilk rangers," was a common appellation for horse soldiers, because, it was said, they were always riding off to some farmhouse for buttermilk. Private George Mosgrove, however, denied this: "The fact is the cavalryman was more of a ranger for cane-reed whisky and applejack than for buttermilk."

For all the rivalry between foot soldiers and mounted men, there was a warm solidarity among all these young men on this particular rainy day. They knew they were approaching a time of testing, an ordeal long delayed. Somewhere up there in the woods along the Tennessee River the enemy waited. It was like going on a dangerous hunt, one of them said afterwards, as if they were invading an unchartered canebrake, "the den of some great bear, hidden in the thicket, with whom momently they expected encounter and mortal struggle."

By nightfall, the column's forward units were near Monterey. Although the showers had ended, low-hanging gray clouds still raced across the sky. They bivouacked along the muddy road, tried to sleep on wet leaves under dripping trees, but after midnight a wild thunderstorm broke suddenly. Torrents of rain drenched them where they lay without shelter, and after an hour of misery the sergeants began calling formations. Marching orders were for 3 A.M., but it was impossible to move in the pitch-blackness over flooded roads and swollen streams, with cold rain driving into their faces.

Along parallel roads a few miles to the west, their comrades of Hardee's, Bragg's, and Polk's corps were enduring the same wretched weather. The Third Corps under Hardee had marched out of cantonments around Corinth Thursday afternoon, with bands blaring "The Girl I Left Behind Me" and "Then You'll Remember Me." Bragg's and Polk's corps had followed and were now strung out along the muddy roads as were Breckinridge's reserves.

By Saturday morning, April 5, it was obvious that no attack could be made on that day. Capricious as springtime, the weather along the Tennessee line had stalled the Army of Mississippi—the latest official designation for Western Confederate forces. Johnston would have to wait.

When they resumed march that morning, the first concern of the men in the ranks was for the condition of their gunpowder. As the forward elements struggled up toward the concentration point at Mickey's,* rifles pop-popped along the columns. The men were testing arms and cartridges.

Hearing the racket, Johnston dispatched orders posthaste to stop all rifle fire. Mickey's was close enough to Federal outpost camps for firing to be heard, and Johnston wanted to preserve the element of surprise. He also wanted to conserve precious ammunition.

When Morgan's squadron reached the high ground at Mickey's Saturday morning, the men found the road choked with troops from Bragg's corps. They turned their horses off into the woods, waiting, nibbling at cold rations, and watching the gray sky hopefully for patches of blue.

Not until late in the afternoon were the roads clear of troops. Breckinridge's artillery and wagons were among the last units to arrive; the cannon rolled in slowly, wheels coated with clay mud, horses badly worn.

With other Kentucky units, Morgan's troopers took the road to the right of Mickey's house and moved through woods to their designated bivouac site, only four miles from Pittsburg Landing.

While the men were searching for dry places to sleep, General Johnston and his staff met for a council of war. The meeting point was a crossroads less than two miles from a small Methodist meeting house which would give the impending battle its name—Shiloh. The building was a one-room, hewn-log structure with two doors and one unglazed window. At the hour of the Confederates' council of war, General William T. Sherman was using Shiloh chapel as his headquarters, unaware of the mighty force that lay beyond the quiet oak forest.

Not so certain of the Federals' lack of knowledge of the Confederate Army's proximity was Johnston's second in command,

* Mickey's was a farmhouse at the intersection of the road from Monterey to Savannah. The proper spelling is Michie, and a village bearing that name stands at the crossroads today, but because all contemporary accounts refer to "Mickey's," that spelling will be used here.

Pierre G. T. Beauregard. The day's delay in attacking caused by the
rainstorm had robbed them of the element of surprise, he feared.
They all knew that General Don Carlos Buell was marching from
Nashville with twenty thousand men; if Buell arrived before Grant's
army could be beaten, the odds would be too great; the Confederates could not hope to win the battle. Polk, Bragg, and Breckinridge argued for a dawn attack. To retreat now, before giving battle,
might be disastrous for the western Confederacy. Beauregard listened, watching them with his sad, deep-set eyes. The element of
surprise was surely lost, he repeated. Johnston listened gravely. "I
will venture the hazard," he said.

In spite of the day's delay, the original battle plan would remain
as it was: turn the Federals' left, cut off retreat to the river, force
the boys in blue back into the bogs of Owl Creek where they could
surrender or be destroyed. The battleground lay between Owl and
Lick creeks; the Confederate front would run three miles across,
parallel to the river, flanks resting on each thicket-bordered stream.
Someone again mentioned the possibility of Buell's army arriving.
"I would fight them if they were a million," Sidney Johnston replied.

Back in the woods, Morgan's men were watching the day ending.
Misty clouds thinned and drifted away, the sun setting in a clear
sky. Final orders assigned the squadron to Colonel Robert Trabue's
1st Kentucky Brigade, and the men were told to be prepared to go
into battle at daylight. Night fell, cool after the rains, the forest
quieting as bone-weary men drifted into sleep. Those who were too
restless for sleep could hear wavering unreal strains of band music in
the far distance—Saturday night marches being played in the Federal camps. And so within sound of each other, two opposing armies
were encamped—nearly a hundred thousand men so young their
average age was less than twenty years. Between them there was
not one trench or earthwork, not even a rifle pit—only the silent
greening forest.

Before dawn the Confederate camps were stirring, though no
bugle note sounded, no drum beat the reveille. While stars paled out
of the sky, Morgan's men ate what was left of their cold rations.
Dawn was a soft gray, the woods fresh and fragrant with spring-

time. Dew lay heavy on the strewn leaves around them. It was Sunday morning, April 6, 1863.

General Johnston had slept in an ambulance, his staff bivouacked around him. In the graying light he joined them at a campfire, shared coffee with them, and as he turned to mount his horse, remarked confidently: "Tonight we will water our horses in the Tennessee River."

He rode off to inspect the forward units forming for skirmish lines. Hardee's men were to lead the first attack, Bragg's the second, Polk's the third, Breckinridge's to be held for reserve calls wherever the fighting grew hottest.

2

At fourteen minutes after five o'clock, Hardee's skirmish line ran into a routine Federal infantry patrol, and the first gun of the battle was fired. Succeeding musketry volleys warned the Federals back in their camps that they were under heavy attack. As the brisk firing increased, the forest in front of the Confederate lines rang with warning bugle calls and the ominous beat of the long roll.

Commands echoed up and down the lines. "Order arms!" "Load!" "Fix bayonets!" "Shoulder arms!" With pennons flying, the Army of Mississippi marched briskly forward through foggy woods, the men in motley garb varying from gray and butternut to the gay blue of one of the Louisiana regiments. The many banners gave the scene an air of pageantry. In the forefront was Hardee's corps flag, a white medallion on a blue field; here and there were regimental and state flags—the Lone Star of Texas, the Pelican of Louisiana.

Lieutenant Basil Duke, waiting in reserve with Company A of Morgan's squadron, was impressed by the spectacle unfolding before him. "The wild cheers which arose made the woods stir as if with the rush of a mighty wind." For a short distance the forest was clear of undergrowth, but as the first wave neared the point of fighting between opposing skirmishers, scrubby brush and dense thickets slowed the advance. Frequent halts were necessary to re-form and dress ranks.

Suddenly the sun rose out of the river mists, burning them away quickly, and to the advancing lines the brilliant morning light was like an omen of good fortune. Their cheers rang and resounded again. At seven-thirty, Hardee's attack faltered slightly as the Federals steadied their defenses, but Bragg's corps went in like a tornado, screaming the Rebel yell, and the Federals' brief stand collapsed.

This was the first time Morgan's squadron had heard the Rebel yell delivered in such concerted volume. But being alligator horses, they recognized its compulsion and its natural origins; most of the boys had developed individual whoops and yawps of their own to be delivered under stress or exultation. The Rebel yell was something primordial, a wild "Haaay-yooch!"—a cry of defiance out of belly and lungs and vocal cords. "A terrible scream and barbarous yowling," Fitzgerald Ross, the British cavalry officer, described it. He believed the Confederates had learned it from the Indians, but it was more Anglo-Saxon than aboriginal, more like the bloodcurdling "Hoochs!" of the Scottish Highlands, modified by the Southlanders.

At ten-thirty, the colors of Polk's corps—a blue cross on a red field—began moving forward to join the battle, and the men of Morgan's squadron knew that they would be next.

For five hours they had waited beside their horses, watching infantry lines march away into the gray-green woods, and some of the boys were beginning to wonder if the fighting would not be all over before the cavalry could get into it. Thus far they had experienced nothing but noise—the sustained volleys of the riflemen, then the artillery joining in the clamor like the growl of an angry monster.

As soon as there was sufficient interval between Polk's corps and Breckinridge's reserves, the cavalry moved out platoon front, keeping abreast as best they could through the trees. In a few minutes they were passing over the first contested ground. Many dead and wounded of both armies lay crumpled or crawling on the brown-leaved forest floor, canteens and haversacks scattered among them.

In a grotesque little heap were three dead men in blue, one with a bayonet thrust through his body up to the cross, one with a bloody hole between his eyes, the third with no face at all.

Morgan's men had seen nothing like this along Green River. "In getting up our glowing anticipation of the day's programme," Basil Duke observed, "we had left these items out of the account, and we mournfully recognized the fact, that many who seek military distinction, will obtain it posthumously, if they get it at all. The actual sight of a corpse immediately checks an abstract love of glory."

When they broke out of the woods into a small open valley, the roar became deafening, the sky filled with artillery shells exploding into puffs of white smoke. Seated unperturbed upon Black Bess, Colonel Morgan began forming the squadron into battle lines across a fallow field.

While they were waiting there for further orders, the 4th Kentucky Infantry Regiment came filing out across their front, the men in close formation, moving with a measured tread. Lieutenant John Churchill of the squadron's C Company recognized some old friends among these Kentucky foot soldiers, and he saluted them by leading his boys in a rousing version of "Cheer, Boys, Cheer." The song seemed suited to that suspended moment of tension; it was as if the blended voices defied even the loudest of the artillery bursts. The infantrymen grinned, and waved, and one of them shouted: "Let's jine the cavalree, boys! Nobody ever saw a dead cavalryman!" And then they, too, joined in the singing: "Cheer, Boys, Cheer, We'll March Away to Battle!"

"The effect," Lieutenant Duke recalled, "was animating beyond all description."

About noon, Colonel Trabue's brigade was ordered to move to the left and join General Hardee. As Morgan's troopers came up to the front, a short distance northwest of Shiloh church, the air suddenly filled with the zip-zip of flying Minié balls. Less than a thousand yards ahead of them across a swale, belching flames and smoke clouds obscured a low knoll surrounded by thickets and underbrush. From the flanking positions of the Confederate infantry, Morgan's men knew immediately that the summit was held by a Federal artillery battery.

A mounted messenger, a lieutenant, appeared abruptly out of the smoke, shouting: "General Hardee wants to know what cavalry this is!" Duke, who was at head of column, replied that it was

Morgan's. The Lieutenant, recognizing Duke, barked back: "General Hardee wants to talk with either you or Morgan."

Following close behind the messenger, Duke crossed through two hundred yards of smoke and found Hardee, grizzled and sweated, beside one of the Confederate batteries. "Well, Duke," said the General, "you young Kentuckians have been anxious to see some war, and I'm going to give you an opportunity. Inform Colonel Morgan that he is to form his squadron and when I send the word, charge that battery on the hill to our right."

As soon as Duke rejoined the squadron and informed Morgan of the order, the men were dismounted, horse-holders moving to the rear. Duke quietly told his company what to prepare for. "The men looked very grave," he recalled, "and lost all pleasure in the pyrotechnical spectacle afforded by the enemy batteries." Everyone's eyes were fixed on the knoll that resembled some violent outpost of hell. They waited for Hardee's final order, and as they watched with fingers tight on their rifles, they saw the long leaping flames disappear, the smoke roll away, and a wave of Confederate infantrymen sprang from concealment in the brush and swarmed over the abandoned position.

A horseman swung over toward them; it was Hardee's Lieutenant. He held his mount only long enough to shout that Hardee's orders had been changed; Morgan was to take his command to the extreme left and "charge the first enemy you see."

Remounting, they wheeled off to the left by twos, following a trail no wider than a bridle path. The first open space fronting toward the battle line was a marsh, and they had just turned into the grassy bog when the front platoon sighted a blue-clad infantry regiment dead ahead. "Halt!" The order came back quickly, repeated by the sergeants, the squadron jerking to a jingling stop. Across the sunlit field, the blue companies were forming, a stocky little colonel flourishing a wicked-looking saber, his commands echoing back from the woods ahead.

Morgan's men, their weapons at ready, were puzzled by the strange accents of the Colonel in blue; they also thought it rather peculiar that the soldiers were facing the wrong way. "First Section, Company A, dismount!" Morgan ordered the dismounted section to approach cautiously. If satisfied the men in blue were enemy troops, they were to open fire and the squadron would immediately support them by coming down on the charge.

As it turned out, the soldiers in blue were not Federals at all; they were Louisianans—Colonel Alfred Mouton's 18th Louisiana— exceedingly proud of their neat sky-blue militia uniforms. These Louisiana Frenchmen had already had trouble with quick-triggered Confederates who were firing at everything blue on the battlefield; the Louisianans had reached the point where they saw no humor in being mistaken for the enemy, and were prepared to answer fire for fire from friend or foe. "We fire at anybody," they told Morgan's men, "who fire at us—God damn!" *

The Louisianans were preparing to charge a Federal camp in a field off to the left, and Morgan decided to join in the assault. While the squadron was circling a deep ravine to get into position for a charge, a company of Texas Rangers came up from the rear: "Hey, Kentucky," one of the Rangers called, "what're you going to do?"

"Go in," was the reply.

"Then we'll go in, too."

As the two cavalry commands faced into open ground, sunlight caught the shiny bayonets of the enemy closing upon the Louisianans. For a minute or two, the spouting flashes of musketry fire were so fast and furious, the sound drowned the distant roar of artillery. A Confederate battery, caught in the open field, was in trouble; a line of Federal skirmishers had appeared as if by magic out of the woods ahead, and their hot fire kept the artillerymen pinned down, unable to unlimber their guns.

"Charge!" The alligator boys had waited a long time for this command, but now at last they were away; they were really in the battle. Before they had galloped twenty yards, the Federal skirmishers vanished back into the woods, but neither Kentuckians nor Texans would stop now to dismount and fight on foot. Headlong they rode into the thickety wood, forcing their horses over tangles of brush, crowding up into confused masses, losing their straight

---

* In his report of the battle, Colonel Mouton said: "Unfortunately our troops on the right mistook us for the enemy, owing, I presume to the blue uniforms of a large number of my men, and opened on us with cannon and musket." He added that he had some difficulty forcing his own men to stop firing back on other Confederate units.

battle lines. But the Federals also had lost their formations and were scrambling through the brush in panic, some being knocked down by the horses of the mounted Kentuckians.

"We came close upon them," Lieutenant Duke recorded, "before they fired—one stunning volley, the blaze in our faces, and the roar rang in our ears like thunder. The next moment we rode right through them—some of the men trying to cut them down with the saber, and making ridiculous failures, others doing real execution with gun and pistol."

A few minutes later Duke was seriously wounded. He was in the act of sabering a Federal soldier on his right when an enemy on his left fired point-blank with an "old-fashioned Brown Bess musket, loaded with ball and three buckshot." One of the shot entered his left shoulder, another tore its way through his right shoulder blade, just missing his spine. As Duke fell unconscious from his horse, Sergeant Pat Gardner shot the assailant through the head with his squirrel rifle.

Dead were Lieutenant James West of A Company, James Chiselin, Archie Moody, and Sam Buckner, the hero of the *Minnetonka*.

The Texans had suffered worse casualties, dashing blindly into a rail-fence ambuscade, and several of their riderless horses came galloping back over the ground where the Kentuckians had placed their wounded.

But the boys had routed the enemy in their first mounted charge of the battle. From the captured Federals they learned they had defeated Colonel John A. McDowell's 6th Iowa Infantry, of General Sherman's 5th Division.

It had been a bad day for Sherman. Although the battle was only hours old, he had already abandoned his headquarters at Shiloh church, which was now occupied for the same purpose by General Beauregard. And Sherman's best regiments were scattered, driven back into the marshy brakes of Owl Creek.

It was midafternoon when the squadron broke off the fighting, for lack of enemies to shoot at. Morgan dismounted his troops, sent skirmishers forward, and moved slowly along the edges of the Owl Creek thickets. But the Federals seemed to have vanished into the greening brushwood.

Then suddenly they heard the first rumors of Sidney Johnston's death, the black news sweeping across the tangled, disjointed battle-field, from division to regiment to company. Almost every soldier in the Army of Mississippi had seen the General sometime during the day, dashing about on his bay Thoroughbred, Fire-Eater, unmindful of flying Minié balls and exploding shells as he urged his men on to victory. Johnston was hit three times before receiving his fatal wound—once by a spent bullet, again by a shell fragment, then by a Minié ball which cut his left boot sole in half. He did not feel the fatal wound, a severed leg artery, until he fell fainting from his mount.

Dismaying as was the effect of their leader's death upon the advancing Confederates, a second piece of news was even more ominous. Late in the afternoon, the first elements of General Buell's Federal relief column of twenty thousand fresh troops were reported to be crossing the river.

Yet there was good news also, as the day wore to an end. After bitter resistance at a place the soldiers afterward would call the Hornet's Nest, General Benjamin Prentiss had surrendered his two thousand Federal survivors. Everywhere along the line other Federal divisions seemed ready to yield. General Hardee was exceedingly jubilant: "The captured camps, rich in the spoils of war—in arms, horses, stores, munitions, and baggage—with throngs of prisoners moving to the rear, showed the headlong fury with which our men had crushed the heavy columns of the foe."

At dusk the fighting ended, the armies disengaging as if by mutual consent. Morgan's squadron bivouacked in the abandoned camp of the 6th Iowa, along Purdy road near the Owl Creek bridge. From captured stores they enjoyed a bountiful supper, and most of the boys had stretched out for some much-needed sleep when the enemy's gunboats, the *Tyler* and *Lexington*, opened up from the river with a monotonous serenade that was to last out the night. At regular intervals of fifteen minutes, huge shells streaked skyward over the Confederate bivouacs, the missiles "screaming louder than steam whistles." Usually they struck the tops of trees, filling the air with dense clouds of smoke as they exploded, doing little damage other than badly frightening those nearest the points of explosion, yet serving to keep almost every man in the Confederate Army awake all night.

Before midnight, rain began falling, and the men blamed it on the big guns; soldiers have always believed that booming cannon and rainfall are cause and effect. "We slept on the battleground as best we could with torrents of rain pouring down on us and with the gunboats on the river firing over us all night to disturb our slumbers. Many of the boys visited the sutlers stores that night and helped themselves to the edibles and as much clothing as they could use or carry off."

While thousands of restless Confederates straggled over the darkened battlefield, tending to their wounded and searching for plunder, their leaders were conferring with the new commanding general, P. G. T. Beauregard. The shock of Sidney Johnston's death was still staggering, and Beauregard was even less sanguine than he had been on the previous day. From the records, it is evident there was indecision in the Confederate high command that night. Certainly, little effort was made to reorganize scattered units and put them into command positions for the morrow's fighting.

The Federals, meanwhile, were straining every effort to repair their disaster. Lost platoons and frightened fugitives were rounded up and put back into ranks. And most vital of all, boats were kept moving steadily back and forth in the rain across the Tennessee River, bringing Buell's twenty thousand fresh troops into Pittsburg Landing.

By daylight the rain had stopped. Morgan's men and the Kentucky regiments near Owl Creek bridge had little ammunition left, but their guns were wet and an order went out to discharge pieces and then clean and dry them as well as could be done. The ordeal of the previous day's baptism of fire, the miserable sleepless night, and the awareness of their half-empty cartridge boxes had taken the edge off the Army of Mississippi. The men were sluggish as they reported to bugle calls sounding assembly.

At six o'clock the combined armies of Grant and Buell launched a counterattack. One of the Texas Rangers, fighting near Morgan's squadron, recorded the events of the morning. "The whole face of the earth at that place and time appeared to be blue. . . . Never did I at any other time hear minie balls seem to fill the air so completely as on this second day's fight."

For four hours, the Kentuckians and Texans along Owl Creek

held their strong positions, then gradually fell back as the remainder of the line gave way before repeated charges of the reinvigorated Federals. Outnumbered and outgunned, with their ammunition virtually exhausted, the Confederates fought stubbornly all the way.

By noon, however, it was apparent to General Beauregard that the contest was hopeless, and he ordered a retreat. During the early afternoon, the Kentuckians fell back to high ground around Shiloh church, holding positions until a strong line of artillery could be placed along the ridge. While these batteries kept up a constant fire on the woods beyond, the Confederate infantry withdrew. So orderly was the withdrawal, Breckinridge's scattered command was able to reunite about a mile and a half west of Shiloh church. There at a crossroads, Morgan's squadron received new orders. They, with the Rangers and Forrest's regiment, were to cover the retreat of Beauregard's army.

During the next forty-eight hours the Army of Mississippi was marching back to Corinth—after tasting victory one day, defeat the next. But Grant was unable to pursue, his army being as badly mauled as Beauregard's, and by midweek the Confederates were digging into solid breastworks around Corinth.

In the meantime Morgan's troopers moved back to Mickey's farm, collecting along the way several wounded men who had fallen out of the retreating columns. Late in the afternoon of April 8, an infantry patrol from one of Sherman's regiments came blundering up the road; the Kentucky boys scattered them back into the woods, netting an easy bag of seventy-five prisoners.

For the next week, the squadron camped around Mickey's where a temporary hospital for serious casualties had been established. They engaged in two or three minor skirmishes, searched the nearby woods for lost wounded men, and buried the dead from the hospital.

4

The Lebanon Races

FOLLOWING ITS ARMY'S withdrawal from Shiloh, the western Confederacy suffered a series of disheartening reverses. On April 11, General Ormsby Mitchel reached Huntsville, Alabama. Island No. 10 on the Mississippi fell soon afterward, leaving the city of Memphis open to eventual capture, bringing all of Tennessee west of the Cumberlands under Federal control. And General Henry W. Halleck, now commanding the combined Federal armies of Shiloh, was moving slowly down toward the main Confederate forces around Corinth.

If there were some among the Confederates who felt that all was lost in the West, they were not to be found in Colonel John Morgan's Kentucky cavalry squadron. From their Tennessee experiences during the winter, these horse soldiers were well aware that the Federal armies massed deep in the South were like huge weights supported by strained and attenuated lines. Any serious blow against these lines of supply and communication could create havoc among the Federals.

After Morgan withdrew his squadron to the temporary base at Burnsville, he went to General Beauregard with a plan for raiding these supply lines far north into Tennessee and Kentucky. Beauregard was sufficiently impressed to order his quartermaster to issue Morgan fifteen thousand dollars to cover expenses for conducting "a military expedition beyond the Tennessee River." The commanding general also authorized Morgan to increase his squadron to five companies as soon as practicable.

On April 23, the raiding party began re-outfitting at Burnsville. As Basil Duke was still hospitalized from the wound received at Shiloh, Lieutenant Sellers took command of Company A. A new fourth company of twenty-five Mississippians and Alabamians under Captain A. C. Brown was added to the squadron, and Morgan persuaded Lieutenant Colonel Robert Wood to join on with a detachment from Colonel Wirt Adams' cavalry regiment, bringing the force to a total of 325 men.

For three days the squadron was busy shoeing horses, putting arms in order, and cooking a supply of rations for the expedition. As they were going deep into enemy territory, extra ammunition and rations had to be transported on pack mules, one mule being attached to a section, or four to a company. Each mule was led by a man detailed from the section to which it was assigned, and all were placed under the command of a former Kentucky legislator, Frank Leathers. Leathers was a private in Company A, but in civilian life he had been known as "Colonel," and often as not his comrades called him by that title. So it was that the squadron's first pack mules were known as "Colonel Leathers' Mule Train," and according to one of the boys in the train, Leathers "made a bigger row in driving his mules than was necessary to align a division of cavalry for action."

Early on April 26, the raiders marched east from Burnsville, passed through Iuka and camped that night six miles from the Tennessee River. When they came up to the river at Oats' Ferry the next morning, they found the stream almost at flood stage. There was only one boat at the crossing, large enough to transport no more than a dozen horses and men each trip. But as there was no other ferry within miles that was free of Federal interference, they settled down to work, spending the better part of two days and nights floating horses, mules and men across the broad, swift-flowing river. "We had the gunboat fever very badly," one of the men reported afterward, "and expected every minute to see one come in sight, for the Federals were patrolling the river for some miles above this point."

From the "home of Dr. Bowles" on the north bank of the river, the morning of April 29, Colonel Morgan wrote his first report of the expedition: "Last of command just crossed river . . . will go to Lawrenceburg, start men to left and have wires cut upon Savannah road . . . determined to reach Lexington." Although his command was still in northern Alabama, he was already thinking of Kentucky and the Bluegrass.

Moving rapidly northeastward, they entered Lawrenceburg, Tennessee, the night of April 30, received a hospitable welcome, an abundance of forage and rations, "and a good deal more whisky than was good for the men." At dawn, they resumed march and were nearing Pulaski about midmorning when they learned that a force of four hundred Federal troops had just passed on the road to Columbia. Considering this number of the enemy a fair match, the raiders swung northward and discovered the Federals in the act of stringing a new telegraph line which was to run to General Mitchel's headquarters at Huntsville.

As soon as Morgan's men appeared, Mitchel's men blocked the road with wagons and teams, and formed a hasty defense line between a wood and a field. But the raiders charged on horseback, overrunning the Federal defenses, and in a matter of minutes captured 268 of the telegraph crew.

Captain Brown's new company chased the remainder up the road to Columbia, then turned back to form the rear guard of the squadron's victory march toward Pulaski.

With the walking prisoners strung out between the advance and rear mounted companies, the column's entrance into Pulaski was a grand parade. Colonel Morgan led the way, mounted on Black Bess, and the Colonel's mare almost stole the show, prancing high and tossing her beautifully shaped head. As soon as Morgan dismounted and fastened Bess to a hotel hitching rail, a crowd gathered to admire her glossy black coat, caressing her and feeding her tidbits. When some of the ladies of Pulaski appeared with scissors to clip souvenirs from Black Bess's jet-black mane, Morgan drew the line and ordered the mare taken to the safety of a stable.

Now the crowd turned its attention to the luckless Federal prisoners, lined up to be paroled. Each captive was required to sign an oath promising not to bear arms against the Confederacy until exchanged, and their names were duly entered on rolls to be forwarded to army headquarters where arrangements would eventually be made to exchange them for captured Confederates. As soon as he had signed his oath, each prisoner was free to return to his home, proceeding usually by foot to the nearest means of transportation. The paperwork required for paroling and exchanging prisoners would grow into a mountain of forms and records before Morgan's men captured their last man, and the shuttling of parolees back and forth from battlefields to home towns and prison camps would become one of the most bewildering complexities of this complicated war.

Bypassing Murfreesboro, the column headed north along familiar back-country roads, crossed Stone's River on May 4, and under dripping skies rode into the friendly town of Lebanon as darkness fell.

With the wet night closing down on the town like a curtain, the mood of the boys was relaxation, to rest weary muscles after the hard day's ride and enjoy the hospitality of the townsfolk. They were deep into enemy-held territory, 170 miles from the Confederate's main army, and the Federal stronghold at Nashville was only thirty miles to the west, but thus far they had met no opposition they could not handle. The raiding party was intact, and another day's march would bring them north of the Nashville supply base where they could strike at a vital railroad.

A, B, and C companies occupied the small college buildings on the edge of town, tying their mounts in the college yard. Captain Brown's company and Lieutenant Colonel Wood's detachment were quartered around livery stables near the town square. Morgan established headquarters in the hotel, and issued orders to company commanders to be prepared to saddle horses about 4:00 A.M. for an early march to Canoe-branch Ferry on the Cumberland River. Pickets were ordered out on all the roads entering Lebanon.

Everything seemed secure on that bleak, rainy night, so secure that no effort was made by the officers to stop the whisky drinking, the singing, the gaiety indoors—from the college dormitories to the stables, and down in the hotel's bar. An alligator horse relaxing prefers to relax with whisky, and Lebanon had an abundant supply. "When the warmth of whisky in a Kentuckian's stomach is added to his natural energy," Timothy Flint once observed, "he becomes in succession, horse, alligator, and steamboat." Another admirer of the Confederate soldier's capacity for alcohol said he had seen few men fonder of spirits. "I do not believe there are many of them who could not finish a bottle of brandy or whisky at one sitting." But he added: "I do not recollect ever to have seen a drunken private soldier in the South, though perhaps once or twice I may have seen an officer a little 'tight.' "

Morgan's alligator horses considered drunkenness a sign of weakness, and most of the boys knew when to leave off the bottle, but the fault of judgment on this particular dismal night was with the pickets. They also joined in the liquid merrymaking.

Out on the Murfreesboro road, the boys were soaked and chilled from the steady rain. At first they took turns going in and out of a nearby farmhouse, drying their clothes by the fireplace and sharing hot toddies graciously offered by the host. Then as the night grew wetter and darker, somehow the entire picket detail found that farmhouse more cozily attractive than the deserted road. After all, they could take an occasional glance out the window, just in case some Federal patrol was bullheaded enough to come riding into Lebanon on a foul night such as this one was.

It was a Private Pleasant Whitlow who saw them first, near daybreak, a whole Federal cavalry regiment plodding by in the slackening rain, heading for town. Whitlow cried a warning to the other pickets, dashed outside, leaped upon his horse, and took off at a fast gait down the road right alongside the enemy column. In the semidarkness none of the Federals paid any attention to his presence; any who saw him pass took him for a courier from one of the rear companies.

Just as the column entered the town, Whitlow reached the forward point; he spurred his horse into a run, and began yelling at the top of his voice, calling out Morgan's name and warning: "The Feds! The Feds!" Guns exploded behind him, and Whitlow pitched off his horse, dead. But Morgan and his officers in the hotel had heard the warning; they dashed out, Morgan running straight for Black Bess's stable.

The next few minutes were indescribable confusion. Although the rain had stopped and dawn was breaking, the light was murky,, creating an illusion of unreality over the frantic town square. From somewhere a bugle screamed boots and saddles, and men were running across the college grounds, from the livery stables, from the hotel—searching for horses, yelling and firing.

2

The Federal force of six hundred cavalrymen which entered Lebanon, Tennessee, on the morning of May 5 was under the command of Brigadier General Ebenezer Dumont; the advance regiment was the 1st Kentucky Union Cavalry, better known as Wolford's Cavalry after its leader, Colonel Frank Wolford.

There in the misty daybreak of a little Tennessee town—which bore the name of a biblical mountain of cedars—it was Kentuckian against Kentuckian, the irony of civil war brought into sharp focus. For many of these men the choice of armies had been fortuitous, the chance of geography, the happenstance of family relations or acquaintances, of being brought up under one mystical shibboleth or other, in which all believed sincerely but few could have clearly explained.

Frank Lane Wolford and John Morgan knew and respected each other; they had served together in the Mexican War. Wolford was the antithesis of the Bluegrass cavalier, a true yeoman who said "hit" for it, "sot" for sit, "fetch" for carry, "thar" for there. His diction was pure Old English poetry, and he loved oratory so dearly that his public speeches endured for three or four hours at a time. Anyone who saw Frank Wolford once never forgot him—his powerful chest, his short thick neck, his oversized head covered with thick black hair, a huge beak of a nose, powerful chin, clear gray eyes that were piercing, hawklike, fiery. "He rode the framework of an ugly roan horse," an observer said of him while he was organizing his cavalry regiment. "He wore an old red hat, homespun brown jeans coat, and his face had been undefiled by water and razor for sometime."

Many of the stories told about Frank Wolford were concerned with his colorful military language. "Colonel Wolford has but two

commands," a Federal general once complained. " 'Scatter, boys!'
and 'Huddle up, boys!' " Like as not he would also shout "Skedaddle!" or "Light out!" Officers on both sides in the western armies
were accustomed to inventing spur-of-the-moment commands such
as "Git up and git!" "By move forward! Put!" "Wheel into line!
Git!" To dismount and fight on foot, one commander used: "Down
and atter 'm, boys!" And for crossing a log over a creek, it was:
"Company attention! In one rank to walk a log! Walk a log!
March!"

On this May morning, Colonel Wolford's advance scouts opened
the firing by shooting Private Pleasant Whitlow off his horse as
he cried the alarm in the town square of Lebanon. Wolford immediately quickened the pace of the main column, but as his regiment
clattered up the pike, Morgan's men began swarming out of the
college buildings on high ground to the right. Not an officer was
present on the campus, but Orderly Sergeant Zelah Boyer barked
Company A into a formation of sorts, and the boys poured a volley
of fire into Wolford's right flank. Wolford responded by wheeling
his men to the right and swarming over the college grounds, surrounding the dormitories, and forcing A, B, and C companies back
into the town.

According to a correspondent of the *Louisville Daily Journal* who
was present, the atmosphere was heavy and the smoke from the
guns hovered low. "After a short time of firing little could be seen
except flashes from the muzzles of guns. The din was terrible. Amid
the crack of rifles, the reports of pistols, and the clatter of hoofs on
the hard wet streets, could be heard hoarse shouts of fighting men,
and at times the shrill shrieks of frightened women and children in
the houses." Several Morgan men were captured in this action, C
Company bearing the brunt of Wolford's first charge.

As the squadron fell back into town, the three companies became
intermixed, but Sergeant Boyer's deep voice kept up a constant call
for A Company platoon leaders, and by the time they reached the
square the sergeant had the Green River veterans aligned for battle.
Suddenly out of the gray dawn, Colonel Morgan appeared on Black
Bess, his voice calmly ordering his men to stand firm and look to
their arms.

Meanwhile Colonel Wolford had rallied his men for a charge

into the square, and they came in now, yelling and firing, breaking through the jumbled lines of B and C companies. But as the first Union platoons galloped into the square, a withering crossfire caught them from the upper windows of the Odd Fellows Hall. Lieutenant Colonel Wood had taken his detachments in there, and this fusillade combined with a blast from A Company's steady line slowed the attackers.

For a minute or so, smoke and mist obscured the square, the smell of horse and dung and leather mingling with the acrid odor of burned powder. Morgan's men could hear Wolford's oratorical voice shouting orders from somewhere near the hotel; those who had reloaded poured a rain of bullets in that direction. Friend and foe became entangled in the succeeding melee, and for a few minutes there were isolated hand-to-hand combats all around the square.

Wounded in the side, Colonel Wolford wheeled his mount. He saw a line of horsemen forming, and dashed toward them. As he swayed from his saddle, Frank Leathers of Morgan's mule train, caught him in his arms. "Frank Wolford!" he shouted. "Old Meat Axe! Well, this is glory enough for me for one day!"

In the brief lull that followed, while Wolford's leaderless men withdrew from the square, Morgan pulled his horse over to greet the distinguished prisoner, and inquire after the wound. Wolford protested that it was nothing, although blood streaked down one trousers leg. When Morgan offered to take the Colonel's parole so that he might go into the hotel and lie down, Wolford stubbornly refused, declared he would take his chances on being rescued by his own men. The fight is not over yet, he warned Morgan, and he was right.

Coming up the Murfreesboro road behind Wolford was General Dumont with elements of the 7th Pennsylvania Cavalry. As soon as Dumont heard the rifle fire of the first encounter, he guessed that Wolford had run into a Confederate patrol of considerable size. He sent companies racing to left and right to seal off all roads leading from Lebanon, and then hurried forward with his main force.

Skirmishing parties from these fresh troops burst into Lebanon while Morgan was still talking with Frank Wolford, and although the squadron stood off the first attacks, it was soon apparent to

Morgan and his officers that they were too far outnumbered to remain much longer in the town.

In one of the first brushes, Private Jeff Sterrett of B Company captured a chaplain, W. H. Honnell. "I am only a chaplain," Honnell protested. "I rode up here to pray for our wounded, and I request permission to rejoin my command."

"The hell you say," retorted Sterrett. "Don't you think Morgan's men need praying for as well as Wolford's devils?"

A few minutes later, Morgan issued the order to retreat from Lebanon, and Chaplain Honnell, taken along as prisoner, described the pell-mell ride: "We were on the wildest race a soldier ever experienced. Sometimes we would jump clear over a fallen horse, and horses would sometimes shy around a man on hands and knees struggling to escape from the road."

Colonel Wolford also was along for the ride—still an unparoled prisoner—but because of his weakened condition, Morgan allowed him to drop behind. When two of Wolford's officers at last overtook him, the Colonel urged them to leave him and press on to capture John Morgan. Blood was dripping from his wound into the road as he spoke. His officers refused the order, and took him back to Lebanon in a buggy. Old Meat Axe Wolford recovered, of course, and he and Morgan—the yeoman and the cavalier—would meet again face to face, a little more than a year later, on a dusty road far north in Ohio.

Racing out of Lebanon on the east road to Carthage, Morgan's men ran into General Dumont's flanking companies, who dashed down on the Confederate rear, attacking with sabers. The Bluegrass boys retaliated as best they could with pistol fire, but it was no easy accomplishment to reload a pistol while keeping a horse going at full gallop. One of them later recalled seeing Colonel Morgan coolly engaging in such a series of duels. "He waited until the foe got within gunshot, wheeled, and emptied his pistols, and then touched up Black Bess until he could reload. The victors tried for dear life to catch him."

In a moment of exertion, Bess broke the curb of her bridle, and Morgan could not control her flight. She ran like a tornado, and although two or three men tried to slow her, there was no heading

Black Bess until she ran through the village of Rome and faced the unbridged Cumberland river.

As swift as the ride had been, the Federals were coming up fast in the rear, and Morgan had only a dozen or so men with him now. The river ferry was too small for loading both horses and men; they had only time to dismount, slap their mounts' rumps, board, and start poling for the opposite shore.

Safely across, they looked back and saw Black Bess running along the river bank, head high, mane flying. "She was the most perfect beauty I ever beheld . . . broad tilted loins, and thighs—all muscle . . . her head as beautiful as a poet's dream . . . wide between the eyes, it tapered down until her muzzle was small enough to have picked a lady's pocket."

Sergeant Tom Quirk could not bear the thought of Black Bess being left behind for some Federal soldier to capture. He jumped into a canoe and started paddling back, intending to bring her over by swimming, but he was scarcely halfway across the Cumberland when Federal pursuers appeared on the opposite ferry landing and began peppering bullets toward his frail craft. Quirk reluctantly turned about and rejoined his comrades.*

There in the woods north of the river was all that remained of Morgan's gay raiders of yesterday—scarcely a squad of unhorsed cavalrymen, safe only temporarily in a country that seemed to be swarming with blue-coated enemies.

And where were the others? Several were casualties back in Lebanon. Dead was Captain A. C. Brown of Company D, and six or seven enlisted men, including the first to die, Pleasant Whitlow. Almost half of the original raiding force had been captured, including Lieutenant Colonel Wood, three captains, and four lieutenants. The remainder were scattered in the forests between Lebanon and the Cumberland.

Among the captured enlisted men were Corporal Tom Logwood and Sergeant William Jones, two of the original five who had driven

---

* The ultimate fate of Black Bess was never known. It was said that she was used for a time by General Dumont, then sold to a civilian who traveled around the country exhibiting her for an admission fee of twenty-five cents. After the war, her original owner, Warren Viley, published advertisements offering a large sum of money to anyone giving information of Black Bess' whereabouts, but to no avail.

the wagonload of rifles out of Lexington on that fateful night back
in September.

3

With the handful of men who had crossed the ferry at Rome,
Colonel Morgan moved on toward Carthage, impressing horses along
the way until all were mounted again. On May 6, after eluding
Federal patrols, they reached Sparta at the foot of the Cumberland
plateau and went into camp. Afterward some of the boys told of
seeing their commander in tears as the full realization of the disaster
affected him. Events had moved full circle; from a handful of loyal
Lexington Rifles he had built a dauntless cavalry squadron, the
beginnings of a regiment. But now all was swept away in one rainy
night. In months to come the boys would refer wryly to the debacle
as the "Lebanon Races," but only among themselves; they never
discussed Lebanon with outsiders.

During the following three days, however, their spirits began to
rise again as several of the "lost" men wandered in to the camp near
Sparta. It reminded them of the old days back at Camp Charity,
when the arrival of one new recruit warranted a whole series of
hearty cheers. They shod their horses, re-equipped as best they
could, and grew homesick for Kentucky.

By May 9, there were almost fifty men in camp, a few from B
and C companies, most of them from the indestructible A, the elite
originals of Woodsonville. Morgan had no difficulty in persuading
them they could make their way into Kentucky; more likely it
was the boys who persuaded their colonel.

Two days and nights of hard riding brought them into the
fringes of their old Green River scouting country—outside Glasgow.
John Hines, a native of the town, volunteered to slip into Glasgow
and size up their chances for spending the night there. He found the
town garrisoned by five hundred Federals.

The boys were disappointed, but Morgan reminded them they had
started on this expedition primarily to damage Federal transportation
lines north of Nashville. Only ten miles away was the L. & N. Rail-

road. This would be as good a time as any to strike a blow against the enemy.

Urging their weary mounts into motion once again, they turned northward toward Cave City. At least they could take some comfort from the sensation of being back in Kentucky, although from the signs of enemies on all sides, they realized now that fifty men stood small chance of riding unchallenged all the way to Lexington.

By morning they were outside Cave City, and could see the twin rails of the L. & N. glistening in the sunshine. With five men, Morgan cantered into the village, intending to pose as Federals if Cave City proved to be garrisoned. They found only a peaceful village, a freight train standing on a siding. Morgan took command of the railway station, and sent a man back to bring in the boys waiting in the woods. During the morning they burned the cars and exploded the locomotive of the captured freight train.

About noon they heard a locomotive whistling from the north, and they took quick action to arrange its capture. After filling a cattle guard near the station with upright ties, a detail hurried down the tracks to block the train's rear in case the engineer tried to reverse his engines when he saw the barricade.

By the time the train appeared in sight, blowing steam and slowing for a stop, everything was in readiness; the men were concealed around the station and along the tracks, weapons prepared for firing. As soon as the wheels ground to a halt, the raiders leaped aboard and found the cars filled with Federal soldiers, some accompanied by their wives.

Among the officers was Major W. A. Coffey, returning from leave to join Old Meat Axe Wolford's regiment. When he realized what was happening, Coffey swung off the platform of the car in which he was riding, his pair of Colt's six-shooters blazing. Private Ben Biggstaff, alert for such resistance, sent a rifle bullet whistling past Coffey's ear, and the Major dropped his pistols. "Stop firing, boys," he said calmly, "I'm out of ammunition and have concluded to quit."

As the raiders corralled the Federal officers, they turned them over to Morgan, who was well acquainted with some of them, Major Coffey in particular. The traveling wives gathered around the group, weeping and sobbing frantically, and one begged Morgan to spare her husband's life. "My dear madam," the Colonel replied with a bow, "I did not know you had a husband."

"Yes, sir," she said. "There he is. Don't kill him for my sake."

"He is no longer my prisoner," Morgan declared. "He is yours."

As a further favor to the ladies, Morgan gallantly agreed not to burn the train—he knew there was no place for them to rest comfortably in so small a town—but he sent a search detail through the baggage cars, seizing several thousand dollars in Federal funds.

After placing a guard on the train, Morgan took the remainder of the boys to the hotel, inviting Major Coffey along as a guest, and they all dined sumptuously, paying the hotelkeeper in United States greenbacks. During the dinner Morgan wrote out a parole for Major Coffey, a rather special parole binding Coffey to remain a noncombatant until such date as the Major could secure an exchange for Lieutenant Colonel Wood, captured at Lebanon. Morgan felt a special responsibility for Wood, having invited him along on the expedition.

After completing the leisurely dinner, Morgan's men herded the paroled captives and their ladies back aboard the train, and ordered the engineer to reverse his locomotive and return to Louisville. Before the locomotive was out of sight, the boys were swinging into their saddles, ready to turn back for the Cumberland. Although they were leaving Kentucky earlier than they desired, their morale was restored. Now they could return proudly to the Confederate lines; they had proved that damaging raids could be made by cavalry deep into Federal-held territory. And if fifty men could do what they had done, what might an entire regiment accomplish? John Morgan was determined to return to Confederate Army headquarters, and recruit such a regiment.

They drifted down through the hills toward Burkesville, avoiding main roads, forded the Cumberland the next day, and after two or three days of easy marching arrived at Chattanooga, which would soon become an assembly point for General Braxton Bragg's new Army of Tennessee.

4

About the time that Morgan's small raiding party was leaving Cave City, forty-one young men of the Bluegrass were gathering secretly some 125 miles to the northeast, just outside Lexington. For weeks they had been planning to slip away from under the watchful eyes of Federal patrols and march south, hoping to find John Morgan and join his cavalry squadron. Now at last, all was ready; the night of departure had come.

Leader of this group was John B. Castleman, who had been a corporal in the Lexington Chasseurs, rivals of Morgan's Lexington Rifles. A number of the Chasseurs had followed their commander, Sanders Bruce, into the Union Army. John Castleman, however, had slipped away to Bowling Green in October, 1861, and after his enlistment in the Confederate Army had returned to Lexington, with Morgan's approval, for the purpose of raising a company of cavalry.

Castleman's recruiting went slowly; he had to work secretly and was also handicapped because most of the men of military age in his neighborhood were already enlisted in one or the other of the contending armies. In the end his recruits were mostly in their teens (Castleman was only twenty-one himself) but by mid-May he had enlisted forty young men, and it was they who were gathered at the Castleman home out on the Newtown pike. By eleven o'clock the company was assembled, all well-armed with rifles, revolvers, and a good quantity of ammunition. Most of these arms had "vanished" months ago from the well-stocked armory of the Chasseurs, mysteriously reappearing on this evening in the Castleman home.

Midnight was set as the hour of departure, but as luck would have it a Federal patrol appeared on the pike as they were mounting up. "No. 2 of each set of fours took the horses to a nearby place of concealment," Castleman recorded, "but nothing happened." At one-thirty they moved out on the deserted Newtown pike, halting before dawn at a friend's farm. At dusk they continued toward Mount Sterling, and hiding by day and marching by night through hills and mountains, they at last reached Knoxville where they found a large Confederate training camp. Reporting to the commander,

General Kirby Smith, they explained they were seeking John Morgan's cavalry. Smith informed them that Morgan was recruiting a regiment at Chattanooga, and sent them on their way.

As they approached Morgan's camp on a day late in May they were recognized from a distance for Kentuckians because of the horses they were riding. All forty-one were mounted on Denmarks —as they were called in that time, after an old race horse whose mating with a pacer produced Gaines' Denmark, the greatest of the American Saddle Horse sires.* In the opinion of most of Morgan's men these were the finest of all cavalry horses, and the eyes of the boys at Chattanooga on that May day in 1862 must have lighted when they saw forty-one of them, with Bluegrass riders up, come cantering into camp. In ten days these Denmarks had marched four hundred miles, and looked as fresh as the night they started from Lexington.

The arrival of John Castleman's company at Chattanooga could not have been more timely. Colonel Morgan had been scouring the Confederacy for uncommitted cavalry companies to build his new regiment, and here, out of the blue as it were, an unexpected one appeared.

Already the empty ranks of A, B, and C companies had been filled with two hundred men of the 1st Kentucky Infantry. These men had enlisted for one year, had served in Virginia, and at the completion of enlistments requested transfer to Morgan's cavalry. Now the remnants of the late Captain Brown's company were assigned to John Castleman, who became captain of Company D. As new volunteers came in, along with about thirty more of the missing veterans who had escaped from the Lebanon Races, Company E was formed with John Hutchinson as captain. About the same time, Captain Thomas B. Webber arrived from Holly Springs with a company of Mississippians; they became Company F. From Alabama, Captain R. McFarland reported with enough men to form Company G. And then from Corinth came Basil Duke, recovered from his Shiloh wound, bringing along two companies of Texans under Captains R. M. Gano and John Hoffman. Both Gano and Hoffman were Kentucky-born, eager for service with Morgan.

* Gaines' Denmark himself, although ten or twelve years old, served for a time in Morgan's command, being ridden by John Dillard.

And so it was that within three weeks after the disaster at Lebanon, the magic name of John Morgan attracted enough men to form a regiment, the 2nd Kentucky Cavalry.

Among the new recruits who would help make the history of the 2nd Kentucky were Gordon E. Niles, former New York editor, soon to found one of the most peripatetic newspapers of the Confederate armies, the *Vidette*, published whenever and wherever a printing press was available; Robert A. Alston, fiery South Carolinian, who would serve as Morgan's adjutant; George Ellsworth, Canadian-born telegrapher, whose tricks on the wires would bedevil Federal commanders in the West for the next two years; Thomas Henry Hines, a mysterious Kentuckian sworn in as a private by John Castleman. Hines and Castleman would experience their most daring adventures behind the Federal lines in a fantastic plot to free Confederate prisoners.

For the veterans of Green River and Shiloh there were promotions in rank; men like Ben Drake and Tom Quirk, for instance, were named sergeants for their daring scouting work. Basil Duke, now second in command, became a lieutenant colonel, relinquishing Company A to Captain Jacob Cassell.

During the latter days of May there was a vast amount of activity around the new regiment's camp, Colonel Morgan hurrying back and forth to army headquarters, seeking arms, equipment, regulation uniforms, and additional mounts. The price of good cavalry horses had risen to two hundred dollars, but Morgan held out for the best, and got them. But when he requested permission to take his regiment immediately into Kentucky, he was reminded that a good portion of his new command consisted of inexperienced recruits. Early in June the 2nd Kentucky was ordered to Knoxville for a month of training under General Kirby Smith.

At Knoxville several companies were armed with the medium Enfield—regular Enfields with the barrel sawed off—a weapon which would remain the 2nd Regiment's favorite through the war because of its ease of handling on and off horseback. Drilling and training was intensive from the first day, the usually easygoing John Morgan driving the men hard, eager to obtain Kirby Smith's early approval for a Kentucky raid.

Officers and non-coms were supplied with new editions of Dabney

Maury's *Skirmish Drill for Mounted Troops*, and from daylight until darkness they drilled and drilled, practicing every evolution in the manual—skirmish drill, open order, close order, by twos and by fours. They practiced wheeling, dismounting to fight, deploying to front, flanks and rear, changing from line into column, from column to line. They learned how to take ground in different directions, how to provide for the employment of supports and reserves.

In the midst of all this hard work, the tedium was relieved one day by the arrival of an extraordinary recruit for the 2nd Kentucky. "Dressed in an English staff blue coat and a red forage cap," this newcomer was riding one mount, leading another, with two or three hunting dogs following along in the rear. His name was George St. Leger Grenfell, a British soldier of fortune, and to the Bluegrass boys nurtured on Sir Walter Scott he might have stepped out of the pages of *Ivanhoe*—the Knight Templar, Sir Brian de Bois-Guilbert. "His bold aquiline features were scorched by the sun to a swarthy hue," said Basil Duke, "and his face, while handsome, wore always a defiant and sometimes fierce expression." Grenfell carried letters of introduction from Generals Robert E. Lee and P. G. T. Beauregard. John Morgan was immediately entranced by the man's exotic personality.

Although he was in his middle fifties, Grenfell looked twenty years younger—being spare of frame, sinewy and athletic. He took to the routine of training like the veteran he was, teaching the boys British cavalry tactics, showing them how to fire pistols from the saddle by the right, left, front, and rear. He explained the fine points of aiming while moving at a gallop, how the trooper should rise slightly in the stirrups, arm half extended, the body turned toward the object of the aim.

It must have seemed rather odd for a Britisher to be instructing Kentuckians in the education of horses, but Grenfell could show the boys a trick or two they did not know about training green mounts to stand under fire. Young horses were like girls, he explained, they must be soothed when excited, and the most timid were more easily trained when matched with more experienced ones.

The Kentuckians were intrigued by this strange old warrior, plying him with questions until they learned he had soldiered all over the world—in Africa with the Moors, in India with the British, in

Turkey with the Bashi-Bazouks, in South America with Garibaldi. As a captain of cavalry he fought in Crimea at the time of the famed Charge of the Light Brigade.

He had been raising sheep in South America when he heard of the American Civil War, and had sailed immediately for Charleston, South Carolina. "If England is not at war," he explained, "I go elsewhere to find one." From Charleston he went to Richmond, offering Lee his services in the "Southern States' struggle for independence," as he put it. Lee had sent him to Beauregard, and as soon as Grenfell expressed a desire for cavalry service, Beauregard forwarded him on to John Morgan.

Grenfell achieved a certain rapport with the 2nd Kentucky on all points except that of discipline. Accustomed to rigid European military standards, he could not comprehend the attitude of these freeborn alligator horses toward their officers. It was impossible for him to understand, for example, an incident that occurred between Colonel Morgan and Sergeant Ben Drake on an occasion when Morgan asked Drake to unsaddle and feed his horse. The sergeant, who had been scouting in the saddle for twenty-four hours, was resentful and performed the service grudgingly. Morgan appeared to ignore Drake's grumblings, and when the sergeant completed tending the horse, the Colonel invited him into a farmhouse to sleep beside a warm fireplace. Next morning, Morgan had to awaken the sergeant, ordering him to get up and eat his breakfast in a hurry; the command was ready to move. "Why didn't you rouse me sooner, Colonel?" Drake asked. "My horse hasn't been fed." "You needed sleep," Morgan replied. "I've fed and saddled your horse."

Perhaps there was more of this camaraderie between officers and men in the 2nd Kentucky than in other regiments. After all, most of the men had known each other as equals since boyhood, and military titles meant little to them. "There was always a sort of free-masonry," John Castleman wrote, "born of close relations between rank, file, and officers."

Every once in a while—whenever discipline tended to break down altogether—Morgan and his officers would tighten the reins on the boys, but these occasions were of short duration. As Basil Duke put it philosophically, a cavalryman was harder to discipline than an infantryman "for the reason that he was harder to catch. It is more difficult to regulate six legs than two."

Eventually St. Leger Grenfell abandoned his efforts to apply British Army discipline to these wild Kentuckians. "I never encountered such men," he once declared, "who would fight like the devil, but would do as they pleased, like these damned Rebel cavalrymen."

5

In mid-June the 2nd Kentucky had another unexpected visitor whose errand was quite different from Grenfell's, but whose arrival was as diverting as that of the Britisher. This visitor to the regiment's training camp was none other than the Union Army Major, W. A. Coffey, who had been captured on the train at Cave City and paroled on the promise that he would arrange for the exchange of Lieutenant Colonel Robert Wood. Coffey, resplendent in a new blue Federal uniform, arrived in a fine carriage, a smile on his broad, good-humored face. He and Morgan shook hands like old friends, and then both broke into explosive laughter. Well-armed with letters of identification and passes from both Federal and Confederate generals, Coffey patiently explained the reason for his presence in Knoxville.

Immediately after Morgan had paroled him, he said, he had journeyed to Nashville where Robert Wood was held as prisoner. But General Dumont, in command there, had refused to recognize the parole and would not release Wood. "I then went to Washington," Coffey continued, "and laid my case before the Secretary of War, and at one time I thought my exchange effected, but I was beaten. I then returned to Nashville, by way of my home in Kentucky, leaving my wife on a bed of sickness from which I fear she has not recovered. I've not heard from home since I left." From Kentucky, Coffey continued to Nashville, obtaining a pass through the lines so that he might report to Morgan as a prisoner in accordance with his promise. He crossed the Tennessee River, went to Huntsville, and then back to Chattanooga, where he had heard Morgan was camped. Discovering that Morgan had gone to Knoxville, he hired a carriage and continued his wandering search. A man of honor, a man of his word, Coffey would have sooner died than suffer the disgrace of dishonoring his parole.

Morgan listened sympathetically to his prisoner's story, expressed regrets over the illness of Mrs. Coffey, and invited the Major to become his guest at the Knoxville hotel where he was staying. Perhaps the matter could be settled satisfactorily, Morgan suggested, by correspondence with Federal authorities. For a week or more, the two men lived together at the Bell House, and when Coffey's funds were exhausted Morgan paid his board bill. Morgan even invited him out to watch the 2nd Regiment drill, and although the presence of a spectator in a Federal major's uniform was rather unusual, the boys did not seem to mind. After all, Coffey was a Kentuckian, a sort of special guest.

After learning of all this fraternizing, however, General Kirby Smith decided he had better call John Morgan in for a talk. It was true, Smith agreed, that Major Coffey had behaved admirably, but as commanding general he felt the treatment of the prisoner was not in exact accordance with military usage. It was his intention, the General said, to send the Major on to Richmond to be disposed of by the authorities there.

Morgan was highly indignant. Coffey was an old friend, he protested, an officer and a gentleman who had given his word not to attempt escape. Kirby Smith, however, was adamant.

Returning to his hotel, Morgan revealed the situation to Coffey. "It's shameful," Morgan declared, and he offered to despatch the Major on a good horse with a reliable escort back into the safety of Kentucky.

Coffey shook his head. "Colonel Morgan, if I consent to what you propose, it may result in your being court-martialed, and I'll never let a friend get into trouble on my account if I can prevent it. Moreover, I don't think I'll be sent to Libby Prison. I believe I will be exchanged, and I'd like to go to Richmond and see the sights there."

And so this Union officer was sent to Richmond under guard, where as he had predicted he was not confined to prison but was allowed the freedom of the city, living in a hotel on his word of honor not to attempt escape. But he waited a long time for his exchange. In Kirby Smith's transfer order of June 27, the General explained that Coffey had been in Knoxville for some time past "and had too much opportunity for informing himself about the affairs of this military department . . . for him to be prudently exchanged at this time. It is just to add that Major Coffey bears a very high character as a gentleman and soldier, and it is with regret that I am constrained to report that any arrangement for his exchange be for the present postponed."

An old soldier, Kirby Smith knew that in war friendships could not matter, and he was taking no chances on information leaking back to Kentucky of an impending military movement of great importance. In another week the 2nd Kentucky Regiment would be ready, he had decided, ready for its big strike into the Bluegrass, its First Kentucky Raid.

5

Return to the Bluegrass

I

ON JULY 4, 1862—a holiday considered appropriate for beginning a raid against Union invaders—the 2nd Kentucky marched smartly out of Knoxville, bound west for Sparta, Tennessee. The command totaled 876 officers and men, some in new regulation gray, others in butternut jeans, most armed with Enfields and a variety of pistols, a few carrying shotguns and sabers.

Over rough winding roads the column moved out of the Clinch River valley and entered the Cumberland ranges. This was guerrilla country—a no-man's-land of family feuds and varying allegiances—and more than once the rear companies were fired upon by unseen bushwhackers.

Moving ahead of the column was a newly organized company of sixty scouts, especially trained by Morgan and Grenfell. Acting as captain was Tom Quirk, with Tom Berry and Charles Rogers as lieutenants. The scouts maintained an interval of four hundred yards to the front, and after the bushwhackers began annoying the column, the best sharpshooters of the company were detailed as a defensive rear guard.

Kelion Franklin Peddicord, one of the members of this special organization, afterward remembered the rapid-fire action demanded of them by Tom Quirk, declaring that the Irishman's favorite command was "Double quick! Forward!" and adding that "he would

75

clap spurs to his horse and be off like a shot, flying up the pike, and then after slowing to reform the line would shout: 'Right wheel, double quick! Forward march!' and on we flew." It was difficult for the Bluegrass boys to reconcile Quirk's military character with that of his civilian occupation; he had kept a candy store in Lexington before the war.

By July 7, the regiment was across the Cumberland plateau, camping for the night at one of their favorite Tennessee towns, Sparta. As on their previous visits to Sparta, the townsfolk were most hospitable, but they had a story to tell that aroused the ire of John Morgan and the veterans of the Cave City raid. It seemed that back in May, after the raiders returned to Tennessee, a certain Major Thomas J. Jordan, commanding a battalion of the 9th Pennsylvania Cavalry, had pursued Morgan's men down to Sparta. According to a report of Jordan's actions in Sparta, "he made an order on the ladies of the town to cook for 600 men in one hour and upon failure he said he would turn his men loose upon them and he would not be responsible for anything they might do. The ladies understood this as a threat of rape. They were forced into compliance with his demands."

As Jordan had come to Sparta in pursuit of Morgan's men, they felt a direct responsibility for settling accounts with this blackguard Major. The next day, after a hard ride to Celina Ford on the Cumberland, they heard again of Major Jordan. Only a few days before, Jordan with his cavalrymen had visited Celina and in crude language told the ladies of the town "that unless they cooked for his command they had better sew up the bottoms of their petticoats."

From civilian informants, officers of the 2nd learned that Major Jordan was based at Tompkinsville, Kentucky, and although this town was some miles west of their planned route of invasion, they resolved to pay a visit there forthwith. They believed it the duty of true knights, when ladies have been dishonored, to seek out the churlish offenders and do battle. Or in the words of "The Hunters of Kentucky":

> And now if danger e'er annoys, remember
> what our trade is;
> Just send for us Kentucky boys, and
> we'll protect you, ladies.

Before leaving Celina, Morgan sent scouts forward to reconnoiter the roads to Tompkinsville. Meanwhile the regiment rested, shoed and curried horses, and enjoyed the July sunshine. St. Leger Grenfell led a bathing party into the Cumberland. "It was one of his habits to bathe himself in almost every stream we crossed," said Tom Berry. "He always wore a fiery red silk cap with cord and tassels of finest Indian silk."

At eleven o'clock that night bugles sounded boots and saddles, and the command moved out for Tompkinsville over a rough road encumbered by fallen timber. Before dawn they were across the line into Kentucky, the boys' spirits rising mile by mile. "On long raids," one of them wrote afterward, "a cavalryman sleeps much in the saddle, but it is a fitful, broken, unsatisfactory sleep." On this night, however, all were wide awake with expectancy. "The cavalryman enjoys nothing more than a long raid into the enemy's country . . . the Kentuckian always had a longing eye for the Bluegrass region, and was never so happy as when marching in that direction. On these wild rides he had a 'high old time!' and enjoyed the constantly varying scenery."

Before leaving Knoxville, Lieutenant Colonel Duke, who was somewhat of a poet, had composed a song designed to be sung by the regiment as it marched into Kentucky. He called it "Song of the Raiders":

> On the Cumberland's bosom
> The moonbeams are bright
> And the path of the raid
> Is made plain by their light.
> And across the wide ripple
> And up the steep bank
> I see the dark squadron
> Move rank after rank.

One difficulty on this night march into their native state was that few of the boys knew the words or music of the song, and without Duke to lead them the verses tended to fade away, although the Colonel's brother, Tom Morgan, lent his fine tenor voice to the choruses.

Back down the column, the alligator horses had a go at "Song of the Raiders," but most of them satisfied themselves with "The Bonnie

Blue Flag," ribald versions of "Rose of Alabama," or such bits of doggerel as:

> Georgia girls are handsome
> And Tennessee girls are sweet;
> But a girl in old Kentucky
> Is the one I want to meet.

When the column was within five miles of Tompkinsville, Morgan sent Gano's squadron of Texans off on a road to the right to get in the enemy's rear and cut off the line of retreat toward Glasgow. Already dawn streaked the sky, and it was broad daylight when the men at the head of the column sighted the church spires of Tompkinsville. A few minutes later they saw Major Jordan's troopers posted on a thickly wooded hill.

The 2nd Kentucky came up fast in single rank, holding fire until within sixty yards. "We had to cross open fields to get at them," Basil Duke recorded. "They fired three or four volleys while we were closing in on them." At the first volley, Grenfell, eager for a taste of action, "spurred his horse forward between the two opposing lines, risking the fire of the enemy, leaped a low fence behind which the enemy were lying, and began lashing at them right and left with his saber."

In ten minutes the fight was all over, Gano's Texans whooping in from the rear, the Pennsylvanians throwing down their arms. The prisoners totaled nearly three hundred. As for the much-sought Major Jordan, he was caught attempting escape on a wounded horse. Brought before Colonel Morgan, he refused to endorse a parole, accusing the Kentuckians of being marauders because regular Confederate soldiers would never be operating so far behind enemy lines. Morgan would hear this argument time and again, but he listened patiently to Jordan's tirade, then ordered a detail to conduct the Major back through the Confederate lines.*

From the Pennsylvanians' camp, the raiders took a number of good Kentucky horses and abundant supplies of coffee and sugar.

---

* Major Jordan was taken to Georgia, then sent by rail to Richmond, where charges were brought against him for insulting the women of Sparta and Celina. In October, 1862, he denied the accusations, admitting only that he had demanded meals cooked for his men. He was later exchanged, and reported back for duty at Louisville in December.

"The guns captured," Basil Duke noted, "were useless breech-loading carbines, which were thrown away," an act which has puzzled some latter-day historians of Confederate cavalry. Actually, early in the war Confederate soldiers were encouraged to exchange their arms for better ones found on the battlefield, but from hard experience Morgan's men had learned that a fine new rifle was useless when the ammunition captured with it was exhausted. Ammunition commonly available in the Confederacy could not be used in Federal breechloaders, and exchange of rifles was eventually forbidden all Confederate soldiers by a general order.

Lighthearted from their easy victory and the capture of the "black knight," Jordan, the boys of the 2nd moved on to Glasgow, home town of several men in C Company. Wives and sweethearts kept cooking-stoves going all night, and Colonel Morgan decided to delay marching orders until late in the morning. During the rest period, he and Gordon Niles—the former New York editor—visited a printing shop to have some recruiting posters printed for distribution along the invasion route.

By midmorning, when the command marched out on the north turnpike toward Green River, fleecy clouds were forming high in the sky. Weatherwise troopers checked their ponchos and oilcloths; shortly after noon the western sky was towering with thunderheads.

Before they reached the L. & N. Railroad, the storm was upon them—wind, lightning, and rain. A half mile below Horse Cave, Morgan ordered the troopers to take shelter where they could find it—in barns, haymows or thickets—while he, Grenfell, the telegrapher Ellsworth, and a few of the scouts continued to the railroad.

In his report of this raid, Morgan recorded a method of obtaining information about the enemy which he was to use increasingly on all his marches. "I caused wires connecting with the portable battery which I carried with me to be attached to the telegraph line near Horse Cave and intercepted a number of dispatches."

The man wholly responsible for operating this interceptor station was George Ellsworth, a jaunty, worldly-wise telegrapher. His eyelids drooped under a high forehead, his nose was aquiline with a bump in the bridge; the expression in his eyes was disdainful, cynical, devil-may-care. Fascinated by Samuel Morse's new invention,

Ellsworth had left his home in Canada to study in Morse's school at Washington, D. C. Graduated as a crack telegrapher, he had taken a job in Kentucky before the war, and while in Lexington became acquainted with John Morgan. In 1860, Ellsworth had moved on to Houston, Texas, but when Morgan first had the idea of tapping wires he remembered Ellsworth and sent for him. The telegrapher had joined the 2nd Kentucky at Chattanooga. He was a prize acquisition for the regiment; he was resourceful, could read rapid-fire code, imitate other telegraphers, and was familiar with the sending styles of many operators who were working for the Federals in Kentucky and Tennessee. He also possessed an astringent sense of humor.

A pocket instrument such as that used by Ellsworth could be cut into a circuit without breaking the current. As long as the operator was content to remain quiet, other telegraphers along the line were unaware of his presence. But if he touched the key to send messages he was likely to arouse curiosity if not suspicion, a telegrapher's operation of a key being almost as distinctive as his voice.

On this first venture into wire tapping at Horse Cave, Ellsworth was daring enough to use a ground wire to cut the southern towns from the circuit, answering for them when the stations to the north made queries. His only difficulty was the storm, the pouring rain and flashing lightning interfering with his work. Once a bolt of lightning danced along the overhead wires and sparked off the key in his hand. Scout Ben Drake, standing by, was both amused and impressed. "Old Lightning himself," said Drake, and the name stayed with Ellsworth through the war—Lightning Ellsworth.

St. Leger Grenfell afterward mentioned that they "were seated for several hours on a clay bank during a violent storm, but the interest was so intense that the time passed like a few minutes."

Ellsworth's own written report of the incident was brief: "Heavy storms, atmospheric electricity. . . . During the whole of the time it was raining heavy; my situation was anything but an agreeable one, sitting in the mud, with my feet in the water up to my knees."

From Ellsworth's intercepted messages, Morgan was able to learn locations and movements of enemy troops along his planned route of invasion, intelligence which on this occasion and others enabled him to confuse and startle the Federals, and on all raids but one to elude efforts to capture his forces.

Leaving the railroad, the regiment turned northeastward, fording Green River and marching by night through wooded hill country. Late afternoon of July 11, the scouts sighted Rolling Fork River, only six miles from Lebanon, Kentucky. Colonel Morgan, coming up with the advance company, was suddenly fired upon as he approached a small covered-bridge crossing. The bullet spun the hat off his head, but he was unscratched.

As soon as the advance took cover, scouts moved out through the woods to reconnoiter. Although the bridge defenders' marksmanship seemed to lack accuracy, they were in considerable numbers, and Morgan decided the time had come to use the regiment's artillery pieces, two mountain howitzers procured shortly before leaving Knoxville. Already the men of the 2nd had acquired a fondness for this pair of small guns, naming them the "bull pups" after their quick barklike reports.

For cavalry use, Basil Duke rated these "bull pups" above the three-inch Parrott guns which the regiment later added. "They can go over ravines, up hills, through thickets, almost anywhere, in short that a horseman can go; they can be taken, without attracting attention, in as close proximity to the enemy as two horsemen can go—they throw shell with accuracy eight hundred yards, quite as far as there is any necessity for, generally in cavalry fighting—they throw canister and grape, two and three hundred yards, as effectively as a twelve-pounder—they can be carried by hand right along with the line, and as close to the enemy as the line goes—and they make a great deal more noise than one would suppose from their size and appearance."

On this day, one vicious bark from a "bull pup" was enough to send the bridge defenders scurrying toward Lebanon. The column crossed, and C and E companies dismounted, driving the Federals back into Lebanon as darkness fell. By ten o'clock the 2nd Kentucky had occupied the town, capturing almost two hundred soldiers who were guarding Federal storehouses.

According to a later report in the *Louisville Journal*, "the destruction was immense . . . sugar, coffee, flour; guns were bent double by hard licks over rocks—powder, cartridges, and caps were thrown into the creek." The same reporter, describing the men of the 2nd, said they "had no general uniforms, and were armed to suit their own taste. They all had Adams' patent six-shooters, an English pistol, received, they said, from England a short time since.* Many of them had shotguns; a few only had sabers, or bayonets."

Not until noon of the following day, July 12, was the 2nd finished with its work in Lebanon, destroying by the Federals' own estimate more than one hundred thousand dollars' worth of military supplies. While the boys were burning these stores, Morgan and his forerunner of the modern propaganda officer, Gordon Niles, were distributing recruiting posters and welcoming new additions to the regiment.

Early in the afternoon the buglers called for formations, and by two o'clock the column was winding out on the Springfield road. At nine o'clock the next morning, after marching all night, they were entering Harrodsburg, which according to Basil Duke was "another stronghold of our friends, and we were warmly welcomed."

2

It was a summer Sunday in Harrodsburg, the townspeople dressed in their best, bound for church in carriages or on foot. As the dusty horsemen moved slowly along the main street, little groups gathered to applaud and cheer. "It was a weird, wild cavalcade," wrote Maria Daviess, who watched the column pass her house, "horses of all kinds and colors; boys of all ages and sizes, and no uniforms, save the general grimy gray, that dust and wear had given. There were shaking of hands and tears and kisses, and such unsoldierly demonstrations, as never were shown."

Deciding to make a brief rest stop, Colonel Morgan turned his men in under the tall elms of the local camping grounds. A small crowd followed them into the shaded greensward, gathering to stare at the legendary Morgan who was mounted on a large chestnut

* Actually only a few carried the Adams' six-shooter, a .44 caliber double-action weapon patented in 1857, and ranked next to the Colt in estimation of Southern ordnance officers.

horse. A woman walked near him, examining the horse. "This is not Black Bess, Colonel Morgan?"

"No, madam," Morgan replied. "Black Bess has 'gone up.' "

A proud mother then lifted her baby for the Colonel to see, explaining that the child was named for General Beauregard. Morgan touched the baby gently, and said: "Beauregard, you're better looking than the General."

In a few minutes the ladies of Harrodsburg had improvised a picnic. "The fat of the land was furnished in rich abundance," Maria Daviess noted. "Milk and honey literally flowed, and the larders of the loyal yielded up their stores as freely as the most rabid 'secesh.' In fact they only saw the return of prodigals in their neighbors' sons, and ate, drank and were merry with them."

As the crowd increased in size, Morgan noticed several men of military age in the background and he seized an opportunity to make a recruiting speech. According to Lizzie Hardin, who recorded the day's events in her diary, he said among other things: "If the men of Kentucky had but the spirit of her women she would have long since been free." *

Morgan cut off his speech; there were matters more pressing. Lexington lay only twenty-eight miles to the northeast, and after five days of driving deeper and deeper into enemy-held territory, there was not one of the raiders who was unaware of the danger surrounding them now. Only by swift marches and deceptive turns and passes had they escaped meeting massed forces of pursuing Federals. After an officers' conference, Morgan sent Gano and his Texans off to the north of Lexington to burn bridges along the Kentucky Central Railroad so as to delay reinforcements from Cincinnati. Captain Allen's Company B was dispatched on a similar mission to cut the Louisville-Lexington Railroad.

---

* According to Maria Daviess' amusing account of the 2nd Regiment's short stay in Harrodsburg, "next day the town was reeking with Sunday's adventures." One pretty girl declared she would never wash her hands again until the boys should come back to imprint them with fresh kisses. A more mature beauty was said to have become engaged to marry St. Leger Grenfell. The daughter of Harrodsburg's most loyal Unionist was wearing on her watch chain a button from John Morgan's coat. "All the town is crying shame on the way the women kissed Morgan's boys," Mrs. Daviess reported, then explained that those who were kissed were "relatives, sons, or college boys."

Hazardous as was their situation, the raiders could take some comfort from telegraphic reports intercepted by Lightning Ellsworth along their line of march. They knew that General Jeremiah Boyle, commanding Union troops in Kentucky from Louisville headquarters, was in a state of panic. Boyle was sending messages in all directions, calling for help to halt the "invasion of Kentucky," and in the few days since the 2nd Regiment had entered the state, Boyle had magnified its strength from one thousand men to five thousand. While the 2nd was enjoying the short Sabbath rest in Harrodsburg, Boyle was telegraphing President Lincoln, pleading for more troops, but Lincoln was having his troubles in the East with General McClellan who was in disastrous retreat before the armies of General Lee. Lincoln did find time to send a message to General Halleck at Corinth, Mississippi: "They are having a stampede in Kentucky. Please look to it."

Unaware of this latest concern in high places about his movements, Morgan started the 2nd out of Harrodsburg before sundown. He and the boys from Lexington still hoped to pay a visit to their home town, and when they reached Lawrenceburg about one o'clock the following morning, the scouts galloped ahead in a feint toward Frankfort, an effort to distract the enemy's attention from Lexington.

At dawn the main column resumed march over a road that brought nostalgic memories to veterans of the old squadron, the Versailles road, and when they reached Shryock's Ferry at midmorning there were some who vividly recalled an autumn night that now seemed like time out of remote past, the night they had brought the hay wagons loaded with rifles out of Lexington.

The ferryboat had been sunk by the Federals, and they had to raise and repair it in order to float the howitzers across. They moved into Versailles cautiously, with patrols out in all directions. During the night the scouts who had made the feint toward Frankfort rejoined the regiment, and the Lexington boys could scarcely contain themselves, knowing that their home town now lay only twelve miles off to the east.

From friends in Versailles, however, Morgan learned the disappointing news that Lexington was a Federal stronghold, with several thousand troops stationed in and around the town. Many of these soldiers were raw recruits in training, it was said, but sheer numbers would outweigh the few hundred troopers of the 2nd Kentucky.

And so instead of marching triumphantly into Lexington, as he had hoped to do, Morgan swung northward. At sundown, July 16, the 2nd Kentucky marched into Georgetown, a bearded, dust-coated, weary band of men. They sat their mounts like centaurs, but after more than three hundred miles of steady marching, horses and riders were bone-weary. Now they would have to stop; every officer and every man knew it; horseflesh and manflesh could endure no more.

Georgetown was no accidental choice for a long rest stop. Morgan and many of the Bluegrass boys had friends and relatives here. "A strong Secesh town," the Federals had labeled Georgetown, but did not bother to garrison the place. Lexington, they thought, was close enough to handle any trouble likely to arise.

Morgan camped his men in line of battle through the night, and after Gano's Texans and Company B came in, he kept alternating detachments moving out of Georgetown in all directions, screening the presence of his main force, giving the troopers an opportunity to take turns at recuperating. Lightning Ellsworth maintained a steady vigil in the telegraph office, creating confusion among the various Federal commanders by sending them fake messages concerning movements of Morgan's men. He also reported to Morgan intercepted information concerning movements of Federal troops.

In the midst of all these activities, Morgan did not overlook one of the prime purposes of this raid into Kentucky—recruiting. He composed a fiery manifesto and ordered Gordon Niles to have it set up in bold black type:

KENTUCKIANS!

I come to liberate you from the despotism of a tyrannical faction and to rescue my native State from the hand of your oppressors. Everywhere the cowardly foe has fled from my avenging arms. My brave army is stigmatized as a band of guerrillas and marauders. Believe it not. I point with pride to their deeds as a refutation to this foul aspersion. We come not to molest peaceful individuals or to destroy private property, but guarantee absolute protection to all who are not in arms against us. We ask only to meet the hireling legions of Lincoln.

The eyes of your brethren of the South are upon you. Your gallant fellow citizens are flocking to our standard. Our armies are rapidly advancing to your protection. Then greet them with the willing hands of fifty thousand of Kentucky's brave. Their advance is already with you.

He closed the broadside with a stirring quotation from Fitz-Greene Halleck's "Marco Bozzaris":

Strike for the Green Graves of Your Sires!
Strike for Your Altars and Your Fires!
God, and Your Native Land.

Although martial law had been declared in Lexington and passes were required to enter and leave the town, Captain John Castleman and others who had lived near there all their lives eluded enemy pickets after nightfall and visited relatives and sweethearts. They also smuggled in copies of Morgan's printed broadside, and passed word around that new recruits would be welcomed at Georgetown.

Awaiting just such an opportunity was a young lawyer-editor, William C. P. Breckinridge and a few of his friends. Because of their Confederate sympathies they had been closely watched by Federal authorities in Lexington, but on this moonlit night they slipped out of town by woodland trails and headed for Georgetown to join the 2nd Kentucky. With other recruits enlisted at Georgetown, Billy Breckinridge—son of a father devoted to the Union—was able to form a new cavalry company the next morning, Company I. "In less than twenty-four hours," Breckinridge said afterward, "I was an enlisted man, a captain, and engaged in a battle."

A battle was certainly overdue for the 2nd Kentucky, but after John Castleman reported early on the morning of July 18 that Lexington was defended by three thousand Federal troops, Morgan definitely decided that his home town was not the place to challenge combat. Instead he proposed to his officers that they strike to the north and destroy Federal stores reported to be concentrated at Cynthiana, then swing south through Paris and Winchester, drawing a half circle around Lexington. At Winchester, they could choose from a number of routes back into Tennessee.

To screen the main movement toward Cynthiana, Captain Castleman was ordered to lead D Company in a daring diversionary march down to the outskirts of Lexington. Castleman was to make every effort to create an impression that D Company was the entire raiding force of the 2nd Kentucky. He was to avoid close enemy contact and take no prisoners. Wherever possible he was to cut telegraph wires and destroy railroad bridges, and some time on July 19—the following day—he was to bring his company into Winchester and rejoin the regiment.

This was quite an assignment for a twenty-one-year-old captain who had been soldiering for only two months, but both John Morgan and Basil Duke were confident that Castleman and the eighty-one men in his company, "each one capable of commanding," could carry it off successfully.

The morning was well along when Morgan gave marching orders to the regiment, and the columns of twos began swinging off toward the sun and Cynthiana. Castleman watched the advance company move out, then wheeled his mounted troop and turned south toward Lexington.

Four miles out of Georgetown, Castleman sent Lieutenant Will Morris and a squad of eight men forward in a fast gallop to scout the approaches to Lexington; then he turned D Company off the pike, sought woods cover, and halted. Within an hour the scouts were back; they had encountered pickets at the tollgate outside Lexington and had driven them in toward the town.

Castleman knew that it would be only a matter of time before a large force of Federals would be marching out of Lexington in pursuit. He formed his company into close columns and reminded the men of their orders: to create the impression that they were the entire force of the 2nd Kentucky. "Pay attention, keep in touch, keep cool," he said. Resuming march, they moved on toward Taylor's Cross Roads.

Suddenly out of the hedges of a country home, they saw three boys appear. One was John Castleman's younger brother, George; the others were Willie McCaw and Allie Cooper, who lived in the house. The three boys excitedly informed Castleman that an advance party of Federal troops, with artillery pieces, was waiting in ambush at the crossroads.

After a brief conference with his lieutenants, Castleman decided it would be foolhardy to ride down the main road into the face of an enemy supported by artillery in position. But he remembered a side road by which they could come in on the flank. Informing his men of his plan, he ordered the column reversed, and in a few minutes they turned off on a dirt track. They moved quietly, the undulating land and its woods cover concealing their presence until they were within three hundred yards of the waiting Federals. As they came up over a rise, Castleman yelled, "At a gallop!" and they thundered down on the surprised enemy, screaming the Rebel yell.

It was too much for the raw troops of Colonel Leonidas Metcalfe's cavalry brigade. After a scattering of return fire and a futile effort to wheel their artillery, the Union troops mounted up and started on the run for Lexington. D Company did not pursue them very far, of course; they turned about and withdrew slowly toward Horeb church.

At the church they turned off into a woodland, familiar to most of them from boyhood, and as they knew they would, found a pond for watering their thirsty horses. It was high noon on a lazy July day in Kentucky, birds calling from the trees, the smell of clover in the air. But for their arms and dress and the urgency they saw in each other's eyes, it was like a hundred other July days they had known in the Bluegrass.

Not a man or horse had been wounded in the charge at the crossroads, and as they recounted the experience, it seemed almost too easy. Had they really tricked the Federals into believing that Morgan's 2nd Regiment was about to descend upon Lexington? Should they go out seeking another fight, or wait for the enemy to come to them? Castleman and Lieutenant Tom Hines agreed that if they waited long enough, concealed around the church, the Federals would come looking for them. The problem was what to do when the enemy advance troop showed on the turnpike. Hines suggested a combined ambush and mounted charge. If the next lot of Federals was as green as the first, they also might panic and run. If not, D Company could make its escape back into the woods behind the church.

Hines volunteered to handle the ambush. He selected five sharpshooters; they left their horses behind the church, walked across the road, and concealed themselves in underbrush where they could deliver a blast of fire into the flank of an approaching column.*

Castleman meanwhile kept the others beside the church. They led their horses out into the burying ground where they could quickly mount and form into a skirmish line. Flies buzzed lazily in the July heat. The horses nibbled at lush bluegrass on the mounds.

Young as these cavalrymen were, the presence of gravestones seemed to sober them, remind them of the brevity of life. Some of their kin were buried here. "My horse stood astride my own father's grave," Castleman remembered. And one of his troopers, Private De Witt Duncan, broke the silence by repeating some verses of Thomas Gray's "Elegy Written in a Country Church Yard":

> "The boast of heraldry, the pomp of power,
> And all that beauty, all that wealth e'er gave,
> Awaits alike the inevitable hour,
> The paths of glory lead but to the grave."

As the young man's voice died away in the shaded stillness, some-one sighted a trace of dust over the glittering turnpike. The enemy . . . *the inevitable hour . . . the paths of glory* . . . They waited. The dust rolled closer. They could see the first horsemen now. Castleman quietly ordered his men to mount and form in battle rank.

Across the road, Tom Hines and his sharpshooters lay on their bellies in the green sunlit brush. The Federal cavalry moved slowly closer, cautious, very alert. A moment before he was certain they would see his men, Castleman shouted: "Charge!" and they came out in a sweeping line, firing by squads. At the first sound of fire, Hines' sharpshooters blasted the Federal flank.

It was a rout, even more complete than the little fight at the crossroads. "The accurate fire of the sharpshooters," said Castleman, "was of great service. Although the enemy gave the mounted men credit, no one can fire rifles accurately in a cavalry charge." D Troop waited only long enough to reassemble, then galloped away, pausing briefly at Castleton—the Castleman homestead—then con-tinuing across friendly farms of the neighborhood. At dusk they halted at Colonel McCann's farm, south of the Winchester turnpike.

---

* One of the sharpshooters with Hines was John Allen, older brother of James Lane Allen, famed Kentucky author.

"At that hospitable home we bivouacked for part of the night and 'man and beast' were well fed."

Some time afterward, Colonel McCann's daughter, Sally, recorded for John Castleman her impressions of that visit of Company D: "I remember, as if it were yesterday, the night you came with your company to my father's house, and with what willingness my father provided for both men and horses. I was then a girl of sixteen. I remember the jokes of John Hines, Lawrence Jones and others, and how silent you were, for we knew you felt the responsibility of your company, so near the enemy. I felt that night as if I were living in the time of 'Robin Hood' with Company D eating supper in the woodland by moonlight, and how quietly you all rode away."

3

While Company D was distracting the Federals outside Lexington, some of the veteran companies of the 2nd Kentucky, twenty-five miles away at Cynthiana, were engaged in their bitterest fighting of the war.

About three o'clock in the afternoon, the regiment's advance flushed out a Federal picket guard, chasing them back to the Licking River and the narrow covered bridge which led into the town. Colonel Morgan knew the terrain well, and had already planned his attack. As usual, he sent Gano's Texans in a sweeping hook around one end, the other arm of the pincers on this occasion being Captain McFarland's Company G. They were to cross at fords a mile or so above and below the covered bridge and get in the rear of Cynthiana.

While these two wing companies were galloping away, companies A and B moved to the right of the road, E and F to the left. These men dismounted while C Company held its position back down the pike, prepared to charge as soon as the bridge was cleared. William Breckinridge's inexperienced recruits, Company I, remained in the rear as reserves.

Here again, as at Lebanon, Tennessee, this was to be a fight largely between Kentuckians. The Union defenders of Cynthiana, under Lieutenant Colonel John J. Landram, consisted of Kentucky infantry and cavalry units and one artillery piece, a twelve-pounder howitzer manned by a company of firemen from Cincinnati. The firemen had their howitzer set up in the Cynthiana square, and they opened up on the 2nd Kentucky while the men were taking positions on either side the covered bridge. Tom Berry, who was preparing to charge the bridge on foot with Quirk's scouts, said afterward that the Cincinnati firemen "went to work with this gun as if they were trying to put out a fire."

It soon became apparent to Morgan's men that they could not take the bridge by frontal assault. In addition to grape and canister flying through the air from the howitzer, heavy rifle fire was now pouring from buildings just across the Licking River.

While E and F moved up to the riverbank on the left, Quirk's scouts and A Company dropped down into the stream, and holding rifles and ammunition above their heads, the men began swimming across. Bullets spattered around them like rain. Some men were hit, some drowned, but most of them gained the east bank and dug in. For a few minutes it looked as if they could not hold their position, with Landram's defenders concentrating upon their little bridgehead, but B Company quickly shifted upstream and opened with flanking fire on A Company's most dangerous assailants.

At this moment, Captain James Bowles' Company C came charging down the pike, St. Leger Grenfell's scarlet skullcap bobbing as he raced with the leaders. They hit the bridge with a thundering of hoofs on board planking and dashed headlong up the main street toward the enemy howitzer. And while the Federals were off balance from the shock of this mounted charge, Morgan's dismounted companies swarmed through the bridge tunnel, each company moving in a different direction through the town. Company A, which had borne the brunt of the assault, charged up the bank from the river, ammunition virtually exhausted. Tom Quirk, noticing a Union soldier taking close aim on Ben Drake, downed the man with a stone.

Meanwhile Gano's Texans and G Company had swept in from the rear, and the Cincinnati firemen seeing Morgan men approaching "by every road, street and bypath . . . were compelled to abandon their piece."

"Old St. Lege," as the boys now called their British comrade, led a second mounted charge against the last enemy stronghold, the railroad depot. Eleven bullets pierced his clothing, his talismanic cap, and in some places his skin, but his attack ended the fighting, and he required no surgeon to patch his wounds. "I cannot too highly compliment Colonel St. Leger Grenfell," Basil Duke wrote in his report of the action, "for the execution of an order which did perhaps more than anything else to gain the battle. His example gave new courage to everyone who witnessed it."

Duke also noted that Company A "covered itself with glory." These former Lexington Rifles, veterans of Green River, Shiloh, and Lebanon, also suffered the most casualties. Private William Craig, first to swim the Licking River, was the first to die, as he mounted the bank. Sergeant Henry Elder, one of the five who drove the hay wagons from Lexington, was too badly wounded to be moved. Tom Berry of the scouts also had to be left behind. All the officers of A Company, except Third Lieutenant Samuel D. Morgan, were wounded.

Lieutenant Colonel Landram, the Federal commander, made his escape on a fast horse. Returning to Cynthiana after the 2nd Kentucky withdrew, Landram reported: "I can give no accurate account of the rebel dead, Morgan having taken off eight burial-cases from this place and his men having been seen hauling off their dead toward Lexington after the fight. . . . Since Morgan left, thirteen of his dead have been taken from the river."

Colonel Morgan reported only eight killed and twenty-nine wounded (the thirteen dead later recovered from the river were probably considered as missing). His estimate of enemy casualties was 194 killed and wounded. As for the damage done to military supplies, he listed the capture of three hundred cavalry horses, a large number of small arms, and the destruction of commissary and medical stores, tents, guns, and ammunition. "Paroled prisoners were sent under escort to Falmouth where they took the train for Cincinnati." John Morgan always made it easy for paroled Federal soldiers to find their way home.

The July sun was still high when the 2nd Regiment marched out of Cynthiana, back over the same covered bridge which they had won at such high cost earlier in the afternoon. With their coffined dead on wagons and their wounded in buggies, they moved cautiously toward Paris. About five miles north of that town they were met by a friendly delegation bringing the good news that the Federal garrison at Paris had been called to Lexington to help fight Morgan's raiders! John Castleman and Company D had done their work well, and thanks to them their regimental comrades spent a quiet night in Paris, camping on the courthouse lawn. Not all of them used the peaceful night for resting, as the pro-Union editor of the Paris *Western Citizen* noted in his July 22 issue: "They took all the good horses that they could lay their hands on, and must have taken thirty or forty in the county and around the town of Paris."

As much as the boys would have enjoyed lingering in Paris, soon after sunrise scouts were bringing in reports of a large enemy force approaching from Lexington. By eight o'clock Morgan started the companies moving south again, and when they rode into Winchester at noon, they found John Castleman's Company D in full possession of the friendly town. There were also fresh rumors of enemy troops in pursuit from north, east and west. At four o'clock they moved down to the Kentucky River, crossed before dark, and marched on through the night to Richmond. Here they were happy to discover a friendly "garrison," a company of recruits under Captain William Jennings, about fifty young men responding to John Morgan's call to liberate Kentucky from the "hireling legions of Lincoln." As soon as the sun rose on the quiet Sunday morning of July 20, Morgan swore them in as Company K of the 2nd Kentucky.

Back in Winchester that same morning, an eighteen-year-old girl, Mattie Wheeler, was writing in her diary: "All is quiet this morning but yesterday was a day that will be ever memorable to me. Col. John H. Morgan, with a great many of his men passed through Winchester. We all went down town and stood in Mrs. Turnbull's yard and talked to some of the soldiers. There was a good many of our acquaintances among them. There was a Dr. Hays whom Bettie had known in Lexington & Johnnie Moore who is a mighty nice gentleman. They got several recruits from this county. Jimmie Price, Marshall and Stonestreet Van Meter, and Joe Croxton. Two boys came in from Lexington. They stole off from there the night before. There were some of the nicest gentlemen among them that I ever saw. They did nothing wrong as far as I could see, except '*swap horses.*' " (Mattie Wheeler explained the meaning of "swapping horses" thus: "When one would brake down, they would change it for a fresh one.")

Late that night she added another entry: "This has been a sad day for me. I hope I may never see a sadder. There is a large army in pursuit of John Morgan, while I am writing. I still hear their tramp, tramp on the Richmond Pike. It is a dreadful sound."

The tramping army, however, did not overtake the 2nd Kentucky. Before dawn of the twenty-first, the regiment had reached Crab Orchard, and quite aware of the hot pursuit, continued to Somerset. The only exciting incidents of this thirty-six-hour march involved Lightning Ellsworth, the swaggering telegrapher. On the way into Crab Orchard, Ellsworth's temper was aroused by a bushwhacker firing into the column. When the regiment halted in the town to feed and water mounts, the telegrapher borrowed St. Leger Grenfell's fine horse—without asking permission—and took off with another trooper to flush out the bushwacker and capture him if possible. Ellsworth and his friend found the bushwhacker back down the road, but the man's marksmanship was too much for them; the telegrapher's companion was wounded, and in rescuing him, Ellsworth let Grenfell's prize steed escape—with a valuable English saddle and a coat rolled behind it, the pockets containing all of Grenfell's gold money.

When Ellsworth rejoined the column with his tale of losing the Englishman's horse, "St. Leger was like an excited volcano, and sought Ellsworth to slay him instantly." According to Basil Duke, "Three days were required to pacify Grenfell, during which time the great 'operator' had to be carefully kept out of his sight."

At Somerset, Ellsworth returned to his regular duties, and sought to make up for his fiasco by composing some masterful farewell telegrams to General Jeremiah Boyle, commander of Federal troops in Kentucky; to George D. Prentice, editor of the *Louisville Journal* and fiery critic of Morgan's raiders; and last, to all the Union telegraph operators in Kentucky. He signed the message to Boyle with Morgan's name:

GOOD MORNING, JERRY. THIS TELEGRAPH IS A GREAT INSTITUTION.
YOU SHOULD DESTROY IT AS IT KEEPS ME POSTED TOO WELL. MY

FRIEND ELLSWORTH HAS ALL YOUR DISPATCHES SINCE JULY 10 ON
FILE. DO YOU WANT COPIES?

His farewell to the telegraph operators was in the form of a general order:

HEADQUARTERS, TELEGRAPH DEPT. OF KY.,
CONFEDERATE STATES OF AMERICA

GENERAL ORDER NO. 1

WHEN AN OPERATOR IS POSITIVELY INFORMED THAT THE ENEMY IS
MARCHING ON HIS STATION, HE WILL IMMEDIATELY PROCEED TO
DESTROY THE TELEGRAPHIC INSTRUMENTS AND ALL MATERIAL IN HIS
CHARGE. SUCH INSTANCES OF CARELESSNESS, AS WERE EXHIBITED ON
THE PART OF THE OPERATORS AT LEBANON AND GEORGETOWN WILL
BE SEVERELY DEALT WITH, BY ORDER OF

G. A. ELLSWORTH

GENERAL MILITARY SUPT. C. S. TELEGRAPHIC DEPT.

For all practical purposes the First Kentucky Raid was now history. The regiment eluded all its pursuers, crossing the Cumberland River at Stagall's ferry, and after five days of slow marching rode into Livingston, Tennessee, on July 28. Here they rested for three days, repairing equipment and shoeing horses, then marched leisurely down to Sparta to establish camp. Leaving Basil Duke in command, Colonel Morgan went on to Knoxville to report in person to Kirby Smith, and to plead for a more ambitious invasion of Kentucky by the combined armies of the West.

4

In assessing the accomplishments of the 2nd Kentucky Regiment's thousand-mile July raid, John Morgan noted that he had destroyed Federal supplies and arms in seventeen towns, recruited three hundred men and several hundred horses, captured and paroled twelve hundred enemy troops, and had lost in killed, wounded, and missing about ninety men.

Some other accomplishments, however, he did not mention; for one, the fear engendered among Federal commanders in the West of other and more damaging raids. Not for many months, at least not until after Morgan's great raid of July, 1863, through Indiana and Ohio, could commanding officers of Union forces between Cincinnati and Tennessee relax in the security of distance from lines of battle. How many thousands of troops were diverted from front-line duty to guard railroads, supply depots, river crossings—every conceivable point of attack or sabotage—cannot be estimated, but the number was large, and would grow larger with each sudden strike of the cavalry raiders.

Even more far-reaching than this was the 2nd Kentucky's contribution to the science of cavalry—the technique of raiding far behind the lines. Although Morgan and his officers did not realize it at the time, they had brought something new to one of the oldest of the combatant arms.

After the First Kentucky Raid, a British student of cavalry wrote admiringly of the style of raiding introduced by John Morgan's men: "By skilful marches, by scattering his forces and threatening several points at once, the Federal officers were entirely bewildered, and did not know where to expect a blow. The extreme mobility of his flying column also rendered it difficult to obtain any correct information as to Morgan's force or his intentions."

In the first year of the war, cavalry on both sides was compact, slow moving, heavily accoutered, moving always with the infantry. Sometimes it was brought in upon a flank at critical moments for charges. The 2nd Kentucky, however—under John Morgan and with the benefit of St. Leger Grenfell's knowledge of irregular military tactics—developed as mounted light infantry, drilled to fight on foot, toughened for long marches. After their experience at Shiloh, the boys of the 2nd wanted no more of the old-style role of hovering around infantrymen, and of trying to fight on horseback in wooded or fenced country. They preferred to cut loose from bases, destroy communications, burn bridges and stores, keep the enemy so busy behind his lines that he could apply only a part of his potential when the battle was joined.

The old basic regimental front for a charge had always been a double rank, but the 2nd Kentucky preferred a single rank. "It admitted of such facility of movement," Basil Duke explained, "it could be thrown about like a rope, and by simply facing to the right or left, and double-quicking in the same direction, every man could be quickly concentrated at any point where it was desirable to mass them." And in mentioning the regiment's preference for dismounted combat, Duke pointed out that while it was easy to charge down a road in a column of fours, it was often difficult to charge across wooded or fenced country in extended line and keep any sort of formation. "We found the method of fighting on foot more effective —we could maneuver with more certainty, and sustain less and inflict more loss."

In dismounted fighting, the role of the horse-holder was as important as that of the rifleman; it was customary in the 2nd Kentucky for one of each set of fours and the corporals to remain with the horses. The men had been carefully drilled by Maury's manual for this operation. At the command, "Prepare to Dismount," the sergeant and numbers two and four in each section moved to the front five yards, the corporal and numbers one and three standing fast. As all prepared to dismount, they took the reins in the left hand with a lock of the horse's mane, carrying the right hand to the right side of the pommel. At the command, "Dismount," all dismounted, leaving the reins over the pommel. The sergeant and numbers two and four stood to horse, while the corporals and numbers one and three led forward and formed rank with them.

To link after dismounting, each man faced about to the rear, took the link which hung from the halter ring of the horse on his left in his right hand, seized his own horse by the bit near the mouth, drawing the horse on his left toward his own until he could hook the snap into the curb ring.

The duties of a horse-holder were not easy, as one student of Civil War cavalry has observed, "especially if he rode one animal and led three others through the woods, for while he went to the left of a tree, the animals he led invariably went to the right of it." It was not the practice in the 2nd Kentucky, as it was in some regiments, to use the least efficient men in the command for horse-holders, for when the animals were needed they were needed at once, and the dismounted men were in trouble if the horse-holders had moved too far to the rear.

Fighting dismounted or mounted, every man in the regiment was aware that horseflesh was the key to success or failure on long raids. They had learned that a good cavalry horse must know how to strike the pace of the column and keep an even gait all day or night, that the speed of a column is not measured by the speed of the fastest horse but by the speed of the slowest. As Private George Mosgrove declared, a real trooper "was more provident for his horse than for himself, because, unlike the Federal cavalryman, he had to furnish his own horse, and should he become dismounted he must go into the infantry, the very thought of which was peculiarly disgusting to the Kentucky fellows. . . . Without any conscientious scruples whatever he could steal forage from his dearest comrades."

Professional cavalrymen at the time of the Civil War maintained that two years were required to produce a seasoned trooper, a rule of thumb unsuited to members of the 2nd Kentucky Regiment, some of whom had not served even half that prescribed period at the end of their July raid. Almost every one of them had been trained from childhood to manage the most spirited horses with perfect ease, and they were also riding the best mounts available. "The Kentuckians are all splendidly mounted," British cavalryman Fitzgerald Ross declared. "The horses are much finer and larger than those I saw in Virginia. . . . Their docility is extraordinary—I never saw a vicious horse the whole time. Every officer or courier coming to a camp will tie his horse's reins to a branch or twig of a tree, and the animal will stand quietly for hours without even attempting to get away."

With these obvious advantages, the 2nd Kentucky boys had at least a year's start in the school of the trooper. They had learned at Shiloh that sabers were not of much use in their style of fighting, that tents were excess baggage for cavalrymen, that a blanket and a waterproof were sufficient sleeping equipment, two men sharing their pairs. "One oilcloth went next to the ground; the two laid on this, covering themselves with two blankets, protected from the rain with the second oilcloth on top, and slept very comfortably through rain, snow, or hail, as it might be."

They had learned that a trooper consisted of one man, one hat, one jacket, one shirt, one pair of pants, one pair of drawers, one pair of socks, one pair of boots (preferably captured Federal jackboots tied with a stout leather string above the knee). As Private Mosgrove declared, the ideal was "a good horse, a Mexican saddle, a pair of big spurs with bells on them, a light long-range gun, a brace of Colt's revolvers, a good blanket, some form of oil cloth, and a canteen of brandy sweetened with honey. When he had these things, or some of them, he was a merry fellow, ready to dash into battle, singing 'I'm glad to be in this army.' "

This final maturation of the veterans of the 2nd Kentucky was another important result of that thousand-mile raid in July, 1862, a fulfillment which must have been so obvious to John Morgan that he saw no reason to mention it in his official report.

6

The Spartan Life

THE CLASSICAL SCHOLARS, of whom there were a number in the 2nd Kentucky, sometimes referred to the regiment's extended stay at Sparta, Tennessee, in August, 1862, as "the Spartan life." For one thing the summer crops were not in; consequently there was a shortage of rations for men, and little grain to bring horses back into condition. But even worse—in the opinion of the alligator horses—than the shortage of provender was the rigid discipline suddenly imposed upon them by Adjutant St. Leger Grenfell with the full support of the acting commander, Lieutenant Colonel Basil Duke.

Duke and Grenfell had two reasons for requiring strict discipline. One was to prevent a second disastrous surprise such as had occurred at Lebanon; the other was to stop the men from wandering off to the numerous whisky stills in the neighborhood and returning to camp in no condition for emergencies. The boys referred to these expeditions as "going on a lark," and the only way Grenfell could stop them was to double and redouble the guards. At one time he had half the regiment posted on guard duty, but as details rotated, the Englishman soon found "some peculiar swaps" being made by the guardsmen.

Finally, with Duke's permission, he resolved to keep them all so busy that none could find the time or energy for "going on larks." Day after day, from dawn until after sunset, the 2nd Regiment

100

provided Sparta with a continuous succession of colorful guard mountings, foot drills, mounted drills, and company and regimental dress parades. Naturally, the boys groused about all this interference with their freedom, but they were fond of Old St. Lege, and to a man they respected Basil Duke. Duke frankly admitted that his men never had much discipline and would obey only those whom they admired and who could win their confidence. They would cheerfully submit to the severest punishment, he said, provided it was not degrading in nature, but would not endure harsh and insulting language or anything that was humiliating.

To alleviate the shortage of bread, and also to keep a few men busy, Duke decided to order a brick bake oven constructed. After a detail had collected some loose bricks from around Sparta, he sent out a call for bricklayers. One of the volunteers was Private Tom Boss of C Company, a fierce-looking, lanky Kentuckian, six and a half feet tall, with bristly black hair. As Boss had been a mason, Duke put him in charge of the construction, and the job was completed satisfactorily within two days.

When the bake-oven detail reported that the job was completed, Duke asked Tom Boss what sort of special reward the boys would like to have for their excellent work. "Three days' furlough," replied Boss instantly, "to go where we please and not be interfered with by that damned provost guard." Although Duke knew where they would most likely go, he granted the furloughs and notified Grenfell to warn his patrols to look the other way if they found Tom Boss and his friends celebrating around one of the nearby whisky stills.

There were other light moments during the period of the Spartan life. After the men learned that "larking" was not to be tolerated, they began devising camp sports of their own, such as footraces. Lightning Ellsworth won a race or two, than began boasting that he could outrun anybody in the 2nd Kentucky. Wiry little Jeff Sterrett of B Company listened to the telegrapher's bragging for a day or two, then invited him to participate in a special race which he was promoting. Ellsworth accepted, but when the contestants showed up, Sterrett announced that each runner was to carry a jockey. Protesting that he had never bargained for such a race, Ellsworth attempted to beg off. Kentucky races, Sterrett insisted, always have jockeys, and he was so persuasive that Ellsworth finally agreed to participate.

"The two men of least weight in the regiment were indicated as riders," Duke afterward recalled, "and Jeff Sterrett was selected to ride Ellsworth. Sterrett surreptitiously buckled on a pair of Texas spurs, with long and exceedingly keen rowels, and when the signal to start was given plunged them into his mount. Ellsworth was naturally disgusted at such treatment, and for a while sulked and refused to go. But as Sterrett continued to ply the spurs, he thought better of the matter and stretched away with an amazing burst of speed. He not only overtook and passed his antagonist and beat him out many lengths, but ran forty yards beyond the goal before he could be pulled up."

During this summer interlude, the regiment had the pleasure of welcoming back several of its veterans who had been captured during the Lebanon Races. For a time there had been some apprehension that these prisoners might be dealt with severely. No less a personage than Andrew Johnson, then serving as Union military governor of Tennessee, strongly objected to their being exchanged. "Morgan and his marauding gang should not be admitted within the rules of civilized warfare," declared Johnson, "and that portion of his forces taken at Lebanon should not be held as prisoners of war. I hope you will call the attention of Secretary Stanton to the fact of their being a mere band of freebooters."

The machinery of prisoner exchange, however, had been well developed by this time on both sides, and each knew that discrimination against one set of prisoners would lead to discrimination from the other side, bringing about a rapid breakdown of the intricate system. Agreement had been made to exchange man for man and officer for officer within ten days after capture, the entire arrangement bearing a remarkable similarity to banking practices, everything being based on a "credit" system whereby records of surplus prisoners were kept on file and balanced against later reports of men captured or exchanged.

To take care of temporary surpluses of men, who were sworn not to take up arms again until notified of a "paper" exchange, the Confederates established a parolee camp for their men near Marietta, Georgia, and the Federals operated a similar one for Union soldiers at Camp Chase, Ohio. This system was devised to halt the practice of parolees going home to await notification and thus becoming too accustomed to the ease of civilian life.

During 1862, the Confederates always had more prisoner "credits" than the Federals, capturing and paroling more men than Camp Chase could hold. General Don Carlos Buell became so annoyed by the excessive number of parolees in his command that he issued a general order forbidding officers and men to give their paroles without his sanction, an order virtually impossible to enforce, of course. General Jerry Boyle, the Union commander in Kentucky, even went so far as to suggest that some of his men were "putting themselves in the way of being taken," and he recommended that parolees be branded by having one half of their heads shaved.

2

In the summer of 1862, after a long series of reverses, the fortunes of the Confederate Army in the West appeared to be improving. Federal forces had been brought to a halt in northern Mississippi, and Braxton Bragg, who had replaced the ailing Beauregard as commander in the West, was left free to rebuild the main Confederate Army around Chattanooga. After General Halleck's departure for Washington to become Lincoln's general-in-chief, the Federal armies which had been combined at Shiloh were divided again, Grant taking command in Mississippi, Buell in Tennessee.

The new Confederate commander in the West, General Bragg, was a West Pointer of wide military experience, a saturnine, humorless, unimaginative man, who sometimes bore personal grudges, and, as his subordinates were soon to discover, possessed a fatal tendency to vacillate in the face of emergencies. His viewpoint on the use of cavalry was decidedly conservative, and his relations with the 2nd Kentucky and other raiding regiments serving under the command of John Morgan would seldom run smoothly.

On July 31, Kirby Smith came down to Chattanooga from Knoxville to confer with Bragg concerning a late summer campaign against Buell's army. Bragg's original plan was to drive for Nashville, wrest that key city from Buell, and thus force Grant to leave

Mississippi. Kirby Smith, however, had a handful of fresh reports in his pocket from John Morgan, giving full and glowing details of the successful raid into Kentucky. Bragg evidently was impressed by these reports, and when Smith pointed out that a massive invasion of Kentucky might have vast political as well as military effects, even Bragg's slow imagination was kindled. Bragg agreed to combine with Kirby Smith in a two-pronged invasion of Kentucky to begin late in August. While Smith was moving north through Cumberland Gap, Bragg would make a feint toward Nashville, then swing around the city and race for Louisville.

It was an audacious plan, and John Morgan was delighted when Smith informed him of the role the 2nd Kentucky was to play in the invasion. On Sunday, August 10, Morgan returned to Sparta from Kirby Smith's Knoxville headquarters with marching orders for the 2nd. The regiment was to move above Nashville and raid the L. & N. Railroad at Gallatin, cutting off Buell's supplies.

Long before dawn of Monday the columns were in motion. They crossed the Cumberland River near Carthage, reaching Dixon Springs late in the afternoon. Somewhere along the way they met by prearrangement a company of thirty men, fresh recruits out of Kentucky. These recruits were led by Captain Joseph Desha, a veteran of infantry fighting in Virginia. In a brief ceremony, Morgan admitted Desha and his men into the 2nd as Company L.

It was nearly midnight when they rode into Hartsville, passing through the town without halting, and day was breaking when they came up to the outskirts of Gallatin and turned off the pike to avoid enemy pickets.

Morgan had planned the capture of Gallatin with great care, having sent a civilian spy, Jim Childress, ahead of the regiment some days before. Childress won the confidence of the Federal commander, Colonel William P. Boone, by a simple ruse. Dashing into Boone's headquarters, breathless and hatless, Childress told the Colonel that he had just escaped the clutches of Rebel conscript officers and begged for protection. Boone not only granted protection to the spy, he also gave him a new hat and complete freedom of movement around the Federal camp. After completing his observations, Childress slipped out through the picket lines and reported to Morgan what he had learned.

And so Morgan knew, as he led the 2nd up to Gallatin early on the morning of August 12, that the town was garrisoned by about 375 men of the 28th Kentucky Union Infantry under command of Colonel Boone. He knew that the off-duty men, probably 150 or so, would be sleeping in the camp at the fairgrounds just west of Gallatin. The others would be on picket duty along roads leading into town, or scattered along the railroad guarding bridges, water tanks, and the twin railroad tunnels (which Morgan had visited some months earlier). Morgan was also aware, from Childress' report, that Colonel Boone was in the habit of sleeping with his wife in a Gallatin hotel, usually without posted guards nearer than the courthouse. He hoped to capture Boone, and force a surrender of the garrison without firing a shot.

Leaving the regiment concealed in woods adjoining the town, Morgan and Captain Desha with a small raiding party slipped through a cornfield into the nearest street. In the dawnlight, neatly painted white houses contrasted against thick groves of evergreens. Lawns and shrubs were heavy with dew. At the courthouse they found two pickets asleep and captured them almost without a sound, then moved along in the shadows of buildings to the hotel. Desha volunteered to take a dozen men and go inside to capture Colonel Boone.

When Desha knocked on Boone's door, the Federal commander was already awake and dressed in preparation for going out to his camp to take morning reports. Upon opening the door, Boone was amazed to find himself confronted by a dozen strange soldiers with cocked revolvers, their gray jeans wet with dew and covered with pollen grains from corn. Desha quietly demanded that he surrender. "By what authority?" Boone asked. Desha informed Boone that Morgan's 2nd Cavalry had captured the town, and that bloodshed could be avoided only if the Colonel would surrender himself and his camp.

After some deliberation, Boone agreed to surrender himself but not the camp. One or two of the men with Desha threatened to shoot Boone if he did not surrender his men, but Desha took him to Morgan for a decision. As the party left the hotel, the streets were beginning to fill with advance companies of the 2nd, and the town of Gallatin was suddenly wide awake. With grave courtesy

Morgan greeted his fellow Kentuckian, Boone, then ordered him to mount up and together they began riding out toward the fairgrounds camp. Colonel Boone, however, held to his first position; he would not surrender his men.

As the 2nd moved rapidly toward the fairgrounds, Morgan sent companies to right and left through woods and fields to surround the Federal camp. About three hundred yards from the grounds, the column halted and Morgan summoned his officers for a conference.

After considerable discussion, Colonel Boone agreed to write a note to the captain on duty in the camp, informing him that he was surrounded by superior forces. Duke and Grenfell then volunteered to take the message forward under a flag of truce.

Thus the garrison at Gallatin surrendered without a shot being fired, and while the prisoners—about two hundred men—were being marched into town to be paroled, detachments of the 2nd Kentucky raced up and down the railroad capturing small details guarding bridges and tunnels.

Meanwhile, Lightning Ellsworth had also won a bloodless victory at the Gallatin telegraph office. Finding the office unlocked, he had climbed a stairway, entered the operator's sleeping quarters, and awakened him with the stern command: "Surrender in the name of John Morgan."

"Certainly," replied the operator, J. N. Brooks, when he saw a pair of huge navy pistols pointed directly at him.

"Dress," said Ellsworth.

When they went downstairs to the office, Ellsworth ordered Brooks to connect his instrument and find out where the trains were. Brooks followed orders, Ellsworth's keen ear and memory recording the operator's style. When Brooks began deliberately tapping the key in an awkward manner to arouse the Nashville operator's suspicions, Ellsworth ordered him to stop, and placed him under guard.

With his usual flair for confusing the enemy, Ellsworth sent off a message to the Federal Commander at Bowling Green, informing him that John Morgan was raiding in that direction with four thousand men, signing the communication with Colonel Boone's name. Then learning that a freight train was moving down from the north, he assumed the role of the Nashville train dispatcher, and brought it in to a siding. In a matter of minutes the boys of the 2nd swarmed all over the freight train, taking what supplies they could use, handing out some to the citizens of Gallatin, and burning the remainder.

But the prize that Ellsworth wanted most, a passenger train from Nashville, escaped because of the alertness of the Nashville operator. The operator held the train, then tapped out a message to Gallatin: "If it's Ellsworth at key, I would like you to protect Brooks." Always respectful of a clever adversary, Ellsworth readily admitted his identity and promised to parole Brooks without harm.

As soon as Morgan learned that the expected passenger train from Nashville would not be coming—but that Federal forces probably would be—he ordered the immediate destruction of the twin railroad tunnels between Gallatin and Nashville. According to Captain John Castleman, whose company participated in the burning of the interior framework, they made certain the south tunnel would be blocked by running the captured freight locomotive inside at high speed, wrecking it upon a heap of cribbed ties. After the tunnel framework burned, slate rock around it collapsed, and as the rock contained coal it continued to burn for several days.*

Leaving the tunnels, the raiders turned to the bridges, burning all of them in the vicinity. Here and there they ripped up rails, laid them across heaps of crossties, and rode on, leaving the heat to do its work of warping the metal.

When the regiment reassembled in Gallatin, darkness was falling. As there was no doubt in Morgan's mind that every Federal unit in the area was alerted and in motion toward Gallatin, he decided to withdraw. Leaving Lieutenant Manley and a few men behind to burn the fairgrounds amphitheater where Colonel Boone's regiment had been quartered, he ordered a night march over the fifteen miles back east to Hartsville.

Having missed two nights' sleep in succession, the boys were permitted to drowse late in their Hartsville camp the morning of

---

* The Gallatin tunnels north of Nashville were closed until December, effectively breaking the Federal rail link from the North, and forcing use of the undependable Cumberland River as a supply route.

the thirteenth. During the day their friends in the community brought in an abundant supply of hams, turkeys and chickens, roasted and ready for eating. The pleasant, lazy August day was spoiled, however, by a report from Gallatin. A Federal force, it was said, had entered the town before dawn, killing Lieutenant Manley and wounding or capturing most of his detail.

Late that night, Morgan sent Sergeant Quirk and fifteen scouts back to Gallatin to make a reconnaissance and determine the fate of Manley and his men. On reaching the outskirts of the town, Quirk discovered that Federal infantry had departed only a few minutes earlier, their rear guard then being in motion around the blocked tunnels.

Quirk decided to follow them, strike a blow for Lieutenant Manley, and then ride away. As he led his men through a cornfield, he saw the Federals boarding a train that was to take them back toward Nashville. Selecting Private John Donnellan as the loudest-voiced man in the squad, Quirk gave him a quick set of orders, and then disposed his men for attack. "Gano's Texans on the right flank!" yelled Donnellan. "Morgan's men on the left flank! Duke's regiment fall on their rear!" With a great yelling and slashing through the high cornstalks, the fifteen men surged out of the field, brought down two or three startled Federals, captured a few more. Instead of having to turn and gallop away, Quirk's troopers sat their mounts and watched the panicked engineer steam his train away.

The scouts rode leisurely back to Hartsville with their prisoners, and when Sergeant Quirk reported to Morgan, the Colonel informed the Irishman that he was now a first lieutenant. While the scouts were away a new company of volunteers had come down from Kentucky. None of these men had seen any service, and the new company, M, needed a commanding officer. Ben Drake, Quirk's constant companion, would be his second lieutenant. Morgan wrote out the commission, citing Quirk's "gallantry, valor and dash," and the former candy merchant went off to celebrate in proper style.

Because Hartsville was a much better defensive position than Gallatin, Morgan decided to remain camped there until the Federals made their next move. As it turned out, the regiment stayed for six days.

During this peaceful week, that incorrigible traveling newspaper of the 2nd Kentucky, the *Vidette*, made its first appearance. Lieutenant Gordon Niles, the New York newspaperman, discovered a plentiful supply of type and a printing press in an abandoned newspaper office, and sent out a call for printers. Four or five men reported, and in a few hours Volume One, Number One of the *Vidette* was being passed through the camp. Editor Niles' biggest handicap was shortage of paper, but his resourceful assistants rounded up enough supplies of wrapping paper and wallpaper to keep the publication going. Among the popular articles was an account of the victory at Gallatin and a salute to the women of the South. Basil Duke contributed a new poem which he hoped would become more popular than his "Song of the Raiders." He called this one "Morgan's War Song," and set it to the air of the "Marseillaise":

> Ye sons of the South, take your weapons in hand,
> For the foot of the foe hath insulted your land.
>> Sound! sound the loud alarm!
>> Arise! arise and arm!
> Let the hand of each freeman grasp the sword to maintain
> Those rights which, once lost, he can never regain.
>
> *Chorus*—Gather fast 'neath our flag,
>> For 'tis God's own decree
>> That its folds shall still float
>> O'er a land that is free.

John Morgan was delighted with the *Vidette*, and sent off copies to relatives, friends and former friends. And instead of laboriously writing out copies of his general orders and reports for Knoxville and Richmond, he merely passed the originals on to Editor Niles, then used the *Vidette* for submission to higher authority. Morgan's were probably the only reports received in Richmond in carefully proofread printed form, and must have unsettled the routines of the clerks in that bureaucrat-ridden city.

Late on the evening of August 19, the easy camp life ended suddenly when a scout reported the presence of three hundred Federal infantrymen in Gallatin. What aroused the boys of the 2nd were rumors that the enemy had arrested every male citizen over twelve years of age in the town—on a charge of collaborating with

Morgan's men in the burning of the railroad tunnels. After months of gallant fighting between soldiers who respected each other, the war was turning brutal. It would become more so in the months ahead.

Marching by night, the 2nd came roaring into Gallatin early on the morning of the twentieth, to discover that the rumor was true—the male citizens were all gone. Gallatin was a town of women and children. A dead man was lying in the street, one of their scouts, and the women told of how he had been kicked and cuffed after being shot. They also whispered darkly of rumors that Lieutenant Manley had been killed after surrendering, and they showed Colonel Morgan a browning stain of blood on the bridge where Manley had died.

"I called my men up to me," Morgan said afterward, "pointed to the blood and told them whose it was."

"We take no prisoners today," one of the men declared angrily.

They moved out south of town, following the track of the Federal infantry, every man determined on revenge. After passing the wrecked tunnels, they came upon a stockade, stormed its defenders fiercely before they could take cover, capturing fifty prisoners. At intervals along the twenty-five miles between Gallatin and Nashville, the Federals had built a chain of these stockades to guard the vital railroad from raiders such as the 2nd Kentucky —heavy upright timbers twelve feet high, surrounded by ditches.

Farther along they overtook the main enemy force, scattering them until their civilian prisoners were freed, pursuing almost to the Cumberland in front of Nashville. At Edgefield Junction, Company A attempted to storm a solidly constructed stockade. The fire of its defenders raked the lines; two officers and three men died, Lieutenants James Smith and Gordon Niles, beloved editor of the *Vidette*. In their anger, the men of Company A were rallying to make another assault when Basil Duke came up and ordered the attack halted. The odds were insurmountable, Duke saw at once; he regretted not having the "bull pup" howitzers along to smash the heavy timbers.

To avoid an attack in force from the strong Nashville base across the river, Morgan and Duke swung the companies about, and they rode back toward Gallatin, carrying their dead slung over saddles.

In the fading light of the day, they overtook a small procession of buggies and wagons which the women of Gallatin had driven out to bring their sons and husbands home. "There was a scene of wild congratulations in town that evening, when they all got in," Duke wrote. "That night the entire command encamped in the fairgrounds."

The entire regiment, of course, did not camp in the Gallatin fairgrounds. Detachments of pickets and scouts were out on every road and bypath, alert for a Federal cavalry attack, which was long overdue. Shortly before dawn, Morgan was awakened by a scout bringing warning of long columns of enemy cavalrymen moving toward Gallatin from Hartsville. During the previous afternoon, according to the scout's informants, the commander of this force had dined in a Hartsville hotel and had boasted publicly that he would "catch Morgan and bring him back in a bandbox." Further, this general had ordered in advance a meal which was to be cooked and waiting for him the following afternoon after he had whipped the 2nd Kentucky.

John Morgan, better than most commanders, could appreciate such gasconade. No doubt he chuckled as he listened to the scout's report, then summoned an orderly to waken the bugler for sounding boots and saddles. "Not wishing, on account of the inhabitants," he wrote in a later report, "to make Gallatin the scene of our contest, I advanced my column, and was greeted on reaching the Hartsville pike by a heavy fire from that direction."

3

The Union cavalry force marching to do battle with the 2nd Kentucky was no ordinary patrolling regiment. It was a carefully selected body of horsemen, the best that General Buell could collect from his divisions posted around the Nashville perimeter. From the first impact of the news that Morgan's raiders had blocked the Gallatin tunnels, cutting the Federal supply line, Buell's headquarters had been in an uproar. And after a day or two, when it was learned that the raiders were so bold as to be still camping

in the vicinity, Buell demanded drastic action. It was not enough
to court-martial Colonel Boone for surrendering Gallatin without
resistance; Morgan's raiders themselves must be destroyed.

To "catch Morgan and bring him back in a bandbox," Buell
selected a West Pointer, Brigadier General Richard W. Johnson,
authorizing him to assemble such cavalry companies as he desired
for the expedition. Johnson started from McMinnville and moved
through Murfreesboro, taking the best companies from the 2nd
Indiana, the 4th and 5th Union Kentucky, and the 7th Pennsylvania. As the column marched north through Lebanon, the 7th
Pennsylvania troopers no doubt recalled the morning four months
past when they had helped Wolford's Kentuckians chase Morgan's
men out of the town square.

This was the enemy column which the 2nd Kentucky moved out
of Gallatin to do battle with on the morning of August 21.

4

Chance, the incalculable quality of man's existence, that morning
led Sergeant Lawrence Jones of D Company to comb his hair before
mounting up and calling for formations. Always meticulous in his
dress, the sergeant had adjusted his uniform neatly, then running
his fingers through his matted hair, decided to comb it before don-
ning his wide-brimmed hat. The other companies had formed,
adjutant's call had sounded, but Jones was working over his hair
with the aid of a pocket mirror which he had suspended from a
pin in the bark of an elm tree.

His captain, John Castleman, strode over toward him: "Sergeant
Jones, the company is formed, the regiment is moving, the enemy
is upon us, we await your readiness. When you report the company will move."

"Yes, sir," said Jones, pocketing his mirror, and mounting deliberately. "Company D all present for duty, sir,"

So it was this element of chance which caused D Company to
fall in late on the left of the column, out of position instead of
being in its proper fourth place in the regimental line of march.

And it was this chance of changed location in column that brought the D Company troopers in position to first strike the enemy's flank, to break the opposing line, and become the heroes of the day.

It came about this way: As soon as Colonel Morgan saw the advance company of the enemy galloping and firing furiously upon his own forward scouts, he ordered Major Wash Morgan, his cousin, to take the first five companies to the left. At the same time, Lieutenant Colonel Duke led the remainer of the column to the right, and Company D being out of position in column, went with Duke. In the first collision of opposing forces, the Federals maneuvered hastily off the turnpike, and D Company found itself facing a woodland thick with bluecoats. Dismounting his men, Castleman took them in, fighting Indian fashion from behind trees and brush until the wing of the Federal line broke, leaving the main body on the right isolated in an open field. These latter horsemen quickly dismantled a rail fence, re-formed, and charged toward the turnpike with drawn sabers.

The men in blue made a fine display of horsemanship, sabers glittering in the early morning sunlight as they thundered across the meadow. Companies B, C, E, and F quickly dismounted, horseholders clattering to the rear, the men on foot dropping on their knees behind a low fence along the road. They held their fire until the blue line was within thirty yards. Then they opened up, rifles blazing in unison. When the smoke cleared the meadow was a tangled mass of thrashing, screaming horses, of dead, dying and wounded men, the survivors recoiling and dashing back toward the gaps in the rail fence.

But before the rout was complete, the Federal officers rallied their men, re-formed them, charging again with sabers up. Company D, meanwhile, swinging back through the woods, struck the enemy flank, enfilading the line. General Johnson, watching from a nearby hill, immediately ordered his battered troops back with a bugle blast.

"At 9:30 o'clock," Morgan recorded, "I had driven them four miles and was preparing for a final charge, when a flag of truce was brought, proposing an armistice in order to bury their dead."

The truce flag was a delaying tactic on the part of the Federals. While Morgan was parleying with General Johnson, the Federal cavalry companies began re-forming in the rear. As soon as Morgan informed Johnson that he would "entertain no proposition except unconditional surrender," the General and his party turned and cantered back to their lines under a fluttering white handkerchief. A moment later the Federal cavalry began withdrawing in orderly fashion.

Morgan ordered immediate pursuit, dividing his regiment into three columns. After a two-mile chase, the Federals pulled up, dismounted, and formed a V-shaped defensive formation at the base of a low hill. Duke and Grenfell came up to them first, with A, B, and E companies, and for once Old St. Lege felt repaid for all the long hours of drilling under the hot sun at Sparta. When Duke gave the command to dismount and form for attack, the boys executed the order with such precision and coolness that Grenfell raised his cap and saluted them with a loud "Bravo!"

After a short but sharp fight of about fifteen minutes, the Federals broke and ran for their horses, most of them escaping into the woods and high corn, heading for the Cumberland River and Nashville. Private Jeff Sterrett caught one of them bounding down the pike on a big sorrel horse, a wild-looking boy with hair on end, mouth wide open, his eyes glazed with confusion. Sterrett grabbed the sorrel's bridle, and decided to frighten the boy into surrender: "I don't know whether to kill you now, or to wait until the fight's all over!"

"For God's sake," replied the captive, "don't kill me at all. I'm a dissipated character, and not prepared to die!"

The haul of prisoners was not large, but it included the boastful General Johnson and several of his officers. When Morgan's men learned from the Federal captives—most of whom were Pennsylvanians and Indianians—that the 4th and 5th Kentucky troops had been the first to break and run, they felt a little ashamed for these Union representatives of their state. The 4th and 5th certainly were not up to the standard of the rugged boys of Frank Wolford's 1st Kentucky Cavalry. Later they learned that the Union Kentuckians had not stopped running until they reached Nashville. Lieutenant Colonel Robert R. Stewart of the 2nd Indiana was especially caustic in his report of the behavior of these two regiments. "I had formed a line," he said, "when they came dashing through in a style of confusion more complete than the flight of a drove of stampeded buffaloes. . . . There appeared to be a question of rivalry between officers and men for which should outvie in the disgrace of their cowardly scamper."

In the opinion of most officers and men in the 2nd Kentucky, however, it was General Johnson's old-fashioned use of mounted saber charges that had brought on the Federals' defeat and an easy victory for the 2nd. "General Johnson was evidently a fine officer," Basil Duke commented dryly, "but he seemed not to comprehend 'the new style of cavalry' at all." At this stage in the development of the regiment, some of the junior officers still carried the shiny blades for show, and Morgan occasionally rode with a sword, but as Kelion Peddicord of the scouts noted: "Sabers were useless ornaments in our service. The trooper that attempted to carry one would be forever after a laughing stock for the entire command."

After Morgan called off pursuit of the luckless foe, the regiment reassembled, and details were assigned to assist the prisoners in burying their dead. The boys also had to bury seven of their own.

In the late afternoon they marched on into Hartsville, Morgan riding beside his prize captive, General Johnson. As they rode along, Morgan must have mentioned the dinner that Johnson had ordered prepared for him that evening in the Hartsville hotel as a celebration for bringing Morgan "back in a bandbox." At any rate, one of the wounded prisoners of Johnson's command who was riding near the General wrote, some years after the war: "Johnson pleaded with Morgan to save him the humiliation of meeting the citizens of Hartsville. . . . Morgan yielded to his entreaties, and took him to a camp two or three miles from Hartsville, at which place he and his men were paroled." Morgan then went on into Hartsville and ate the luxurious feast which had been prepared for the now-humbled General Johnson.

One of the first tasks undertaken by the former printers in the regiment after their return to Hartsville was publication of a special edition of the *Vidette*. Major Robert A. Alston, the South Carolinian who had recently joined Morgan's staff as adjutant, took over the duties of the late Gordon Niles as editor, with occasional assistance from Texan R. M. Gano. Alston's first issue featured a victory proclamation which Morgan read before the assembled regiment on August 22:

> Soldiers: Your gallant bearing during the last two days will not only be inscribed in the history of the country and the annals of this war, but is engraven deeply in my heart. Your zeal and devotion . . . your heroism during the two hard fights of yesterday, have placed you high on the list of those patriots who are now in arms for our Southern rights. . . . All communications cut off between Gallatin and Nashville, a body of three hundred infantry totally cut up or taken prisoners, the liberation of those kind friends arrested by our revengeful foes . . . would have been laurels sufficient for your brows; but, soldiers, the utter annihilation of General Johnson's brigade . . . raises your reputation as soldiers and strikes fear into the craven hearts of your enemies. Officers and men, your conduct makes me proud to command you. Fight always as you fought yesterday and you are invincible.

Another *Vidette* account described the unexpected arrival on the twenty-second of Brigadier General Nathan Bedford Forrest with his cavalry division. The Confederates' efficient intelligence system in central Tennessee had warned Chattanooga headquarters of Johnson's combined forces moving to trap the 2nd Kentucky, and Forrest had been dispatched to aid Morgan. Forrest was regretful that he had arrived too late to join in the victory, but the commanders celebrated in high style, this being their first leisurely meeting since they had joined in the policing of Nashville during the winter.

"We were pleased to see General Forrest," the *Vidette* commented. "He looks to be in the enjoyment of excellent health, and happy as you could expect so noble a patriot, enjoying the good news that crowds upon us from every quarter. I thought as I looked upon the manly forms of Forrest and Morgan that nothing could excel that picture except the groups, everywhere to be seen, of our lovely countrywomen. They excel all the universe contains. . . . Oh what can equal the women of the South? They are the noblest works of God. I must leave this dull sanctum to look once more upon them."

5

Some of the gaiety prevalent in the regiment during its short stay in Hartsville was diminished by two somber incidents involving deserters turned over to the 2nd for punishment. The first deserter, a native of Gallatin scarcely twenty years old, had been taken while bearing arms for the Union. The sentence was inevitable: to be shot to death.

The boys of the 2nd had no taste for this side of war; they understood its necessity, but were revolted at having to carry out the action. Twelve men were selected for a firing squad, six with loaded rifles, six with unloaded, so that none would know if he were the executioner or not. Lieutenant Sam Morgan, the colonel's cousin, was in command of the squad, and he directed the execution with obvious reluctance. A native of Tennessee, himself, young Morgan addressed the prisoner briefly: "Die like a Tennessean!" then barked out the fatal commands: "Ready! Aim! Fire!"

The second incident concerned a deserter who had not joined the enemy, being, as Basil Duke observed, "too cowardly to fight on either side." This man was sentenced to receive thirty-nine lashes on the bare back, a method of punishment that seemed even more revolting to the men of the 2nd than death by firing squad. The day before sentence was to be excuted, a deputation of ten men, one from each company, called on Duke for a conference.

"Colonel Duke," said the spokesman, "we are instructed by our comrades to say that no man in the regiment will consent to flog this man. We feel no sympathy for the scoundrel, but we think such an act would be degrading to ourselves. It isn't on his account we refuse, but on our own. We never expected to disobey any order you might give us, and we very reluctantly tell you that we will disobey this one if given. If you see fit to punish any of us for refusing, well and good; we'll make no complaint. But none of us will flog that hound, mean as he is."

Duke was disconcerted by this turn of events, but he understood the feelings of his men. "Very well, gentlemen," he replied firmly, "I appreciate your frankness. As for punishing any one of you for disobedience, I only say that no order has yet been disobeyed.

Go back and tell your comrades that I've received their message."

For some hours the young Lieutenant Colonel pondered the problem, wondering how it might be solved. He had an order to carry out, but how could it be done if no one in the regiment would consent to be the executioner? Unexpectedly the solution came in the person of a second lieutenant, recently elected to that rank by the men of Captain Desha's company. The Lieutenant announced that he had learned of the resolution taken by the enlisted men of the regiment, and that he was willing to help Duke "out of a difficulty" by flogging the prisoner himself.

Duke could scarcely restrain his indignation. "Don't you understand, Lieutenant, that the private soldiers have expressed a disinclination to perform such service because they regard it as degrading? Will you, an officer whom I cannot order to do such a thing, volunteer for duty so abhorrent?"

The Lieutenant assured him that he was doing it as a matter of duty, and Duke, although he could barely contain his anger, finally decided to grant permission.

Next day at the appointed hour the prisoner was brought forth stripped to the waist, and was bound to a stake in front of the regiment which was drawn up on parade to witness the flogging. The Lieutenant than made his appearance, walking in a pompous strut and flourishing a long thick leather strap. At a signal from Captain Desha, Officer of the Day, the flogging began, the Lieutenant applying his blows with apparent relish, the victim screaming and circling the stake in his agony. After the thirty-ninth lash had been delivered, the Lieutenant raised his arm with the evident intention of striking again. A roar of anger arose almost in unison from the regiment, and Captain Desha spurred his horse forward, threatening to shoot the Lieutenant if he struck again.

That afternoon Duke summoned the Lieutenant to his headquarters. The man came swaggering in, obviously expecting that his lieutenant colonel intended to thank him for the service he had rendered. Instead Duke curtly informed the man that he was no longer an officer of the 2nd Kentucky. Furthermore he was not to remain with the regiment in any capacity.

The Lieutenant was astonished, first expressing disbelief, then accusing Duke of injustice, of having no right to dismiss him so summarily. Duke calmly admitted that his accuser was probably correct, but insisted that he had meant what he said. He was resolved, he explained, to protect the men of his command from the humiliation of serving under such an officer. "I believe," added the soft-voiced Lieutenant Colonel, "that if I preferred charges against you for conduct unbecoming an officer and a gentleman, a court-martial would convict you, and you would be regularly dismissed from the service. As it is, I simply tell you that you cannot serve as an officer in this regiment. You can go where you please."

The man saw that Duke was adamant. Some time that night he left the Hartsville camp—and the boys of the 2nd Kentucky never saw him again.

7

Dark and Bloody Ground

I

FROM HARTSVILLE, TENNESSEE, late in August, 1862, John Morgan wrote to a clothing manufacturer in Alabama, ordering one thousand new uniforms. "My men are nearly out of clothes. Have them made full size and very strong. Our service is very hard upon clothes." Although he gave no address for delivery, he was quite hopeful of accepting these uniforms somewhere in Kentucky.

On August 28, Morgan received support for these hopes in the form of a message from Kirby Smith ordering the 2nd Kentucky in motion "to meet him in Lexington about September 2." Smith's advance infantry units were already into the passes of the Cumberland Mountains, heading for Lexington. And southward around Chattanooga, Bragg was starting his army across the Tennessee River with Louisville as the goal.

Marching out of Hartsville the morning of August 29, the nine hundred troopers of the 2nd were in their most ebullient spirits—cheering, laughing, joking, singing. They said their farewells to good friends in Hartsville with special meaning. They were sure that if they came back again, they would come as civilians; the war would be ended. This time they were going home to Kentucky with the intention of staying there.

As they rode northeastward, some of them even felt a sense of lingering regret at leaving this lovely Tennessee countryside of

120

green pastures and yellow fields ripening with grain, of blue hills, shady forests, and cool clear watercourses. They knew they would forever remember the lazy summer bivouacs, the excitement of chase and combat, the moonlit rides, the lovely girls of Gallatin and Hartsville. On this particular August day the war they had endured for almost a year bore a transitory illusion of romance, peopled by legendary Maid Marians, Sheriffs of Nottingham, and such chivalric heroes as they knew from reading the Waverley Novels.

Before nightfall they crossed into Kentucky at Red Sulphur Springs, and camped that night a few miles beyond Scottsville. Around cooking fires they sang Basil Duke's new war song, and some variations of "The Girl I left Behind Me":

> "If ever I get through this war
> And Lincoln's chains don't bind me,
> I'll make my way to Kentuckee
> To the girl I left behind me."

With all the rumors and talk of the "big" invasion and a feeling of portentous events in the air, sleep did not come easily that first night on Kentucky soil.

By daybreak Morgan had them moving again, and at ten o'clock they were entering Glasgow. For the benefit of the home-town boys of C Company, the regiment rested there through the noon hours, then marched up toward the familiar woods along Green River.

By noon of the thirty-first they were in Columbia. As yet they had seen not one blue-coated soldier, but Morgan was wary, and he ordered the regiment into camp. There were two reasons for delaying the march at Columbia; first, the Colonel's brother, Charlton, was somewhere in the rear, bringing up the two "bull pup" howitzers from Knoxville where they had been sent for repairs; and second, information was needed from scouting parties sent out along the roads toward Lexington.

Thirty-six hours later, Charlton Morgan arrived with the howitzers, and most of the scouts had returned with reports that routes toward Lexington were all clear except for occasional annoying bushwhackers. The night of September 2, when the regiment marched into Houstonville, Confederate sympathizers there were celebrating news of Kirby Smith's great victory over the Federals a few miles south of Lexington.

The boys of the 2nd were elated to hear of the victory, but disappointed with the realization that General Smith's columns would likely arrive in Lexington before they did. There was little sleep among the Lexington contingent that night, and every man of them was saddled and ready to ride at the first sign of dawn.

By late morning they were in Danville, and all afternoon they rode hard, excitement mounting, everyone wondering where the enemy could be. Kentucky seemed swept clean of Federals. It was dusk when they reached Nicholasville, with Lexington only twelve miles to the north, and the Bluegrass boys were eager to march on up the pike. But Morgan ordered a halt, passing the word to the men to wash up, brush the dust from their uniforms, and curry horses. He wanted to enter Lexington by daylight, on parade.

At ten o'clock the morning of September 4, John Morgan, in full dress uniform of a Confederate colonel, rode proudly into Lexington at the head of his regiment. Here the 2nd Kentucky had begun its career, almost a year ago on an early autumn evening with a handful of men on two hay wagons rumbling unnoticed out of town along Main Street. Along this same street the full regiment marched now, a high moment for the boys of the Bluegrass, with bands playing, Confederate flags fluttering from the buildings, and sidewalks crowded with old friends cheering them wildly as they marched on down Main to Cheapside, the square, where they halted and dismounted.

"The wildest joy ruled the hour," said one observer. "The bells of the city pealed forth their joyous welcome, whilst the waving of thousands of white handkerchiefs and tiny Confederate flags attested the gladness and joy of every heart. Such a scene—I shall never look upon its like again!" At every street corner baskets of provisions and buckets of water had been placed for the troopers' refreshment; gifts of every kind were pressed upon them.

"John Morgan could scarcely get to his home, the people almost carried him," Mattie Wheeler of Winchester wrote in her diary. "I went to Lexington last Sunday with Lee [her brother] and spent the day. Lee went on business, he was raising a company to go in John Morgan's brigade. I dislike for Lee to go, very much, but I know there is no use to say anything, his mind has been made up for some time. Every young man in the State is going that are not Union, and they [the Unions] are very scarce."

As Miss Wheeler predicted, recruiting was active around the 2nd's headquarters, and Major Robert Alston wasted no time taking over a printing office to publish broadsides appealing for more men to join up. "Arouse Kentuckians!" one began in bold type, over Morgan's name. "I have kept my promise. . . . Young men of Kentucky flock to my standard!"

Understandably they all wanted to join the cavalry, all wanted to go with Morgan's 2nd Kentucky. Although Kirby Smith had won the race into Lexington, the General obtained barely enough recruits for his infantry to fill up a single company. Courtland Prentice, son of Morgan's bitter enemy, editor George Prentice of Louisville, came in to volunteer for the Confederacy. Young Prentice was immediately commissioned a lieutenant in the 2nd Kentucky. Among other unexpected arrivals was one of Tom Quirk's former scouts, Tom Berry, who had been severely wounded at the Cythiana bridge in July. Captured and imprisoned, Berry had escaped and made his way back to Kentucky. He arrived in Lexington with several recruits, but as the 2nd was at full strength, Berry took his followers into a new regiment being formed around R. M. Gano's Texans.

Other volunteers were coming in so rapidly that Morgan gave Captain William Breckinridge permission to withdraw Company I from the 2nd and begin the organization of a third regiment.

It was John Morgan's day, and he enjoyed every moment of it. He established headquarters at Hopemont, the Morgan family mansion at the corner of Mill and Second streets. Friends pointed out to him where Federal sentinels had lurked in the Hopemont shrubbery night after night in the belief that the cavalry leader would be bold enough sooner or later to visit his mother. A delegation of Bluegrass ladies called to make him a present of regimental colors sewed by their own hands. Some of his male admirers gave him a set of silver spurs. His old friend, Keene Richards, a Bluegrass breeder, brought him a beautiful charger, a Thoroughbred gelding named Glencoe. (A year later Morgan would be riding Glencoe on a fateful march across Ohio.)

"Have spent the day in Lexington," one of Kirby Smith's infantrymen recorded, "wandering about the beautiful streets and feasting my eyes on the pretty rosy-cheeked girls. The great chieftain, John Morgan . . . is a splendid type of the *genus homo,* and seems to be a perfect idol with the people. They gather around him in groups and listen with wondering admiration to the recital of his daring adventures. Recruiting is going on rapidly, and Kentucky is enlisted in the cause for freedom."

It was a glorious, buoyant week, and there was even some wild talk of riding on to Chicago and marching down the streets of that city. But wiser heads knew that Louisville must be taken first, and acting with that end in mind, Kirby Smith ordered Morgan to send a small raiding force against a Federal stockade guarding the Salt River bridge on the L. & N. Railroad. Captain John B. Hutchinson was assigned the mission, and having had experience with stockades before, he took the howitzers along with four companies of the 2nd.

By the time this expedition returned to Lexington, after successfully burning the long bridge and capturing its defenders, Kirby Smith was ready to threaten Cincinnati—a move designed to keep Federal forces occupied there while Bragg was coming up toward Louisville. To screen his infantry units, Smith needed cavalry, and again the 2nd Regiment drew the assignment. Captain Hutchinson, with six companies, marched up within five miles of Covington, creating a cold shock of fear in Cincinnati which lay just across the Ohio River.

A few days later, Basil Duke followed with the other companies of the regiment. For the first time the 2nd was going into a combat area without Morgan. General Smith had ordered the Colonel into eastern Kentucky with Gano's and Breckinridge's new regiments to intercept the Federal commander, General George W. Morgan.

On his way to the Covington lines, Duke met Captain Hutchinson near the little town of Walton. A heavy Union force was advancing out of Cincinnati, and for the next two or three days the regiment zigzagged back and forth across the "camel's hump" salient of northern Kentucky, avoiding contact with the enemy, successfully deceiving him as to the actual Confederate strength in the area.

While swinging back toward Walton early one morning, an advance party of Company A suddenly overran an infantry patrol. Lieutenant Greenberry Roberts, in command, ordered the Federals to surrender, and sent Sergeant Will Hays ahead with six men to pick up stragglers. Sergeant Hays and his men galloped right into the midst of an entire company, sixty-nine Ohioans in brand-new blues, obviously raw recruits. Dressed in dusty blue jeans, Hays pretended to be a Union cavalryman, but the ruse failed. The Federal lieutenant ordered his men to cock their rifles. Hays instantly leveled his own rifle at the head of the lieutenant, and the six men with Hays grouped around their sergeant, threatening to shoot any man who should raise a rifle against him.

"I thought it the finest sight I had ever seen," said Duke who arrived about this time at the head of Company A. The Federals surrendered immediately, and were sent back to the rear of the column to be paroled.

That evening while in bivouac outside Falmouth, the regiment first heard the news of Lee's brilliant victory over McClellan at Antietam Creek in Maryland. The star of the Confederacy was rising, the battle lines moving northward now, and most of the boys of the 2nd Kentucky were even more confident the war would end before the year was out.

Basil Duke shared their hopes. With Lee in Maryland, the time had come for the western armies to strike at Ohio. Shortly before Morgan had been ordered off to eastern Kentucky, he and Duke had discussed the possibility of a raid across the Ohio River, and they took their plan to Kirby Smith. Smith in turn had queried Bragg, but the latter was opposed to a crossing in force, advising only a feint by a small raiding party to draw off reinforcements from Buell's army.

Now, late in September, Duke pondered the possibility of a crossing by the entire 2nd Regiment. If the Federal commanders around Cincinnati could be panicked by a few cavalry companies appearing outside Covington, what would they do if faced by an entire regiment on their side of the river?

With this unanswered question in mind, he sent John Castleman and Company D to scout possible fords along the Ohio. Castleman and his men came up to the river near Foster's Landing, a point where the westward rolling stream turns north toward Cincinnati. Scouting toward Augusta, Castleman found the river running low in the late summer season. A mile or so below Augusta he discovered a series of sand shoals lying almost the width of the river, an excellent place for a cavalry crossing.

2

At the Treaty of Wautauga in 1775, when the Cherokees sold Kentucky to the white settlers, Chief Dragging Canoe warned the purchasers that there was a "dark cloud" over the land. Another Cherokee nodded solemnly and said the ground was bloody there, and they were glad to be rid of it. "Dark and bloody ground," the settlers called it then, and remembered the words afterward with good cause, passing the descriptive phrase on to their descendants. By "dark cloud," the Cherokee chief was referring to Northern tribes who continuously invaded the Kentucky country to hunt and fight.

For a year the boys of the 2nd Regiment had lived with one aim in view, to drive the "dark cloud" of their time out of Kentucky. On the morning of September 27, as they rode toward Augusta, they had high hopes that an invasion of northern soil would help mightily to bring this about.

From friendly informants Duke had learned that Augusta was defended by a strong company of Union militia, and he decided that to insure the safety of his men during the precarious river crossing, it would first be necessary to capture the town and subdue its garrison.

Although it was yet early morning, the sun burned into their faces, the air turning sultry so that perspiration dripped from the riders' faces and clung to their bodies. It was more like a late summer day than early autumn.

Passing through a hollow, the column slowly climbed a high hill overlooking the town. From the summit a hazy panorama unfolded before them—the river valley bordered by green trees, the Ohio running straight from left to right as far as they could see, and directly below, the neat little river town of Augusta.

Two small stern-wheelers lay quietly at the board wharf. Duke raised his field glass and studied them, the U. S. S. *Belfast* and the *Florence Miller*. Bales of hay were stacked along the sides of each vessel; the pilothouses were boarded up with heavy oaken planking. A twelve-pounder was mounted on each deck. As Duke watched, he saw armed riflemen taking positions on board.

Shifting his glass, he caught other movements in the streets of Augusta, saw rifles glinting in the sunlight. The Union militiamen had received warning of the 2nd Kentucky's approach, and were taking defensive positions.

Duke ordered his men to dismount and conferred briefly with his captains. All agreed that the gunboats presented the greatest obstacle; if they could be driven away, the town probably could be taken easily. Accordingly, Captain Jacob Cassell was ordered to take Company A across the turnpike and approach the other side of the town where direct rifle fire could be opened upon the stern-wheelers. While Company A was in motion, gunners set up the howitzers on the highest point of the hill, aiming them directly down upon the boats. As soon as Cassell got his men into position, the howitzers opened fire, one of the first shells penetrating the hull of the *Belfast*. The continuous bombardment from the "bull pups" and the sharp rifle fire of Company A quickly put the gunboats to flight. The Union Navy men fired only three charges from their twelve-pounders, and then steamed off up the river, the howitzers flinging shells in their wake.

With the gunboats out of the way, Duke was confident he could bring the militia to terms with a mere show of force. As he came down the hill with B and C companies, dismounted, he was surprised to find the streets totally deserted; there was something ominous in the muggy air, an unnatural quietness. He ordered B Company down Main Street, dividing C Company so as to cover both Elizabeth and Upper streets.

When B company reached Front Street, the advance platoon turned east, surrounding the home of Major Joshua Bradford, commander of the local militia. Bradford was watching from a window. He realized at once that he was too far outnumbered to offer resistance, and immediately began waving a white handkerchief from the window, calling out that he was surrendering the town.

Almost at this very moment, however, other B Company troops turned into Upper Street and were met by a fusillade from the up-stairs windows of the houses. The fight which Duke had not ex-pected and which the defending commander, Major Bradford, had tried to avert, now suddenly exploded.

At the first burst of fire, Captain Cassell sent Lientenant Green-berry Roberts forward with a platoon from A Company's position. Nineteen-year-old Roberts, forgetting everything he had been taught, brought his men all the way into town mounted, adding to the confusion in the smoke-filled streets. At the same time, the ser-geant left in charge of the howitzers on the hill mistook Roberts' charging troopers for the enemy; he opened up on them with the deadly "bull pups."

Suddenly everything was going very badly for the 2nd Kentucky. Lieutenant George White was shot from his horse as he dashed down Upper Street. Captain William Kennett and Lieutenant Court-land Prentice* were wounded fatally. Lieutenant Whip Rogers fell at the door of a house on Upper Street, and as he lay dying he called for Lieutenant P. T. King to give a message to his father. King was shot from the hallway and died before Rogers. Private C. T. Puckett, rushing to aid both of them, was killed instantly, falling across the officers' bodies. Captain Sam Morgan fell bleeding on Elizabeth Street, and his brother, Major Wash Morgan, witnessing the shoot-ing, ran toward Bradford's house in a rage, crying vengeance. "He was a most vicious-looking man," one of the Augusta witnesses re-called, "with a revolver almost as long as his arms, clasped in one hand, and with a feather sticking in his cap."

White flags began fluttering in several windows now, but they were as meaningless as Major Bradford's first effort to surrender.

---

* Learning of his son's death, editor George Prentice of the *Louisville Jour-nal* ran two black rules in his editorial column of October 2. "An intense Southern sympathy," the grieving father wrote, "in spite of the arguments, the remonstrances, and the entreaties of those who dearly loved him, made him an active rebel against his country. . . . After a brief five weeks' service in the rebel ranks, he fell. . . . And yet we shall love to think of Courtland Prentice, that brave and noble though misguided youth, during the little rem-nant of our lives."

My men were infuriated by what they esteemed bad faith, in a continuance of the fight after the flags of truce were displayed," Duke said. "I never saw them fight with such ferocity." Mary Coburn, who lived in Augusta, corroborated this unco-ordinated use of truce flags: "The women and children waved their white flags out the winders and the men was behind them and done their shooting out of the winders."

Duke saw no way to stop the slaughter except by smashing in doors of houses in which the militiamen had fortified themselves. The howitzers were brought down from the hill and, double-shotted with canister and grape, tore great holes in the doors and walls, but even so some of the buildings had to be set on fire before the tenacious defenders would surrender.

The bitter fight in Augusta ended all hopes of the regiment's crossing into Ohio. Ammunition for the howitzers was exhausted, dead and wounded must be cared for, and prisoners paroled. When the echo of the last shot died away, the regiment counted twenty-one dead and eighteen wounded, some of the best of the veterans of the old Green River squadron.

Kentuckian against Kentuckian had created a dark and bloody ground of their own in the streets of Augusta. Mary Coburn, in her letter describing the fight, blamed the Union militia: "They tried so hard to have a fight in Augusta and they accomplished it to their sorrow. I don't pitty them one bit for it was their own fault, they have no one to blame but their selves. . . . Of all bloody sights you ever saw I never witnessed such a scene. . . . I have often heard of war and read of it but now I witnessed it." Miraculously, no women or children had been harmed.

Heartsick over his losses and the miscarriage of his plans, Duke ordered a withdrawal about four o'clock in the afternoon. With their dead and wounded in a line of wagons and carriages, the troopers turned back west for Falmouth. Behind them smoke still floated over the low hills, over the fading summer day.

At Brooksville the column halted, and after pickets went out to guard the roads the others bivouacked for the night, "the gloomiest and saddest that any man among us had ever known." Next morning Duke began paroling prisoners, and was almost captured when a Federal cavalry patrol overran the 2nd's pickets and broke into town. As soon as the men recovered from surprise, they scattered the attackers. Shortly afterward the sergeants began calling formations, and the 2nd moved slowly down to Cynthiana—a town most of them remembered well—to encamp for several days.

3

On October 4, Duke received a message from John Morgan ordering him to march the 2nd to Lexington. Morgan had been unsuccessful in intercepting his Federal namesake, General George Morgan; the latter had escaped by marching his men out of eastern Kentucky into the safety of Ohio. This seemed like good news to the men of the 2nd, and when they rode into Lexington they found the city filled with rumors of Confederate victories and of Buell's dismissal by President Lincoln. But there was also an inexplicable rumor that Lexington was about to be evacuated.

As soon as Duke arrived at Hopemont to report, Morgan confirmed the last rumor. When Duke expressed the belief that the abandonment of Lexington might be only temporary, Morgan laughed scornfully. "I shall never forget his laugh," Duke wrote, "and the bitter sarcasm with which he spoke of the retreat, which he seemed to certainly expect." In Morgan's viewpoint, General Bragg was the villain of the piece, a commander-in-chief utterly demoralized.

During the month following Kirby Smith's and Morgan's occupation of Lexington, Bragg had moved his Army of Tennessee north from Chattanooga up the Sequatchie Valley through Sparta, then swiftly crossed the Cumberland at Carthage and Gainesboro. By September 13 he was in Glasgow, Kentucky, and on the seventeenth was at Munfordville on Green River, squarely across Buell's communication system. It was an unusual situation—a Confederate army in strength, dug in north of a Union army. Certainly, a bold Confederate commander might have brought disaster to Buell, cut off as the Union leader was from supplies and reinforcements. But when Buell began moving northward from Nashville, Bragg was worrying about his own lines of supply and retreat, and made no attempt to offer a fight. Those close to him at the time described him as a man alternately exhilarated and dejected.

While Bragg dawdled, moving his army slowly toward Bardstown, Buell raced for the safety of Louisville, arriving there unchallenged on September 29. Two days later, his divisions reinforced, Buell was already sending patrols out of Louisville, feeling for Bragg's positions, determined to drive the Confederates back into Tennessee. On October 4, while Bragg and Kirby Smith were in Frankfort installing Richard Hawes as provisional governor of the Confederate State of Kentucky, the ceremonies had to be cut short when couriers arrived with warnings that Buell was advancing in force from Louisville.

This then was the military situation when Basil Duke met John Morgan in Lexington. The word was out that Braxton Bragg had lost his nerve and was about to order a general retreat.

Confirmation came on October 6—orders for the 2nd Kentucky to leave Lexington and operate as a screening force for Kirby Smith's retreating infantry, their first position to be along the Versailles-Frankfort road. Morgan's bitterness was quickly shared by the men of the regiment. Once again they were leaving the Bluegrass, without even engaging in a full-scale battle. Would they ever again have such an opportunity? "With the failure to hold Kentucky," Duke afterward declared, "our best and last chance to win the war was thrown away. . . . With this retreat a pall fell upon the fortunes of the Confederacy. . . . All the subsequent tremendous struggle was but the dying agony of a great cause, and a gallant people."

Disillusioned as they were, the boys could still swap snatches of barbed humor. One story going the rounds of the companies concerned two cavalrymen, one of whom was about to exchange his worn mount for a white-faced animal. "That one won't do," warned his companion. "The enemy could see that white face a mile." "That's no objection," replied the first trooper. "It's the tail end of Bragg's cavalry that's always pointed toward the Yankees!" He took the white-faced horse and went his way.

While the 2nd Kentucky was moving into its screening position outside Lexington, some forty miles to the southwest Bragg was being outmaneuvered by Buell. With the two wings of his army divided, Bragg blundered into battle on October 8 at Perryville.

The fighting was fierce, the Federals suffering four thousand casualties, the Confederates more than three thousand. It was a tactical victory for Bragg's army, and his reinforcements coming up late in the day expected to renew the battle at dawn. But Bragg ordered the columns back to Harrodsburg, and after two days of vacillation, ordered a general retreat set in motion.

The 2nd Kentucky, with Gano's and Breckinridge's regiments, meanwhile moved down to picket the Confederate Army's left flank. On the night of the tenth, they patrolled in a chilly rain, close enough at times to look enviously upon the enemy's long lines of campfires glaring in the gloomy darkness. On the twelfth they fell back to Nicholasville, and the next day as Bragg's army began its slow retreat, the cavalry regiments went into skirmish formations. For three days in weather as dismal as their sunken spirits they screened Kirby Smith's infantrymen who were marching toward the Cumberland passes.

On the fifteenth the cavalry halted at Gum Springs. As it was apparent now that the Union Army did not intend to press pursuit, Morgan requested permission from Kirby Smith to make a quick reverse raid into central Kentucky. He proposed to damage Buell's supply lines and then swing back through western Kentucky into Tennessee.

Smith was astonished by this proposal, but he held no higher opinion of Buell's cavalry than Morgan did, and he knew the Federal infantry could never offer any serious danger to raiding horsemen. Although Smith's reply was somewhat ambiguous, he did not deny the request and on the seventeenth, Morgan's regiments turned about in a forced march for Lexington.

Perhaps it was Kentucky pride that impelled the boys to make one more daring thrust at the enemy invaders. Perhaps they wanted one more look at the bluegrass which was springing into new color after the October rains, wanted to ride once more across the rolling green and russet land they loved.

Along unfamiliar back roads they galloped northward, and after nightfall became utterly lost. To find a river crossing they impressed a local guide of obvious Union sympathies, Morgan posing as Colonel Frank Wolford until they came out upon the Lexington turnpike. As soon as he was certain of where he was, Morgan revealed his true identity, advising the startled guide "to be careful in future of how he confided in soldiers."

According to a story in the *Louisville Journal* of October 22, Morgan was wearing at this time "a plain suit of green cloth, without any distinction of rank, patent leather jackboots, and was mounted on a superb horse." This same correspondent noted that Morgan's men carried only weapons and blankets, and none of the usual encumbrances favored by Union cavalrymen. "They fight recklessly, travel rapidly, and do an immense deal of mischief."

By two o'clock in the morning the 2nd was within three miles of Lexington, and Lieutenant Quirk was ordered forward to scout the approaches and discover what he could of the strength of enemy units posted in the town. From friends near Lexington, Quirk learned the strength, identity, and exact locations of the enemy—one of their old antagonists of Green River days, the 4th Ohio Cavalry. Two companies of the Ohio regiment were guarding the courthouse and other points in town, the remainder were camped on the rich pastures of Henry Clay's estate, Ashland, two miles out of Lexington.

At dawn, Captains Cassell and Bowles of the 2nd marched in with their companies to take the town. Duke, with the remainder of the regiment, moved directly out toward Ashland, while Gano and Breckinridge hurried their regiments around to the rear to completely surround the Clay estate.

What followed was largely a comedy of errors that could have turned to tragedy. As Duke's companies came up to the enemy camp in the gray light, Breckinridge's troopers mistook them for the enemy and opened fire. A few moments later when Breckinridge's dismounted men charged the Ohio camp, one of the 2nd's gunners sent a howitzer shell into their midst. No casualties resulted from either error, but no sooner had Breckinridge marched his bag of prisoners out upon the pike for Duke's mounted men to guard than Gano's regiment came dashing up and fired into the 2nd's forward line.

At this crowning blunder, Duke's adjutant, Captain Patrick Thorp, lost his temper. He wanted to bring Gano to court-martial, charging the Texan had twice deliberately shot at him. Gano claimed that in the dim light he had not recognized Thorp, but the Captain was not immediately pacified. "Colonel Gano may not have recognized my face," Thorp cried hotly to Duke, "but he couldn't have failed to recognize my buttons!" The adjutant always wore a zouave jacket, the sleeves thickly studded with bright red coral buttons.

Duke at last managed to soothe Pat Thorp's injured feelings. He knew well enough that it was not only the poor light of dawn that had caused all the mistakes, it was also lack of brigade experience among the officers. Morgan's men had grown into too cumbersome an organization to continue using their old regimental tactics.

In the last of the fighting—before the 4th Ohio completely surrendered—Major Wash Morgan was seriously wounded. Only a few days before, Wash had watched his brother, Sam, die at Augusta. Now another Morgan saddle was empty. John Morgan took his fierce-visaged cousin into Lexington in a buggy, Wash protesting vehemently that no Yankee bullet could finish him. When he was laid out on a bed in Hopemont, the ancestral home of the Morgan clan, he insisted upon being propped up with pillows so he could smoke a big black cigar. The cigar was still in Wash Morgan's mouth when he died.

In the afternoon, after paroling prisoners, the regiments formed and began marching out of Lexington, heading west on the familiar Versailles road, camping that night at Shryock's Ferry. During the night their old enemy, General Ebenezer Dumont, who had given the 2nd a bad time at the Lebanon Races, attempted to bypass the ferry route with his cavalry and form a juncture with infantry units coming from Louisville. Dumont was intent upon entrapping the whole Morgan brigade, but alert pickets warned the bivouac and Morgan had his regiments moving within twenty minutes. They raced through Lawrenceburg and turned down into thick forests around Bloomfield, where the Lexington Rifles had established Camp Charity back in the early autumn of 1861.

On the night of the nineteenth, Lieutenant James Sale, who was out on a routine patrol with E Company, ran into one of Buell's supply trains rumbling southward on the Louisville turnpike. A brief rattle of rifle fire was enough to frighten the surprised drivers into surrender. None of them had dreamed there were Confederate troops within a hundred miles. The boys of E Company ransacked the wagons, burning all except two, which they brought back into camp next morning loaded down with everything from cavalry boots to gingerbread.

At ten o'clock that morning they resumed march. On the twentieth they were in Elizabethtown, and that night burned a culvert and stopped a troop train on the L. & N. They gave the train-riding soldiers a "lively greeting" and then galloped off on the Litchfield road. By the twenty-second they were across Green River at Morgantown, moving always westward, sure that strong Federal forces would be guarding all routes to the south.

On the twenty-fourth, near Greenville, they rode into the fury of an autumn snowstorm blowing out of Illinois. As darkness fell the men went into camp, wrapping themselves in gum cloths and blankets. "I rode out early in the morning to the camp of the 2nd Kentucky," Basil Duke said afterward, "and had some difficulty in finding anyone except the camp guards. Inasmuch as we proposed to let them rest that day, the men had not yet arisen, and the level field in which they were encamped was marked by white mounds, under each of which lay one or more sleepers. The field really looked like a graveyard enshrouded in snow." A loud outcry awakened the sleepers, and what followed reminded Duke of biblical stories of the resurrection. "On all sides and throughout the encampment the mounds opened, and men sprang up, as one may imagine the dead will rise from their graves on the last day."

Long after the fights and skirmishes of this long October ride were forgotten, the men remembered that snowfall, recalling the sound restful sleep, the warmth under the snow, the bracing air of morning, their frozen boots which had to be thawed out over cooking fires, and the contrast of sparkling white ice against green leaves only faintly streaked with the first yellow and scarlet of autumn.

Learning that Colonel Thomas G. Woodward was camped at Hopkinsville with his Confederate Kentucky cavalry regiment, Morgan decided to pay a visit to this comrade in arms. Through one of those strange mix-ups that frequently occurred in the Richmond military records office, Woodward's regiment had also been numbered 2nd Kentucky Cavalry, a situation that had already caused much confusion in the bureaucracy. By the time the error was discovered, neither regiment was willing to relinquish its numbered identity, and sometimes Woodward received credit for Morgan's activities, and sometimes it was the other way round. Morgan had already considered that the best solution to the problem was to merge the two regiments. As he was now engaged in organizing a brigade—with an eye toward a brigadier general's commission—he decided that this would be an excellent opportunity to make the proposition in person to Tom Woodward.

Hopkinsville was primarily Confederate in sympathies, and when Morgan led his regiments into town, the people gave him an ovation. Confederate flags were flying in the bright October sun, and cheering crowds lined the streets. It was almost as wonderful as the day they had marched into Lexington, and Morgan and his boys enjoyed the Hopkinsville conviviality so much they lingered there for five days.

Colonel Tom Woodward was also hospitable, but firmly refused all offers to join his 2nd Kentucky with Morgan's legendary regiment. In his way, Woodward was even more independent-minded than Morgan, determined to fight his war where and when he pleased, and it was only the threat of having his regiment labeled as guerrillas by the Federals that led him eventually to subordinate his command to one of the official Confederate armies.

Refreshed from their stay in Hopkinsville, Morgan's men at last said farewell to Kentucky, and on the first day of November once again crossed the line into Tennessee. For two days they camped at Springfield, only twenty-five miles northwest of Nashville which was again a strong Federal base under a new western commander, Major General William S. Rosecrans.

While waiting at Springfield for scouts to find a route around Nashville, Robert Alston and R. M. Gano published another issue of the *Vidette*, reviewing the Kentucky campaign and poking fun at Union leaders for removing Buell as commander in the West. They also printed an account of court-martial proceedings against a private soldier accused of "horse pressing" without authorization. The trooper was drummed out of the command. As an indication that Morgan was becoming concerned over the loose way in which his boys "swapped" horses from friends as well as foes, he authorized a signed statement for the *Vidette*, outlining his rules for horse pressing. In enemy country no horse was to be taken by a trooper until he had the written consent of his captain; in loyal territory no exchange was permissible unless made in the presence of a commissioned officer and with the consent of the owner of the horse.

Morgan deeply resented the sobriquet "King of the Horse Thieves" which had been given him by the Northern press, and he concluded his statement with an invitation to all offended horse owners "to call upon me at my headquarters and reclaim their property and assist in bringing to justice those men in the garb of soldiers who are a disgrace to the service." Although Morgan no doubt made this promise in good faith, civilian readers of this issue of the *Vidette* may have wondered exactly where they might find the headquarters of a cavalry commander who never seemed to remain in one place long enough to pitch a tent.

For example, two days later the brigade was thirty miles away, quartered in its adopted town, Gallatin, and the men had scarcely removed their saddles when Morgan received orders to raid Edgefield Junction, just north of Nashville. Rosecrans had collected several hundred freight cars there in expectation of using them as soon as the Gallatin tunnels were reopened.

To assist Morgan in carrying out this assignment, General Forrest was to create a diversion south of Nashville; the time of the raid was set for dawn of November 6. The 2nd Kentucky moved out of Gallatin during the night of the fifth, approaching the railroad yards before daybreak. The men waited impatiently in the darkness, listening for sounds of Forrest's rifle fire across the river.

Dawn broke slowly, but all was quiet in Nashville and, at the first light, enemy pickets sighted the Confederate horses drawn up below the railway embankment. A sharp fight followed, the advance guard of the 2nd falling back to the main body. A few minutes later they heard the rifles of Forrest's troopers rattling off across the river, and Tom Quirk and Ben Drake led a detail across the tracks, running crouched forward until they took cover among the freight cars.

At the same time Federal infantrymen—the 16th Illinois—came trotting across a pontoon bridge out of Nashville, preventing Quirk from setting fire to more than a dozen cars. And before Quirk could withdraw his men, seven were captured by the Illinois infantrymen. Duke held the 2nd in position until it became evident that the enemy was paying no attention to Forrest's diversionary attack across the river; then he ordered a retreat to Gallatin.

The boys of the 2nd considered their Nashville expedition a total failure. Some were almost ready to admit they were too exhausted to fight well. After three months of constant movement, their cartridge boxes were empty, their rifles in need of repair, and their mounts badly worn. They needed time to refit, to obtain proper winter clothing, to recondition horses before engaging in another hard fight.

Aware of this, Morgan took his three regiments south of the Cumberland and went into camp four miles below Lebanon on the Murfreesboro turnpike, with hopes that he could stay long enough for the 2nd Regiment to secure fresh mounts and re-equip.

But Rosecrans was pushing cavalry patrols out of Nashville, probing for Bragg's army, and the Murfreesboro turnpike was no place for a rest camp. On November 13, in a message to General John C. Breckinridge, commanding at Murfreesboro, Morgan announced that he was falling back to Stone's River. "I sent five companies last night under Lieutenant Colonel Hutchinson to the pike below Silver Springs for the purpose of catching enemy foraging wagons. He returned this afternoon after capturing a lieutenant and nineteen men of the 4th Michigan Cavalry. Colonel Duke also went in pursuit of a body of cavalry approaching Lebanon, and chased them back within two miles of Silver Springs. My headquarters is to be at Stone River, but one regiment will remain at Lebanon until the last possible moment."

It seemed that the 2nd Kentucky had been as busy as ever.

Late in November, the 2nd Regiment was finally ordered to Fayetteville with the assurance of a period of continuous recuperation. Around Fayetteville grain and forage were plentiful, and with Bragg's Army of Tennessee based at Murfreesboro, there was no likelihood of Federal patrols appearing anywhere in the vicinity to disrupt the peace. Sick and slightly wounded men were quartered in country houses; the others rested, occupying their time with grooming and pampering their mounts. A few new horses were obtained to replace those worn out from long campaigning.

During this rare period of inaction for the 2nd, several exchanged prisoners reported for duty, some of them members of the old squadron who had been in Federal prison camps for several weeks. As A, B, and C companies had been filled to quota during the Kentucky invasion, these returnees were organized into a company of scouts. To lead them, Tom Quirk was relieved from command of M Company and promoted to captain of scouts.

One day early in December, Quirk and his scouts mounted up and rode off toward Murfreesboro. Basil Duke and St. Leger Grenfell also went with them, leaving the 2nd in command of Lieutenant Colonel John Hutchinson. There were rumors that Morgan was planning something interesting for "Old Rosy" Rosecrans, but the boys were rather certain that John Morgan would not attempt a real raid without calling for his veterans of the 2nd.

When they learned on December 9 that Morgan had raided Hartsville and won a great victory, the troopers of the 2nd were unforgiving. As much as they had enjoyed their rest at Fayetteville, they felt let down, and on later occasions when the victory was mentioned by those who had been present, the 2nd Regiment was inclined to pass it off by belittling the Federal garrison at Hartsville.

For his Hartsville raid, Morgan acted as a brigadier general, commanding the 7th, 8th and 11th Kentucky Cavalry regiments, the 2nd and 9th Kentucky Infantry, and a battery of artillery. The fifty-mile march was made in wintry weather, the ground frozen with ice and snow. To cover the distance rapidly, Morgan ordered a "ride and tie" march, the cavalry riding five or six miles, then leaving their horses and proceeding on foot; the infantry then coming up would mount the horses and ride until they overtook and passed the grounded cavalrymen, when the same routine would begin over again.

Grenfell, snuggled inside an oversized poncho, kept to the front with Duke and Quirk, and these three were given the honor of leading the river crossing and the first assault upon the surprised Federal garrison. Kelion Peddicord, one of the recently returned scouts, later said that Morgan had promised them horses and overcoats as rewards for accompanying him on the expedition, and when the first Federal cavalry appeared in view, Morgan shouted to them: "Boys, yonder are those horses I've been promising you!" And he added: "Be careful how you take them, each horse has an armed man on his back!"

An hour after the first shot was fired the Hartsville defenders surrendered, a bag of almost two thousand prisoners for "Brigadier General" Morgan. Among the captured units were elements of the 104th Illinois Infantry, the 106th and 108th Ohio Infantry, the 2nd Indiana Cavalry, and the 12th Indiana Battery. Along with the Indiana batterymen, the raiders captured two Parrott guns, one with an extraordinarily long barrel which the victors quickly named "Long Tom." (This gun was later to travel all the way across Indiana and Ohio before falling into Federal hands again.)

To obtain the overcoats promised the scouts, Morgan ordered the 104th Illinois drawn up in line and given a command found in no military manual: "104th Illinois, attention! Come out of them overcoats!" In the cold snowy weather, the captives obeyed somewhat reluctantly. "The overcoats," reported Private Peddicord, "were dyed black and worn by our men afterward."

Also captured were three regimental standards and five cavalry guidons, all of which were fluttering at the head of Morgan's column as he came marching proudly into Murfreesboro the next day with his two thousand prisoners.

By one of those coincidences of wartime, President Jefferson Davis arrived in Murfreesboro a few days later, and Davis found even the reticent Braxton Bragg waxing enthusiastic over John Morgan's Hartsville victory. Bragg recommended a brigadier general's commission be given the Kentucky cavalry leader immediately. Morgan's old friend, General Hardee, suggested that it be a major general's commission, but Davis demurred. "I do not wish to give my boys all of their sugar plums at once," he said.

Morgan had the satisfaction of receiving his brigadier's commission from the hand of Jeff Davis, and it was dated back to December 7, the day of the Hartsville raid.

Basil Duke also received a new commission as colonel and commander of the 2nd Regiment, an action which only made official a post he had held unofficially since the formation of the two new regiments during the recruiting period in Lexington.

Thus, the 2nd Kentucky was now only one of John Morgan's cavalry regiments. By mid-December there were six others in the brigade, the 3rd, 8th, 9th, 10th, and 11th Kentucky, and the 14th

Tennessee, which with attached batteries totaled almost four thousand men camped around Murfreesboro.

And when the 2nd Regiment moved up from Fayetteville to join these new comrades, the boys heard rumors going around the campfires that General Morgan was about to wed his Murfreesboro sweetheart, Miss Martha Ready. If some of them believed this indicated a long cozy winter for the soldiers of a bridegroom reluctant to leave a warm marriage bed, they were in for a rude surprise.

8

Christmas Raid

THE WEDDING of General John Morgan and Martha Ready on Sunday, December 14, 1862, was a gala affair. Morgan set the date himself, declaring that everything important always happened to him on Sundays. The two-story Ready home just off the Murfreesboro square was decorated with evergreens, the walls of the parlor encircled with mistletoe and holly, with green wreaths spelling out the names of towns in which the bridegroom had won victories. President Jefferson Davis and all the high-ranking generals of the Army of Tennessee were present—Bragg, Hardee, Breckinridge and Polk. Leonidas Polk, with the vestments of an Episcopal bishop over his lieutenant general's uniform, performed the marriage ceremony.

Although St. Leger Grenfell had frankly opposed the wedding for fear it would make Morgan less daring, the Englishman was in good form, offering numerous toasts to bride and groom, and then entertaining the company by singing "Moorish songs with a French accent to English airs." According to Basil Duke, the Britisher "was as mild and agreeable as if some one was going to be killed."

Along the street outside the brilliantly lighted house, Morgan's men gathered by hundreds around bonfires, and while two regimental bands played sentimental and martial tunes of the Confederacy, the boys cheered lustily for John Morgan and his bride.

142

One might have found it difficult to believe, with music ringing clear and bonfires and chandeliers burning brightly, that the Army of Tennessee was in any danger. But the high generals present were acutely aware of their precarious position at Murfreesboro, and even while the singing and dancing were at their merriest, Bragg was planning an important assignment for Morgan's brigade.

For several days it had been evident that the new commander of the Union's Army of the Cumberland, General Rosecrans, had no intention of keeping his soldiers idle through the winter. His divisions were massing below Nashville, his patrols were constantly probing, and with the Gallatin tunnels repaired, his railroad trains were bringing down a stockpile of rations and arms to Nashville. It was this supply line which was most vulnerable; without supplies Rosecrans could not sustain a long winter campaign.

Sometime during the week following his wedding, Morgan conferred with Bragg and the staff of the Army of Tennessee. From personal observation and from information obtained by spies, Morgan and the army's staff officers knew that the L. & N. Railroad now had a chain of almost impregnable stockades built along its length from Nashville to Bowling Green. Bridges were under full guard, rail towns strongly garrisoned. The Gallatin tunnels were heavily defended. After studying a map of the rail line, Morgan selected the weakest point, a pair of long high trestleworks just north of Elizabethtown where the road cut through Muldraugh's Hill. Each of these trestles was about five hundred feet long and one hundred feet high, and if destroyed would effectively cut Rosecrans' rail supply line for most of the winter.

The tricky condition of this plan was that Muldraugh's Hill was only a few miles below Louisville, a good seven-day march from Murfreesboro. With average luck a cavalry brigade could reach the trestles, but something more than luck would be required to overcome the defenders, burn the structures, and then march out again. Evidently Bragg and his generals believed Morgan's cavalry could do it. They authorized a Christmas raid against the Muldraugh's Hill trestles.

In preparation for this adventure, Morgan divided his regiments into two brigades to permit greater flexibility of movement. The 2nd Kentucky, Gano's 3rd Kentucky, Colonel Leroy Cluke's 8th

Kentucky, and a four-piece battery formed the 1st Brigade under command of Basil Duke. John B. Hutchinson was moved up from E Company to command of the 2nd Kentucky. The 2nd Brigade was offered to Adam Johnson of the 10th Kentucky, but Johnson declined and the command went to William Breckinridge.

On December 20, the new organization moved from its camps around Murfreesboro to Alexandria. Next morning farriers completed last-minute shoeing of horses; the men cleaned their rifles, burnished boots and leather equipment; officers inspected arms and horses.

That afternoon the regiment passed in review before General Morgan and his bride. The weather was pleasant, the columns marching against a background of dark cedars and leafless trees topped by mistletoe white with its blossoms of the holiday season. "It was Sunday, and a clear lovely day," Lieutenant James McCreary recorded. "As company after company moved forward into line with horses prancing, firearms glistening, bugles blowing, and flags waving, and with our artillery on the right flank and finally halted in a beautiful valley with bright eyes and lovely faces gaping at us, it formed a grand and imposing scene." Never again would John Morgan command such a body of men, four thousand strong, the majority seasoned veterans mounted on the best Kentucky and Tennessee horseflesh left in the South.

For some reason, St. Leger Grenfell chose that grand Sunday at Alexandria to say farewell to the boys of the 2nd Kentucky. He mounted his best horse, and with his hunting dogs trailing after him rode back toward Murfreesboro to ask Braxton Bragg for another assignment. Few were ever certain why Old St. Lege departed their company so suddenly. One story had it that he disliked Billy Breckinridge and had quarreled with Morgan because the General appointed Breckinridge commander of the 2nd Brigade. Another belief was that he had a bellyful of the lack of discipline in the ranks. Grenfell himself said afterward that he and Morgan "had a conflict on a point of duty, in which he got exceedingly angry so I left him and reported to General Bragg, who made me inspector of cavalry."

Most of the boys would see him again briefly during the winter, and then again toward the end of the war some would become intimately acquainted with this romantic swarthy knight under rather strange circumstances. The troopers of the 2nd would never forget Old St. Lege. From him they had learned the principles of courage combined with those of survival, and horse soldiers could ask for little more.

Before daybreak on the twenty-second, reveille sounded in the Alexandria camps. Horses were fed, watered, and saddled, and breakfast fires lighted. The march out was set for nine o'clock. It was a soft mild morning, like early autumn, the sun bright in a cloudless sky, birds twittering in the cedars. The order of march called for Quirk's scouts and the 2nd Kentucky to take the advance, Duke riding with John Hutchinson at the head of his old regiment. Except for the regimental commanders none knew exactly where they were going, but all were sure they would be in Kentucky for Christmas and that was enough.

For two hours columns of fours marched out of the frost-browned, cedar-fringed meadows until regiments were strung out for seven miles. Suddenly above the steady hoofbeats and the creak of leather, tremendous cheers broke far back down the column. The boys of the 2nd knew what the cheering meant; Morgan had bid his bride farewell and was coming up front to join them. "Alongside the column," said Bennett Young, "with a splendid staff, magnificently mounted, superbly dressed, riding like a centaur, bare-headed, with plumed hat in his right hand, waving salutations to his applauding followers, the general came galloping by."

Just before winter's dusk, the 2nd, with both Morgan and Duke forward, reached Sand Shoals ford on the Cumberland. The men crossed without incident and went into camp on the north side.

At daylight they were moving again, Morgan aiming for Tompkinsville, but the plodding artillery held the columns back. When they crossed the Kentucky line, the short December day was closing, a full moon lighting the sky. "Cheer after cheer and shout after shout echoed for miles toward the rear of the column, breaking the stillness of the night," James McCreary noted in his journal. "Tonight we are camped on the sacred soil of old Kentucky and it fills my heart with joy and pride to know that I am once more on my native heather . . . campfires illuminate every hill and valley and the fires burn brighter, seemingly are more cheerful, because it is the fatherland."

To celebrate the Christmas Eve march from Tompkinsville to Glasgow, several of the boys foraged some "swell head brandy," and a few overdid their seasonal imbibing, growing "too heavy for their saddles," and had to be strapped on by their more sober comrades.

During the afternoon the 2nd Regiment overtook an enormous wagon drawn by twenty Percheron horses, "perhaps the largest wagon ever seen in the State of Kentucky." The driver was a Union sutler, bound for Glasgow with Christmas delicacies for the Federal camps there; consequently the boys captured it immediately. According to Tom Berry it contained "a fabulous variety and quantity of good things to eat," and that night every mess in the brigade had something to brighten their otherwise drab Christmas suppers.

The regiments bivouacked that night five miles below Glasgow, scouts having brought reports of strong Union cavalry movements in the area to the north. " 'Tis Christmas Eve," wrote James McCreary. "I am sitting with many friends—around a glorious campfire. Shouting, singing and speechifying make the welkin ring, for the boys have a superabundance of whisky and are celebrating Christmas Eve very merrily. We have not seen an enemy yet."

2

While the main body of the expedition was making camp south of Glasgow, Tom Quirk and his scouts approached the town. From friends along the way, Quirk learned that the 2nd Michigan Cavalry was patrolling in the vicinity, but the enemy's exact location was unknown.

Quirk, having a mighty Irish thirst and a desire to celebrate Christmas Eve, took his scouts in to a Glasgow saloon. As the advance platoon was dismounting and hitching horses to the front rail, a patrol of Michigan boys came cantering down the street with the same objective in view—a glass of Christmas cheer. Scout Kelion Peddicord laconically described the unexpected meeting: "A collision was the result, then a skirmish, then—a stampede of all parties!"

In their hasty "stampede" the scouts captured a pair of Michigan stragglers, then turned back toward camp. Along the way, Quirk and Peddicord stopped at several Christmas parties, "long enough to enjoy a dance with some of the girls, very much to their surprise—and gratification, they said. They had not the remotest idea that Morgan was near. But we danced our set, though the whole country was alive with the enemy."

With Quirk's company of scouts on this raid was seventeen-year-old Johnny Wyeth (later to serve with General Forrest and become his first biographer). Quirk had refused to enlist Wyeth because of his age, but allowed him to ride along as a sort of "independent" member of the company.

Wyeth afterward recorded the events of Christmas Day, how the scouts marched early through Glasgow, then swiftly up the pike toward Munfordville. "About two o'clock in the afternoon, at Bear Wallow, our company was well in front of Morgan's command when the vidette came back with the information that the road was full of Yankees just ahead. With his usual reckless dash, Quirk drew his six-shooter and, yelling to his company of about forty-five men to draw theirs, he dashed down the road toward the enemy. War was a new experience to me, and it was very exciting as we swept down the road at full tilt. Right ahead of us, as we swung around a turn, stretched across the turnpike, and field to one side of the road, was a formidable line of Federal cavalry. The number in sight evidently checked the enthusiasm of our plucky captain, for, as they opened fire upon us and one or two of our men were wounded, he told us to dismount and fight on foot, which we promptly did, leaving our horses with 'No. 4' and advancing some hundred yards further down the lane."

The Federals, however, had set an ambush, and as the horse-holders formed a corral in a corner of the field, the concealed enemy rushed up to an adjoining rail fence, firing into the horses and stampeding them. "Our one chance," said Wyeth, "was to climb over the fence on the other side of the lane which we speedily did. Quirk and I went over the same panel, with the Federals shooting at us from the fence across the road, no more than thirty or forty feet distant. We got over safely without any delay and ran across the field, making the best possible time to take refuge in a thicket."

As soon as they were under cover, Johnny Wyeth turned around and was shocked to see blood spurting down Quirk's face. "The damn Yankees've shot me twice in the head," Quirk growled in his thick brogue, "but I'll get even with them before the sun sets." He wiped the blood out of his eyes and swore an Irish oath. "Johnny, I want you to go back to the rear as fast as you can. Tell my men if they don't come back here and help me clean these fellows out, I'll shoot the last damn one of them myself."

Johnny Wyeth worked his way back to the rear, and met Duke and Hutchinson coming up with Company A. A few minutes later the Federals were surrounded and forced into surrender.

When Morgan arrived on the scene and found Quirk with a bloody handkerchief around his head, he ordered the Irishman to see a surgeon. But Quirk only grinned and declared he had a head built in County Kerry, so toughened by shillelaghs that a couple of bullet wounds were mere trifles. He gathered his scouts and resumed march in advance of the 2nd.

All afternoon the wintry skies had been thickening, and before dark a cold rain began falling. The regiments crossed Green River in a downpour, and turned toward Hammondsville over a road which was quickly churned into mud, yellow torrents foaming down the side ditches. That night they camped under beating rain only seven miles from the enemy's dry and cozy stockades along the L. & N. Railroad.

At reveille the icy rain was still falling, men fumbling for saddles in the winter dark, trying vainly to dry their weapons. On the chance that the Federals might have guessed the raiders' main objective—the Muldraugh's Hill trestles thirty miles to the north— Morgan and his staff decided to take advantage of the proximity of the Bacon Creek bridge and strike a damaging blow there. If Muldraugh's Hill turned out to be unassailable, at least they could turn back south with one good bridge out on the railroad. Some of the junior officers who had been in the old squadron recalled that they had destroyed that Bacon Creek bridge twice before; it seemed to be becoming a habit.

Lieutenant Colonel Hutchinson and the 2nd drew the bridge assignment, the other regiments proceeding slowly northward toward Elizabethtown. Basil Duke accompanied Hutchinson, but left the command responsibility to the latter, and on that day the twenty-four-year-old Lieutenant Colonel proved himself a capable successor to Morgan and Duke.

John Hutchinson was well over six feet tall, powerfully built, with a head like a hawk's—an aquiline nose, dark piercing eyes, close-cropped black hair. Mounted on his oversized gray charger, he led his men confidently down to the railroad bridge at Bacon Creek. Since the 2nd's last visit a year before, the Federals had constructed a massive stockade within a hundred yards of the bridge, close enough so that the bridge's entire length could be covered by loop-hole fire.

In the bleak December rain the bridge appeared invulnerable, but Hutchinson ordered up one of the Parrott guns captured at Harts-ville, and while heavy shells smashed away at the sturdy stockade, he sent details in to fire the bridge. Several times fires were started, to drown in the incessant rain. Hutchinson himself crawled up behind the railroad embankment, tossing lighted brands upon the structure only to see them shot away by the accurate Federal sharp-shooters.

As a last resort, a truce party was sent into the stockade, informing the defenders that they were surrounded by Morgan's men. The magic name of Morgan turned the trick; the stockade surrendered.

The bridge was now quickly set ablaze, and for good measure the men built huge fires along the tracks for several miles, ripping up rails to heap upon them. They knocked down telegraph poles, adding them to the fires, twisted the wires around trees and tossed rolls of it into nearby streams.

For a few days at least, Rosecrans' Nashville base was cut off from Louisville, and now nothing lay between Morgan's men and the Muldraugh's Hill trestles but thirty miles, and well-defended Elizabethtown.

On the morning of December 27, the advance regiments were within six miles of Elizabethtown, and a quick sweep around would have brought them to the trestles by late afternoon. Morgan, however, decided that it would be wiser to capture the town's garrison, rather than risk being caught between the forces there and those at the trestles.

In the line of march that morning, Duke and Morgan were up front with Colonel Cluke's 8th Kentucky, the 2nd having fallen in at the rear after the raid at Bacon Creek. During the night the skies had cleared, and it was "a lovely sunny day, all nature seemed to be sparkling and smiling."

As the forward scouts approached the outskirts of Elizabethtown, they saw a Union corporal coming down the muddy road; he was waving a truce flag. The scouts held their horses warily until the corporal came up and asked in a thick Dutch accent for their commander. They took him into custody and hustled him back to Morgan, the corporal saluting stiffly and handing over a message scrawled on the back of an envelope:

ELIZABETHTOWN, KY., Dec. 27, 1862
To the Commander of the Confederate Forces:
SIR; I demand an unconditional surrender of all your forces.
I have you surrounded, and will compel you to surrender.
    I am, sir, your obedient servant,
                                    H. S. SMITH
                                Commanding U. S. Forces

Morgan could barely conceal his amusement, but he was in no mood for joking, and quickly sent a reply back to Colonel Smith informing him that it was *his* forces which were surrounded, not the Confederates, and that the Federal garrison should surrender. In a second message Smith refused to capitulate, and Morgan replied briefly that he would give the defenders time to remove women and children, and then would attack.

Duke had already dismounted Cluke's 8th, keeping the 2nd in reserve, and Morgan had sent the battery up on a hill to the left of the road, from where the gunners could fire down into the town. Colonel Smith's six hundred Union soldiers were concentrated in brick residences and in two or three large warehouses facing the south, and it was into these that the Parrott guns and howitzers began to drop their shells while the dismounted men of the 8th moved in.

The fighting was brisk and noisy for a few minutes, and the six hundred Federals soon had enough of grape and canister. Even before Colonel Smith gave the final order to surrender, his men began waving white flags from windows.

Mounting up, Lieutenant McCreary rode down past one of the brick houses which had been heavily shelled. To his surprise "several very handsome young ladies" appeared in the front yard. They asked him to come in and have some refreshments. "I dismounted and went in. Saw that a shell had entered the window, exploded and killed three Yankees, who were then weltering in their blood on the floor, and I was informed it wounded others. With hair disheveled, these ladies like proud Spartans walked contemptuously through the blood of those who had insulted them and invited me into a room where there were many quarts of wine, cakes, etc. I did justice to Christmas, and a hungry stomach, and ample justice, I hope to the dear fair ones. At another place I met five or six ladies, had refreshments, and wrote a letter home. These so dear Kentucky ladies have a charm which no others possess."

As the work of rounding up scattered Federals, and disarming and paroling them, delayed the raiders until late in the afternoon, Morgan decided to make a temporary fortress of Elizabethtown and wait out the night. His men had six hundred extra rifles at their disposal now, and an abundance of Federal ammunition. Except for the unlucky ones who drew vidette and patrol duties, all spent a pleasant evening in Elizabethtown. As Lieutenant McCreary noted: "An old Southern friend gave our quartermaster a barrel of superb whisky. It was reasonably dealt out and now all goes merrily as a marriage bell."

Next morning they were bugled out early, Quirk's scouts and the 2nd in advance again, and before noon both brigades were in position around the two long wooden trestleworks—the principal objective of this Christmas raid. Morgan sent truce parties in to both stockades, offering the defenders a chance to surrender, but again as at Elizabethtown the Federals were determined to make a fight of it.

The attacks began simultaneously, Duke's brigade against the upper trestle, Breckinridge's against the lower. After two or three hours' shelling, the 71st Indiana Infantry ran up white flags on both stockades, and 650 prisoners marched out to surrender.

Sergeant Henry L. Stone, one of the few Indianians in Morgan's command, chose this opportunity to write a letter to his mother in Greencastle, hoping to have it delivered by one of the Indiana parolees. "Dear Mother . . . At the railroad trestleworks we captured the 71st Indiana, including Billy Brown and Court Mattson. Lt. Col. Brown appeared very glad to see me indeed. I was surprised to see him. . . . I happened to go up to the house in which Gen. Morgan had his headquarters and I hadn't more than seated myself by the fire when I looked around and recognized Brown sitting by the same fire. I says 'Hello! Brown, what are you doing here?' He looked for some time and recognized me at last and shook my hand heartily. After talking a little I took my canteen and called him aside to take a heavy horn of good old Cogniac brandy. I think he took about three drinks. Next morning I wrote a letter and he said he would take it home to you for me, and I think he will.

"Mother, to say I've never wished to be at home and sleep once more in a feather bed would be telling an untruth, but I never enjoyed any life as well as this. . . . When we'll leave the state I don't know, neither do I know where General Morgan expects to concentrate his forces. . . . I'm well now excepting a cold. Not a day's sickness or a dose of medicine have I taken since joining the service. . . . I know it'll prove a great benefit to my health and I'll try to prevent its seriously injuring my morals. It is true that I take a little spirits occasionally, for these cold mornings it is beneficial. I've seen almost the infernal regions on earth since I left home but have endured it all and today rejoice that I'm a Confederate soldier. . . . I wish I could have been home at Christmas and took some turkey."

A few minutes after the Indianians surrendered, both trestles were afire, flames licking high, black smoke spiraling into the light blue December sky. For the men of both brigades, December 28 was a day of high accomplishment. After a week of hard marching, hard fighting, and some bad cavalry weather, they felt as if their lost Christmas had been well sacrificed. Morgan summed it up for them in his official report: "I had the satisfaction of knowing that the object of the expedition was attained, and the railroad was rendered impassable for at least two months.* The two trestles were the

* Morgan's estimate was conservative. It was mid-March, 1863, before the Federals could rebuild bridges and trestles and restore service on the L. & N.

largest and finest on the whole road. Neither had been destroyed before during the war."

Now that his mission was accomplished, Morgan faced an even greater problem—that of marching back into Tennessee through all the swarms of Union troops bent upon intercepting him. As soon as he was satisfied that the trestles were destroyed, he formed columns and turned eastward. At the mouth of Beech Fork on the Rolling Fork River, the regiments bivouacked for the night, Quirk taking his scouts across the stream for outpost duty watch.

During the night Colonel John M. Harlan, commanding a brigade of five Union infantry and cavalry regiments fell upon the raiders' trail. Shortly after daybreak of the twenty-ninth, while the last of Morgan's men were crossing the flooded Rolling Fork, Harlan's pursuit force was close enough to begin shelling the rear regiment.

Basil Duke, who was still on the south bank attempting to hold Harlan in check while the last companies forded the stream, was struck suddenly by a shell fragment. He fell unconscious from his horse, blood flowing from the side of his head.

Shouts and cries of dismay ran through the line of men holding the last defensive position. Duke lay where he had fallen, motionless, shells bursting all around, and his men were certain their beloved young commander was dead.

Captain Tom Quirk, who had been assisting Duke, ran forward and lifted the apparently lifeless Colonel upon his horse, then mounted behind and splashed across the Rolling Fork. At the first farmhouse, Quirk impressed a carriage, filled it with feather mattresses and blankets, eased the yet-unconscious Duke into the soft bedding, and set out at a fast pace for Bardstown and medical aid.

At the moment Duke was struck down, the forward attackers of Colonel Harlan's Federals had been close enough to overhear the excitement created, had heard Morgan's men shouting that Colonel Duke had been killed. In his report to division headquarters that day, Harlan wrote that among the Confederate casualties was "Colonel Basil W. Duke, commanding a brigade under Morgan, and who is believed to be the life and soul of all the movements of the latter. . . . Near where he was seen during the engagement, ten dead horses were found within a space of twenty feet square . . . the work of the section of battery on the left."

When this information was passed on to General Boyle, commanding Kentucky Union forces, Boyle was so excited he could not restrain himself from forwarding the news to President Lincoln: "Colonel Duke died of wounds. . . . Morgan has paid dearly for what he has done."

However, the tough little half-cavalier, half-alligator horse was far from being dead. His arrival in Bardstown was chronicled by a circuit-riding preacher, J. W. Cunningham: "About dark Morgan's men began to throng the streets. Among the arrivals was Basil Duke. . . . He had been wounded. It was necessary for him to be helped by others into the hall of Dr. Cox's two-story brick house and up the stairway to the north end room where he was laid on a thick pallet on the floor. Dr. Thomas Allen [surgeon of the 2nd Kentucky] attended Duke. I stood by and witnessed. The wound was on the right side of the head, and when the doctor had washed the blood from it, I was invited to examine a cannon's work . . . a piece of skin and bone behind the ear was gone."

As the Reverend Cunningham bent down, Duke opened his eyes and said cheerfully: "That was a pretty close call."

Next morning the circuit rider watched the regiments marching out of Bardstown on the Springfield road, Morgan at the head of the column dressed in a close-fitting roundabout and pants of green woolen. "On his head was a black low-crowned soft hat with a broad brim . . . a splendid-looking man." Duke rode far back down the column in the feather-bedded buggy, one of Quirk's scouts handling the reins like a proud coachman.

By midafternoon the scouts were in Springfield, finding the town ungarrisoned, and the regiments filed in until twilight, to camp in and around the town. With the early darkness came a slow rain which began freezing to the trees, and as ominous as the weather were reports coming in from patrols which had been ranging southward.

Lebanon, nine miles to the south, was a concentration point for Federals in pursuit of Morgan, the scouts reporting several thousand bivouacked there, and probably ten thousand more were in motion between Glasgow and the Cumberland River crossings. Among the various pursuing units was Colonel Frank Wolford's 1st Kentucky, a regiment which Morgan's veterans warmly respected.

One of the axioms of cavalry raiding is that it is always easier to get in than to get out, and it was never truer than on that bleak December evening. According to Bennett Young, Morgan saw that "the best way of escape was the longest way; that he could not whip the eight thousand Federals at Lebanon and he must manage to get around them. He determined to make a detour to the right of Lebanon, swing back on the road to Campbellsville, and rush to Campbellsville with all possible speed." Consequently a forced march was ordered at 11:00 P.M.

When the advance reached the road fork four miles from Lebanon, the main column bore off in the darkness along a rough side trail toward St. Mary's. At the same time Quirk's scouts and a few companies of the 2nd and 11th regiments were making a feint toward the Federal camps. "This was done in gallant style," Kelion Peddicord reported, "and the pickets were driven back into Lebanon in great disorder." The skirmishers then stacked fence rails for a mile through the fields and fired them, the reflection of flames on the low clouds convincing the Federals in Lebanon that Morgan's men were camping by their fires, awaiting battle at dawn. "It was bitter cold," said Lieutenant McCreary, "but it was certain death to stand before the firelight."

Every Morgan man who afterward recalled this march around Lebanon described the weather as the worst experienced during the entire war. The darkness was intense, the freezing rain turning to sleet and cutting into their faces. Although most of them wrapped blankets around their bodies and covered their feet with strips of cloth, this was but slight protection against sharp penetrating winds whistling and rattling through the naked trees. Boot soles froze to stirrups, fingers and toes turned blue with frostbite.

"Icicles gathered on the horses' manes and breasts, covered their bridles and halters, and dangled from their nostrils. Ice coated the beards and moustaches of the men. Half the time they walked by their steeds, stamping their feet, swinging their hands and beating their bodies to drive away the stupor which extreme cold imposes upon flesh and blood. There was no loud word spoken. Commands, if given, were uttered in soft tones, and all were directed to ride, walk or march in absolute silence." Even the wounded Basil Duke in his insulated buggy suffered from the intensity of the cold.

When day dawned, the column looked like a ghostly army, men sheeted in ice, horses steaming from exertion as they moved silently through the woods. It was the last day of the year, December 31, 1862.

3

Before the 2nd Kentucky marched out of Springfield on the previous evening, Lieutenant George Eastin of D Company had dined with friends, a family which included several charming young women. During the meal the conversation revolved mainly about one Colonel Dennis Halisey of the 6th Kentucky Union Cavalry, a thoroughly hated officer who had arrested a number of Confederate sympathizers and sent them to Northern prisons. Halisey was accused of adopting the methods of the Federal commander at New Orleans, "Beast" Ben Butler, who issued an edict declaring that all Southern women who showed contempt for Union soldiers would be treated as common prostitutes.

Under the soft candlelight of the dining room, twenty-one-year-old George Eastin listened sympathetically, and when one of the prettiest of the young belles declared with emphasis that she would marry any Confederate soldier who killed the tyrant Halisey, Eastin gallantly rose from his chair. "I accept the challenge, miss," he declared smilingly.

After some applause and gay laughter, the conversation had turned to another subject, and by the end of his regiment's terrible night march, Lieutenant Eastin had completely forgotten Colonel Dennis Halisey.

Shortly after daybreak, Captain Castleman of D Company suggested that Eastin should take a side road off to New Market and make an effort to obtain boots from a shoemaker known to live there. Lieutenant Alexander Tribble of Company K requested permission to accompany Eastin, as some of his men also were badly in need of new boots.

Turning away from the column, Eastin and Tribble reached New Market without incident, but their mission was fruitless. "We found nothing we cared to buy, even for Confederate money," Eastin said later. But when they were riding back to join the rear of their column, they were overtaken by three Union cavalrymen. One of them was none other than Colonel Dennis Halisey.

As soon as the three Federals saw the Confederate officers' gray uniforms, they galloped in pursuit, firing several shots. Eastin and Tribble, being on an open road, decided to make a dash for a nearby woods.

"We had gone this way for perhaps half a mile, running just fast enough to encourage our pursuers to follow us without trying to get entirely away from them. I saw we were approaching a small, sluggish stream. . . ." The next moment Eastin noticed a side road offering concealment. "I therefore turned as abruptly as possible into this open space, and called to Tribble to do the same, but before he understood my purpose his horse had carried him into the stream.

"We had scarcely time to face about when the front man of our pursuers, an orderly on Halisey's staff by the name of Edwards, dashed around the corner, and though he endeavored at once to check his horse, he did not succeed in doing so until he had run squarely up to Tribble."

What followed was as dramatic as a combat scene involving Little John or Friar Tuck in Sherwood Forest—with pistols rather than quarterstaves. Tribble and Edwards exchanged shots, but their horses' stumbling about in the muddy stream spoiled their aim. A moment later, Tribble grappled with Edwards, dragging him backward from his mount, the two men sprawling into the water. Both had lost their weapons, but Tribble forced Edwards down into the stream until he yielded, sitting up in the muddy water, gasping for air and announcing that he was the Confederate's prisoner.

All this had happened in a matter of seconds, and even before the struggle in the water ended, Colonel Halisey came dashing up, reining in his horse, the animal swerving into the open space where Eastin waited. The two men were not more than ten paces apart.

"I at once fired at him," Eastin said, "and demanded his surrender. He returned my fire, and urging my horse a little nearer to him, I fired again, and saw the dust fly from the shoulder of his overcoat, though, as I afterwards discovered, the shot did not wound him. He then fired again; and spurring my horse towards him, was about to fire again, when he threw up his hand and surrendered to me saying twice, 'I am your prisoner, sir; I am your prisoner!' I extended my hand and demanded his pistols. Instead, however, of giving them up, he dropped his bridle rein, and reaching over with his left hand, grabbed me in the collar, and, at the same time, without taking special aim, firing under his left arm, fired at me again. The discharge burned and blackened my face, and the flash for an instant blinded me, but almost instinctively, and at the same moment, I grappled with him, and putting my pistol firmly against his temple, fired again.

"In the excitement caused by the unexpected shot in my face, I held on to Halisey's body for a moment, and both horses being loose, moved side by side down to the pool of water. Here I released him to reach for the bridle of his horse, but missing this, Halisey's lifeless body fell over against me and down between his horse and mine into the water. In the fall, his head caught my bridle rein, which was hanging loose. This kept his head out of the water, but jerked my horse up and made him plunge around, dragging Halisey's body through the pool, until we reached the other bank where it became disentangled.

"I had scarcely time to look around and take in the situation as to my friend Tribble, when the third man on the Federal side came dashing around the corner. Tribble was completely disarmed. The pistol that I had been using and still held in my hand was then entirely empty. I leveled it at the lieutenant who had just arrived, and he seeing the fate of his companions, rode up and handed me his carbine and a pair of army pistols."

Not until the Federal Lieutenant identified the dead Colonel did George Eastin know he had unintentionally carried out his knightly vow to the young lady of Springfield. Although he did not—as his models of the Arthurian legends would have done—dash away to claim the lady's hand, young Eastin did take as trophies the sword and pistols of the dead tyrant, Dennis Halisey.

A few months later the sword would come to a strange resting place in southern Indiana, but the derring-do of George Eastin was memorialized for posterity in a ballad, one verse of which runs as follows:

And now is Eastin, for 'twas he,
With air of proudest chivalry,
That dared defy the Federal knight
Who challenge gave for mortal fight,
Free to go and end this feud
By work of death—at least, of blood.

Not many junior cavalry officers achieved such literary renown. The boys of the 2nd Kentucky must have been as proud of George Eastin as he was of being a subject for Bluegrass metrics.

4

While Lieutenant Eastin was engaged in his duel to the death, General Morgan with the advance column was climbing the heights of Muldraugh's Hill, some miles southeast of the burned bridges. Although the raiders had marched steadily for almost fourteen hours, their route had been so circuitous that they were still not out of danger from the Federal concentration at Lebanon. "I could see Lebanon with a glass distinctly," Morgan wrote in his report, "and the enemy's skirmishers deployed in the valley below."

Ordering a short halt to rest horses, Morgan sent George Ellsworth down to the spur line railroad running from Lebanon to a junction with the L. & N. Ellsworth tapped the telegraph wire, "obtained all the news afloat," and as soon as Morgan was assured that the road south was clear of enemy troops, a double-quick march was ordered to Campbellsville.

New Year's Eve was spent in Campbellsville—after the boys had routed a small detachment left there to guard commissary supplies while the main Union force was marching somewhere to the north in pursuit of these turn-about raiders. The captured supplies included both food and forage. "Tonight we are camped in a lonely woodland on the edge of Campbellsville. A big log fire is sparkling . . . here we found abundance of corn, hay, molasses, crackers, and ham, and all are doing well."

Dawn broke on a gray new year, 1863, the men celebrating by rising to early reveille bugles and beginning a rapid march toward

Columbia. As the column was winding down a high hill that afternoon, they heard a rumble of faraway cannon—a trick of sound
waves against leaden winter skies—carried and deflected from a
bloody artillery duel at Stone's River many miles to the south. While
Morgan's raiders were cutting the Union supply line, Rosecrans had
marched out of Nashville to challenge Bragg. The continuous rumbling was haunting and foreboding, like some inexorable burden of
the future. In Washington that day, Abraham Lincoln was signing
the Emancipation Proclamation.

With Federal cavalry pressing hard in pursuit, the raiders did not
dare halt for the night in Columbia, but marched on several miles
south of town. During the short bivouac, Henry Stone wrote a letter
to his mother in Indiana for mailing at the last United States post-
office on their route. "We are now on the retreat from Kentucky
and are thus far on our road back to Tennessee. I'm now seated by
my campfire among the ordnance wagons with pen, ink and paper,
and a lamp light and a valise to write on. It is eight o'clock at night
and the other boys are fixing to go to bed, and quarreling about who
shall spread down the bed, &c. . . . We came to destroy the Louisville & Nashville Railroad, and through the Northern papers you've
no doubt ere this heard how well and fully we accomplished our
mission. It will take two months at least to repair the damage. The
Feds of Nashville will for a while now have to go *unfed.*

"We'll try starvation on them a while as they've been trying it on
us since the war began.

"You've no idea, mother, of the rapidity with which we travel. We
think nothing of traveling 40 miles, and often 50, sometimes and
even quite often lately till 12 at night. We never stop for rain, snow,
or obstacles of any kind, not even a heavy force of blue-coated
Yankees."

The next day James McCreary noted in his diary: "Still onward
and onward we go, our column, with glittering arms and wearied
horses, winding far out in front and far back in the distance like an
immense anaconda . . . in the distance I see the blue hills that border
the Cumberland." On January 3, they crossed the Tennessee line.
"Here we are with oil cloths up and the rain falling in a perfect
deluge. The raid may be considered ended for we are again on Ten-

nessee soil . . . railroads, telegraphs, Yankees and commissary stores have received a blow they will long remember."

On the fifth they rode into Smithville, men and horses utterly exhausted, and for the first time in two weeks, they could take stock of what the raid had accomplished. Their own losses were incredibly light—only two killed, twenty-four wounded, and sixty-four missing. Most of the missing would find their ways back to the brigade; on long cavalry raids the heaviest losses were expected to be in the "missing" classification—patrols forced to detour around enemy forces, foraging parties temporarily lost on unfamiliar side roads, and the inevitable stragglers who may or may not have been captured by the enemy.

On the other hand, Union forces engaged against the raiders had sustained total losses approaching two thousand, most of them paroled prisoners. The damage inflicted upon Rosecrans' communications and supply lines was incalculable. Even before Morgan's men rode into Smithville on January 5, Major General Horatio G. Wright, commanding at Cincinnati, was desperately attempting to deliver one million overdue rations to Rosecrans' army. Wright shipped the rations down the Ohio River to the Cumberland, but the Cumberland was at low water stage and there was only one light-draft boat available for transport to Nashville. "We must open the railroad soon," Wright telegraphed General Boyle at Louisville, "or Rosecrans will starve."

The Christmas raid had come too late, however, to hinder Rosecrans' assault on Bragg's army. By the time the raiders reached Smithville, the Stone's River campaign was ended, both armies withdrawing from the field badly blooded. Each side claimed victory, but Lieutenant McCreary noted in his diary of January 6: "Received dispatch of 'victory' of Bragg's army. Bragg deemed it expedient to fall back towards Tullahoma. I don't believe in such victories. Bragg's talent seems to be all on the retreat."

Weary as they were, Morgan's men found no prospect of rest at Smithville. Bragg ordered them to immediate duty covering the left of his retreating army.

It looked like another long hard winter in Tennessee.

9

Winter of Discontent

I

By MID-JANUARY 1863, the Army of Tennessee was dug in for the winter along Duck River from Shelbyville to Tullahoma, with its cavalry guarding front and flanks. General Morgan established headquarters at McMinnville, and John Hutchinson took the 2nd Kentucky out to Woodbury, "a beautiful and rebellious village" on the Murfreesboro turnpike.

During this early period of what was to be a long stalemated winter, Morgan's men found themselves in the midst of a "paper war" between Rosecrans and Bragg. Couriers were kept busy carrying vitriolic messages back and forth between the lines, and much of the subject matter concerned Morgan's raiders. Even before the Christmas raid, the two generals had been arguing about the proprieties of guerrilla warfare, and during the brigades' absence in Kentucky, Rosecrans had composed an indignant message relating to Morgan's action in taking overcoats from the 104th Illinois Infantry. "Whether your idea of humanity consists in robbing them of their overcoats, I know not," Rosecrans wrote, "but such they assure me was the treatment they received from your troops." Rosecrans also added a repetitive complaint that Morgan's cavalry did not always wear recognizable Confederate uniforms, and must therefore be considered guerrillas.

162

To this, Bragg replied tartly that "we aim to clothe them as uniformly as the exigencies of our situation will admit. Whenever you will afford us the facilities to obtain the requisite material, we shall be most happy to make the desired change. In the meantime we shall use the best to be procured." Apparently Bragg considered "the best to be procured" were Union overcoats and the best means of procuring them was to capture the wearers.

The overcoat incident was only one minor facet of the question as to whether Morgan's cavalrymen were or were not guerrillas—in essence, whether they were or were not to be treated as regular troops subject to the rules of war when captured. Rosecrans attempted to settle the matter by issuing an edict that all Confederate soldiers caught without uniforms would be treated as spies, but this only added fuel to the controversy.

One of the incidents swirling out of this "paper war" was an accusation that Lieutenant George Eastin of the 2nd Kentucky had killed Colonel Dennis Halisey after the latter had surrendered and should therefore be turned over to Union authorities as a murderer. Eastin, with his youthful ideals of knighthood, was outraged by the charge. The accusation was a half-truth, he maintained, which overlooked the fact that Halisey had attempted resistance after surrendering.

And even though Union authorities placed a price on his head, Eastin continued wearing the dead Colonel's sword as a talisman, a sword with Halisey's name engraved upon the hilt, and which would prove to be an embarrassing possession when Eastin found himself trapped in an Indiana woods a few months later.

As if to balance all these charges and denunciations, the raiders received a paper accolade during the winter, a resolution of thanks from the Congress of the Confederate States of America:

> The thanks of Congress are due, and are hereby tendered to General John H. Morgan, officers and men of his command, for their varied, heroic, and invaluable services in Tennessee and Kentucky immediately preceding the battles before Murfreesboro—services which have conferred upon their authors fame as enduring as the records of the struggle which they have so brilliantly illustrated.

2

As for the boys of the 2nd Kentucky out on daily patrols in rain
and sleet, they were too busy to be concerned with what generals
and congressmen were writing about them. These veterans of the
oldest Morgan regiment, as usual, were stationed on the hottest
outpost corner, facing Union headquarters at Murfreesboro.

Early on the morning of January 24, Lieutenant Ben Drake, acting
as officer of the guard, reported to Lieutenant Colonel Hutchinson's
headquarters that Union troops were reconnoitering on the Murfreesboro road. Drake had withdrawn his videttes to the edge of
Woodbury, and suggested that the regiment be bugled out for an
expected attack from at least four enemy infantry regiments with
an accompanying battery.

Hutchinson received the news calmly, although he realized this
might be the first real testing of the 2nd under his sole command.
Duke was convalescing somewhere in Georgia, and Morgan was at
McMinnville. Turning to John Castleman who was acting as his
second in command, Hutchinson said that he would take charge of
the pickets replacing Drake's night guard. "We'll hold the enemy in
check, Castleman, until you can bring out the regiment."

Castleman remonstrated politely, pointing out that Woodbury
with its surrounding rough hills was a better defensive position than
the Murfreesboro road. Hutchinson shook his head. He looked older
than his twenty-four years, his weather-beaten aquiline features
always serious. Dropping a hand on Castleman's shoulder, Hutchinson replied bluntly that he had "promised the people of Woodbury
that no live Yankee should come into their town unless over my
dead body. I'm going to keep my promise. Form the regiment and
come ahead."

A few minutes later Castleman had the 2nd in motion. As he led
the way across a ravine, he could hear brisk exchanges of gunfire
between Hutchinson's pickets and the Union advance. Dismounting
the troopers, Castleman moved them by companies up a slope and
along the right of the road until they joined with Hutchinson's
men.

They were one regiment against four—the 6th and 24th Ohio,

the 23rd Kentucky (Union) and the 84th Illinois. The 2nd Regiment, however, held a terrain advantage, digging in behind a stone fence, the Union infantrymen clinging to a hill crest opposite. After an hour or so of firing which inflicted little damage upon either side, the Union troops appeared to be withdrawing.

It was then that John Hutchinson, forgetting or disregarding his towering form, recklessly rode out into the open, calling to Captain Castleman. A moment later a bullet whined out of the brush, striking him in the temple, and he fell from his horse.

Castleman was so shocked that for a few seconds he scarcely realized that command of the 2nd Regiment was now his responsibility. His first concern was for Hutchinson. Corporal Charley Haddox, Hutchinson's orderly, had already reached his commander's side, and it was obvious from the orderly's actions that Hutchinson was dead. Castleman's first order as acting commander of the 2nd was to Private George Keene, who was in firing position behind the stone fence. "George," he said softly, "help Charley Haddox put Colonel Hutchinson's body on his horse and carry him back to camp."

All of a sudden Captain Castleman discovered that commanding a regiment under attack by superior enemy forces was no slight responsibility. The Union troops who had appeared to be withdrawing had only been shifting positions while their batterymen were bringing two pieces of artillery into range of the 2nd's stone fence. Charley Haddox and George Keene had scarcely departed with Lieutenant Colonel Hutchinson's body when the first shells whistled over. As soon as the enemy gunners found the range, the stone fence began to fly apart.

"It was a hopeless engagement," Castleman reported. As he had no artillery for retaliation, he ordered a withdrawal to the Woodbury camp on the double-quick. The retreat was swift but orderly, and the strategic position of the camp site discouraged the Union attackers. After the enemy withdrew from Woodbury, acting regimental commander Castleman noticed a burning sensation in his right ankle. A Yankee sharpshooter had found his mark, but Castleman had been luckier than big John Hutchinson.

Hutchinson's death was a severe blow to the 2nd, not only because as Duke said "he was the best field officer in Morgan's command," but because the vacancy created temporary dissension among the companies. Some men wanted John Castleman for permanent commander, others James Bowles, and others Thomas Webber. Morgan had to settle the argument, and he commissioned Captain Bowles probably because Bowles had the longest period of service, having left his studies at Yale University in the summer of 1861 to journey to Richmond and enlist.

After a few days virtually all agreed that Morgan had arrived at the best compromise solution, and the command functioned smoothly again.

About this time, however, Morgan made a serious error of judgment in accepting a new officer, one John T. Shanks, who claimed he had been in a Texas regiment so badly cut up in the Stone's River fighting that he was left without a command. Shanks became acquainted with St. Leger Grenfell while the latter was inspecting cavalry, and through the Britisher secured introduction to Morgan. In this chance encounter Grenfell sealed not only his own doom but that of several others in the 2nd Kentucky, for John Shanks was to become the instrument of destiny in a wild sequence of events to unfold in future months. Forger, embezzler, liar, cheat, traitor—John Shanks claimed to be a captain; he was not even a commissioned officer. But John Morgan, accustomed to dealing with honorable men, accepted Shanks on his word and sent him out to Woodbury for picket duty with the 2nd.

As the winter deepened, Morgan's front line lengthened, running all the way from Woodbury for more than a hundred miles along an irregular curve into the hills of eastern Kentucky. For lack of sufficient forage around Woodbury, the 2nd was forced to spread out by companies into a thin line that invited constant hit-and-run attacks from roving Union cavalry.

Only the worst weather brought respite, and sometimes it was so bad the boys would have preferred receiving Yankees. Rains, sleet, snow and biting winds were so frequent that diaries of that winter are filled with such entries as: "Coldest day of the season. Ground frozen hard. . . . This country seems flowing with whisky and mud. . . . Snow. Below zero . . . Many a night have I slept with a sheepskin under me, a blanket over me, and my hat over my face to keep the frost off."

For the first time, however, the men of the 2nd remained camped in one place long enough to construct shelters against the weather. They had a good supply of blankets captured on the Christmas raid, and almost every man had a gum cloth or poncho. Four or more troopers would combine their equipment, and by stretching blankets and ponchos across fence rails were able to erect weatherproof substitutes for tents.

To insure dry beds they drove forked sticks in the ground and laid rails and pieces of planking across. A fire blazing in front of the open fly furnished a certain amount of warmth. Favorite shelter sites were cedar thickets which broke the bitter winds and furnished aromatic wood for fires. On cold winter nights, the orange smoke of these fires glowed against a ceiling of greenery, the groves glittering with showers of sparks flitting upward like swarms of fireflies.

When Basil Duke—recovered from his wound—came out to Woodbury to visit his old regiment, he was amused by the "apparently inextricable confusion of these camps. . . . Men and horses were all huddled together, for the men did not fancy any arrangements which separated them by the slightest distance from their horses, and the latter were always tied close to the lairs of their masters."

Yet, in spite of the comparative coziness of the winter camps, there was a growing discontent among the men during that cold, dragging winter of 1863. Lack of supplies—particularly boots and clothing, coffee and sugar—lowered morale and discipline. Ammunition was so short at times that patrols were forced to turn and run, after the men had emptied their cartridge boxes. What little clothing could be obtained by the regimental quartermaster was usually made of coarse, yellowish brown homespun which wore out quickly. Arms replacements were varied and undependable in action, and new issues of cartridge boxes, saddlebags and saddleskirts were made of cotton rather than leather. Paper for records keeping was so rarely available that it was not unusual for orderly sergeants to make out morning reports on wooden shingles.

A visitor to one of the mid-Tennessee camps that winter noted four or five different kinds of rifles and shotguns, "all sorts of saddles, some with rope stirrups, many of the saddles without blankets, all sorts of bridles, and in fact a conglomerate get-up fairly laughable."

Cooking vessels were as hard to come by as food with which to fill them. "If a cavalryman had any flour," wrote Private George Mosgrove, "he mixed it with salt and cold water, plastered it on a board and set it before the fire to bake, or he would wind the dough around an iron ramrod and hold it over the fire. With the iron ramrod it was also an easy matter to broil a piece of meat." By the end of winter the beef supply ran short, and when meat was available it was tasteless. "There was not an ounce of salt, and it was not to be got for love or money." When only hardtack was available, the boys taxed their ingenuity to devise new ways of preparing it, a popular method being to soak it in carefully hoarded grease. "Prepared thus," one man commented, "hardtack was a dish which no Confederate had the weakness or the strength to refuse."

For some time the policy of the Army of Tennessee had been to furnish rations only to the infantry; the cavalrymen were supposed to be mobile enough to obtain food for themselves and forage for their horses. During the early months of 1863, however, with the Federals constantly threatening below Nashville, Bragg dared not permit any sizable force to be removed even temporarily from the cavalry screen protecting his army. Tied down to stationary camps, the cavalry was expected to maintain fighting efficiency without being clothed, shod, fed, or even paid—although if the men had received any money that winter there would have been little to spend it for except raw corn whisky.

By late February no oats or fodder could be procured around Woodbury, and corn had to be hauled thirty miles, each horse receiving a ration of only two or three ears per day, some days none. Every blade of grass around the 2nd Regiment's camps was gone, and bark had been stripped from the trees as high as the horses could reach. Before spring, all of mid-Tennessee was stripped of meat, grain and everything edible. "It was as if a cloud of Titanic and omniverous locusts had settled upon the land," wrote Duke.

The most discouraging feature of all was the condition of the horses. So many cavalrymen were without serviceable mounts—some doing picket duty on foot—that Bragg suggested transferring them to the infantry, thus creating a state of incipient mutiny throughout Morgan's camps and inspiring a number of men to take unofficial leave to go into Kentucky in search of horses. General Rosecrans took note of one of these unauthorized "horse expeditions" on February 22 in a message to General-in-Chief Halleck: "Morgan has sent some men into Kentucky—a party to steal horses."

All these desperate pressures for food, supplies and horses naturally led to large numbers of temporary delinquencies from duty by men forced to go in search of needs which the Army of Tennessee could not supply. For instance, so many of the boys in the 2nd traded their rifles for smokehouse meat and whisky—against the day when the long-absent paymaster appeared—that when a regimental arms inspection was held almost half were found unarmed. Major Thomas Webber, acting as regimental commander in James Bowles' absence, was so outraged by this unsoldierly practice that he ordered every man without a rifle to carry a heavy fence rail upon his shoulder until the missing Enfields and Springfields were found. Most of the boys "found" their rifles rather quickly in nearby farmhouses, and Webber let them off with a warning that they would be transferred to the infantry (the direst of threats) if they were ever caught unarmed again.

Even with all the discontent, however, the more irresponsible alligator horses of the 2nd managed to have some fun that winter. On bad days they played cards under their gum-cloth shelters, handling the packs tenderly because they were scarce and irreplaceable. On good days they raced horses, clandestinely because racing was forbidden in order to save the horses' strength. And on off-duty nights they could visit girls in the neighborhood. "Beautiful daughters and good whisky," wrote one diarist. "Miss Brown gave me some very sweet music on the piano." And again: "I attribute my cure [from an insect bite] to the beautiful Miss Della and her sweet music. She sings 'Bonnie Blue Flag' to perfection."

Perhaps the incident which afforded the most amusement to the entire regiment involved Jeff Sterrett, Jack Trigg and Tom Ballard. These three were the regimental jesters, "the chartered libertines," who moved in and out of one scrape after another, and whom neither Bowles, Duke nor Morgan could bear to punish severely because they had all been together since the Green River days. Late in the winter a faro dealer set up operations at McMinnville, and so many men began riding in from camps to gamble that in order to preserve both horses and discipline, Morgan ordered the dealer to cease operations. The gambler, however, moved into a nearby barn and continued running his game under cover. Learning of this, Morgan ordered his provost guard to raid the place and arrest all men caught there. Among the players arrested were Sterrett, Trigg and Ballard, and they were brought before Morgan for punishment.

Forcing a stern manner, Morgan ordered the culprits to stand at attention, and demanded: "What were you doing there, Trigg?"

"Why, sir," replied Trigg, "I only went there to find Ballard."

Morgan turned to Ballard, repeating the question.

"Sir, I went to find Sterrett."

Barely able to repress a smile, Morgan asked wiry little Sterrett what he was doing at the faro dealer's. As there was no one else to shift the blame to, Sterrett drawled, "I was coppering the ace, sir."

"Very well," said Morgan. "And what punishment do you think you should receive?"

Sterrett answered without blinking an eye: "About thirty days' furlough from this place of temptation, sir."

3

With the coming of March and more tolerable weather, skirmishes became more frequent along the cavalry front. "There were frequently days and nights passed," wrote Leeland Hathaway, "in which I did not take off my clothes for sleep. Every day and night brought its skirmishes somewhere and we had quite a number of men killed and wounded."

On March 1, Lieutenant Colonel Bowles took the 2nd Kentucky on reconnaissance down toward Bradyville for his first experience of command under heavy attack. The attackers were the regiment's oldest antagonists, the 4th Ohio Cavalry with some companies of the 3rd Ohio. The Union troopers closed in on all sides, forcing the regiment to fight its way out. The 2nd lost several men as prisoners, and Company C in rear-guard action had to stand off a saber charge.

One man especially irritated by the saber wielders was Tom Boss, the bristly black-haired giant who had constructed a bake oven for Colonel Duke during the episode at Sparta. It was Boss' habit to carry a short-handled axe strapped to his back, and when a Federal captain lunged at him with a saber, Boss snatched his axe from its sling and drove it into his assailant's skull.

The boys could not count Bradyville as a victory, nor did they admit any defeat, although some of them thought Jim Bowles had been a bit rash in his actions that day.

About three weeks later the 2nd was back in action near Liberty, losing two of its best officers in a minor skirmish, Captain James Sale of Company E and Captain John Cooper of Company L. Spring was in the air that day, peach and cherry trees in full bloom, the grass greening, buds swelling on the trees, and a few summer birds singing. But the 2nd's saddles were emptying, the ranks of the old Green River boys thinning There was no bright lifting of hopes in the springtime of 1863 as there had been in 1862.

April brought more skirmishes, more blood letting. The first nights of the month were cool and clear, with full moonlight falling softly on the greening hills. After such a night, the regiment was hit hard at daybreak of the third, Bowles' camp near Liberty being overrun by Colonel Robert Minty's 1st Cavalry Brigade. D Company bore the brunt of the attack. Captain Castleman's beloved Denmark mare was shot, her legs broken, and Private Charley Wilson afterward told of how he found Castleman weeping beside the dying horse with bullets still flying all about. Tom Quirk and his scouts fought a brilliant delaying action that morning, but the 2nd was badly scattered, strung out along the road back toward McMinnville.

After this engagement there was a lull of several days in the skirmishing, giving Colonel Duke an opportunity to reorganize his brigade in the hills north of McMinnville. During the following three weeks, Duke's regiments were in almost constant motion around Liberty and Smithville, then were ordered north to guard the Cumberland River crossings from Stagall's ferry to Celina. Most of the time the weather was fine, in sharp contrast to the desolation and decay that lay across the familiar countryside. In the once-thriving little towns, some of the finest residences had been wrecked, doors and sidings torn away, trees and shrubbery cut or trampled. In many places a fearful stench arose from decaying horses and mules left unburied in the woods during the winter, the warm weather now revealing their presence.

It was while the 2nd was on picket duty along the Cumberland that the boys heard the astounding news of General Morgan's narrow escape from capture at his McMinnville headquarters. All through the winter, McMinnville had been considered as impregnable as a moated castle, Morgan bringing his bride there for safety. Officers on leave met their wives at McMinnville, brought up from Chattanooga or Georgia to brighten the week-ends with social evenings, dinners and dancing.

In mid-April the Federals decided to have a try at breaching John Morgan's headquarters fortress. Colonel Minty's cavalry brigade, supported by infantry, broke through the McMinnville picket line at dawn of April 21 and charged into town eight abreast. Morgan barely had time to bundle his young wife into a carriage and send her off toward Sparta with the headquarters wagon train. He was able to escape himself only because of the loyalty and quick thinking of Lieutenant Colonel Robert M. Martin and Major Dick McCann. Afterward, Corporal John Williams of the 7th Pennsylvania, who led the first charge into McMinnville, reported that McCann held his horse steady in the middle of the street and shouted, "Come on, you Yankee son of a bitch!" Corporal Williams accepted the challenge, spurred his horse forward, and knocked McCann from his saddle with a saber stroke across the head. McCann, struggling to his feet, shouted in a loud voice: "I am Morgan! You've got the old chief at last!"

While Corporal Williams was making McCann a prisoner under the impression that he was General Morgan, the Union charge halted in confusion, and Lieutenant Colonel Martin chose this moment to further delay the enemy. With his bridle in his teeth and a pistol in each hand he dashed down upon the Pennsylvanians, firing until his weapons were emptied. A bullet burned into his lungs, but Martin swerved down a side street, hoping to divert the enemy long enough to give Morgan an opportunity to escape.

Morgan did escape, and so did the wounded Martin, taking refuge in a farmhouse out in the hills. That night, Major McCann also escaped, after getting his guard drunk on a ration of brandy which had been allowed him because of his painful head wound.

Along the road to Sparta, however, a Union patrol had bagged Morgan's fleeing wagon train, capturing the General's wife. But when her captors learned her identity, they gallantly freed Martha Morgan and sent her back to join her still-lucky husband.

4

"In this year," Basil Duke wrote in retrospect, "the glory and prestige began to pass away from the Southern cavalry. It was not that their opponents became their superiors in soldiership, any more than in individual prowess. . . . But it was daily becoming more and more difficult to keep the Confederate cavalry in good condition. . . . One special cause of the degeneracy of the Southern cavalry was the greater scarcity of horses and the great difficulty of obtaining forage within the Confederate lines, and consequently of keeping the horses which we had in good condition."

Duke's opinion was shared by most of the other cavalry leaders in the South. 1863 was the last year the Confederate *beaux sabreurs* held center stage; soon the Yankee raiders would be stealing their thunder, and until the end it would be largely an infantryman's war for the Rebels.

It was difficult enough for a man to retain his spirit and endurance on short rations; for a horse it was impossible, and the more spirit a horse had, the worse it was for such an animal when sustenance was withdrawn. The best of horses losing a shoe on rough roadways became utterly unfit for service in half a day's march. "I have seen my men many a time have strapped to their saddles the hoof of a dead horse," said General T. T. Munford, "which they had cut off at the ankle with their pocket knives, and would carry them until they could find a smith to take the shoes off with his nippers, and thus supply their sore-footed steeds."

With the border states and the upper South occupied by Union armies, the Confederacy had lost its best source of riding horses.

The South's horse breeders, in fact, had been supplying replacements for both armies, as the South's farmers were now being forced to feed both armies.

It is no wonder that as conditions grew worse instead of better in the first months of 1863, a wave of pessimism swept through the camps of Southern cavalrymen, a weariness and a disillusionment with war that even the bright springtime could not banish.

5

Late in the spring, however, two isolated events occurred which in different ways seemed to lift John Morgan and his men from the lethargy of winter's discontent, to bring them out of despondency and inspire them into attempting their greatest raid of the war.

First, there was the publication of a book, *Raids and Romance of Morgan and His Men*, by Sally Rochester Ford. Mrs. Ford was a Bluegrass belle who had attended a Georgetown seminary, married a Baptist preacher, and become a fairly popular novelist. *Raids and Romance* was fiction woven around the actual adventures of Morgan and the 2nd Kentucky, most of the action taking place during the raids of 1862. Printed in Mobile, Alabama, by Sigmund H. Goetzel in an edition limited by the Confederacy's short paper supply, it was widely sought by Southerners, and was banned as seditious by Union authorities in Memphis and St. Louis.*

The alligator horses must have been fascinated to read of their heroic deeds in a romance wherein John Morgan rode as a sort of Richard the Lion-Hearted, surrounded by a band of flesh-and-blood knights that included Duke, Grenfell, Castleman, Gano, McCann, Ellsworth, the younger Morgan brothers, and other real characters.

The second event in the spring of 1863 which came like an electric shock was the successful raid of Colonel Benjamin Grierson and his Union cavalrymen through the heart of Mississippi to Baton Rouge,

---

* In 1864 a New York publisher reprinted the book with appendices to bring the reader up to date with the raiders' later misfortunes, and it was no longer considered dangerous literature.

a raid which according to Grierson, proved the South to be "a hollow shell."

Both these events—the book and the enemy raid—were stimulating challenges; each must have had a profound effect not only upon John Morgan but upon his officers and men. Sally Ford's book was a pattern of glory to be lived up to; Grierson's raid was a dare to be emulated. If Yankee cavalry could ride through the South with impunity, then surely Confederate cavalry could ride through the North.

Not long after the appearance of *Raids and Romance of Morgan and His Men*, and the first startling news of Grierson's raid, Captains Tom Hines and Sam Taylor were sent north on separate missions. Hines took a number of men into Indiana, scouting practicable river crossings west of Louisville and raiding routes around Cincinnati. According to Duke, Hines was also instructed "to stir up Copperheads" and locate other Southern sympathizers who might be useful while a raid was in progress. Captain Taylor's * mission was to scout fords and other escape routes along the Ohio River east of Cincinnati.

On May 26, Morgan ordered all his regiments concentrated between Liberty and Alexandria. Many men who had been on long furloughs or convalescent leaves reported for duty, filling up the vacant ranks, their renewed enthusiasm cheering the winter-weary veterans. After a few days of grazing on rich spring grass, the horses fleshed into condition. Miraculously, wagons loaded with uniforms and weapons began rolling up from Chattanooga. Fresh horses were driven down from eastern Kentucky by troopers who had been stationed on the northeastern end of the long winter front.

Working his old magic, John Morgan brought a new regiment into his division—Colonel D. Howard Smith's 5th Kentucky Cavalry. In a few days the division's total strength increased from two thousand to almost three thousand men.

Something big was in the wind. The men could sense it, although even their officers were not sure what it was, and Morgan was still down at Tullahoma headquarters working out the plans with Braxton Bragg.

* Captain Samuel Taylor was a nephew of "Old Rough and Ready" Zachary Taylor.

With renewed zest the men cleaned and polished their weapons, refurbished equipment, tended their horses and drilled, drilled, drilled. From eight o'clock until sundown they went through evolutions in the meadows, fighting flies and swarms of bees in the clover. Dress parades followed inspections, and inspections followed dress parades. Strict vigilance was maintained at all times against Yankee spies, the camps being spread apart and concealed as much as possible to avoid revealing the presence of so large a concentration of cavalry obviously preparing for something out of the ordinary. Diversionary patrols were kept moving far out to avoid any large-scale contact with the enemy.

On June 10, John Morgan appeared suddenly in Alexandria, dressed in a resplendent new uniform and flashing his confident smile. That evening he called his staff together, brigade and regimental commanders, and told them he had orders from Bragg to make a raid far north into Kentucky. If all went well they would cross the Ohio River into Indiana and strike eastward for Ohio. The time had come for the North to feel the lash of invasion.

10

The Great Raid Begins

ALTHOUGH GENERAL MORGAN was confident in early June of 1863 that he would receive authorization for a raid across the Ohio River, Braxton Bragg never issued such an order. Bragg only wanted Morgan to enter Kentucky and make a threat against Louisville— a mere diversionary raid to take pressure off the Army of Tennessee for a few days.

Bragg's forces had been seriously weakened by the sudden removal of several divisions under General Joseph E. Johnston, rushed to Mississippi in hopes of relieving besieged Vicksburg. Fearing for the safety of his army after Johnston's departure, Bragg decided to withdraw to more easily defended positions below the Tennessee River. To accomplish this maneuver without inviting attack, he needed action elsewhere to distract the enemy's attention. A raid by Morgan, he thought, would be sufficient distraction, and it was for this reason in the main that Bragg granted Morgan permission to march north.

When final orders reached Morgan's headquarters at Alexandria, instructing him to move into Kentucky—but not to cross the Ohio River—Morgan decided forthwith that he had had enough of Bragg's timidity. He was determined to strike for Indiana as planned. He revealed his decision to disobey Bragg to only one officer, his brother-in-law, Basil Duke. In recording the incident afterward,

177

Duke made no apologies for his commander, stating simply: "So positive were Morgan's convictions that in order to be of any benefit in so grave a crisis, his raid should be extended to Northern territory, he deliberately resolved to disobey the order restricting his operations in Kentucky."

On June 11, Morgan started his regiments north to the Cumberland, where he planned to capture the Federal garrison at Carthage and clear the river crossings before beginning a lightning dash across Kentucky. Late in the day, however, a courier arrived from Bragg's headquarters with a message which delayed all his well-laid plans. A heavy Union raiding party was reported pushing into eastern Tennessee, threatening General Buckner's small defending army, and Bragg ordered Morgan's cavalry to intercept.

As a result of this order, the following three weeks were utterly wasted in hard marches over rugged country and bad roads, the division moving east through Gainesboro and Livingston, and then north across the Kentucky line to Albany, only to discover that the Federal force—if it ever existed—had completely vanished.

This wild-goose chase not only delayed Morgan's raid for three weeks, it wore down horses and used up carefully hoarded rations. Under pouring rains that flooded roads and creeks, the regiments swung back westward through the hills to the Cumberland approaches near Burkesville, camping long enough to commandeer grist mills for grinding corn and blacksmith shops for shoeing horses.

By July 2 the rains had stopped. Morgan held a final conference with his regimental commanders, informing them definitely that they were going across the Ohio. He traced the route on a map, indicating four main danger points—the crossing of the flooded Cumberland just ahead of them, the crossing of the Ohio west of Louisville, the long march north around Cincinnati, and the recrossing of the Ohio east of Cincinnati. Later he told Duke privately that they might not have to recross the Ohio River; he had learned that General Lee was invading Pennsylvania, and if all went well Morgan's men might keep marching eastward and join Lee.

All were cautioned to secrecy concerning the invasion of Indiana and Ohio, and the colonels evidently kept tight security. None of the men suspected that they were going beyond Kentucky, although at least one was hopeful of it. Sergeant Henry L. Stone, whose family lived in Greencastle, Indiana, writing from the "South Bank of the Cumberland, 5 miles from Burkesville" mentioned that he had heard "Captain Hines with 90 men is in Indiana. . . . I wish I was with him. . . . I wish our whole command could go into Hoosier."

Below Burkesville that day, Morgan had ten regiments assembled, all far under strength, one of them the hastily organized 14th Kentucky Cavalry, scarcely larger than a company, commanded by the General's brother, Colonel Richard C. Morgan. The 2nd Kentucky was led by its acting commander, the fiery Major Thomas B. Webber, Colonel Bowles being unable to make the journey. Four three-inch Parrott guns and a section of twelve-pounder howitzers comprised the division's artillery support under Captain Ed Byrnes. Total present for duty was 2,460 men, about 1,500 of them in Duke's 1st Brigade, the others in Colonel Adam Johnson's 2nd Brigade.

"In high feather and full song," reported George Mosgrove, "Morgan's gallant young cavalrymen formed in columns, looking toward Kentucky." When General Morgan, smartly uniformed and mounted on his favorite, Glencoe, rode along the column to the front, the men cheered and sang:

> "Here's the health to Duke and Morgan
>   Drink it down;
> Here's the health to Duke and Morgan
>   Drink it down;
> Here's the health to Duke and Morgan,
>   Down, boys, down, drink it down!"

Morgan rode on, smiling and waving. Behind him came Duke, a flowing plume in his hat, and they all marched out for the Cumberland singing "My Old Kentucky Home."

The river was rain-swollen, more than half a mile wide, running out of its banks and filled with driftwood tumbling and rocketing through the foam. The 2nd Kentucky moved above Burkesville, the men out searching for boats, finding nothing but a few frail canoes. They lashed these together and made crude floorings of fence rails.

"We turned the horses in," Sergeant Stone wrote a few days

later, "and the men came over in the canoes with their saddles—
the wagons were put on canoes, piece at a time and brought over."
At some places driftwood covered almost the entire surface, and
to secure their animals the men had to enter the water, holding
to a canoe-raft with one hand and to their horse's mane or tail with
the other.

As bad as was the flooded stream, it had one beneficial effect;
there was no organized resistance to the crossing. The Federals
were confident the river would stop Morgan, and only a few scattered patrols were on the north bank.

Bennett Young, crossing with Quirk's scouts, described one of
the few encounters with the Yankees: "Those who had clothing
on rushed ashore and into line, those who swam with horses, un-
willing to be laggard, not halting to dress, seized their cartridge
boxes and guns and dashed upon the enemy. The strange sight of
naked men engaging in combat amazed the enemy. They had never
seen soldiers before clad only in nature's garb."

The Union soldiers opposing the dangerous Cumberland crossing
were of Frank Wolford's Kentucky regiment, and Morgan's men
were thankful there were so few of them. With Tom Quirk's
scouts in the lead and the 2nd Regiment close behind, the columns
of dripping horses and men moved on toward Marrowbone Creek.
Here, about midafternoon, the scouts charged a Union encampment, and the dauntless Irishman took a bad bullet wound in the
arm. "Only one man received a wound," Kelion Peddicord noted
laconically, "Captain Tom, whose rein arm was broken."

But the scouts regarded Quirk's misfortune as an ill omen; they
had come to consider their bold leader as indestructible. Over his
profane protests, Quirk was ordered back to Burkesville to con-
valesce, and for the first time the 2nd moved into Kentucky without Tom Quirk up front to serve as eyes and ears for the regiment.

By nightfall of the following day the regiment was seven miles beyond Columbia, with other units of the division strung out far
behind. It was three o'clock the morning of July 4 before the
rear regiment entered Columbia, bivouacking in the streets. Duke
in the meantime had sent Captain Franks and the scouts forward
to reconnoiter the Tebb's Bend bridge at Green River. Franks re-

ported back before dawn that the Yankees at the bridge appeared to be expecting an attack. They were as busy as beavers, he said. All through the night the scouts had heard the ringing of axes and the crash of falling timbers.

At daybreak of July 4, the meaning of all this night activity was revealed to Franks and his men. Across the narrow peninsula entering Tebb's Bend, a hundred-yard breastwork blocked the neck of land, facing south and barring access to the bridge. It was a sturdy abatis of logs and tangled brush, with rifle pits protected by fence rails, wire and sharpened pieces of wood.

Morgan was up front before the sun rose, ordering Captain Byrnes to open with his battery. After one round was fired into the barricade, Lieutenant Joe Tucker was sent forward under a truce flag with a message to the Union commander, demanding unconditional surrender. Tucker found the commander to be Colonel Orlando H. Moore of the 25th Michigan Infantry, with about two hundred men dug in shoulder to shoulder. Moore read Morgan's message, smiled, and said to Tucker: "Lieutenant, if it was any other day I might surrender, but on the Fourth of July I must have a little brush first." He then wrote a brief note to Morgan: "It is a bad day for surrender, and I would rather not."

The 2nd Regiment took no part in the fight at Tebb's Bend bridge, the 2nd Brigade having passed through Duke's regiments during the early morning march up from Columbia. Colonel D. W. Chenault's 11th Kentucky, being in advance, led the assault dismounted, a straight frontal attack across open ground with bugles blaring. As the first wave ran into fallen timbers and brush, it collapsed under the close fire of Moore's determined Michigan infantrymen. Chenault was killed as he climbed the barricade, falling back into the debris. Two succeeding attacks also failed.

"Many of our best men were killed and wounded," Major McCreary noted in his journal that night. "It was a sad, sorrowful day, and more tears of grief rolled over my weatherbeaten cheeks on this mournful occasion than have before for years. *The commencement of this raid is ominous.* Total loss in killed and wounded—71." Among the dead was Alexander Tribble, Lieutenant Eastin's companion in the celebrated duel with Colonel Halisey. Tribble had only recently been promoted to captain and transferred to Chenault's regiment from the 2nd Kentucky.

After three hours, with the morning still young, Morgan called the useless fighting to an end. Under another flag of truce he sent a second message to Colonel Moore, requesting permission to bury his dead. Moore gave consent, delivering the bodies to the front of his line.

After burying their dead and bypassing Tebb's Bend, the regiments moved north through Campbellsville and out on the road toward Lebanon. They knew it had been a bad Fourth of July for Morgan's raiders, but they did not know how terrible a day it had been for the Confederacy. In Pennsylvania, Lee's army was beginning its retreat after disaster at Gettysburg; on the Mississippi, Vicksburg was surrendering to Grant. Morgan's raiders, instead of invading a country wavering and divided after two years of indecisive war, would find the people celebrating their first real victories, reunited in a determination to bring the war to a triumphant end.

Completely unaware of these portentous events, the raiders camped that Fourth of July night five miles west of Lebanon.

2

From reports of scouts, Morgan and Duke learned before six o'clock the morning of July 5 that Lebanon was defended by Lieutenant Colonel Charles Hanson's 20th Kentucky Infantry with detachments from three other Kentucky Union regiments, a total force of nearly five hundred men. Hanson was a brother of Roger Hanson, the Confederate leader who had welcomed Morgan's Lexington Rifles when they first came down to Green River from the Bluegrass. The 20th Kentucky was also a Bluegrass regiment, containing former friends, near relatives, and even brothers of men in Morgan's command.

Hoping to take Lebanon without a clash between brothers and friends, Morgan decided on a bold show of force. Ordering his regiments to form a two-line front, he marched them up to the edge of town, the forward skirmish line spread out for two miles across open fields bordering the turnpike, Byrnes' battery at center on the road. Hanson had thrown up a crude breastwork where the pike entered the town, and Morgan ordered Byrnes to shell it. As soon as the breastwork's defenders scurried back into town, Morgan sent his adjutant and occasional editor of the *Vidette*, Lieutenant Colonel Robert Alston, forward under a truce flag to demand a surrender.

To Alston's discomfiture, he was fired upon as he approached Hanson's headquarters, and when his own men attempted to cover him with retaliating fire, negotiations almost came to a sudden end. After the tense situation finally quieted, Hanson informed Alston that he had no intention of surrendering. "Then notify the women and children to leave immediately," Alston replied. "The town will be shelled."

As soon as Alston departed, Hanson concentrated his men in a sturdy brick railroad depot, an excellent defensive position according to Sergeant Henry Stone: "Our artillery could not bear on it, only at the roof." Colonel Roy S. Cluke's 8th Kentucky opened with a vigorous assault, but this was to be no quick victory. Before Morgan's scouts had circled the town and cut telegraph wires to Louisville, Hanson had received orders to hold out on the assurance that reinforcements would arrive in a few hours.

July 5 was a torrid summer day, the temperature soaring into the nineties by midmorning, and the 8th Kentucky was pinned down around the depot in patches of high weeds that held the heat. Lying on their bellies, half-smothered and choking for want of water, carefully hoarding their diminishing supply of ammunition, Cluke's men could neither advance nor retreat.

Although Lebanon was completely surrounded now, Morgan could neither take the town nor withdraw until Cluke's men were extricated from the weed patches around the depot. Basil Duke, watching the deadly duel, was reminded of the 2nd Regiment's fight in Augusta, and realized that what was needed was a regiment experienced in street fighting. With Morgan's permission he ordered Major Webber to bring the 2nd Regiment into the siege.

"The 2nd had tried that sort of work before," Duke said. "Major Webber skillfully aligned it and moved it forward."

Kelion Peddicord, who went in with the scouts in the 2nd's first attack wave, said they charged all the way up to the rear of the depot, with the boys of the 8th cheering them on. Some ran their rifles and pistols through windows, firing blindly inside, others stormed the doors and broke them down. "A street fight," commented Peddicord dryly, "is one of the most desperate modes of warfare known to a soldier. The advantage is strongly against the storming party."

Colonel Hanson surrendered, but the 2nd and 8th regiments paid a high price for the victory. Almost at the moment Major Webber gave the 2nd orders to charge, nineteen-year-old Lieutenant Tom Morgan, the General's favorite brother, was killed. "Poor Tommy Morgan," Robert Alston wrote in his diary that day, "ran forward and cheered the men with all the enthusiasm of his bright nature. At the first volley he fell, pierced through the breast." His brother Calvin caught him as he fell, and he died in Calvin's arms; his only words were: "Brother Cally, they have killed me."

By three o'clock on that hot afternoon, Adjutant Robert Alston and Captain William Davis had the prisoners lined up and were issuing paroles. In the midst of these activities, scouts brought warnings of approaching Union cavalry in strength—Hanson's promised reinforcements arriving too late to save him. To avoid another costly fight, Morgan ordered regiments formed and started columns moving rapidly north toward Springfield. Alston and Davis herded their unparoled captives together, marching them on the double-quick along the same route.

About halfway along this dusty eight-mile stretch of road, a raging rainstorm overtook the prisoners and their guards. "Hardest rain I ever experienced," Alston commented. The water-soaked, bedraggled column did not reach Springfield until after dark.

While Morgan's raiders moved on through the night toward Bardstown, Alston and Davis established paroling headquarters in a comfortable Springfield house, the owner's lovely daughters, Frances and Belle Cunningham, watching the proceedings with fascination. For William Davis and Frances Cunningham it was love at first sight, and when the last prisoner was released, Captain

Davis reluctantly obeyed Alston's order that he move out and rejoin his command.*

But Alston himself delayed departure. "Wet and chilly, worn out, tired and hungry," he fell asleep, was aroused by his orderly just before dawn, and started hurriedly for Bardstown. When he reached a point on the road where he expected to find Morgan's rear guard, a party of cavalrymen appeared out of the gray morning fog. "Supposing them to be our pickets," he explained later, "I rode up promptly to correct them for standing in full view of anyone approaching, when to my mortification I found myself a prisoner. My God! how I hated it, no one can understand." Like a true cavalryman, Alston's first thought was for his fine mare, "Fannie Johnson, named after a pretty little cousin, of Richmond, Va. I said, 'Poor Fannie, who will treat you as kindly as I have?' I turned her over to a captain and begged him to take good care of her, which he promised to do."

One by one, Morgan was losing the officers he most depended upon, and he was not yet across the Ohio.

3

The 2nd Kentucky and other regiments of Duke's brigade were in Bardstown by daylight of the sixth, and enjoyed the benefit of a six-hour rest while Adam Johnson's 2nd Brigade marched on through town to take the advance. Most of Duke's boys lounged in the shade of a sycamore grove, but Lightning Ellsworth rode off with a detachment to Bardstown Junction on the L. & N. Railroad.

Ellsworth was amused to find the operator there wearing a uniform—recently issued to Union telegraphers—dark blue blouse, blue trousers with a silver cord on the seam, a natty buff vest, a forage cap with no ornaments or marks of ranks. "Hello, sonny," said Ells-

* The romantic wartime letters of William Davis to Frances Cunningham, which began as a result of this meeting and led to their marriage in 1866, were carefully preserved by the recipient, and are now in the Filson Club, Louisville, Kentucky.

worth as he showed his cocked revolver. "Move an inch except as I tell you, and you'll be buried in that fancy rig."

In a few minutes Ellsworth learned that strong Union cavalry forces were gathering in the rear, no more than twenty-four hours behind Morgan's main column. From every message he intercepted, it was evident the Yankees were certain that Morgan's raiders were bound for Louisville, and troops were being concentrated there for an expected attack.

John Morgan, meanwhile, was preparing the way for his river crossing into Indiana, the selected jump-off point being Brandenburg, Kentucky, on the Ohio River. He started Captains Sam Taylor and Clay Merriwether and their companies of the 10th Kentucky by forced march direct to Brandenburg. They were told they would probably find Captain Tom Hines, who had been scouting the area for several weeks, somewhere around that town. They were to join forces with Hines and capture Brandenburg, as well as any boats which might be lying at the landing.

At the same time Morgan ordered the love-smitten captain, William Davis, to take Company D of the 2nd Kentucky and Company A of the 8th Kentucky on a diversionary expedition east of Louisville. Davis' mission was to cut telegraph wires, burn railroad bridges, and create the impression that his two companies comprised Morgan's entire raiding force. They were to aim for Twelve Mile Island above Louisville, cross the Ohio River there, and attempt to rejoin Morgan's raiders at Salem, Indiana.

Lieutenant George Eastin of D Company was second in command. When he rode off with Captain Davis at the head of his company, Eastin was still proudly wearing his talisman, the sword of the Union colonel, Dennis Halisey.

In a letter to Frances Cunningham, Davis told of how he first learned of Morgan's plans to invade Indiana. "When within ten miles of Shepherdsville [on the afternoon of July 6] Gen'l Morgan explained to me his intention of crossing the Ohio at Brandenburg, and ordered my detachment to create a diversion by operating between Louisville and Frankfort. Rapidly pushing forward ahead of the column, I crossed Salt river at an almost impracticable ford three miles above Shepherdsville and directed my course towards the railroad some thirty miles above Louisville."

At the same time, the main column was turning northwestward, away from Louisville, still twenty-four hours ahead of the Union cavalry massing behind. Morgan was rather certain that no attack would be forthcoming from Louisville where the enemy was gathering in fearful anticipation of the raiders' striking there.

4

Early on the morning of July 7, Sam Taylor and Clay Merriwether led their companies into Brandenburg. Being so far north, the town was not garrisoned. The people appeared to be either apathetic or Confederate in sympathy, and no fight was offered. The only vessel at the landing was a small wharf boat, but Taylor and Merriwether learned that a packet steamer running between Louisville and Henderson was due in early that afternoon. A faster mailboat usually passed about the same time, but made no scheduled stops.

Brandenburg was a small town built high on a hill. From the crest the winding river could be observed for several miles in either direction. After placing lookouts on the highest points and pickets along roads entering the town, the two captains permitted their men to laze away the morning on the river front. Shortly after noon, a boarding party was ordered on to the wharf boat. Around one o'clock lookouts signaled that a steamer was coming, and the men on the wharf boat were instructed to ready their weapons and keep under cover.

Promptly on schedule the steamboat *John B. McCombs* rounded the last bend, sounded its hoarse whistle, and slowed its chugging engines. With paddle wheels splashing silvery in the July sunshine, it turned in to the Brandenburg landing.

The instant the packet eased alongside the wharf boat, forty fully armed Confederate cavalrymen leaped aboard, much like the pirates of a certain seagoing Morgan. In a matter of seconds, the *John B. McCombs* was in Rebel hands. Captain Ballard, the crew and fifty passengers, caught by surprise, were without arms and offered no resistance.

A few minutes later a fast mailboat, the *Alice Dean*, came puffing upriver. From the pilothouse of the *McCombs*, Clay Merriwether watched until he was certain the *Alice Dean* did not intend to stop, then ordered Captain Ballard to steam out toward her.

Some accounts of the capture of the *Alice Dean* claimed the Confederates ran up distress signals to lure the second boat alongside. According to a report in the *Cincinnati Gazette*, however, which was based on witnesses' stories, "the *McCombs* was headed out just in time to touch her bows, when the Rebels who were concealed on the *McCombs*, jumped on board the *Dean* and effected the capture of that boat also."

The Cincinnati newspaper also reported that passengers were assured their private property would be respected. Ten thousand dollars in the boats' safes were returned to the various owners, and all were liberated with instructions not to try to leave Brandenburg. Guards of course were placed on both vessels, officers and crews being held aboard.

About nine o'clock the next morning the 2nd Kentucky, with Morgan and Duke riding in the advance, came trotting into Brandenburg, the other regiments strung out in columns of fours under a long dust cloud in the rear. The town's main street sloped straight to the river which was still covered by a streamer of early-morning fog concealing the Indiana shoreline. This was the first time the boys of the 2nd had looked upon the Ohio since their fight at Augusta in 1862, and from what they could see of it the dark greenish brown stream was running full.

Captains Taylor and Merriwether rode out to meet the column, giving Morgan the good news of the capture of the two passenger steamers. They also informed Morgan that Captain Tom Hines had brought in what was left of his command to Brandenburg.

The officers rode on down to the landing where they found Hines "leaning against the side of the wharf boat, with sleepy, melancholy look—apparently the most listless, inoffensive youth that was ever imposed upon." Morgan dismounted and talked with Hines for several minutes. The young captain had much to report of conditions in Indiana, the roads, the towns, what help or resistance might be expected from the people. At the end of their conversation Morgan informed Hines that he was to take command of the scouts, the third officer to replace Tom Quirk within the week.

Establishing headquarters in a many-windowed house on the town's highest hill, Morgan began issuing orders for the river crossing. Captain Ballard of the *McCombs* and Captain Pepper of the *Alice Dean* were given instructions, a Parrott gun was placed aboard each steamer, and bales of hay were stacked along the bulwarks for defense.

The veteran 2nd Kentucky, with Hines leading the scouts, was chosen to make the first crossing on the *Alice Dean*. Colonel W. W. Ward's 9th Tennessee would follow on the *McCombs*. There would be no room for horses; they would come over on the second trip.

While the men were loading, the river mist thinned slightly, then suddenly burned away under the sun to reveal a line of enemy riflemen along the Indiana banks. A few moments later the Indianians opened fire, flashes spouting from a hundred weapons, quickly followed by a long leaping flame and the sullen roar of a fieldpiece.

Across the thousand yards of rippling brown water the background was incongruously peaceful and pastoral, like a Currier and Ives color print—two or three neat farmhouses with tan haystacks in yellow fields, strips of trees and underbrush in two shades of green, fresh light green near the river, dark green on the farther ridge.

The enemy's big gun flashed again, the shell whistling across, a piece of it wounding one of the 1st Brigade's quartermaster officers. Through his field glass Basil Duke found the gun; it was an ancient cannon mounted on the chassis of a farm wagon, propelled by hand. The riflemen were dressed in a mixture of militia uniforms and rough farm clothing. They fired another volley, but their range was less than the river's width.

From the hilltop where Morgan had his headquarters, Captain Byrnes opened up now with blasts from his Parrott guns, followed by repeated barks of the howitzers. As the Indiana defenders broke and ran for the ridge in their rear, the steamboats were signaled to move out. Paddle wheels churned on the *Alice Dean;* she shuddered briefly and slid away.

On board at that moment, Major Tom Webber was entering the pilothouse. He curtly instructed the pilot as to where he wanted the 2nd Regiment landed, warning the man that any attempt at delay or sabotage would be dealt with severely. The pilot tipped his cap respectfully, then as he turned to watch Webber leave, he saw a Kentucky giant looming in the doorway, a sun-scorched soldier with an axe slung over his shoulder, a long rifle in one arm, a big navy revolver in his belt. This was Tom Boss of C Company. "I'm here as guard to see you act right," Boss growled sternly. "I don't want no nonsense."

Boss found a seat in a corner, hitched his revolver into reach, and placed his rifle across his knees. As the *Alice Dean* chugged across the river the pilot attended strictly to business, easing the bow in for a perfect landing. As soon as the plank was pushed out and the first platoon of cavalrymen began hurrying ashore, the man breathed a sigh of relief. He turned to Boss and said: "My name is Smith. Would you object to telling me yours?"

"Oh, no," replied Boss affably, "I don't mind who I make acquaintance with. My name's Tom Boss."

To make conversation the pilot asked: "How long do you remain on your post when you're on guard duty?"

"Well," Boss answered, "we cavalry stand four hours on and eight off. The webfoot infantry stand two on and four off. But we generally do twice as much work as they do so we need twice as long rest." The big Kentuckian raised up to see how the boys were doing ashore. They were forming lines and keeping a close watch on the wooded ridge where the Indianians had disappeared. Everything was quiet. "Mr. Smith," Boss drawled, "you got anything on this boat to drink stronger'n water? I'm beginning to feel powerful dry."

"Certainly," replied the pilot. "I'll get it for you." Mr. Smith excused himself, dropped down the ladder to the ship's bar and returned after a minute or so with two strong toddies. He intended to drink one of them himself, feeling an acute need for a restorative after the strain of crossing with that fierce-looking giant at his back.

But when the pilot came within reach of his guard, Boss thrust out both long arms, grasped a glass in each hand, and drained one after the other with scarcely a pause between drinks. Smacking his lips, he thanked the pilot, then added casually: "You needn't bring any more, Mr. Smith, until just before I'm relieved. I don't like to drink too much while I'm on duty."

Tom Boss' comrades, meanwhile, had established a bridgehead on the sloping riverbank, and the *Alice Dean* was reversing engines to make room for the *McCombs* which was coming in with the 9th Tennessee.

The *Dean* had scarcely recrossed to the Brandenburg landing when an unexpected intruder appeared in the bend of the river, the gunboat *Elk*, a snub-nosed craft boarded up tightly with heavy oak planking, three howitzers thrust out of embrasures. "A bluish-white, funnel-shaped cloud spouted out from her lefthand bow and a shot flew at the town, and then changing front forward, she snapped a shell at the men on the other side."

Horse-holders of the 2nd Kentucky who were waiting at the Brandenburg landing to load the regiment's animals drew them hurriedly back out of view. Across the river the dismounted cavalrymen, feeling lost and helpless without their horses, took cover in the forested ridge.

From his headquarters vantage point, General Morgan had been watching the approach of the *Elk* for several minutes. He now ordered Captain Byrnes to change the position of his biggest guns, and shortly thereafter solid shot was skipping all around the *Elk*, followed by bursting shells. After about an hour's dueling the *Elk* turned and headed back upriver toward Louisville to spread the alarm and summon reinforcements.

As soon as the gunboat was out of range, the 2nd's horses were led aboard the *Alice Dean*, and the work of crossing the regiments was resumed. About sundown, Duke's brigade was on the Indiana shore, and Adam Johnson's regiments began moving across.

By midnight the rear guard was landing on the Indiana bank. When the last man stepped ashore, Morgan issued orders to burn both boats, but Basil Duke intervened and saved the *John T. McCombs*, Captain Ballard being an old acquaintance. Ballard promised to take his boat upriver to Louisville so that it could not be used to ferry pursuing Union troops, who already were beginning to appear on the Brandenburg wharf.

As the flames of the *Alice Dean* lighted the river, a few of these advance enemy troops fired a futile round of rifle fire toward Indiana. The alligator horses in Morgan's rear guard only laughed, waved their hats, and rode off into the dark woods.

There is no record of how John Morgan felt as he watched the last of his men come ashore into Indiana, knowing that he had successfully invaded the enemy's country. But as he watched the *Alice Dean* burning brightly and the *McCombs* splashing away toward Louisville, he knew there was now no turning back. He was cut loose from Kentucky, he was acting against orders, but he had accomplished what other western commanders had only dreamed of doing, and there must have been elation with that realization.

Sergeant Henry Stone, the boy from Greencastle, Indiana, who was attached to Hines' scouts, recorded that he "experienced some peculiar sensations as I set foot on Indiana soil." Stone found time to write a letter to his father, beginning it "On the Ohio River 30 Miles Below Louisville, Wednesday 8th July 1863." After describing the crossing, he wrote: "Wake up old Hoosier now. We intend to live off the Yanks hereafter and let the North feel like the South has felt of some of the horrors of war—horses we expect to take whenever needed, forage and provisions also. In fact it is concluded that living is cheaper in Indiana and Ohio than Tennessee. . . . I hope I'll get close enough to pay you a visit. This will be the first opportunity of the Northern people seeing Morgan and they'll see enough. I just imagine now how the women will bug their eyes out at seeing a Rebel army."

Crossing with the 2nd Regiment, Stone helped establish the first bridgehead, then moved on into the deserted countryside—the morning's defenders on the riverbank having completely vanished. They burned a flour mill, marched inland six miles, and went into camp in a meadow, waiting for the other regiments to build up behind them. As twilight came on, the liquid July heat intensified, became heavy with the smell of horses and smoke from cooking fires. Fireflies blinked in the dark foliage; bugles rang in the summer night. Voices of many men mingled as they sought their proper outfits in this strange Yankee country.

"Some of the boys gave champagne parties that night," said Kelion Peddicord, "which doubtless was taken from the stores of one of the steamers, as also were a few other luxuries that had so mysteriously come into their possession. After satisfying their unnatural appetites, all took a sly snooze, dreaming of home and of the fair fields beyond the waters."

5

Before daylight of the ninth, bugles were blowing boots and saddles. Although Colonel Adam Johnson's 2nd Brigade led the order of march, out in front was that short-lived scouting regiment, the 14th Kentucky Cavalry, which contained a number of men and officers from the 2nd Regiment. General Morgan had formed the 14th as a special command for his brother, Dick Morgan, who had recently transferred from Virginia.

Operating with the 14th were the scouts, now under Tom Hines, along with other veterans from the 2nd Regiment's Company A. In addition there were twenty men from Billy Breckinridge's 9th Regiment, which had been serving as a delaying force far in the raiders' rear, and failed to reach Brandenburg in time to make the crossing with Morgan. Several of these men were originally members of the 2nd Kentucky.

Among the scouts that morning who rode in the van singing, "Here's to Duke and Morgan," were Kelion Peddicord, Henry Stone, Winder Monroe, Leeland Hathaway, Jack Messick, and the shifty James T. Shanks. Each of them was riding into strange adventures which would extend far beyond the few days of the great raid—into events involving espionage, dramatic prison escapes, gallantry, romance, dungeons and betrayal.

This summer morning, however, they were chiefly concerned with discovering the presence of the enemy as they rode straight northward toward the town of Corydon past alternating patches of woodland and cornfields, carefully scouting farmhouses from which the occupants had fled, seemingly vanished from the earth, leaving doors wide open in their precipitate haste.

About ten o'clock that morning they met the first resistance point, a party of home guards—the same force which had appeared on the shore opposite Brandenburg the previous morning—who were posted behind a heap of fence rails on the Corydon road. Bringing up his regular regiments, Colonel Johnson overran these inexperienced defenders, pursuing them all the way to the outskirts of Corydon.

Here, Johnson found a solid barricade of logs, rails and underbrush piled high across the road. A cavalry charge was out of the question, and after the first dismounted company was repulsed with several casualties, he waited until the 2nd Kentucky and 9th Tennessee came up. "A flank movement to the right and left," Johnson reported, "gallantly led by the 2nd Kentucky on the right and Ward's on the left caused the enemy to disperse in confusion."

One of the Corydon defenders describing this action said "the enemy opened upon our forces with three pieces of artillery, making the shells sing the ugly kind of music over our heads. . . . In the meantime the enemy had completely flanked the town . . . the fighting was very sharp for the space of 20 minutes. . . . After the field was taken by the enemy they moved forward, and planted a battery on the hill south of town, and threw two shells into the town, both of them striking near the center of main street, one exploded but did no damage. Seeing the contest was hopeless . . . Col. Jordan wisely hoisted the white flag and surrendered."

According to the Corydon *Weekly Democrat*, the raiders lost eight killed and thirty-three wounded in the attack, and took their revenge by seizing "everything they wanted in the eating and wearing line and horses and buggies. The two stores were robbed of about $300 each and a contribution of $700 each was levied upon the two mills in town."

Morgan arrived in Corydon in time for lunch, and during a casual conversation with the hotelkeeper's daughter learned the startling news that General Lee had been defeated at Gettysburg and was in retreat. If this were true—and the newspapers he was shown corroborated the story—he knew he must now abandon plans to march into Pennsylvania.

As he rode northward out of Corydon he found small comfort in reports from some of his officers that a few houses along the way were displaying the lone-star flag of the Knights of the Golden Circle, and that his own picture had been seen in one or two windows. John Morgan had little use for Copperheads. If these so-called Northern friends of the South really wanted to help, he reasoned, they should join the Confederate Army and fight.

By nightfall his regiments were within sixteen miles of Salem. He ordered the men into camp, with pickets doubled. Lee may have been beaten at Gettysburg, but John Morgan was resolved to continue the raid as planned.

Using all his tricks of deception, he had already spun an intricate web of confusion as to his intentions. In Brandenburg he had permitted known Union sympathizers to overhear elaborate plans for marching to Indianapolis to burn the State Capitol and release Confederate prisoners at Camp Morton. He also spread a story that General Nathan B. Forrest with two thousand more Confederates was close behind him. All day the telegrapher, George Ellsworth, had ridden beside Morgan, and at every telegraph line Ellsworth swung aloft with his portable set, tapping the wires and transmitting misleading reports as rapidly as Morgan could dictate them. Wires were always cut behind them, so that nowhere in southern Indiana could Union forces check the raiders' whereabouts or coordinate their own movements.

It was no wonder that as the day wore on terror rolled northward across Indiana, newspapers printing extra editions, every rumor increasing the size of the invading force. (Although Morgan crossed only two thousand men at Brandenburg, no Northern paper during the raid ever used a figure of less than four thousand, and often it was increased to as many as twenty thousand.)

By nightfall every city and town in the Middle West was looking for Morgan's terrible raiders, and even three hundred miles away on the Illinois prairies a village became panic-stricken when a charivari party serenaded a bride and groom with trumpets and tin pans. Residents not in on the affair were certain the noise heralded the advent of Morgan's bloodthirsty raiders, and ran helter-skelter in their night clothes to hide in the cornfields until daybreak.

6

Unaware of the widespread panic they were creating, Morgan's men awoke that same morning (July 10) in the peaceful dewy fields below Salem, Indiana, and resumed their steady march straight northward. In Indianapolis, Governor Oliver P. Morton had declared a state of emergency and was posting warnings throughout the city: "In order to provide against possible danger it is requested that all places of business in Indianapolis be closed this afternoon at 3 o'clock, and that all ablebodied white male citizens will form themselves into companies and arm themselves with such arms as they can procure, and endeavor to acquaint themselves with military tactics." At Brandenburg that morning, pursuing Union cavalry began crossing the river in strength, still twenty-four hours behind the raiders.

As there were two roads running north to Salem, one through Greenville, the other through Palmyra, Morgan separated his brigades. Tom Hines' scouts led one column, the 2nd Kentucky the other, and the march turned into a race along parallel roads between these old regimental comrades. Occasionally during the morning they could see each other's dust trails across the green countryside, and rival flankers met each other as they sought provisions and fresh horses at farms off the main roads.

As Sergeant Henry Stone had written his father in Greencastle, they intended "to live off the Yanks hereafter." Regimental quartermasters had already worked out a method for procuring rations. Thomas M. Coombs described the system in one of his letters: "Every morning the Captains of Companies would appoint a man for each mess to go ahead and furnish provisions. They would all go ahead of the command and scatter out to the farmhouses for miles on each side of the road, and by ten or twelve o'clock they would overtake us with sacks full of light bread, cheese, butter, preserves, canned peaches, berries, wine cordial, canteens of milk and everything good that the pantrys and closets of the hoosier ladies could furnish."

As on the previous day, the forward parties saw very few people, but they knew the driving columns had been observed, and warnings passed on far ahead. From every village to the right and left of them, church bells were tolling urgently. By the time they sighted Salem, that town was a bedlam of church bells, fire bells, and shrieking whistles. It was as if the townspeople somehow believed that a vast amount of noise might frighten these devil raiders away.

The 2nd Kentucky won the hot dusty race into Salem. Lieutenant A. S. Welch of Company L led his platoon of twelve men in at a brisk gallop, their yells and fierce momentum scattering a force of frightened home guards. Before the defenders could re-form, Captain W. J. Jones brought his company pouring into a side street, overturning an ancient swivel gun, which was loaded and ready to fire, in the public square.

By noon both brigades were swirling around the little town. They fed and watered horses, burned the railroad depot and a bridge over Blue River, ripped up tracks for several hundred yards, and then descended upon the Salem stores.

Basil Duke frankly admitted that his men pillaged Salem, "actuated by a desire to pay off all scores that the Federal Army had chalked up in the South. . . . Calico was the staple article of appropriation—each man tied a bolt of it to his saddle. . . . One man carried a bird cage with three canaries in it for two days. Another rode with a chafing dish, which looked like a small metallic coffin, on the pommel of his saddle, until an officer forced him to throw it away. Although the weather was intensely warm, another slung seven pairs of skates around his neck, and chuckled over his acquisition."

Morgan's provost marshal attempted to stop the plundering, but nothing short of mass courts-martial would have been effective on that hot July day in Salem. The alligator horses literally cleaned out every drygoods store, saddle shop, and liquor store in town. "The ragamuffins were particularly delighted," commented the New Albany *Ledger* the next day, "with the style of Salem clothing and the quality of Salem whisky."

The only thing that stopped the mad celebration was an order to march out, and by two o'clock that afternoon the dusty horsemen were gone, vanished as quickly as they had come, leaving Salem, Indiana, its one day of Civil War to be talked about for years to come.

7

Under a blazing cloudless sky the raiders turned straight eastward now, marching to Canton where they paused only long enough to wreck a stretch of railroad and tangle several sections of telegraph wire. "We then rapidly moved on," James McCreary recorded in his diary, "like an irresistible storm to Vienna." Here for the first time they found a town filled with women and children, the able-bodied men having departed northward to help guard Indianapolis from expected attack. Also for the first time the Kentuckians learned how deep ran the awesome dread of Morgan's "terrible raiders" among these people. "The women were soon crying," Sergeant Peddicord reported, "begging and imploring us to spare their children. The boys heard this with amazement, and asked the women if they thought we were barbarians that they should think we could hurt women and children. The men assured them that not a hair of their heads would be injured, nor would they wound their feelings in any way."

While the columns continued on through Vienna in the dusk, George Ellsworth went to work in the telegraph office. He learned that Union forces were concentrating around Indianapolis, that home guard companies had been working through the day felling timbers and blocking roads south of the city, and that pursuing cavalry forces were still crossing at Brandenburg. Morgan was especially pleased that his Indianapolis ruse was working so well, and saw nothing alarming in reports of enemy cavalry still a day's march behind him.

Six or seven miles east of Vienna, near the village of Lexington, the advance companies began moving off the road for a short bivouac. They were only thirty miles due north of Louisville, yet for all that Union commanders anywhere knew of their whereabouts, they might as well have been on the moon.

That night John Morgan commandeered a house in Lexington and slept in comfort, guarded only by a small escort. Just before daylight a dozen or so Federal cavalrymen blundered into town, were challenged by Morgan's guards, and three of the Yankees were captured before they could gallop away.

Awakened by the clatter, Morgan decided he might as well start the columns moving again, and this day he chose to march north on a winding road through rolling country toward Vernon. A few miles above Lexington he sent Colonel D. Howard Smith's 5th Regiment east in a feint toward Madison. He also issued orders to seize every saddle horse in sight; the raiders' mounts were still holding up well, but he did not want to leave any replacements behind for his pursuers. Before noon, each regiment had a sizable horse herd bringing up the rear.

It was midafternoon when the scouts sighted Vernon, and a cautious reconnaissance indicated that the town was prepared to fight. Sturdy barricades had been thrown up in the streets, and several hundred militiamen were waiting with rifles at ready. When Morgan sent in a truce party demanding surrender, the colonel in command flatly refused.

Morgan moved up to the front, joining Basil Duke and Adam Johnson for a conference. None of them liked the looks of the town. They believed they could force their way in, but feared the cost would be high, and to lose more men now might endanger the success of the raid. They decided to shift the brigades over to a side road leading back southeastward toward Dupont.

To gain time while his straggling columns were re-forming for the turnabout, Morgan sent in a second demand for surrender. In the meantime, however, a long railroad train had rolled in from the north, bringing General John Love and more than a thousand volunteer troops. After taking command in Vernon, Love immediately sent out a reply demanding Morgan's surrender.

It was now late in the day, shadows of mounts and riders falling in tall black slants across the dusty roads. Morgan purposely delayed his answer until the sun was down. Then, about nine o'clock, he sent a message in to Love informing him that he would give the Federals thirty minutes to remove women and children, after which time the raiders would begin shelling Vernon with artillery.

While Love was frantically rounding up noncombatants and hurrying them to safety north of Vernon, Morgan's rear guard slipped away, and concealed by darkness hurried on after the forward columns. The division was miles away to the southeast before Love, waiting for an artillery barrage that never came, realized he had been outbluffed by a master of military legerdemain.

"We traveled all night to Dupont," wrote James McCreary, "where we rested and fed our horses. Like an avalanche we are sweeping over the country. Man never knows his powers of endurance 'till he tries himself. The music of the enemy's bells is now as familiar and common as the caroling of the spring bird which, unknowing of death and carnage around, sings today the same song that gladdened our forefathers."

At midnight they went into camp, but Morgan had them in their saddles again by three o'clock in the morning. Since crossing the Ohio River they had averaged twenty-one hours a day on horseback, and fatigue was beginning to take its toll. They were hungry, too, this Sunday morning, July 12, and after daylight when they passed a meat-packing plant near Dupont, the boys could not resist falling out of column to "capture" some Indiana hams. Most of them slung the hams to their saddles and resumed march, but several laggards in the rear guard stayed too long and were captured by a band of militiamen.

Sunday morning church bells were ringing in all the villages—whether to summon worshipers or to warn them of the approaching raiders, the men could not tell. About noontime, Tom Hines' scouts and the 2nd Kentucky rode into Versailles at a walk, men and horses suffering from dust and sultry weather. After subduing a halfhearted force of home guards, they watered their horses and sought food and drink from the terrified householders.

While waiting for the rear regiments to come up, many men fell asleep on the streets beside their horses, but when a rumor was passed around that Frank Wolford's 1st Kentucky Union Cavalry had been reported only a dozen miles to the rear, they all mounted up willingly to resume march. The pursuing forces had closed the gap as a result of the division's delay and reversal of march at Vernon. All day Saturday the raiders' route of march had been like an inverted V, Morgan's men traveling both sides, the Union cavalry only the short base.

Leaving Versailles, Morgan put his columns on parallel roads again in an attempt to gain upon his pursuers, marching northeastward at a steady gait. Near Milan sheer weariness forced a halt, Bennett Young describing how he passed his dust-begrimed comrades "scattered along the fence corners for four miles." And James McCreary, the faithful diarist, was so weary that night when he tumbled off his horse, he could write but one sentence: "We moved rapidly through six or seven towns without resistance, and tonight lie down for a little while with our bridles in our hands."

The point where the two columns came together long after

nightfall was just outside a village called Sunman. They bivouacked there, only fifteen miles from the Ohio state line.

8

While Morgan's main columns had been successfully eluding enemy forces in both front and rear, the detachment of two companies under Captain William J. Davis and Lieutenant George Eastin had not been so fortunate. After leaving Shepherdsville, Kentucky, this diversionary party of about one hundred men marched rapidly around Louisville to Shelbyville, then swung north through Smithfield to Sligo, cutting telegraph wires, burning railroad bridges, and attempting to create the impression that they were Morgan's entire raiding force.

On the night of July 10, while their comrades were bivouacked scarcely twenty miles north across the Ohio near Lexington, Indiana, Captain Davis' men were approaching Westport on the river. The latter part of their march was over a corduroy road—poles laid crosswise on muddy earth—the clattering of their horses' hoofs breaking the stillness of the night.

About daylight of the eleventh, at the time Morgan's raiders were beginning their drive north toward Vernon, Davis' detachment reached the river. While his men were searching for boats, Davis stopped in at the residence of a Dr. Barbour, accepted an invitation to breakfast, and enjoyed making the acquaintance of the host's lovely daughter.

When Davis returned to the riverbank, Lieutenant Eastin reported that two small flatboats had been found opposite Twelve Mile Island. The bottoms not being particularly sturdy, Davis decided the safest method of crossing would be to use one boat to ply between the Kentucky shore and the island, the other between the island and the Indiana shore.

By eight o'clock all were off the Kentucky landing except Lieutenant Josiah B. Gathright of Company A, 8th Kentucky, and an eight-man platoon posted to guard the rear. As Gathright was calling the rear guard down to cross to the island, he saw three steamboats turning the river bend. A moment later puffs of white smoke rose from the decks, and shells roared toward the Indiana shore where Davis, Eastin, and about forty men were waiting along the grassy flats. About fifty other men were trapped on Twelve Mile Island with their horses.

Gathright acted promptly, taking the boat out quickly to the island. He made two turns to the island and back to the Kentucky shore, narrowly escaping a direct hit on the second run, rescuing thirty-four men before the gunboats moved up too close for risking another try. But in their haste, these men left not only their horses but also their arms and accouterments on the island.

And so at nine-thirty the morning of July 11, Lieutenant Gathright found himself the sole officer in command of forty-two men, only eight of them mounted and armed. They were cut off from their command across the river, and in their rear a dozen irate Federal patrols were searching for them. (As several of these men were of D Company, 2nd Kentucky, their subsequent adventures will be recorded in a later chapter.)

Meanwhile, Captain Davis and Lieutenant Eastin had moved away from their exposed position on the Indiana shoreline, and with their little band of forty set out to find John Morgan. If they had continued straight northward they might have overtaken the column's rear guard, but Morgan had underestimated by one day the time he expected to be in Salem. Unaware of this, however, and obedient to orders Davis turned west toward Salem, only to run into the hornet nests stirred up in the wake of the swift-moving raiders.

"While crossing a small creek near Pekin," he later wrote to Frances Cunningham, "we were attacked by the 73rd Indiana Volunteers and a detachment of 5th U. S. Regulars in ambuscade." Outnumbered, Davis ordered a retreat into a nearby woods where he hoped to make a stand. In the fight which followed, Davis' horse stumbled over a fallen tree, throwing its rider. Davis fell unconscious, and most of his men, believing him killed, surrendered.

Among those surrounded was George Eastin, still wearing the captured sword of Dennis Halisey. Aware that a price had been put on his head for the alleged murder of Halisey, and knowing that identification of the sword was certain, Eastin quickly hid the shiny blade under a log somewhere in that little patch of woods near

Pekin, Indiana. He also concealed all articles of identity and marks of rank, and when the Yankee captors asked his name, he told them he was Private George Donald, and it was under this *nom de guerre* that Lieutenant George Eastin went into a Northern prison camp.

A few hours later Captain Davis was revived by a cool evening breeze. He was still lying beside the log which doubtless had concealed him from the victorious Yankees. Davis hid in a thicket until morning, then set out on foot, alone in enemy country. After walking about five miles he met a small boy in a field. The boy volunteered the information that a wounded Rebel soldier was in a house nearby. Davis walked to the house, entered, and surrendered to six militiamen who were carefully guarding the wounded captive. It would be fifteen months before Captain Davis could rejoin Morgan's raiders.

11

Farthest Point North

I'm sent to warn the neighbors, he's only a mile behind;
He's sweeping up the horses, every horse that he can find.
Morgan, Morgan, the raider, and Morgan's terrible men,
With Bowie knives and pistols are galloping up the glen.

I

MONDAY MORNING, July 13, 1863, the state of Ohio was invaded by Confederate troops for the first time in the war. The next two weeks for many Ohioans, particularly those in isolated farming areas and villages, was to be a time of self-induced terror which often approached the comical in its absurdities. As Bennett Young put it, the raiders in gray were pictured as "real sure enough devils, horns, hoofs and all. Even rhyme was put under conscription to help tell how awful Morgan's men were."

Actually, during most of their drive across Ohio the raiders were in flight. Rather than being bent upon destruction of the enemy, they sought to avoid him, dodging militiamen in front and racing to escape from an army of Union cavalry pounding at their heels.

About noon of the thirteenth, the 2nd Kentucky, heading Duke's brigade, rode into Harrison, Ohio, without resistance. "The most beautiful town I have yet seen in the North," James McCreary

204

noted. "A place, seemingly, where love and beauty, peace and prosperity, sanctified by true religion, might hold high carnival. Here we destroyed a magnificent bridge and saw many beautiful women."

Waiting in Harrison for John Morgan was a man in rough civilian clothing, Sam Taylor, one of the captains who had captured Brandenburg and the steamboats. Taylor had been on another special mission—this time into Cincinnati. He reported to Morgan that Cincinnati was stampeded, the city under martial law and expecting attack, and Union troops were pouring in from Kentucky to defend it.

But Morgan had no intention of attacking Cincinnati, of risking disaster in its labyrinth of streets and hills. What he was looking for was an escape corridor between Cincinnati on the south and Hamilton on the north. As soon as the last of his companies was across the Whitewater bridge, he ordered the structure burned in order to delay his immediate pursuers, then marched out of Harrison on the road toward Hamilton. A few miles out he cut the telegraph lines, sent scouts north in a feint toward Hamilton, and turned his main column in the direction of Cincinnati. By thus threatening both points in the same afternoon, he kept his enemies waiting for him, leaving the intervening area free for his columns to slip through during the night.

The Union troops pursuing the raiders—including Wolford's Wild Riders—were so close behind that as they rode down the hill toward the river west of Harrison they could see a long line of Confederate cavalry stretching away toward the east. But the Federals could come no closer in the fading twilight; the bridge over the Whitewater was a mass of charred timbers.

2

On that afternoon of the thirteenth, the raiders started their longest continuous march, the severest test ever endured by Morgan's men and their horses. Yet it was not a rapid cavalry march, the dark night and unfamiliar roads holding them to a plodding pace much of the time.

To fight off sleep, the men talked, slow and easy, recalling events of their four days in Indiana. Already there were dozens of stories swapped back and forth among the companies of little incidents which would be forever remembered. . . . One of the boys entering the kitchen door of a farmhouse asking for food, the lady of the house flourishing a butcher knife in his face and shouting: "I'll let you know I'm from the State of Virginia and if you make any further attempt to enter here, I'll cut your heart out!" The cavalry-man retreating, apologizing: "Ma'am, I know you Virginians will fight like the devil, and I have no doubt you mean what you say." . . . The hams captured at Dupont; some of the boys at a rest-stop broiling theirs over a fire, the aroma tantalizing just as a warning of approaching Yankees came. "Mount up!" They strung the half-cooked hams to their saddles, galloping away at top speed, hams flapping, breaking loose, strewing the road, delectable suppers lost in the dust. . . . And Colonel Duke's story of the pies: everywhere they went they found bread and pies left in deserted kitchens like propitiatory offerings to fierce gods. The boys were suspicious of such gifts, uneasily passing them by until the day Duke rode up and caught several of his forward scouts standing around a table filled with apple pies cooling from the oven. "Why don't you eat them?" Duke asked. "They might be poisoned," replied one of the wary troopers. "I've always been fond of pies," said Duke. "Hand me one of the largest." The little Colonel downed the pie with relish, and when he appeared to be suffering no ill effects, the boys dived in and finished the lot. After that, Duke seldom arrived in time to find any pies left over by the ravenous scouts. . . .

As they rode eastward into the night they also worried aloud about the condition of their horses. Those who had already been forced to "swap" for Indiana farm horses grumbled over the sluggish movements of these "big-bellied, barefooted, grass-fed beasts." They would find as they moved across Ohio that these horses could endure no more than a day's march, sometimes less than that, Henry Stone reporting that he rode down eight horses before he was captured.

Another question they pondered was how much longer they could keep going. Nobody knew for certain how many men were left, but company sergeants comparing notes knew that about one out of every five of the men who had started the raid was no longer reporting for duty.

There was talk also of Butternuts, Copperheads, Peace Democrats, and Knights of the Golden Circle—those alleged friends of the
Southern cause who, some had predicted, would rise up and take
over Indiana and Ohio at the first strike of a Confederate invasion.
The boys decided these people must be phantoms, for they had seen
precious few friends on this raid. One of the stories going around
concerned General Morgan and an Indiana farmer who wanted his
horse returned, claiming that he was a Knight of the Golden Circle.
"Good," replied Morgan, "then you ought to be glad to contribute
a horse for the use of a Confederate soldier." *

Another topic of conversation as the raiders began that long night
ride around Cincinnati was the whereabouts and strength of the
enemy. They knew that Wolford's cavalry was in their rear, and
could guess there were other Kentucky Union regiments. They
could not know, of course, that Michigan, Ohio, Indiana and Illinois
cavalry were also moving in on the chase, nor that sixty-five thousand home guards in Indiana and fifty-five thousand in Ohio were,
or soon would be, armed and determined to kill or capture them.
If they had known these awesome facts, the alligator horses doubtless would have considered this massive force a flattering lot of
Yankees to be occupied with catching a few Kentucky boys out on
a mild spree.

3

After they crossed the Miami River, they burned another bridge
behind them. "As the red flames created by the great burning tim-

---

* Although certain historians have hinted at a secret political link between
Morgan's Indiana-Ohio raid and the so-called Copperhead conspiracy, there
is little evidence to support such a theory. General Sherman, who understood
his opponents better than most Union leaders, wrote on September 17, 1863:
"They scorn the alliance with the copperheads. They tell me to my face that
they respect Grant, McPherson, and our brave associates who fight manfully
and well for principle, but despise the copperheads and sneaks who profess
friendship for the South and opposition to the war as mere covers for their
knavery and poltroonery." Eyewitness observers along the raid route confirmed Sherman's belief. For instance, Miss Attia Porter of Corydon, Indiana,
recorded: "The rebs were pretty hard on the copperheads but they did not
take a thing from us."

bers rose skyward," said Bennett Young, "they illumined the entire valley, and in the flickering shadows which they cast for several miles around . . . huge, weird forms, born, it is true, of the imagination, filled the minds and hearts of the invading horsemen for the moment with apprehensive awe and depressing forebodings."

Before midnight they were brushing the northern outskirts of Cincinnati, all houses darkened, the night extraordinarily black and airless. On this march, Duke's brigade followed Adam Johnson's, the 2nd Regiment bringing up the rear—where Morgan expected an attack would most likely come.

Because of the intense darkness it was impossible to keep columns closed up. Men could not see horses immediately forward, and several times Colonel Duke was uncertain as to which of the many roads and byroads Johnson's regiments had followed. He ordered flares lighted from paper or bolts of calico—still carried by many of the men—so that it would be possible to examine hoof tracks or see the direction of movement of suspended dust kicked up by the passing horses.

Sleep was the enemy now, stragglers falling from their saddles, awakening and stumbling after their mounts. Kelion Peddicord sometimes saw in the light of flares "both man and horse nodding together, and at such times the horse staggering like one intoxicated." Bennett Young said that men lashed themselves to their saddles, only to have their mounts collapse under them. "The crawl of the artillery and a large number of buggies bearing sick and wounded comrades over a hilly and woody country amidst almost absolute darkness, with here and there an unfriendly shot, made an ordeal which rarely if at all had come into soldier life."

General Morgan, who seemed to need less sleep than most men, rode up and down the line of march, "laughing with this one, joking with that one, assuming a fierce demeanor with another." As they moved through Glendale and crossed the Reading pike in the first gray of dawn, they surprised an occasional farmer out early for morning chores. One man described what he saw, later that day for a newspaper reporter: "They were uniformed, many of them having linen dusters over their coats . . . appeared to be very much fatigued."

With daybreak came a welcome breeze and the first songs of

morning birds. At convenient meadows and streams along the way companies dropped out of column for short halts to graze and water horses. But there could be no stopping for breakfast fires or sleep— so close to Cincinnati.

As regiments were re-forming, Duke's men hurrying through to the advance, the scouts ran into a militia outpost at a railroad bridge. They skirmished briefly, driving the enemy away and capturing a few fresh horses fully equipped. Hearing a train whistling, the scouts stacked crossties into a cattle gap, cut the telegraph wires, and concealed themselves in a cornfield near the tracks. The train's engineer, meanwhile, had sighted Morgan's main column on the road, and put on a burst of speed.

"The train shot past us like a blazing meteor," said Lieutenant Peddicord, "and the next thing we saw was a dense cloud of steam above which flew large timbers. Our next sight startled our nerves, for there lay the monster floundering in the field like a fish out of water, with nothing but the tender attached. Her coupling must have broken, for the passenger carriages and express were still on the track, several yards ahead. Over three hundred raw recruits were on board, bound for Camp Dennison. They came tumbling and rolling out in every way imaginable. . . . All submitted without a single shot, and were sent under guard to the General."

The bridge defenders had been based at nearby Camp Dennison, and by the time Morgan's column crossed the railroad, the camp's complement of soldiers was in earnest pursuit. During the morning these untrained troops peppered away at the rear guard, but near Batavia they abandoned chase and began felling trees across the road to block the raiders in case they turned back. (Morgan of course did not turn back, and the felled trees only served to delay the regular Union cavalrymen when they arrived.)

About four o'clock that afternoon under a windless July sky, the weary, dusty raiders rode into Williamsburg—twenty-eight miles east of Cincinnati—ending the longest continuous march ever made by Morgan's men. They had covered ninety miles in thirty-five hours. As soon as the order was passed along to fall out for bivouac, the men tumbled from their saddles, tended briefly to their horses, and except for the unfortunate pickets all slept like dead men until bugles awakened them at dawn.

All day July 15, as they continued eastward, forage parties scoured the countryside for food and horses, especially horses. A few miles out of Williamsburg, Dick Morgan and Tom Hines led the scouts off in a fast march twenty miles south to Ripley on the Ohio River, to search out possible crossings, but when they rejoined the main column late that evening at Locust Grove their report was negative. The Ohio was running full and ferries were under heavy guard. They would have to march on to Buffington Island, one of the fords selected by Captain Sam Taylor when he made his secret journey to Ohio back in the spring. And Buffington was almost a hundred miles to the east.

On Thursday, July 16, they were continually harassed by home guards who ripped up bridges, felled trees across narrow roads, sometimes fired into the advance from concealment. "The enemy are now pressing us from all sides," James McCreary wrote that day, "and the woods swarm with militia. We capture hundreds of prisoners, but, a parole being null, we can only sweep them as chaff out of our way." At sundown they were in Jasper on the Scioto River. After ransacking the town they crossed the river to Piketon, breaking up a futile attempt by home guards to stand them off.

But behind them, Michigan and Kentucky Union cavalry regiments were regaining ground lost in the long ride around Cincinnati, and Morgan ordered another all-night march. For forty-five miles they rode steadily and at dawn on the seventeenth were in Jackson. Buffington Bar was still fifty miles away.

They halted in Jackson only long enough to take what they wanted from the stores. Some of the boys of the 2nd Regiment appropriated one drygoods establishment's stock of women's blue veils to use as sunshades. The veils proved to be useful accouterments as the troopers faced into the brilliant morning sun, but Ohioans were astonished when they saw this group riding by, looking for all the world like a company of harem ladies on parade.

During the past two days the column had acquired a number of odd pieces of rolling stock for transporting baggage and ailing members of the division—old lumbering omnibuses, a monstrous two-story peddler's wagon, a dozen or more hackney coaches used as ambulances, a number of barouches, top and open buggies, and several ordinary farm and express wagons. A Buckeye citizen forced to act as a guide reported after his release that he had ridden near the front with General Morgan in a barouche, and that the General was carrying "a pair of lady's fine kid boots suspended by their tiny silk lacings from one of the posts which supported the top of the vehicle." Morgan evidently had also visited a drygoods store to obtain a present for his young bride.

A short distance east of Jackson, the brigades took separate routes, Duke's men proceeding northeastward through Wilkesville, Johnson's following the southerly route through Vinton. Local militia again were felling trees in front of the 2nd Regiment, and the constant cry was "axes to the front" as the advance slowed down to cut away the blockades. At Wilkesville there was token resistance in addition to log barricades, delaying Duke's column until long after midnight.

Day was breaking as the 2nd passed through Rutland, and when the advance joined Johnson's brigade near Pomeroy they found their comrades engaged in a sharp skirmish with regular Union troops. The latter were under command of General Henry M. Judah—Indiana and Illinois cavalry brought upriver from Louisville by steamboats to head off the raiders.

General Judah had arrived too late, however, to do more than brush Morgan's flanks. Shielded by hills, the raiders were around Pomeroy at a trot before the pursuit could engage them. Major Webber marched the 2nd Kentucky in the rear, fighting off darting attacks from militia and units of regular Ohio troops.

Throughout the morning the column was virtually running a gantlet past strongly defended crossroads and hills, but Adam Johnson afterward recalled a reassuring meeting with General Morgan during a five-minute stop to rest horses. "I found him sitting on the gallery of a crossroads store, where there was a fine well; the boys were filling their canteens from the pump. The General greeted me with his bright smile, asking me to get down and rest a little, remarking: 'All our troubles are now over, the river is only twenty-five miles away, and tomorrow we will be on Southern soil.'"

About one o'clock that afternoon advance regiments were entering Chester. They quickly invested the town, preparing for an attack which never came. It was here that Morgan ordered a halt of about two hours—a delay which many of the men afterward believed was the turning point of their luck. The Ohio River was still eighteen miles away, and because of the long stop the raiders were unable to reach Buffington Island until after dark—forcing them to postpone their planned river crossing until the following morning.

Yet Morgan could scarcely have avoided a halt in Chester. Because of continual harassment from enemies along the way, his regiments had become intermixed, long gaps had broken the columns, men were marching in complete disorder, and horses were at the point of exhaustion.

By midafternoon they were out on the road to Portland, the sun scorching their backs, local militia active as hornets in their front. "Every bridge had been destroyed," said Lieutenant Peddicord, "and at every pass and ravine the road was blockaded and defended by troops in concealment. A large number of 'blockaders' were captured and compelled to clear away the obstructions that many of them had assisted in making. Poor fellows, they felt their time had come, so badly were they frightened. Oftentimes the boys would dismount, and go in pursuit of these bushwhackers and command them to halt, but on they ran . . . never stopping until the boys laid violent hands upon them, holding them fast by main force. Even then they would strive hard to get away, just as some wild animals would do."

It was eight o'clock when the scouts fumbled their way into Portland on the Ohio River, under a sky veiled with a scud of clouds that brought early darkness. The first thing that most of the men wanted to do was stare across the liquid blackness of the river to vague shapes of hills that were Virginia.*

"All were now on the *qui vive*," Major McCreary noted upon his arrival, "for the Ohio river is full of gunboats and transports, and an immense force of cavalry is hovering in our rear. . . . A dense fog wraps this woodland scene."

In the blackness of night and fog, the raiders could learn little more than that the approach to Buffington ford was defended by three hundred Union infantrymen with two pieces of artillery, dug

* Only a few weeks earlier this part of Virginia had become West Virginia, a Union state, but few of Morgan's men were aware of the change in status, nor would have accepted it, if they had known, as anything more than Yankee pettifoggery.

in behind a strong earthwork. Should they attack and try for the river? Or should they wait until morning? It was a difficult decision for Morgan and his officers to make. After some discussion they finally agreed that even if they could capture the earthwork without severe losses, the dark river probably would claim many lives. The Ohio was running much higher than normal because of unseasonably heavy rains upstream, and Buffington Island and its sand shallows were indiscernible.

Deciding to wait, Morgan ordered Warren Grigsby's 6th Kentucky, D. Howard Smith's 5th Kentucky, and Captain Byrnes' battery to approach within four hundred yards of the earthwork. At the first light of dawn these units were to storm the Yankee defenders. In the meantime scouts moved out in both directions along the river, searching for other possible fords. One of these parties found a number of leaky flatboats about a mile and a half upstream, and as best they could in the darkness set about caulking the seams.

Most of the boys in the 2nd Kentucky had no special duties on this night. Junior officers and sergeants making a hasty check of ammunition supplies found that some men had no more than two or three rounds left. But no one worried too much about that; Virginia and safety lay just across the ford. After engaging in rear-guard action all day, they should have fallen into exhausted sleep, but somehow sleep would not come easily. Here and there musicians with guitars, banjos, and fiddles—confiscated from luckless Ohio merchants along the way—began playing sentimental tunes. In the darkness the musicians drew together, and a few of the boys came to listen. Soon they were all singing and playing "My Old Kentucky Home," then "Juanita," and "The Hills of Tennessee." To show off his dexterity a fiddler played a fast version of "The Arkansaw Traveler," and some of the listeners tried to dance a mock reel on the wet stubble of the wheatfield in which they were camped.

When weariness overcame the last of the music-makers, the foggy night lapsed into silence broken only by the occasional snort of a horse, a soldier calling out in his sleep, and the muddy river murmuring unceasingly in the darkness.

4

"Everything important always happens to me on Sundays," John Morgan often said, and something very important was about to happen to him on the foggy Sunday morning of July 19, 1863.

The day began as planned, Grigsby and Smith starting their dismounted regiments cautiously through river mists toward the enemy earthwork. Not a sound could be heard on their front, and when the skirmish line dashed forward they found the earthwork abandoned, the two fieldpieces rolled over a nearby bluff.

Officers had just given the command to mount, when a rattle of musketry tore along the flank like a noise of ripping canvas. Fog still shrouded everything, but there was little doubt from the direction of firing that the attackers were General Judah's river-borne cavalrymen coming up after a night march from Pomeroy. A moment or so later, Judah's artillery boomed from behind the milky curtain of fog. And then as if on signal another fusillade of rifle fire broke from the opposite direction—revealing the presence of the raiders' constant pursuers in the rear, Union cavalry led by Generals Edward Hobson and James Shackleford, converging upon Adam Johnson's 2nd Brigade guarding the road from Chester.

While Morgan's forces formed to return fire from two directions, a gust of air "hot as the breath of an oven" rushed down the valley. The white fog lifted like a curtain going up, and for the first time the raiders could see the battlefield. They were in a V-shaped valley a mile long, about eight hundred yards wide, regiments scattered across meadows, cornfields and among tan-colored shocks of wheat. Along one side of the V was a wooded ridge thick with Shackleford's cavalry; in the wide opening was Judah's mounted skirmish line. As they looked toward the other side of the V—the river running north and south—they were startled to see two menacing enemy gunboats. The raiders were trapped from three sides, the only way of escape being a narrow opening at the angle of the V.

As the 5th and 6th regiments began moving toward the river, the Union flagboat *Moose* opened fire with her powerful twenty-four-pounder Dahlgren guns. A minute later Judah's artillery in the valley and Hobson's on the ridge joined in the thunderous barrage. Now the raiders were caught in a three-way crossfire of exploding shells. In addition, several thousand dismounted Union cavalrymen were pressing closer, joining in with small arms fire. "The scream of the shells," Basil Duke afterward wrote, "drowned the hum of the bullets . . . and bursting between the two lines formed at right angles—a disposition we were compelled to adopt in order to confront both ground assailants—the air seemed filled with metal, and the ground was torn and ploughed into furrows."

There was little that Morgan's men could do to beat off the attacks. Although the 2nd Regiment was probably worse off than the others in regard to ammunition supply, few companies averaged more than five rounds in cartridge boxes. As for Captain Byrnes' battery, the bores of several pieces were so clogged they could scarcely be loaded with the few shells remaining, and the gunners in position to retaliate were quickly driven away by fire from the *Moose*.

Most disheartening of all was the rain-swollen river, its swift waters rippling over the sand shallows of Buffington Bar. A few men of Grigsby's and Smith's regiments rushed into the muddy current, tossing away their arms and stripping themselves of clothing, but less than thirty made it across under close fire from the *Moose* and *Allegheny Belle*. Farther upstream, some of the 9th Tennessee troopers managed to launch one of the repaired flatboats and crossed before the enemy discovered them.

The attack now heightened in fury, the Dahlgrens belching from the river, continuous small arms fire whining like an angry overtone. In the midst of this inferno, Duke and Morgan held a quick consultation. The only way of escape was through the narrow pass at the north end of the valley. Morgan would attempt to lead out as many men as possible, while Duke and Johnson made a last-ditch stand.

Duke galloped back to his brigade, and in the next few minutes watched his regiments break before one charge, rally to fight off another. He knew that many of the men had used their last cartridges. Several times he sent off couriers for the 2nd Kentucky, which had been camped about midway down the valley. But the 2nd was trapped in a maelstrom of men and horses, its companies being sucked off first in one direction and then the other, the men becoming hopelessly entangled with other regiments and separated from their sergeants and officers.

Farther up, Morgan was withdrawing rapidly through the narrow gap, his first companies in good order, the rear bunching, breaking ranks and clogging the road. Officers struggled vainly to re-form columns, bugles screamed quick urgent calls at cross purposes. Over all the field a thin blue haze of smoke was slowly spreading.

A shell struck the road where the 2nd was attempting to rally, throwing up a cloud of dust. A solid burst of shot danced around the heels of the horses; the pict-pict-pict-pict of bullets in flight made the men duck their heads clear to the saddle bows. A shell burst into a column, and then all around them was an eddy of men and horses in panic flight.

Troopers began unloading their booty of the raid—cutting loose shoes, parasols, skates, sleighbells and bird cages, scattering them to the winds. Long bolts of muslin and calico spun out in banners of brilliant colors, streaming in the morning sunlight. "The upper end of the valley," said Duke, "was filled with wagons and ambulances, whose wounded and terror-stricken occupants urged the scared horses to headlong flight. Often they became locked together, and were hurled over as if by an earthquake. Occasionally a solid shot, or unexploded shell would strike one, and dash it into splinters. . . . The remaining section of artillery was tumbled into a ravine, during this mad swirl, as if the guns had been as light as feathers. The gunboats raked the road with grape. . . . In a moment the panic was complete, and the disaster irretrievable."

Among the last to escape through the jumbled gap were scattered units of the 2nd Kentucky, Major Webber leading out the better part of companies A, C, E, F, I and L.

5

As soon as he realized that further resistance was useless, Duke ordered a flag of truce sent to the nearest of the Federal regiments, the 7th Ohio Cavalry under Colonel Israel Garrard. In a few minutes firing ceased, and Garrard sent Captain Theodore Allen forward with a platoon escort to accept Duke's surrender.

Shortly afterward a *Cincinnati Gazette* reporter, who had come upriver with the gunboats, went ashore to see the captives. "The rebels were dressed in every possible manner peculiar to civilized man. . . . They wore in many instances large slouch hats peculiar to the slave States, and had their pantaloons stuck in their boots. A dirty gray-colored coat was most prevalent, although white dusters were to be seen. . . . On the battlefield of Buffington Island, one could pick up almost any article in the drygoods, hardware, house furnishing or ladies' or gentlemen's furnishing—linen, hats, boots, gloves, knives, forks, spoons, calico, ribbons, drinking cups, carriages, market wagons, circus wagons. . . ."

Meanwhile Basil Duke and D. Howard Smith were meeting with Captain Allen of the 7th Ohio. "Colonel Duke," Allen recorded, "bore himself with great dignity, and I would not have known I had him if one of his own men had not accidentally disclosed his identity to me."

Of the approximately seven hundred men who surrendered at Buffington, one hundred and sixteen were of the 2nd Kentucky, a large part of G Company, the others representing almost every other company in the regiment. There are no accurate records to show how many of the hundred or so dead and severely wounded were 2nd Regiment men. The scouts—officially of the 14th Kentucky—also suffered heavy losses, both Dick Morgan and Tom Hines being captured. Hines was among those who surrendered to the 7th Ohio, and to show that he bore his captors no personal animosity he presented Captain Allen with a small Confederate flag.

While other Federal regiments were disarming scattered bands down the mile-length of the valley, the 7th Ohio moved its prisoners over to a tree-shaded strip beside the river. "As we sat on the river bank," Captain Allen said, "first one man and then another asked permission to go to the water's edge to wash his face, till pretty soon about one-half the men, both Union and Confederate, were at the river's edge, washing their faces, and digging the dust out of their ears, eyes, and nostrils. This proved to be such a halfway sort of business, and so unsatisfactory, that the men asked permission to go in swimming."

Allen decided to grant permission for one half the prisoners and one half the guards to swim together, the others to stand by and take turns later. The men stripped, plunging into the cool shallows. Only a few minutes before they had been enemies determined to kill each other; now they were splashing happily together in the water, ridding themselves of two weeks' accumulation of sweat and dust.

While the men were swimming together one of Duke's officers standing beside Allen pointed to the naked soldiers and remarked philosophically: "It's difficult to tell one from the other when they're like that."

After the river bathing was finished, the Ohio boys shared the contents of their haversacks with Duke's troopers. "We spread out on the grass under the shade of the trees," said Captain Allen, "in regular picnic fashion, resting and waiting for orders." The captives soon fell asleep, sprawling like dead men. A few curious souvenir-hunting civilians wandered up to stare and search around, and when the guards were not looking they cut buttons off the uniforms of "Morgan's terrible men."

6

A few more than eleven hundred men escaped with General Morgan, including about two hundred and fifty of the 2nd Kentucky. They galloped away to the north, rounding a wide bend in the river, searching for another crossing. Close behind them came Shackleford and Wolford with Kentucky Union cavalry.

Fifteen miles upstream opposite Belleville, West Virginia, the river narrowed. It was deep for fording, but Morgan ordered the forward sections to plunge in and begin swimming their horses. Colonel Adam Johnson later told of leading the first group across: "Forming the men who were with me in column of fours, I appealed to them to keep their ranks . . . there was hardly a company in the whole division that was not represented in this body of men."

The first horses had scarcely touched hoofs upon the West Virginia shore, when the gunboat *Moose*, like an unrelenting Nemesis, shoved its ugly nose into view downstream. It was a moment of bitter despair for the men on the Ohio shore. Only a few more minutes of precious time, and every man and horse could have been safely across! Without hesitation the gunboat opened fire, shelling columns forming on the Ohio shore, then dropping two or three heavy explosives into the stream where Morgan's men were swimming their horses four abreast.

"Looking back across the river," said Adam Johnson, "I saw a number of hats floating on the surface, and knew that each represented the life of a brave and gallant Confederate who had found a watery grave. . . . We reached the woods, where the men were now gathered, a little over three hundred."

When the gunboat opened fire, General Morgan was in midstream, swimming his prize steed, Glencoe. "He could have easily escaped," one of his officers declared afterward, "but seeing that the greater portion of his command would be left behind, he returned against the urgent protests of some of his officers and men, to share their fate."

Only three hundred and thirty crossed safely, including two colonels, Adam Johnson of the 10th Kentucky and Warren Grigsby of the 6th. Two companies of the 2nd Kentucky were fairly well intact on the West Virginia side, F and L, with their captains, N. M. Lea and John Cooper. Captain Byrnes, an artilleryman with no guns, rode ashore, and as might have been expected the always-nonchalant George Ellsworth also escaped with his portable telegraph. As quickly as possible these men mounted up and vanished into the West Virginia forest, bound south for the Confederate lines.

Driven away from the Ohio shoreline, Morgan's remaining force of eight hundred (about one-fourth of them were now 2nd Regiment men) gathered in the sheltering hills and quickly reorganized. Morgan named Major Tom Webber an acting colonel, combining the two hundred men of his 2nd Regiment with about the same number surviving from other regiments of Duke's brigade. Roy Cluke replaced Adam Johnson as commander of the 2nd Brigade.

Webber assumed the duties of his new command with grim earnestness, still determined to escape and take his men out with him. For several days he had been painfully ill, disregarding his surgeon's advice to drop out of column and give himself up. Already the boys of the 2nd were calling him "Iron Man" Webber. As darkness fell over the Ohio hills, he set his men to work building large camp-fires, and when Morgan gave the signal all were lighted at once.

A few minutes later the reorganized companies mounted up, formed in columns of twos and rode quietly away. The old camp-fire trick was successful. Enemy patrols sighted the winking lights from afar, and all through the night Union cavalry units were moving into positions to surround what they believed was John Morgan's last camp of the raid.

But when morning came the raiders were far to the west, doubling back away from the river. For forty-eight hours they followed obscure trails through isolated hill country, avoiding all towns. Their whereabouts during this time were so much a mystery to Union pursuers that even General Burnside, who was commanding the entire pursuit operation, reached the conclusion that Morgan and most of his men had escaped into West Virginia.

Then suddenly early in the morning of the twenty-second, they were reported sighted in a heavily forested section near the town of Zaleski, thirty-five miles west of the river. A few hours later the report was confirmed; several hundred Confederates were approaching Nelsonville. All of eastern Ohio, which had been breathing easier since the victory at Buffington, again became a bedlam of rumors and alarms. Never in the war had eight hundred poorly armed and badly mounted men frightened so many people over so large an area.

For three more days and nights, Morgan, Webber and Cluke kept their boys moving northeastward into the heart of the Union. On Thursday, the twenty-third, they crossed the Muskingum at Eagleport after fighting off some of Shackleford's cavalry which had moved north across their front. "The enemy had fallen back on all the roads," Major Webber recorded, "guarding each one with a force in ambush much larger than ours—and to make our way out seemed utterly impossible."

The tireless Frank Wolford also got across their path in the hills beyond the Muskingum, and captured more than a hundred men, leaving Morgan with less than seven hundred. According to Major Webber's account, the entire command narrowly escaped by climbing a high bluff "up which nobody but a Morgan man could have carried a horse."

Early Friday morning, the twenty-fourth, they rode boldly out upon the National Road, a few miles east of Cambridge. By questioning frightened farmers, they learned of an Ohio river ford called Coxe's Riffle a few miles below Steubenville. All day Friday and into the night the desperate horsemen marched eastward, through Harrisville and Smithfield.

Ten o'clock Saturday morning they were only five miles from the river, but their horses were utterly exhausted and a rest stop was ordered. The raiders sprawled under trees along the road near Wintersville, some of the officers entering a farmhouse and demanding breakfast. According to the terrified farmwife, Morgan and his officers collapsed upon her beds, stretching out for a few minutes of rest in their dusty clothes and boots. When a messenger brought Morgan warning of militia approaching from Wintersville, the General showed no concern. But a second report of regular cavalry moving up from the south—Shackleford and Wolford—caused a hurried departure.

Riding on toward Wintersville, the raiders charged the waiting militia, cleared the town, hurriedly collected foodstuffs from a general store, and swung away from Steubenville on the road to Richmond. A comedy of errors on the part of the Steubenville militia now saved them from immediate attack by Shackleford and Wolford.

As the Union cavalry came galloping after Morgan, Colonel James Collier was just arriving out of Steubenville at the head of five hundred proud Minute Men. Sighting Shackleford's approaching dust cloud, the Minute Men immediately assumed it signaled the approach of Morgan's raiders. Forming line of battle along a hill on the east side of Wintersville, Colonel Collier opened fire with a six-pounder loaded with scrap iron. The metal whistled through the air, one piece thwacking into the side of a Wintersville tavern and sending General Shackleford's troopers scurrying for cover.

As soon as Shackleford recognized the Minute Men for what they were, he sent an officer forward under a truce flag to enlighten their commander of his error. Approaching the militia's defense line, Shackleford's courier shouted: "What are you fools shooting at?"

And then in colorful military profanity, he explained to the abashed Colonel Collier that he had been firing on Union soldiers.

All this delay won more than an hour of time for Morgan's raiders. They cut away from the main road, fended off two or three attacks from scouting parties during the late afternoon, and while Shackleford and Wolford were combing the countryside all night in search of them, they enjoyed a few hours of luxurious sleep, hidden in a patch of woods near Bergholz.

7

July 26 dawned bright and clear, a languid morning, the men rising without animation, wondering what another day would bring. It was a Sunday, the day on which everything important always happened to John Morgan, a week since the disaster at Buffington Island.

There were no more than six hundred of them now, the ranks thinning daily as men dropped out for lack of horses or from sheer exhaustion. Most of them had no exact idea of where they were, and with Ellsworth and his telegraph gone the officers could only guess at the enemy's movements. From his tattered map, Morgan knew that Lake Erie was only sixty miles away, a hard two days' march, but even if they reached the lake their chances of escape by boat were poor indeed. And any hope of fighting their way around the shoreline to Canada was but a wild dream.

They had discussed surrender, rejecting it because they knew the Federals had suspended paroles and exchanges. Victories at Gettysburg and Vicksburg had surely filled the Northern prison camps with a surplus of Confederates, and if they surrendered now they could look forward to long periods of confinement. To a man they determined to fight on to the end.

What they did not know on this Sunday morning was that two fresh regiments of cavalry had entered the chase during the preceding twenty-four hours. Majors George W. Rue and W. B. Way had arrived at Mingo Station by rail from Cincinnati, each commanding about three hundred and seventy-five veteran cavalrymen mounted on the speediest Kentucky saddle horses available.

Major Way and his 9th Michigan troopers struck Morgan's column at eight o'clock in the morning near Salineville, and in a severe running fight inflicted about seventy-five casualties and captured two hundred prisoners. Most of those captured were mounted on ungainly farm horses which failed miserably, the luckless riders firing off their last cartridges at the attackers and then surrendering. One group of Webber's brigade made their escape in front of a country church by hurriedly exchanging exhausted mounts for horses which had been hitched outside by the churchgoers.

At the time of the attack Morgan was riding in a carriage drawn by two white horses, and he escaped capture only by leaping out, mounting a led mare behind the carriage and galloping away. When the Michigan boys overtook the abandoned carriage they found inside "a loaf of bread, some hard-boiled eggs, and a bottle of whisky."

According to Major Webber's records, the surviving "old regulars" of C Company under Captain Ralph Sheldon made the last charge of the Great Raid during this Sunday morning fight. The troopers dashed valiantly down upon the enemy, but their tired horses breasted a fence without being able to clear it, knocking off the top rails. The boys of C Company stood their ground, firing their revolvers until chambers were empty. Some were killed, several wounded, and the most of them captured by the onrushing Michigan regiment.

With his command reduced to less than four hundred men, Morgan broke away during this rear-guard charge, and continued northeastward. Riding parallel with him, however, on a secondary road, was another fresh enemy regiment—Major George Rue's assemblage of crack horsemen drawn from five different Kentucky and Michigan regiments, including a few of Frank Wolford's Wild Riders.

About noon the raiders collided with a small band of home guardsmen out of Lisbon. There was no fight, Morgan quickly sending forward a truce flag and promising to pass through the county without disturbing property if the Ohioans offered no resistance. Being completely outnumbered and unaware that Morgan's men were almost out of ammunition, the guardsmen agreed. When Morgan asked for a guide to the next county line, James Burbick, acting as a temporary captain, agreed to accompany the raiders as far as Elkton.

A few minutes later, his column in motion again, Morgan sighted the dust of Major Rue's troopers off to the right across a broad valley. He turned immediately to Burbick and asked him if he would accept the surrender of the sick and wounded soldiers who were struggling to keep up with the fast pace. Burbick agreed to do so. While they were discussing terms, Rue's fresh horses pushed far ahead, swerving down a dry creek bed and cutting across Morgan's front.

John Morgan knew now that the end had come to his Great Raid. His men did not have enough ammunition to sustain a five-minute encounter; his horses could not outrun the force in his front, and he knew the pursuers in his rear would soon overtake him. But he had one more card to play—he wanted paroles for himself, his officers and men.

He ordered a halt and asked Burbick abruptly if he would accept his surrender. "On what conditions?" asked the astonished guardsman.

"On the condition that my officers and men be paroled to go home," replied Morgan.

"I don't understand the nature of a surrender," Burbick stammered. "I am not a regular officer."

"I have a right to surrender to anyone," Morgan insisted. "I want an answer right off, yes or no?"

"Yes," said Burbick.

Morgan took a handkerchief from his pocket, reached for Burbick's riding stick, and tied the white cloth to the end of it. He then ordered Burbick to ride out in company with two of the raiders' officers and inform the Federals that General Morgan had already surrendered.

It was two o'clock, July 26, 1863, a bright Sunday afternoon on the Crubaugh farm south of Lisbon, Columbiana County, Ohio, when Major George Rue, a six-foot-three Kentuckian came riding up to John Morgan. Rue had to guide his mount through Morgan's troopers who were lying in the grass along both sides of the road, some already asleep in the shade of fence corners. Morgan smiled when he recognized Rue; they had soldiered together in the War with Mexico.

Without preliminaries, Morgan informed Rue that he had already given his parole to Captain James Burbick. Then as a sort of conciliatory gesture, he offered the Union commander a sorrel mare for a trophy.

Rue had little to say, but it was evident that he felt cheated over losing the honor of capturing General John Hunt Morgan. He ordered his officers to disarm the Rebels and collect their horses. He had three hundred and sixty-four prisoners and almost four hundred horses.

The endurance of the 2nd Kentucky Regiment is apparent in the records of Rue's prisoners. More than one third of them were of that rugged organization. At the beginning of the Great Raid, one in five of Morgan's men was a 2nd Regiment trooper; after Buffington it was one in four; at the final surrender the ratio was better than one in three. The hard training given them by Basil Duke and St. Leger Grenfell had paid off for the veterans of the old 2nd. The Lexington Rifles, the Green River boys, the Lebanon Racers—they had shown the Yankees that Kentucky boys are alligator horses.

Years afterward a marker would be placed at the site of surrender, bearing the inscription:

> This Stone Marks the Spot Where the
> Confederate Raider, General John H. Morgan
> Surrendered His Command to Major Geo. W. Rue
> July 26, 1863, and is the Farthest
> Point North Ever Reached by Any Body of
> Confederate Troops During the Civil War

Whether Morgan surrendered to Rue, Burbick, or General James Shackleford is one of those moot points of history. To the end of his days Shackleford would claim the honor. Rue, he said, was operating under his command, and he even took away from Rue the sorrel mare given by Morgan, as well as the great Glencoe, which he shipped off as a gift to old General Winfield Scott. As for Burbick, Shackleford dismissed him as a mere civilian with no authority to accept a surrender from anybody.

Only a few minutes after Rue reached Morgan's side, Shackleford and Wolford arrived at a fast trot, and a strange reunion occurred there in the quiet Ohio farm country, all four men being Kentuckians. Wolford slid off his horse, limping with pain from the old wound Morgan's men had given him months before, his scorched meat-axe face breaking in a great grin at the sight of John Morgan disarmed.

Shackleford's manner, on the other hand, was cold and disdainful. Upon Morgan's insistence that Burbick had given him a parole, Shackleford declared that such a proposition was "not only absurd and ridiculous, but unfair and illegal." When Morgan saw that Shackleford had no intention of letting him go, he demanded to be put back upon the field to fight it out. "Your demand," Shackleford retorted, "will not be considered for a moment."

According to one of Wolford's men who was present at the meeting, "General Shackleford's passion got the upper hand of his judgment and he began to bestow some caustic epithets upon the conquered chieftain. Colonel Wolford interrupted, and rebuked the irate General, and told him that it was wrong to speak harshly to one whose hands were figuratively confined. Morgan as a token of appreciation of his kindness presented to Wolford his fine silver spurs."

During the afternoon the captives were marched down to Wellsville for transport by railroad to Cincinnati. Frank Wolford, in charge of the officers, put his prisoners at ease, and invited them all to share chicken and dumplings with him at the Whittaker House. "Gentlemen," he is reported to have said, "you are my guests. This hotel together with its bar, cigar stand, and other accessories is at your service and my expense. Do not go off the square in front of the hotel."

8

Basil Duke and the raiders captured at Buffington Island meanwhile had already been taken to Cincinnati. On that hot Sunday afternoon after the defeat at Buffington Island, they were marched ten miles on foot down the river to board two waiting transports. The overland march told severely on them, several almost fainting on the road from heat and exhaustion, and Duke himself became so lame he could hardly walk.

As the two boats bearing the prisoners approached Cincinnati, the levee filled wtih a throng of men, women, and children eager to see "Morgan's terrible men."

The sixty-eight captured officers disembarked, the boats then moving on down to the foot of Fifth Street where the enlisted men were marched to a special train which would take them to Camp Morton at Indianapolis.

Duke, because of his lameness, and Dick Morgan, because of an infected leg wound, were ordered into an open carriage. Their fellow officers formed in two ranks behind them, and with guards four deep on either side were marched through Cincinnati to the City Prison on Ninth Street.

"Colonel Duke seemed to have many acquaintances in the city," one observer reported, "for as he rode up the street he was frequently recognized by persons in the crowd, to whom he would respond by lifting his hat."

For a brigade commander, the twenty-five-year-old Duke made a most unimpressive appearance, being dressed in plain blue jeans pants, a white linen shirt, and a dusty, wide-brimmed hat. He wore no marks of rank whatever. Yet he attracted the attention of everyone, including a reporter for the *New York Post*. "He is of small stature, weighing scarcely 130 pounds, well built, erect, with angular features, dark hair brushed carelessly aside, sparkling and penetrating eyes of the same color, a low forehead, moustache and goatee. He has a sweet musical voice, a pleasant smile continually on his face, and is very free and cordial in his manner. There is nothing commanding in his appearance, though he has been termed by some the 'brains of the raid.' "

This same reporter also arranged to visit the other prisoners, "huge brawny men, most of them, while not a few of a more lithesome form, lying on blankets, jumped up and courteously greeted us, evincing in their manner good birth and education. They were dressed in all styles of costumes, but few Confederate uniforms being worn, as they were mostly clad in linen coats appropriated from the wardrobes of Ohioans or from clothing stores, the property of which they had confiscated. One huge six-footer was clad in a dress-

ing robe, and sported a huge black sombrero, looped up at the side
with a plume of the same color. His immense black whiskers, which
reached nearly to his waist and his heavy moustache, gave him a
brigandish-looking appearance, as he strode in a theatrical manner
around the room, smoking a cigar."

John Morgan's arrival after dark a week later, with Webber,
Cluke and his other officers, provided another Roman holiday for
Cincinnati. A mob of five thousand milled around the railroad station, some brandishing pistols and shouting, "Hang the cut-throats!"
But no effort was made to storm the glittering bayonets of the
guard, Union regulars of the 111th Ohio Infantry, who formed a
hollow square and marched the prisoners quickly through the
crowds, the regimental band playing "Yankee Doodle."

At the jail, newspaper reporters were permitted to interview the
prize captive of the raid. "Morgan appeared in good spirits," one
wrote, "and quite unconcerned at his ill luck." He was dressed in a
linen coat, white shirt, black trousers, and a light felt hat, "a well-
built man, of fresh complexion and sandy hair and beard." The alert
New York Post correspondent quoted a request Morgan made to
General Mahlon Manson: "General, I wish you would intercede and
get a drink for me. I'm terribly dry." After this remark, the reporter
said, Morgan bowed courteously to the newspapermen, and with
cigar in mouth walked away with his jailer.

9

And what did it accomplish—the Great Raid of July 1863? Mili-
tarily it forced General Burnside to delay his planned move into
eastern Tennessee to join Rosecrans against Bragg at Chattanooga.
Bragg never forgave Morgan for crossing the Ohio, but the absence
of thousands of Burnside's troops occupied in pursuing Morgan's
raiders enabled Bragg to win the battle of Chickamauga—the only
great victory the Confederacy was to win in the western theater of
war. In addition, during the crossing of Kentucky, Indiana and
Ohio, the raiders inflicted almost six hundred casualties and captured
and paroled six thousand enemy troops. They destroyed bridges,

railroad equipment, telegraph wires and military stores, the total value of claims public and private approaching ten million dollars.

Yet neither Bragg nor the Confederate high command considered all this a fair exchange for two thousand of the Confederacy's best cavalrymen.

As for the 2nd Kentucky Cavalry, it was never to regain its full strength. In late July the remnants of Company D, escaping from Twelve Mile Island, were making their way south by stealthy night marches through Kentucky and Tennessee. Sections of A, F and L companies and a scattering of men from other companies were with Adam Johnson in western Virginia, searching for the Confederate lines. Four hundred and ninety-three men of the 2nd Regiment were prisoners in Camp Morton, their officers locked in cells in the Cincinnati jail.

Almost two more years of war, however, were yet to come, and many 2nd Kentucky cavalrymen would play exciting parts in the struggle, even into the turbulent weeks following Lee's surrender at Appomattox.

12

The Captives

Oh, Morgan crossed the river
And I went across with him;
I was captured in Ohio
Because I couldn't swim.

I

DURING THE STEAMBOAT JOURNEY down from Buffington Island to Cincinnati, several prisoners among the enlisted men of Morgan's command took advantage of the dark rainy night to leap overboard from the crowded hurricane deck and swim to the safety of the West Virginia shore. They were the last to escape by crossing the river.

Sergeant Henry Stone stayed aboard, and next morning wrote a letter to his father in Indiana:

> On Board the Ingomar
> Bound for Cincinnati
> Tuesday July 21, 1863.

DEAR FATHER

I am now with 700 others of Morgan's men a prisoner of war. . . . So far I have been treated fairly well by our captors, but I can't tell you how long such treatment will last.

230

I have but one suit of clothing and that is on my back. As to money I have none that will buy anything in Abolitionland. . . . I have deck passage now and last night when it rained I got wet through and through.

I'll bet we are the gayest lot of prisoners ever taken. . . . Last night we had hard crackers and raw bacon . . . this morning we had the former and coffee. We meet with a little sympathy now and then. Some ladies cheered us on the Virginia side this morning.

At Cincinnati, the men were loaded in boxcars and moved north to Camp Morton, Indiana, only forty miles from Sergeant Stone's home in Greencastle. To his surprise, Stone found himself in the keeping of old friends and neighbors, the boys of the 71st Indiana. "They all seemed rejoiced to see me *there*," he wrote. "Through their intervention I received clothing and other necessities from home, and obtained an interview with my brothers and some of my old friends who learned of my capture while at Indianapolis and came out to see me."

Camp Morton was badly overcrowded, recent arrivals being packed into earthen-floored stables crawling with vermin. At their first roll call, Morgan's men provided considerable amusement for the guards, lining up in variegated costumes collected during the raid—stovepipe hats, linen dusters, jeans pants stuffed into cavalry boots, or in a combination of Confederate gray and civilian summer wear. Almost all were miserably dirty from an accumulation of sweat and dust.

Squads were soon assigned to laundry duties, however, and in a few days clothes were clean and bodies washed. A week later when their comrades were brought in after Morgan's surrender in northeastern Ohio, the first arrivals had settled into prison ways. They had learned to defy the ever-present "graybacks" in their barracks, a few had managed to escape, and others were watching every opportunity to do so.

In a move to relieve overcrowding and prevent additional escapes, the Federal prison authorities decided to transfer the Morgan prisoners elsewhere. On August 15, Henry Stone scribbled a hasty note to his father: "Understanding whether reliable or not that we leave here for some other prison today. . . . I guess if we leave here it will be for Fort Delaware, or to be exchanged."

The hopes of Sergeant Stone and his companions for immediate exchange were considerably dampened a day or so later. After a night rail journey, daylight revealed the flat prairies of northern Indiana, and the rising sun told them their train was moving westward rather than to a Delaware exchange camp. At Michigan City they had their first glimpse of Lake Michigan, and not long afterward the train halted outside Chicago where Federal soldiers were waiting for them alongside the tracks. To the sharp commands of blue-coated sergeants, they unloaded and began what for some would be their last march. Their destination was Camp Douglas, the North's worst military prison.

2

Camp Douglas had been established in the spring of 1862 to house Confederate prisoners taken at Fort Donelson and elsewhere in Tennessee and Kentucky during the Federal offensive of that year. Constructed on land originally owned by Stephen A. Douglas, the camp was named for him. Its location on low ground which flooded after every rain, and in winter became a sea of frozen mud, was a poor choice for any sort of concentration of human beings. The camp was four miles from the center of Chicago, about four hundred yards from Lake Michigan.*

Conditions in Douglas became so wretched in January, 1863, that Federal soldiers stationed there to guard prisoners almost mutinied; they expressed their loathing of the place by rioting, and wrecked some of the barracks and fencing. In the following month, 387 prisoners died, a mortality rate of ten per cent, which according to official records was the highest monthly death rate of any military prison during the war.

After an official investigation in March, a medical officer strongly recommended removal of the camp to another site, but General Halleck rejected the proposal. Death and disease rates among both

---

* Its present-day placement would be between Thirty-first and Thirty-third streets, near the Douglas monument just off Lake Shore Drive.

prisoners and guards continued to run so high, however, that in April another investigation was made by the Sanitary Commission. "In our experience," the inspecting officers reported, "we have never witnessed so painful a spectacle as that presented by the wretched inmates . . . the ground at Camp Douglas is most unsuitable, being wet and without drainage. We think it ought to be abandoned."

Although the camp was not abandoned, no more prisoners were assigned there until August, 1863. In that month the gates were reopened, and prisoners came into Douglas like a flood, the first of the thousands being the men of the 2nd Kentucky Cavalry Regiment and their comrades of the Great Raid.

Barracks were in poor repair when the Kentuckians arrived on August 19, and there was no shade except along the sides of buildings. But cool winds usually blew off the lake to relieve the heat, no rain fell to leak through the roofs, and the broken walls provided comfortable summer ventilation. At first, most of the boys considered Douglas an improvement over crowded Camp Morton. Colonel Charles V. De Land, the commandant, quartered the prisoners by their old company organizations, each with a sergeant for spokesman. Through the sergeants the men were informed of rules and regulations, and were told they should make the best of the situation as they would be confined in Camp Douglas until the end of the war. Few prisoners believed this latter assertion, and during the first week or so not many escapes were attempted, even though the broken fencing was tempting. Almost to a man they were certain that exchange was only a matter of days. Why risk being shot while trying to escape, when exchange with transportation provided back to Confederate lines was bound to come soon?

By September, however, hints in letters from friends, rumors and newspaper stories combined to convince them of the hard fact that prisoner exchanges had indeed broken down. They learned that on July 3, Secretary of War Stanton had issued a general order declaring all paroles null and void; a short time later all exchanges were stopped. To the prisoners in Camp Douglas, it became clear that escape was the only way to freedom.

Once the Kentucky boys made up their minds to escape, they overlooked no opportunity to do so. "Prisoners have slid out fence holes in the dark," Colonel De Land reported in October to his superior, Commissary General William Hoffman. "They have passed out as workmen, and in a variety of ways have eluded vigilance of guards." On the rare occasions when prisoners were recaptured, De Land's method of punishment was to make them carry board signs on their backs marked *ESCAPED PRISONER RECAPTURED*. After the Chicago newspapers printed statements by military officials advising the prisoners to accept their fate and not attempt escape, one prisoner wrote a caustic letter to the *Tribune:* "The commanders seem to expect us to stay here. It is not our business to stay. It is theirs to keep us."

Escapes continued through the autumn, so many that one official privately remarked that "the authorities at Washington might as well turn Morgan's men out in a body, as they will all get out singly, anyhow." Exactly how many escaped is not clear from the records, but probably one third of the eighteen hundred Morgan men captured during the raid forced their way to freedom before the war's end.

Those who did not escape adjusted as best they could. They were permitted to receive presents from home—clothing, food, tobacco and a little money. A photographer set up a studio in the enclosure and did a thriving business making ambrotypes and miniatures which the boys mailed to their sweethearts back in Kentucky and Tennessee.

"Don't be at all concerned for my welfare," Henry Stone assured his parents in one of his frequent letters. "You can't hurt a Morgan man." But late in September, after the weather turned bad and sickness broke out among the prisoners, he mentioned that "one or two poor fellows are dying daily."

On September 29, Stone attempted to cheer his mother by writing her that he hoped to be exchanged very soon, though by that time he certainly could not have believed it possible. "Imagine to yourself a long mule-shed, weather-boarded; on the inside bunks put up three deep one above another, also at places whole rooms to themselves with bunks in them; these are our barracks, back of them are cooking-houses with large fireplaces, cooking utensils furnished. We get up at 7 o'clock, have roll call; then comes breakfast, composed generally of warm bread, coffee, butter, with milk to go in our coffee; vegetables we have with beef or bacon, for dinner at 4 p.m. Our mess composed of nine live in a nice little room to ourselves, two cooks per day, one ration-drawer and the other noncooks carry water. During the day we read the news, books, etc. [Stone had been reading Victor Hugo's *Les Misérables*, the war prisoners' favorite classic], play marbles, cards, checkers, chess—in fact all games are played here. We have two sutler's stores, a barbershop and daguerrean room."

By mid-October, however, conditions within Camp Douglas deteriorated to the point where a medical inspector ordered it closed for the third time. Six thousand prisoners were packed into barracks space intended for four thousand. Typhoid, pneumonia and measles were prevalent. Open slit trenches were in filthy condition, facilities for cleanliness deficient, and some barracks were without doors, roofs or flooring. More than a thousand prisoners had not a single blanket, and many had no winter clothing. "The commander would not use U. S. Army clothing sent him," the inspector reported, "because he feared prisoners would escape if so clad . . . some 150 sick men are lying in the barracks who should be in the hospital receiving attention."

The inspector was especially disturbed by Colonel De Land's dungeon which was used for punishments. "A close room about 18 feet square, lighted by one closely barred window about 18 by 8 inches, about 6 feet from the floor, and entered by means of a hatchway in the ceiling. The floor is laid directly on the ground and is constantly damp. A sink occupies one corner, the stench from which is intolerable. In this place at the time I visited it were confined twenty-four prisoners, the offense of all, I believe, being attempts to escape. The place might do for three or four prisoners, but for the number confined there it is inhuman. At my visit I remained but a few seconds and was glad to get out, feeling sick and faint."

In taking note of this report, the Commissary General of Prisoners, William Hoffman, warned Colonel De Land to put his camp in order, and scolded him for not issuing Union clothing to Confederate prisoners. "Cut the skirts of the coats short," he ordered, "and cut off the trimmings and most of the buttons, which will sufficiently distinguish them from Federal soldiers."

It was during this period that ten men of the 2nd Regiment escaped, records indicating that two sergeants from B and I companies and eight privates from four other companies made their way out. On October 9, Henry Stone wrote another reassuring letter to his mother, adding one significant line: "We have everything we want but *freedom*." On a dark night one week later, Stone decided he had seen enough of Camp Douglas. He tied his boots around his neck with a bandanna handkerchief, climbed a twelve-foot fence between two pacing guards, and escaped.

He walked into Chicago, looked up his younger brother who conveniently was studying medicine at Rush College, borrowed some money and clothing, and spent the next day sight-seeing. After dining sumptuously at the Adams House, young Stone boarded an Illinois Central train, rode to Mattoon, transferred to Terre Haute, and was soon visiting with his family at Greencastle.

Not all of Stone's comrades could count on such a run of fortune; for many of them their luck ran out at the fence. "Erection of new fence," Colonel De Land reported late in October, "has made prisoners desperate. Several have been killed, others wounded, yet some escapes could not be prevented. New fence will be completed this week and then escape will be next to impossible. Has been bribery, no doubt, constantly a throng of disloyal men and women here from Kentucky to test the virtue of every soldier they meet with money. Three or four days more will make Camp Douglas so safe and secure that not even money can work a man out."

But De Land reckoned without the resourcefulness of the alligator horses. In November, Lieutenant George Eastin, still posing as Private George Donald, and two genuine privates of D Company made a successful break. And on December 3, De Land was writing Hoffman again: "It is my disagreeable duty to report to you the circumstances of a serious break of the Morgan prisoners in this camp."

This big escape the night of December 2 was a triumph for the boys of the 2nd Kentucky who engineered construction of a tunnel from one of their barracks to the outside of the fence. For fifty feet they burrowed a narrow hole under frozen ground crust, secreting the dirt under floors of barracks and cook-houses. By covering the tunnel entrance with board flooring during the day, they avoided all suspicion, and waited patiently for a night with fog off the lake.

At eight o'clock the night of December 2 the first men started through the cramped tunnel, and an hour and a half later when guards first discovered what was happening, about one hundred prisoners were gone.

Colonel De Land sent mounted troops out for twenty miles on roads leading north and west, and recaptured some of the fugitives. "This is the eighth attempt," he noted despairingly in his report, "to escape from here by tunneling under fences. . . . I have ordered all floors removed from barracks and cook-houses and spaces filled with dirt to the top of the joists. Will undoubtedly increase sickness and mortality, but it will save much trouble and add security."

By a strange coincidence, at the same time the Camp Douglas boys were digging their escape tunnel, General Morgan and his officers also were digging out of their prison in Columbus, Ohio. The news of John Morgan's escape reached his boys only a day or so before they made their big break, and no doubt helped steel their courage to begin the long dragging crawl through that fifty-foot airless passage which led to dangerous freedom.

3

Soon after their confinement in the Cincinnati jail late in July, most of Morgan's officers were transferred to military prisons—Johnson's Island and Camp Chase. But when Ohio's Governor, David Tod, insisted that Morgan and his officers should be treated as civil prisoners accused of crimes against citizens of his state, General Burnside offered no objections. Nor did General-in-Chief Halleck interfere with this unusual decision. Halleck was determined to make an example of "Morgan's guerrillas, this band of robbers and murderers," as he called them. In this climate of vindictiveness created largely by lurid stories in the Northern press, rules of warfare were put aside. Orders went out to transfer all captured Morgan officers to the Ohio state penitentiary at Columbus, where they were to be treated as common criminals.

On the morning of July 30, Morgan and those of his officers still in Cincinnati were brought out into the street before the jail. The

111th Ohio formed a hollow square around them and began the march to the railroad depot. "First came John Morgan dressed in blue jeans pants, and having on a new grass linen blouse, his towering form prominent in the procession. . . . Most of the prisoners were smoking cigars, and we noticed a canteen freely circulating among them on their way down Ninth Street to the depot."

Upon arrival at Columbus, the officers' first experience of convict life was to be stripped and ordered into water barrels where they were scrubbed vigorously with horse brushes. After these rough baths they were seated in barber chairs, and beards and hair were close-shaved. The loudest objector to this indignity was Colonel D. Howard Smith, who was proud of owning the longest beard and suit of hair in the Morgan division. "This morning," he wrote in his diary, "as if our degradation and humiliation was not sufficiently complete, we were marched out of our cells to the public washroom, our persons stripped and washed by a convict, and our heads shorn, and our beards taken entirely off!"

Arriving from Johnson's Island a day or so later, Basil Duke failed to recognize John Morgan when the General spoke to him. "He was so shaven and shorn that his voice alone was recognizable."

The prisoners were assigned to a double-tiered cell block, each man confined to a single room three and one-half feet wide by seven feet long. During the day they were allowed the freedom of a hallway that ran the length of the lower cell block, but each evening before sundown they were locked in their individual compartments.

Accustomed for two years to rigorous outdoor life and continual movement, the young officers found this close confinement—without exercise, sunlight or fresh air—almost unbearable at first. "A long ladder, which had been left in the hall, leaning against the wall, was a perfect treasure," Duke wrote. All day while they were out of their cells they took turns practicing gymnastics upon this ladder, "cooling the fever of their blood with fatigue."

Gradually they turned to more sedentary time killers—chess, marbles, reading, letter writing. Duke and Morgan both wrote poems, Duke composing subtly satirical verses belittling the prison guards and wardens. But most of Morgan's writing was in the form of indignant letters to high officials of the Union, demanding that he and his officers be treated as military rather than civilian prisoners.

During the first few weeks conditions were endurable; then one by one privileges were taken away. Food became abominable, newspapers and other reading matter were forbidden. As a special form of cruelty they were handed empty envelopes from wives or sweethearts, the letters removed.

For the slightest infraction of rules—talking in the dining room, for instance—they were transferred to a dungeon. As punishment for writing a letter critical of the United States government, Major Webber was confined for several days in a cell sealed on the inside with sheet iron which excluded all light and air. In the hundred-degree summer weather, the box was like an oven, and he was forced to subsist on two slices of bread and one cup of water per day. When Webber was released his face was hollowed, his gaunt frame more wasted than ever.

In one of Dick Morgan's confiscated letters he told of how four officers, including his brother Calvin, and Basil Duke, were put in the "black hole" as punishment for talking after lights were out. "They were all released this morning except Basil, who they say is not humble enough yet to let out. I suppose he will remain there until Monday, if not longer. Cally says it is the most terrible place he was ever in and was covered with green mold when he came out."

Major J. B. McCreary, who spent five days in "the hole" for having a knife in his possession, called it "this living death, this Hell on earth." For the entire period he was kept in total darkness, "all the time nauseated by the terrible stench of the night bucket, which, though the only furniture in the cell, had seemingly not been cleaned for weeks. When I was taken out I was scarcely able to stand up, and some of my comrades had to be helped to their cells, with their feet swollen and the blood oozing out of their fingernails and toenails."

As the men at Camp Douglas had done, Morgan and his officers gradually came to the realization that the doom of imprisonment was upon them; there could be no release except by their own efforts and ingenuity. They must force an escape.

They discussed the subject occasionally during October, yet in the face of their barred cells, the heavy brick walls, a courtyard guarded by vicious dogs, and an outer wall twenty-five feet high, escape seemed utterly impossible.

Various plans were advanced, then rejected. At last Tom Hines suggested one, an idea which he said had occurred to him while reading *Les Misérables*. He had noticed that the concrete floor on which the hallway and lower row of cells rested was always dry. As this was the ground floor, the concrete should be moist on warm humid days—unless there was an air chamber below. During a deliberately casual conversation with an elderly deputy warden, Hines learned that there was such an air chamber.

When Hines revealed his findings to a small group of escape plotters and suggested they start digging, Morgan laughingly called him "Count of Monte Cristo." But they decided to try. After securing two or three table knives from the prison dining room, they sharpened these dull instruments as best they could and took turns chipping away at the concrete floor in Tom Hines' cell.

Lookouts were assigned to watch unobtrusively for the approach of guards at the hallway entrance. As noise had to be kept to a minimum, work went very slowly. The concrete was six inches thick, with a six-layered arch of bricks below. The workers carefully concealed all rubbish in their handkerchiefs, later thrusting the large pieces inside Tom Hines' mattress and dropping the dust and grainy mortar into the coal stove in the hallway.

To cover the floor opening in his cell, Hines used a carpetbag in which he kept his change of clothing. Fortunately for the plotters, the prison authorities made no careful inspections during this period, and after the diggers broke through into the four-foot air chamber, a system of rapping signals was devised to warn workers below of the approach of any guards.

When they had forced an opening through the brick sidewall below, they ran into a section of hard-packed earth and grout. What they needed now was a spade, and some of the more observant had noticed one with a broken handle lying rusted beside a coal heap in the outer yard through which they passed three times each day to the dining room. The problem was how to obtain the spade without being observed by the guards.

A plan was worked out in great detail. Captain Jake Bennett would wear his long loose coat, and as they marched out into the yard, several others near him would pretend to engage in a playful scuffle. During this horseplay, Bennett would be shoved to the ground, fall upon the coveted spade, and slip it inside his coat.

The scheme worked to perfection, Bennett sitting stiffly upright through breakfast to prevent the spade showing against the folds of his coat.

With this spade the digging went much faster, but there were other problems to be overcome. As the tunnel's exit would be inside the prison yard, they had yet to devise a method for scaling the twenty-five-foot outer wall. A rope and a hook would be required. In the darkness of their cells, several of the plotters tore their bed coverlids into strips, and Calvin Morgan took on the job of plaiting them into a thirty-foot rope. For a hook, they took the poker from the hall stove, bent it, and attached it to the end of the rope.

Other necessary preparations included the acquisition of a railroad timetable. Knowing that local newspapers usually carried timetables, Morgan asked a guard for one, but as newspapers were still forbidden the man refused. Morgan had to bribe him with fifteen dollars in gold before the newspaper was finally secured. After studying the timetable, Morgan and Hines realized that escape to Canada would be too risky. Trains leaving Columbus at night did not reach the border until long after daylight. Any escape would certainly be discovered at dawn, and the alarm would be out to all border points before the fugitives could cross. They would have to go south for Kentucky.

After long discussions it was decided that no more than six men should attempt to make the breakout with Morgan. Any more than that might jeopardize all, and all agreed that the important objective was to get John Morgan back through the Confederate lines to re-organize what was left of his old command and recruit new regiments. The six selected to try for escape with Morgan were Tom Hines, Ralph Sheldon, Sam Taylor, L. D. Hockersmith, Jacob Bennett, and J. S. Magee. They would separate, Hines accompanying Morgan on the train to Cincinnati, the others moving in different directions.

As escape time would be after dark when each man would be locked in a separate cell, it was necessary to prepare openings in the floors of the other six compartments. Rather than risk discovery of any one of these holes, they were cut from underneath, leaving a thin crust of cement which could be knocked out with a sharp kick of a boot heel.

On November 24 the tunnel was completed. Now they would wait for suitable weather. For two reasons they wanted a rainy night; first, to deepen the darkness; second, to keep the watchdogs in the prison yard in their kennels. On the twenty-sixth they learned from guards' gossip that a new military commander had been appointed in Columbus. Suspecting this change of authorities might bring on a thorough inspection of the prison, Morgan decided they would wait only one more day. At sunset of the twenty-seventh the sky was clear, but before midnight a drizzling rain was falling.

With the exception of John Morgan, the seven who were to escape were confined to the lower tier. Just before lock-up time, Morgan exchanged cells with his brother, Dick, on the lower level. They were both about the same size and bore a close resemblance, but to make certain the substitution went unnoticed, each entered the other's cell and lay down immediately, face to the wall. (Basil Duke also was confined to the upper tier and refused to jeopardize the others' chances by a similar exchange of cells.)

Ten minutes past midnight was selected as deadline for escape, so that Morgan and Hines would have time to board the one o'clock train south. From past observation they knew that shortly before midnight a guard usually made a routine check with a lantern, holding it up to each cell door and peering in at the sleepers. This night guard, being a furtive sort, wore India rubber soles and sometimes made unscheduled appearances. To foil him, they sprinkled small particles of coal over the hall floor.

Between eleven and twelve they heard him making his rounds, the coal crunching under his rubber soles. As soon as the guard was gone, Sam Taylor slipped out of his bunk and made a dummy from his pillow and extra clothing. Then he broke out his crust of concrete, dropped down, and signaled Hines and the others to join him in the air chamber. A few seconds later they were into the tunnel.

The first man up, Captain Hockersmith, used a razor to cut away the sod and they crawled out into the courtyard, the welcome rain wetting their faces. Not a dog was to be seen. Armed only with Hockersmith's razor and their digging knives, they crossed the dark

yard, determined to fight if discovered. They climbed a low wall
and faced the high outer one.

Without hesitation the hook was tossed up, clanking dully against
the brick coping, catching firmly. They held their breaths, listening.
They knew that guards walked the wall by day but not by night,
yet they were certain guards were somewhere near.

Sam Taylor swung up first, crouching at the top, looking down
at the glow of a fire a few yards away—guards gathered around it
trying to keep dry. Hines, Morgan and the others pulled up one by
one. They were on a wing wall and had to move a short way along
a catwalk to the outer bulwark. Here in the darkness Morgan's
hands touched a cord. He felt it gingerly, guessed its purpose: a bell
alarm. While two men held opposite sides of the cord, he cut it with
his knife.

They had no gloves, and as they slid down to their first taste of
freedom the rope burned their hands. Sounds carried far in the driz-
zle. They could hear the guards talking around the fire sixty yards
away. In whispers they wished each other luck, and then moved off
into the wet blackness of the autumn night.

Half an hour later Hines and Morgan reached the railroad depot,
Morgan keeping to the shadows of the platform while Hines boldly
entered the waiting room and purchased two tickets for Cincinnati.
When they boarded the passenger cars no one paid them any attention; they were both dressed in the plain civilian clothing worn in
prison. They took separate seats, Morgan finding himself beside a
Federal major in full uniform.

The train was only ten minutes late when it pulled out of Columbus. As the cars rattled past the penitentiary walls, the Federal major
remarked brightly: "Over there is the prison where they put the
Rebel, General Morgan, for safekeeping." Morgan smiled and replied: "I hope they'll always keep him as safe as he is now."

At Dayton the train was delayed almost an hour by track troubles, and long before they reached Cincinnati, Morgan and Hines
anxiously watched the sky turning gray. The train was due in at
seven; they could not make it now before eight o'clock. During that
intervening hour the empty cells surely would be discovered, and
Cincinnati police and military authorities would probably be waiting at the station.

When he noticed the first houses outside Cincinnati, Morgan rose from his seat, motioned Hines to follow him, and they made their way back to the last car. Morgan pulled the bell cord signaling the engineer to stop, then both men stepped out on the rear platform, each turning one of the hand brakes. While the train was slackening speed, wheels shrieking against rails, they leaped off. The train went shuddering on down the track for a hundred yards, its bell clanging furiously. With only a brief glance in its direction, Morgan started to move off after Hines. Two Federal soldiers rose up suddenly from a pile of lumber. "What in hell are you jumping off the train for?" one demanded suspiciously.

"What in the devil is the use of a man going on to town when he lives out here?" Morgan countered quickly. "Besides, what matter is it to you?"

"Oh, nothing," said the soldier, sitting back on the lumber.

In a few minutes they found the river, which had defied all their efforts to cross it back in July. They saw a small boy paddling a skiff near the bank. Morgan called to the boy, offering him two dollars to row them across.

Before noon they were with friends in Newport, Kentucky.

As the day ended, news of John Morgan's escape was spreading across both North and South. In Canada, a pro-Southern Irishman named Joseph H. Morgan, learning of the escape, deliberately walked into a Windsor hotel and registered as "J. H. Morgan." In a short time telegraphers were relaying this tidbit of information from city to city, effectively throwing Federal searchers off Morgan's trail for at least twenty-four hours.

Political forces in the North immediately seized upon the escape as a dark and mysterious plot of the Copperheads, charging conspiracy and bribery. The tunnel was a blind, it was claimed, the prisoners had been deliberately turned loose. In answer to these wild accusations, four separate investigations were made by responsible authorities, but no real evidence was ever discovered to indicate that Morgan's men received direct aid from outside accomplices. The only bribe on record was the fifteen dollars Morgan paid a guard for the Columbus newspaper with its railroad timetable.

As Governor Tod of Ohio admitted, the real fault was "a failure to examine and inspect the cells. The civil authorities connected with the prison insist that this was the duty of the military authorities, and the military authorities claim that it was the duty of the warden and his assistants."

The clamor would go on for months, even years, but "Morgan the Raider" was free again, bound for the Confederacy to form a new command.

13

The Survivors

I

Late on sunday afternoon of July 19, 1863, after Captains John Cooper and N. M. Lea successfully forded most of F and L companies of the 2nd Kentucky across the Ohio near Belleville, West Virginia, they with other remnants of Morgan's raiders disappeared into the forests of the Little Kanawha Valley. As ranking colonel over Lawrence Grigsby, Adam Johnson assumed command of these 330 survivors, pushing them south at a rapid pace.

Not wishing to show themselves until they were deep into the mountains, they avoided main roads and towns. Subsistence was a real problem, but it was solved by the slaughter of a few "captured" steers. "From the crossing of the Ohio to our entrance into Greenbriar County," wrote Adjutant S. P. Cunningham, "our men lived on beef alone, without salt and no bread."

After five days and nights of hard marching they were across the mountains and safe from pursuit. "When we first came in sight of fields of wheat and green, waving corn," Colonel Johnson recorded, "I am sure each one of us felt as much pleasure as Moses of old when he first viewed the Promised Land."

As soon as authorities in Richmond learned that Johnson and Grigsby had salvaged more than three hundred of Morgan's men from the disaster in Ohio, the two colonels were invited to military headquarters for consultation as to what should be done with the remnants of a command which was scattered from Virginia through Kentucky, Tennessee and Georgia.

Colonel Grigsby's suggestion was to take the dismounted men—and there were now many of them—dismount the others, and form a new infantry regiment. Johnson was opposed to this course of action, and so were other Kentucky military leaders, including General Buckner, who strongly recommended forming a new cavalry regiment with Johnson as commander. Early in August it was agreed that this would be done, and Morristown, Tennessee, was selected as rendezvous camp.

Morristown was an excellent choice, being isolated in a fertile valley easily defended, and geographically most accessible to all the known surviving units of Morgan's division. The area had seen little devastation from war; a few remounts were available; food, forage, wood and water were plentiful.

Official notices announcing the rendezvous camp and ordering all men belonging to Morgan's command to report to Morristown were published in newspapers throughout the mid-South. The Confederate War Department also notified all officers in the army to release and transfer any Morgan men who might have drifted into their commands after the raid.

Within ten days Johnson had almost five hundred troopers assembled for duty. Then, late in August, about three hundred men who had been left behind at the beginning of the raid—because of illness or other reasons—were marched up from Gadsen, Alabama, where they had been stationed since July. Captain Tom Quirk came up with this group, his wounded arm still in a sling, but he eagerly claimed the handful of survivors from his old scouting company.

Another smaller group, attracting considerable attention when they rode in, were the boys from Company D who had been led to safety by Lieutenant Josiah Gathright following their narrow escape at Twelve Mile Island. After leaving the Ohio with eight mounted and armed men, and thirty-four dismounted and without arms, Gathright had moved back into the hills south of the river. Appointing non-coms, he placed four of his mounted men in advance and the remaining four in the rear and began a series of night marches across Kentucky. By the time Gathright's little army reached Taylorsville they were all mounted, but most of them were still without arms when they crossed the Clinch River and entered the Confederate lines near Knoxville.

Enough men of the old 2nd had reported for duty in early September to form a respectable battalion. Also by that time they had become well acquainted with their new commander, Adam Johnson. Johnson was a firm but mild-mannered man, not yet thirty, one of the many Kentuckians who had gone out to Texas before the war.

One of Johnson's first official acts, which won him the warm support of the impoverished boys of the 2nd, was to arrange for them to be paid. Many of them had received no money for fourteen months, and when Johnson performed this miracle for them even the most skeptical of the alligator horses was willing to accept him as a first-rate colonel.

Johnson also won their loyalty by placing all the 2nd Regiment men in the same battalion, under Captain J. D. Kirkpatrick. It was soon evident, however, that Johnson was a disciplinarian, more like Duke than Morgan. He had orders read before each group of new arrivals, requiring them to remain in camp unless they had official permission to leave, and drills were held each day.

By mid-September Johnson had seven hundred men mounted, and about five hundred more waiting for horses. No doubt he would have had the others in saddles within another month, but time had run out.

Rosecrans was beginning to move around Chattanooga in his long-expected offensive against Bragg, and orders came for Johnson to march his cavalry south to Dalton, Georgia. "We rode our horses day and night," wrote Private Carl Sager, "arriving at Dalton about the 15th of September."

This patched-up, poorly equipped regiment of Johnson's was in sharp contrast to the plumed and gaily caparisoned horsemen of Morgan's old command. Many used blankets for saddles, and some had stripped bark from pawpaw trees to make crude bridles and stirrups. When they rode through Dalton, the 2nd Regiment troopers were so ashamed of their unmilitary appearance they replied to questions as to what regiment they were by saying "East Tennessee cavalry."

General Bragg was so unimpressed by their tatterdemalion appearance he wanted to dismount the lot of them and make them infantrymen. But Nathan B. Forrest would not hear of it. In a hasty reorganization to save the Morgan cavalry, Johnson agreed to keep only the dismounted men, while Forrest took over the mounted companies. For the impending battle, Captain Kirkpatrick's battalion (survivors of the 2nd Kentucky) was put under command of one of John Morgan's old cronies, Lieutenant Colonel Robert M. Martin, who with Major Dick McCann had saved Morgan from capture back in the spring at McMinnville by dashing down upon the 7th Pennsylvania and taking a bullet in the lungs. Fully recovered, the reckless Martin was eager to prove to Bragg just how good Morgan's men really were.

On the evening of September 18, Forrest moved up from Dalton toward Chickamauga Creek, Martin's cavalry camping near Reed's Bridge. The night was clear and cool, katydids piping a farewell to summer. At dawn, wisps of fog lent a ghostly quality to the quiet forests and fields; dew was so thick on the pastures it looked like frost.

Martin's boys were ordered to mount up, and as they rode past a fork in the road they were surprised to see General Forrest sitting a horse there. At a sudden command they pulled to a halt, and Forrest gave them a short rousing talk. "You're Morgan men," he said. "Braver men never went to battle. Remember, boys, your commander is now in a felon's cell. Let 'Morgan' be your battle cry and give the Yankees hell!" In an added gesture of confidence, Forrest let Martin's battalions take the advance.

And so it was that the survivors of Morgan's 2nd Regiment fired the first guns of Chickamauga, at Reed's Bridge over the creek. Dismounting, they crossed the bridge and drove the enemy cavalry out of fortified positions, pursuing them into a tangled undergrowth of pine. Breaking out of the forest, they saw the blue-coated enemy forming across an open field, and those few who had been at Shiloh remembered the day there when they made their first mounted charge. This day they fought on foot, advancing and retreating, advancing and retreating, until the enemy fell back into another patch of woods.

All around them they could hear the rumbling of caissons, the shouts of unseen men. By midday the firing was furious, artillery in the distance, small arms fire close at hand. "How wickedly the bullets sound," wrote Will Dyer, "as they come in with their 'spat' and now and then strike some unfortunate with a thud that sounds horrible in the extreme, and now and then a shell comes along with its terrible scream, *Johnnie whar is ye*, and you feel like you want to be home with mother."

Late in the afternoon, with opposing forces scattered and disengaged along much of the ill-defined line of battle, the noise lessened. By dusk all was silent except for an occasional artillery burst. Smoke and dust drifted over the Chickamauga bottoms.

The night was ominously quiet. Horse-holders brought up the mounts and the men camped in combat readiness, lying on dry leaves and brush, waiting for orders. No one seemed to know how the battle was going, but there were rumors that General James Longstreet had brought up two fresh brigades to throw against Old Rosy Rosecrans.

The second day, September 20, dawned clear, but there was no attack from the Yankees. The sun rose, but there was no sound of battle. It was midmorning when Martin received orders to move up in support of General John C. Breckinridge's division. At eleven o'clock the battle was joined. "The roar of hundreds of cannon," said Lieutenant Josiah Gathright, "was something awful, and the rattle of tens and thousands of small arms swelled through the woods into an uproar almost as deafening as that of the artillery."

All afternoon the sun burned like midsummer. Dust swirled everywhere, mixing with battle smoke, creating tortuous thirsts. But bloodstained Chickamauga Creek was far behind them now, and the rapidity with which lines were moving westward indicated victory. It was more than a victory, they learned that evening. Rosecrans' army was in full retreat. Only one Union general had stood firm, General George Thomas, who that day earned the name "Rock of Chickamauga."

Next day, Captain Kirkpatrick's battalion rode with Forrest over Missionary Ridge into the valley before Chattanooga. After a few light skirmishes with scattered Union cavalry, they captured some frightened infantrymen. The boys of the 2nd later claimed that in this engagement they fired the *last* shots of the battle of Chickamauga, as they had fired the first at Reed's Bridge.

Following a reconnoitering scout up Lookout Mountain, Forrest ordered his cavalry formed to celebrate the victory. As he came down the front of Kirkpatrick's battalion, he pulled his horse up and saluted the troopers. "Any man who says that Morgan's men are not good soldiers and fine fighters," he roared, "tells a damn lie!"

The boys cheered themselves hoarse at that; they knew Bedford Forrest was making a reply to General Bragg's recent disparagement of their abilities.

Apparently every man in the Army of Tennessee except Braxton Bragg knew the Confederates had won a great victory. Certainly Rosecrans knew he had suffered a defeat. "The Army is simply a mob," wrote one of his officers that evening. "There appears to be neither organization or discipline. The various commands are mixed up in what seems to be inextricable confusion. Were a division of the enemy to pounce down upon us between this and morning, I fear the Army of the Cumberland would be blotted out."

But no Confederate division pounced upon the beaten Yankees. Polk, Breckinridge, Longstreet, Buckner, Hood, Wheeler, Forrest— all the fighting generals waited for an order to follow up Rosecrans' disastrous retreat and sweep the Union Army out of Tennessee. But as usual Bragg vacillated. He wrote out an order for pursuit, then quickly countermanded it. The Confederates formed a siege line on Missionary Ridge facing Chattanooga, and again waited for the enemy to take the initiative.

2

As soon as the two opposing armies settled into positions, Bragg again began talking of dismounting the cavalry—not only Morgan's men but many other regiments in need of replacement mounts. When Forrest learned that Adam Johnson had been ordered to march his dismounted men into eastern Tennessee, the General advised Johnson to take Kirkpatrick's mounted battalion along with him "to get them as far as possible from the Old Man's clutches."

This ruse worked until the Kentuckians were ordered back to Missionary Ridge in November—when it became obvious that the Federals were preparing for a second great battle. In a desperate effort to shore up his infantry positions, Bragg dismounted most of Johnson's men.

The Federals meanwhile were preparing to throw a powerful army against Bragg. General Grant, who had been named commander of all Union forces in the West, arrived in Chattanooga to take personal command. From Mississippi, Sherman bought his crack divisions; from Virginia, General Joe Hooker brought two corps by rail and boat to give Grant heavy numerical strength over the Confederates.

On November 23, the Union armies launched a massive assault against Missionary Ridge. Although the Confederates held the high ground, they were outmanned and outgunned. They had been existing on tough beef and rancid bacon for weeks, and morale was low, especially among the dismounted cavalrymen.

The first sight of the immense army in blue—superbly equipped, well-fed, nattily uniformed—was startling, almost frightening, even to the most hard-bitten veterans on Missionary Ridge. One of Adam Johnson's troopers, Will Dyer, described Sherman's divisions as they appeared to him on the morning of November 25, the decisive day of the battle. "We who had the fortune, or misfortune, to be on top of Missionary Ridge on the forenoon of November 25, 1863, witnessed one of the grandest military pageants ever seen. . . . From early morning till Sherman's lines were formed, brigades, divisions and corps of his troops were moving across the valley and over the opposite hills in long blue lines with arms glistening in the sunshine, halting here and there till there was one long blue line in plain view in the order of a dress parade. Everything was calm and peaceful and although we knew that this line would soon be hurled at us with death dealing force we could not withhold exclamations of admiration."

The dismounted troopers of the 2nd Kentucky might have read the future there on that bright autumn morning. They were witnessing power the South could no longer resist; they were watching the beginning of Sherman's dream, the Great March to the Sea which would end the war in the West.

Before that day was over, Bragg's veterans were reeling in defeat back down the east slopes of Missionary Ridge toward Chickamauga Creek, where they had won their hollow victory only a few weeks earlier. The next day the retreat became a stampede back to the camps at Dalton. Dogged rear-guard action and rainy weather saved the Confederates from total disaster, but it was the end for Braxton Bragg. Richmond headquarters at last had had enough of his retreats, and named Joseph E. Johnston commander of the Army of Tennessee.

3

Receiving fresh assurances from Richmond that he was to continue the reorganization of Morgan's men, Colonel Adam Johnson now established headquarters in Decatur, Georgia, and set out in earnest to remount his veterans of Chickamauga and Missionary Ridge.

In mid-December a patrol of mounted men under Lieutenant Josiah Gathright, who had been on picket duty above Dalton, was ordered to Decatur by way of eastern North Carolina. Johnson had hopes that Gathright might collect a few horses in the isolated mountain communities and bring them in to the Decatur camp.

While en route on this dog-leg march, Lieutenant Gathright halted on a raw December day in Franklin, North Carolina. Noticing a cobbler's sign above one of the wings of the town's single hotel, Gathright decided to stop long enough to have a pair of boots mended.

He was waiting comfortably in the warmth of the little shop when a stranger entered and announced excitedly: "General Morgan is in the hotel!"

"What General Morgan?" asked Gathright.

"Why, General John Morgan, the great cavalryman."

Gathright was amused. He was certain that Morgan was in an Ohio prison. Suspecting that somebody was masquerading as the General, the young Lieutenant decided to unmask the fraud.

"Please take me to him," he said, and followed the man through a side door into the hotel and on to an inner parlor. Gathright was astounded at what he saw. "Imagine my surprise," he wrote afterward, "when I stepped into the parlor and found myself in the presence of the real thing—our general. He was surrounded by a bevy of ladies, and was looking as 'chipper' and gay as though he had never been in a penitentiary."

Morgan was delighted to see Gathright. He inquired about Captain William Davis and Lieutenant Eastin, and was pleased to hear how Gathright had escaped with forty-two men from Twelve Mile Island. He also wanted to know the fate of other survivors of his regiments, and declared that he would come to Adam Johnson's camp at Decatur as soon as he had visited with his wife in Columbia, South Carolina.

The only thing Morgan seemed to be distressed about was the fate of Captain Tom Hines, who had allowed himself to be captured in Tennessee in order that Morgan might escape and continue southward. (Unknown to Morgan, Hines had already escaped again, and was that day making his way toward Confederate headquarters at Dalton.)

4

John Morgan was in Columbia with his wife for Christmas, learning for the first time that Martha had lost an expected child in pregnancy—as a result of her recent flight from Tennessee to South Carolina. He stayed with her during the holidays, trying to console her. By the year's end he had changed his mind about going directly to Johnson's camp at Decatur; instead he would go first to the seat of power in Richmond.

On January 7, 1864, he and Martha made a triumphal entry into the capital of the Confederacy. Although the high command did not receive him warmly—his old enemy, the deposed Bragg, was now there acting as a special military adviser to President Davis—the Richmond populace went wild with enthusiasm. Women asked for locks of his hair, editors wanted the exclusive story of his escape, soldiers begged for his autograph, presents were showered upon him, and poems written in his honor.

A special reception was held in the city hall with such notables on hand as Provisional-Governor Hawes of Kentucky, and Generals Jeb Stuart and A. P. Hill. St. Leger Grenfell came with Stuart, and Morgan persuaded the Englishman to remain in Richmond as a special agent to intercede for him with the War Department. Lieutenant Colonel Robert A. Alston, who had just been exchanged, also was there, and Morgan immediately promised him a post in his yet unformed command.*

After the band played the "Marseillaise," Morgan was called upon for a speech, the *Richmond Enquirer* reporting it as follows: "Fellow citizens, I thank you for this reception and hope that my future career will prove that I am not unworthy of the honor you have done me. Not being accustomed to public speaking, I will give way to others who are."

During most of January he remained in Richmond seeking authorization for a new command, struggling with the military bureaucracy and attempting to thaw the coldness of the few powerful men who opposed him.

There was one delightful surprise—Tom Hines appeared suddenly one day, none the worse for his adventures after being captured and separated from Morgan in Tennessee. Hines' successes in making escapes had led him to devise a mysterious plan for freeing the Morgan prisoners in the North, and he was in Richmond to secure authority for this dangerous venture.

Neither Morgan nor Hines overlooked calling upon anyone who might help them. "General Morgan came to my office during the week," General Josiah Gorgas, the Confederate chief of ordnance noted in his diary of January 17. "His hair has not quite recovered from the cropping it received in the Ohio penitentiary. Captain Hines, one of his escaped comrades, was with him, a modest young-looking man of active build. These men will be heroes of history."

On the twenty-seventh, Morgan wrote Secretary of War James Seddon, requesting permission to assemble a command in southwestern Virginia and proposing an invasion of Kentucky to capture horses. "The Yankee government," he said, "has now in Kentucky some 15,000 cavalry horses, sent to recruit their condition in the comfortable homesteads and on the rich grass of that country." He believed that a sudden raid into Kentucky would also draw off a portion of "the Yankee army from J. E. Johnston and Longstreet."

---

* Alston secured his exchange by proving to Federal authorities that he had been captured by soldiers he had paroled a few hours earlier, and an exception to the new policy of allowing no more exchanges was made in his case.

But in the face of threats by Bragg to order Morgan court-martialed for crossing the Ohio River, the War Department would promise him nothing. He was advised that he belonged to the Army of Tennessee and therefore should report directly to General Johnston for orders.

At last he departed Richmond in disgust, leaving Grenfell behind to serve as his agent, and taking Colonel Alston to Georgia as his temporary adjutant. He would have liked Hines to go with him also, but the mysterious captain had secured the backing he needed for his plan to free war prisoners and was already assigned to duty in the Signal Bureau, learning how to send and read cipher.

Early in February, Morgan and Alston arrived at Decatur, finding conditions in the Georgia camps much worse than they had expected. They were shocked at the lack of supplies, the ragged uniforms, the shortages of rations and arms.

Their first act was to publish and circulate a proclamation:

> SOLDIERS: I am once more among you, after a long and painful imprisonment. I am anxious to be again in the field. I therefore call on all the soldiers of my command to assemble at once at the rendezvous which has been established at this place. . . . Come at once, and come cheerfully, for I want no man in my command who has to be sent to his duty by a provost-marshal. The work before us will be arduous, and will require brave hearts and willing hands. Let no man falter or delay, for no time is to be lost. Every one must bring his horse and gun who can.

> JOHN H. MORGAN
> Brigadier General Provisional Army Confederate States

Official:
R. A. Alston,
Lieutenant Colonel and Acting A.A. General.

Confronted by shortages of everything, Morgan's determined survivors established their own quartermaster department. From their ranks, tailors, blacksmiths and saddlemakers were organized to reoutfit the command, the Texans turning out a number of excellent Mexican saddletrees, preferred by all Morgan troopers.

As the winter wore away, several additional veterans drifted in from Kentucky, men who had escaped and had been hiding out in the hills. Lieutenant Colonel James Bowles, nominal commander of the old 2nd Kentucky (but who had been unable to ride on the Great Raid) reported for duty and was placed in charge of one of the camps.

When Morgan returned to Richmond early in the spring, he won at last his long battle with the military bureaucrats. He was promised the Department of Southwestern Virginia, and not only was he given his mounted men at Decatur, but the dismounted men at Dalton also were ordered transferred to him.

While in Richmond, Morgan was surprised to meet Colonel D. Howard Smith, commander of the 5th Kentucky, who had been suddenly exchanged. After falling seriously ill in the Columbus penitentiary, Smith had been transferred to Johnson's Island, and then through the intercession of Union Kentuckians who had been his lifelong friends, he was granted a special exchange. Although Smith was still ailing, he gladly accepted Morgan's invitation to join the new command at Abingdon, Virginia, as soon as he was fully recovered.

In April, Adam Johnson received orders to march all the Morgan men from Decatur to Virginia. It was a leisurely springtime ride up through the hills of the Carolinas, and the knowledge that at last they were to be trooping together again under the old Morgan banner brought a buoyancy of hope to these veterans who had endured so long and uncertain a winter. They rode into Wytheville, Virginia, on a bright pleasant May day. "The birds were chirping in the trees as we marched into the fair grounds," said John Fields, "and everything indicated that spring had opened. We were thinly clad and had only one thin blanket, and no tent or protection from the weather; and when we awakened next morning we were all covered with snow."

But the snow melted quickly in the warm sunshine, and they went to work willingly reshoeing horses and preparing defenses for the lead mines at Wytheville and the saltworks at Saltville. With regrets the boys now said farewell to Colonel Adam Johnson, who had held them together for eight of their most difficult months of the war. Johnson had been ordered on a special recruiting mission to his old home territory in occupied western Kentucky.

In addition to the survivors brought up from Georgia, Morgan received a full-strength regiment, the 4th Kentucky Cavalry, under Colonel Henry Giltner. To form the nucleus of a brigade, he divided his old command into two battalions under Captains Jacob Cassell and J. D. Kirkpatrick, with Lieutenant Colonel Alston acting as regimental commander.

For Morgan's men, prospects seemed much brighter in that late spring of 1864. Some of Tom Quirk's scouts went into Kentucky to gather information concerning concentrations of cavalry mounts and dispositions of enemy forces. By May, Morgan's brigade had increased to two thousand men—a third of them dismounted—and there was open talk of a raid into the Bluegrass.

5

Late in that month, John Morgan quietly began concentrating his brigade near Wytheville, and on the thirty-first he dispatched a message to Richmond informing the War Department that he was starting a raid into Kentucky. By the time Confederate Army headquarters learned of his plans, his columns were through Pound Gap into the Cumberlands.

For the invasion—which would be known as Morgan's last Kentucky Raid—he had organized his force into three regiments. Colonel D. Howard Smith replaced Alston as commander of the original Morgan men, who were divided into three battalions. The old 2nd Kentucky, now known as the 2nd Battalion, was commanded by Major Jacob Cassell; the 1st Battalion was under Lieutenant Colonel James Bowles, and the 3rd under Major J. D. Kirkpatrick. The other two regiments were Colonel Giltner's 4th Kentucky and a dismounted group led by Lieutenant Colonel Robert M. Martin, with Alston second in command.

Strength of Cassell's 2nd Battalion was about two hundred, including such veterans as Tom Quirk, George Ellsworth and John B. Castleman. For seven days they marched over rocky roads, the men on foot struggling vainly to keep up with the horsemen as they climbed mountains, followed meandering valleys and waded innumerable streams. According to John Castleman there was "little for man to eat and nothing for horse."

At dawn of June 8, they sighted the town of Mount Sterling. For many of them it was their first view of Bluegrass country in almost a year, and as the column came to a halt the men broke into cheers.

Morgan ordered Colonel Smith to take his battalions forward, Giltner's regiment to hold in reserve. In a few minutes, as the sun brightened the landscape, the enemy's tent camp became plainly visible. The morning was summery, with lazy sounds—stamping horses, twittering birds, crowing roosters. Smith ordered his men into mounted skirmish lines, then sent Cassell and Bowles forward in a charge.

It was hardly a fight, three hundred Federals surrendering in a matter of minutes. Giltner's regiment came in at a canter, the men going out of control of their officers as soon as they were in to the streets. Not a store escaped looting, and some private houses were entered in search of food, clothing and valuables.

The worst of these discreditable acts, insofar as Morgan's later career and the reputation of his command were concerned, was the robbery of the Mount Sterling bank. Morgan apparently first learned of the robbery early in the afternoon when a delegation of citizens called upon him and asked that the stolen money be returned; they pointed out that the deposits belonged to the people of the town, many of them being Confederate sympathizers. They showed Morgan a written order signed by his adjutant, Captain Charles Withers, demanding delivery of the money under penalty of setting fire to every house in Mount Sterling.

According to Captain Withers, who was present, Morgan showed intense anger, turned upon him and demanded: "What does this mean?" Withers was dismayed by the accusation. He examined the paper and swore that it was neither his handwriting nor signature. One of the bankers then volunteered the information that the demand had been presented to him by a man with fair hair and beard who spoke with a German accent. The description fitted only one man in the command, Surgeon R. R. Goode.

Morgan immediately ordered Goode brought to him, but the surgeon was missing. Goode would never return, but his disappearance did not end the affair of the Mount Sterling bank robbery. It would plague Morgan to the last day of his life.

About four o'clock that afternoon as Morgan was preparing to start D. Howard Smith's regiment out on the road to Lexington, Colonel Smith approached him and suggested that the march be delayed until a complete investigation was made of the bank robbery. "I have just heard of it," Morgan replied. "I have no time to attend to it now, but will." He felt that it was more important to continue the raid, rather than risk a fatal delay by a lengthy investigation, and he ordered Smith to lead his battalions out toward Lexington.

Giltner's troopers and Martin's dismounted regiment were left behind to complete destruction of Federal stores and search for horses to remount Martin's regiment. But before dawn the bivouac camp at Mount Sterling was surprised by a slashing attack from General Stephen Burbridge's command. Colonel John Mason Brown's 45th Kentucky Union Infantry overran Martin's pickets, killed or captured most of them, and was into the Confederates' bivouac area before the men could crawl out of their blankets.

Under a fog cover Giltner and Martin made a hasty withdrawal through Mount Sterling. A courier racing westward toward Lexington overtook Smith's regiment near Winchester, and Morgan turned back. About ten miles out of Mount Sterling, he met Giltner and Martin. They had lost about two hundred and fifty men, but Burbridge's horses were too exhauted to pursue; the Federal cavalry had been under forced march for twenty-four hours in an effort to overtake the raiders.

After a brief consultation with his colonels, Morgan gave the order to march on to Lexington. From reports of friendly informers, he knew that five thousand of the best Bluegrass saddle horses were waiting there for the taking; he was also eager to see Hopemont again.

It was two o'clock in the morning when the 2nd Battalion, with Quirk's scouts in advance, walked their horses slowly into the darkened outskirts of Lexington. "I volunteered to test the enemy by going into Lexington under a flag of truce," John Castleman later recorded. For escorts he chose his brother, Humphrey, and sixteen-year-old Key Morgan, the General's youngest brother. They went in on Winchester Street, calling out repeatedly, "Bearer of flag of truce," but the Federal garrison evidently felt so secure that no pickets had been posted around the town. At Limestone Street a window raised suddenly and a woman's voice asked if they were Morgan's cavalry. When Castleman replied that they were, she said she was Mrs. John George. Her husband was with the raiders. She warned the flag-bearers to be careful, that Captain Hawes' Union battery was posted a short distance down the street.

"I advised the boys to pull their horses well up on the sidewalk," Castleman said, "and we halted and announced our mission with unusual vehemence." A few minutes later Captain Hawes himself approached with a lantern, wanting to know the purpose of the truce party. "To demand the surrender of Lexington," Castleman replied. After some delay, Hawes declined to surrender, and the flag-bearers turned back.

Confident that Lexington was not heavily garrisoned, Morgan now ordered Castleman to take a number of the Lexington boys and scatter through the town, setting fire to the railroad depot and military warehouses. While the Federals were distracted by these blazes springing up on all sides, Morgan led his column into Lexington, captured Hawes' battery, and seized a number of outposts.

As day was breaking, Tom Quirk led a detachment from the 2nd Battalion out to Ashland, raiding John Clay's stables and capturing several Thoroughbreds, including Skedaddle, one of the great racers of the times. Before noon they had more horses than they could handle, and more were being brought in from Federal stables every hour. "My entire command," Morgan noted in his report, "was then elegantly mounted and the greater portion clothed and shod."

After paying a visit to Hopemont (it was the last time he would see his ancestral home) Morgan ordered companies formed for marching. The best of the surplus animals were gathered into a horse herd to be driven at the rear of the column, and by midafternoon they were riding out of Lexington.

Before daylight of the eleventh, they were approaching Cynthiana, the boys of the old 2nd recalling their bitter fight at the covered bridge back in July, 1862. On this day it was much easier. Bowles and Kirkpatrick led the attack, dismounting and charging through a wheatfield, while Cassell was galloping the 2nd Battalion around to the right to outflank the small garrison. In a sharp little fight in the downtown streets, a fire broke out in a livery stable, spreading through several business buildings before Morgan's men and the townspeople could stop it.

After the excitement was over, Morgan and his officers expressed their regrets for the fire, and then would have resumed march had they not learned of heavy infantry reinforcements approaching Cynthiana. Morgan quickly divided his regiments, Giltner meeting the enemy in dismounted skirmish formation while Smith circled to the rear. In a mounted charge, "yelling the infernal Rebel yell," Smith's troopers stampeded the rear of the Federal line, and truce flags went up.

Commander of these surrendered troops was General Edward Hobson, who had pursued Morgan's raiders across Ohio in July, 1863. Here was a prize indeed! Morgan's first thought was that perhaps a parole exchange might be arranged for some of his officers in Northern prisons. Hobson, however, could sign no valid parole, nor could any of the thirteen hundred ninety-day volunteers who had surrendered. Federal War Department regulations forbade further acceptance of paroles, with penalty of court-martial for any Union officer or soldier who did so.

On that late Saturday afternoon of June 11, General Morgan thus found himself burdened with more than a thousand prisoners. If he released them, they would quickly return to fight him; if he held them, they must be marched back to Virginia.

The question now before Morgan and his staff was whether or not to leave Cynthiana at once, with or without the prisoners. Evidently there was sharp division of opinion. Two enlisted men, Sergeant G. D. Ewing and Private George Mosgrove recorded that there was a long wrangling officers' conference during the evening. Morgan was in favor of staying until morning. He still hoped to work out some sort of special exchange arrangement with the captured General, Hobson. He also felt that his men and horses needed rest. But Colonel Giltner wanted to march without delay. He was certain that General Burbridge, outrun at Mount Sterling, was long overdue.

As it turned out, Giltner was justified in his fears of an attack from Burbridge. And if Morgan had been more superstitious, he should have realized that the next day was a Sunday—the day of the week on which everything important happened to him.

Before sunrise, General Burbridge struck with a force twice as strong as Morgan's. Four cavalry regiments, the 9th and 17th Michigan, and the 7th and 12th Ohio came in out of the gray light, overrunning the pickets, hoofs drumming, their long skirmish line crescent-shaped. Giltner's men were preparing breakfasts in a field beside the town, and some were trapped before they could reach their horses. As soon as he heard the firing, Colonel Smith sent Bowles and Kirkpatrick forward, but Bowles' battalion was hit hard, his troopers falling back to the Licking River. The covered bridge jammed with panic-stricken horses, their riders leaping off and swimming the stream.

As best he could, Smith re-formed his lines in the street, but he soon saw that it would be impossible to hold, and ordered the men to attempt escape by squads.

"I saw General Morgan," Private Mosgrove said, "skimming along at an easy pace, looking up at our broken lines and—softly whistling. I was glad to see him getting away, for had he been captured he would doubtless have fared badly—as the Federals had not forgiven him for his daring escape from the Ohio prison."

Carl Sager, one of the boys trapped at the river, told of jumping his horse over a stone fence and landing in the water. "As we crossed, the enemy farther down gave us a heavy enfilade fire, killing many of our horses. To avoid the enfilade fire, we hung over the side of our horses, using them as shields from the bullets while crossing. My horse was shot through the neck, but succeeded in swimming the river and jumping the bank. Due to the loss of so much blood he fell to the ground. I had no difficulty in getting another horse, as many of them came out without riders."

Miraculously, all but about two hundred and fifty men escaped from Cynthiana, but the survivors were so badly scattered that weeks would pass before all found their different ways back to Virginia. Among those captured was George Ellsworth, the telegrapher. The boys would miss his sardonic humor, but they guessed correctly that Ellsworth was too slippery a character for the Yankees to hold for long in prison.

Moving through the hills by nights, constantly searching for food for men and horses, Morgan led the 2nd Battalion along the valley of the Big Sandy, picking up scattered bands here and there. On June 20, the survivors rode into Abingdon, a much smaller force than had left there three weeks earlier. But John Morgan was still wearing a plume in his hat, he had horses to spare, and he was confident that most of his missing men were resourceful enough to escape from Kentucky.

6

July and August, 1864, were cheerless months for the Confederacy, with Grant hammering at Lee's armies around Petersburg and Sherman slicing away at Johnston in Georgia. In their little corner of southwestern Virginia, Morgan's men were almost forgotten in a temporarily quiet eddy of the giant struggle.

Singly and by squads the men who had been separated at Cynthiana continued to come in to Abingdon. By August, Morgan not only had most of his men back at Abingdon headquarters, he also acquired two additional regiments—formed from the broken brigades of Generals John C. Vaughan and William E. Jones. Determined to build up another cavalry division, he listed his four regiments as brigades in his table of organization, although their total strength was less than three thousand. Survivors of the 2nd Kentucky continued under Major Cassell as the 2nd Battalion of D. Howard Smith's "brigade."

On the surface everything seemed to be going well. Morgan's wife had come up from South Carolina to live at headquarters, and she accompanied the General on his inspection tours about the camps. He dressed impeccably, he could still flash a smile at his boys, and would always stop for a word of good humor or encouragement.

But underneath, John Morgan was a troubled man. He could shrug off the censure from Richmond concerning his June raid, but not the many adverse reports from Kentucky. Some of his staunchest civilian supporters in his home state had turned against him, denouncing him for the looting in Mount Sterling and Lexington, the burning of Cynthiana. The robbery of the Mount Sterling bank was the sorest point of all.

Before John Castleman left Abingdon to join Tom Hines' secret mission in Canada, he said that Morgan was "low-spirited, embarrassed by misfortune. He had not the buoyancy, nor the self reliance, which was his wont, and had not any longer his accustomed faculty of inspiring enthusiasm."

What hurt Morgan most was criticism from his own officers, criticism which turned to direct accusations. Giltner, Smith, Martin and Alston, in attempts to clear themselves, all went over Morgan's head to report to Richmond what they knew about the Mount Sterling bank robbery. "Appeals have been made to Morgan by Cols. R. A. Alston, and R. M. Martin and others," Giltner reported, "to institute proceedings of investigation, but he has failed to do so."

Alston had learned many details about the robbery from enlisted men in Company A of the 2nd Battalion who volunteered the information that they had been ordered to assist Surgeon Goode in robbing the bank. John Castleman's brother, Humphrey, who was not yet twenty years old, was named as a key participant. According to Alston, when he passed this information on to Morgan's inspector-general, Captain Bryant Allen, the latter "called on Humphrey Castleman, and instead of taking his evidence told him that 'mum was the word.' I use his language."

Alston then discovered that all the volunteer witnesses among the enlisted men were being transferred away from Abingdon, that "all privates who dared to speak openly . . . were arrested." Affidavits and other papers which he had collected on the robbery mysteriously disappeared from his quarters.

When he persisted in his demands for an investigation, Alston himself was transferred to Gladesville, Virginia, on the pretext that he was needed there to inspect troops. At this point, Alston decided the time had come to confer with his fellow officers, and together they submitted their charges to the Confederate War Department.

Instead of making an explanation of the bank robbery or defending his failure to investigate, Morgan wrote out a mild statement on August 21 for Secretary of War Seddon: "The facts developed thus far are not sufficient to a full exposé of the matter, and I have delayed any public action in regard to it until the whole thing can be thoroughly sifted."

During the following week, Richmond headquarters studied the submitted reports. Morgan's old enemies, including Braxton Bragg, no doubt considered these charges by the General's own officers an excellent excuse to bring the incorrigible cavalry leader to account. On August 30, Richmond ordered that "Brig-Gen. J. H. Morgan be suspended from command and a court of inquiry . . . be at once constituted and convened, to meet at Abingdon, in Southwestern Virginia, on the 10th day of September next." In addition, court-martial proceedings were drawn against Private Humphrey Castleman and Surgeon R. R. Goode. Significantly the charge against Goode read: "Brig. Gen. John H. Morgan, commanding, ordered the said Surg. R. R. Goode, then serving on his staff, to enter the Farmers Bank of Kentucky, located in Mt. Sterling, and seize the public funds in said bank for the use of the Confederate States, whereupon said Goode took from said bank $72,000, and failing to account for the same, applied said money to his own use."

Did Morgan *order* Goode to take the money? And if so, did the surgeon abscond with it, or was he sent to Canada to turn the funds over to Captain Tom Hines for use in freeing Confederate prisoners in the North? Hines was in need of negotiable funds, and the money taken from Mount Sterling was in specie and U. S. treasury notes, instead of Confederate paper which was as worthless in Canada as it was in the North. Goode, with his foreign accent, would have been an ideal messenger.

Neither Goode nor Humphrey Castleman was ever brought to trial. Goode vanished immediately after the robbery, young Castleman about the same time that his brother left Abingdon to join Hines in Canada.

If the money was to be used for secret cloak-and-sword activities in the North, why did Morgan not hint at this in his letter to Secretary of War Seddon? Did he assume that Seddon knew this already? Was he covering up for someone higher in authority? Or did he consider the bank's deposits fair spoils of war and therefore nothing to be overly concerned about?

The answers to this mystery will probably never be known. Before the court of inquiry could meet, John Hunt Morgan was beyond the reach of any mortal judges.

7

On the same day the Confederate War Department ordered a court of inquiry to investigate the robbery of the Mount Sterling bank, Brigadier General John C. Echols was named to replace Morgan as commander of the Department of Southwestern Virginia. But before Echols could arrive in Abingdon to take over command, scouts brought warnings of a Union column moving toward Bull's Gap on the department's defense line to the southwest. Morgan immediately ordered the troops—which Echols was supposed to be commanding—to march out toward Tennessee. He would join them later, if Echols did not arrive in time.

In the midst of this turmoil, Basil Duke arrived suddenly from the south. He had been unexpectedly exchanged at Charleston, South Carolina, reaching Abingdon only a few hours before the deadline Morgan had set for leaving. Duke was shocked by Morgan's appearance. "He was greatly changed. His face wore a weary, care-worn expression, and his manner was totally destitute of its former ardor and enthusiasm." The brothers-in-law briefly discussed events which had occurred since they had last seen each other in the Ohio penitentiary, then it was time for Morgan to board a train which would take him across the Tennessee line to Jonesboro, where he planned to join the troops for a march toward Bull's Gap. Duke expressed a willingness to go with the expedition, but Morgan suggested he stay in Abingdon. He knew Duke was looking forward to a reunion with his wife, Henrietta.

Morgan's train reached Jonesboro September 2, and he joined his waiting troops that afternoon on the road south of town. He had sent sixteen hundred men out of Abingdon, Giltner's 4th Kentucky, Colonel William Bradford's regiment from Vaughan's old Tennessee brigade, and D. Howard Smith's battalions. For this expedition, Captain James E. Cantrill was in command of the 2nd Battalion.

On the afternoon of September 3, with the Great Smokies hazy in the distance, they were approaching Greeneville. Scouts rode far in advance, on the flanks, and beyond the town, but could find no trace of the enemy.

At a grist mill outside Greeneville, the column halted long enough for quartermaster details to obtain meal and flour. The weather had turned warm and humid, with dark cloud banks rolling up from the Smokies. At a turn in the road just before entering Greeneville, Morgan detached a battery and a company of the 2nd Battalion. The artillery was pulled up on a hill overlooking the town, and the column moved on.

In disposing his forces for the night, Morgan sent Smith and the remainder of his regiment out southwest of town to bivouac along the Bull's Gap road, Giltner's 4th to the northwest on the Rogersville road, and Bradford's Tennesseans to the fork of the Newport and Warrensburg roads. He thus had troops covering every main entrance to Greeneville.

General Morgan and his staff established headquarters in the largest house in town, the home of Catherine Williams. Mrs. Williams professed to be a pro-Confederate, but her house had often been used as a stopping place by both Confederate and Union officers. She had two sons in the Confederate Army, one in the Union Army. Greeneville, the home of Andrew Johnson, was a town of divided loyalties.

Catherine Williams' house occupied almost an entire block, shaded by large trees, bordered by a boxwood hedge, with a board-fenced garden at one side extending to a small church. As John Morgan and his staff officers entered the front yard late that sultry afternoon, the air was filled with the fragrance of roses blooming in profusion around the gallery.

About the same time that Morgan entered the house, Mrs. Williams' daughter-in-law, Lucy, left in a buggy for the purpose of driving out to the Williams farm to obtain watermelons. Because Lucy Williams was married to the Union soldier of the family, and happened to depart at about the same time Morgan and his staff arrived, she was to become a legend, one of the enduring myths of the Civil War.

An hour or so after Lucy Williams started out, a hard rainstorm swept across Greeneville, catching many of the troopers before they could unsaddle and find shelters in woods and fields. Their flour was soaked before they could build fires to cook it; their horses, frightened by thunder, almost stampeded.

Morgan and his staff—including Majors Harry Clay, C. W. Gassett, and Charles Withers—dined leisurely, waiting for the storm to let up. But the rain continued, and Morgan finally ordered his officers to don their ponchos and accompany him on an inspection tour of the outlying camps.

They returned to the Williams house just in time to escape another downpour with lashing winds. Logs were blazing in the parlor fireplace, and the officers stood before the fire drying their damp uniforms. They began swapping jests, drinking a little, and singing ballads. Morgan, who usually joined in this sort of merrymaking, did not participate on this evening. He sat silent before the fire, his face drawn and solemn. Suddenly he rose, ordering two of the officers to make another ride around the picket lines. He was afraid the pickets might have become careless in the heavy weather.

Perhaps he also remembered that it was Saturday night. In another hour or so it would be Sunday—the day everything important always happened to John Morgan.

Before he went to bed, he stepped out on the long gallery in the flashing lightning to make certain that sentinels were on duty all around the house.

A few hours later one of these faithful sentinels was knocking on Major Withers' door, informing him that dawn was breaking. Withers pulled on his trousers and walked across the hall to Morgan's room, calling him awake.

"It's still raining, is it not?" Morgan asked sleepily.

"Yes, sir," Withers answered.

"Let the boys have time to get their guns dry; better say seven o'clock."

Withers replied that he would send couriers immediately to the camps, informing the colonels of a delay in marching orders until seven o'clock so that the men might dry their weapons.

While Withers waited for the couriers to return with receipted orders, he could hear the rain slackening. Thunder rumbled far away to the east. The long night storm was passing over.

Suddenly he heard another sound somewhere down the street; he listened carefully. It was rifle fire, increasing in intensity and coming closer. He stepped out into the hall, and saw Morgan with Major Gassett hurrying toward a door leading to the garden. Morgan was still fastening his clothes; he wore only a white night shirt, trousers and boots. There had been no time to put on his green underjacket, a present from his wife which he often wore as a charm against danger.

Withers followed Morgan and Gassett out into the board-fenced garden. Morning mist shrouded the rain-washed vines and shrubbery; water dripped from the grape arbors. The air was cool after the rain, heavy with the scent of blossoms.

Rifle fire exploded loudly in front of the house, and they started for the stable across the street to get their horses. But suddenly the street was filled with blue-clad horsemen, indistinct in the gray light. The three Confederates hurriedly took cover inside the small church at the end of the garden.

After a few minutes, Withers made a quick return to the house to try to signal the battery on the hill east of town. But low-lying mists screened everything; he could not even see the hill. The street outside was thick with milling Union cavalrymen. Some of Morgan's sentries had been killed; others were inside the house, firing from the front windows. When Withers dashed back through the wet garden to inform Morgan of the situation, the mounted Federals saw him, opening fire. He had barely reached the shelter of the church when the enemy began pounding on the street doors.

Withers and Gassett wanted to surrender, but Morgan refused. "It's useless," he said. "They've sworn never to take me prisoner again." He suggested they return to the house, join the surviving sentries, and make a stand until help could come. Morgan went out first, crossing behind the grapevines. His white nightshirt betrayed him. One of the Federal cavalrymen shouted, and a dozen or more began firing at once. Withers, racing for the house, heard Morgan moan "Oh, God!" and then saw him fall forward on his face into a clump of gooseberry bushes. A moment later the Federal troopers clubbed a hole through the board fence, urging their mounts into the garden, trampling the shrubbery. In all the confusion, Gassett escaped, but Withers was captured.

As he surrendered, Withers heard one of the cavalrymen shouting: "I've killed the damn horse thief!"

Morgan was dead; there was nothing Charles Withers could do now. It was a Sunday—the last day anything important would ever again happen to John Hunt Morgan.

The trooper who was first to reach Morgan's body was Private Andrew Campbell of the 13th Tennessee Union Cavalry. Campbell threw the body across his horse, and for years Morgan's men believed he then paraded it around the town. Actually, Campbell turned back toward his command to show Morgan's body to his general, Alvin C. Gillem. There was no proof Campbell had killed Morgan; the dead leader had been struck by a fusillade from several rifles. Campbell's purpose was to gain reward or promotion by presenting the dead body of Morgan as evidence of his prowess as a soldier—and he was given a lieutenancy later.

But according to Colonel James W. Scully, who was riding with General Gillem that morning, Gillem denounced Private Campbell for his treatment of the dead, and "had the remains placed upon a caisson and carried back to Mrs. Williams' house, where they were decently cared for."

8

In the meantime, Morgan's men on the roads outside Greeneville had been alerted into action. Bradford's Tennesseans were in retreat, their camp having been overrun by General Gillem's attacking force. When Giltner and Smith first heard the gunfire from their distant positions, each assumed that men in one of the other camps were firing off their weapons to dry them. The firing continued in intensity, however, and Smith ordered his battalions to saddle up. They moved out at a gallop toward Greeneville. Down the road, Smith met one of his lieutenants who had been sent into town earlier to obtain a brandy ration for the rain-soaked troopers. As the lieutenant reined up, he shouted: "The town is full of Yankees!"

Smith then ordered his column to make a flanking movement into the Jonesboro road, and moved up to the battery on the hill where the 2nd Battalion men were mounted and waiting for orders. The morning fog had cleared by now. "I saw the streets of the town full of Federal soldiers," Smith afterward reported, "and on the

farther side, General Gillem's whole command in battle array."
Smith immediately ordered the battery to open fire on the Federal
lines, and sent the 2nd Battalion charging into Greeneville in a
desperate effort to rescue Morgan. None of these men dreamed that
John Morgan was already dead.

The charge, led by Lieutenant Lewis Norman's company, was
repulsed, several of the men being captured before they could withdraw to the battery on the hill.

It was some of these captives and certain pro-Confederate citizens
of the town who saw Lucy Williams returning to her mother-in-
law's house later that morning. Because she was conducted in by
Federal pickets, it was assumed by those who knew her that Lucy
Williams had been an informer, had betrayed Morgan to the enemy.
The rumors would grow, and because Lucy Williams at first did
nothing to disprove them, in fact cherished the notoriety and hoped
to ingratiate herself with the Federals, the story grew into a legend
accepted by many for years. Basil Duke, for instance, still believed
Lucy Williams was Morgan's betrayer when he wrote his history
of the command.

But in none of the Federal accounts of the attack on Greeneville
is there any evidence that General Gillem or his officers knew for
certain that John Morgan was in the town. There was an informer,
however, a young boy named James Leddy, who rode into Gillem's
bivouac about nine o'clock Saturday night and told him "Morgan's
men were all around his mother's place"—a farm west of Greeneville.
As one of Gillem's officers knew the boy well, the story was believed. An hour later the 13th Tennessee Union Cavalry was marching, with two other regiments and a battery close behind.

Through torrents of rain and vivid lightning flashes which il-
luminated the flooded road, the Federal column moved eastward.
About daylight the advance was challenged by Colonel Bradford's
outer videttes; they were answered with shots which killed them.
The next set of pickets was found fast asleep and captured. (In
spite of Morgan's precautions it was his pickets who failed him in
the end.)

A few minutes later, the 13th Tennessee had broken through
Bradford's bivouac, and the advance company was already into the
town before the Federals learned for certain that Morgan was

there. This time the informer was a Negro boy on a mule who volunteered the information that "General John Morgan was fast asleep at Mrs. Williams' house." At that same time Lucy Williams, the legendary informer, was also fast asleep at the Williams farm.

9

After the 2nd Battalion made its reckless charge into Greeneville and was thrown back to the battery on the hill, Smith, Giltner and Bradford joined forces and began a cautious retreat of fourteen miles to Rheatown. At any moment they expected to see the imperishable John Morgan come galloping down some byroad, smiling, and waving his plumed hat. But he did not come.

At Rheatown they held a consultation and sent Captain John J. McAfee of the 4th Kentucky with an escort party under a truce flag back to Greeneville to learn for certain what had happened to Morgan. When McAfee reached the town it was deserted; the Federals had turned back toward Bull's Gap. He rode on down to the Williams house, and there found his general laid out for burial.

McAfee obtained a neat walnut coffin, commandeered a one-horse wagon for a hearse, and began the slow sad journey back to Rheatown.

The boys in the ranks—the survivors of the old Green River days, the long marches into Kentucky, the Great Raid—could scarcely believe their leader was gone. They had known for weeks that Morgan had changed, that he bore little resemblance to the light-hearted, smiling captain they had known when he was commander of the 2nd Kentucky. But so had they all changed, the war was changing, their world was changing.

For all his human faults they would never lose their admiration for the man who had brought them together. "Any one of us—all of us—would gladly have died in his defense," Lieutenant Kelion Peddicord wrote after his death, "and each one would have envied the man who lost his life defending him. So much was he trusted that his men never dreamed of failing him in anything that he attempted. In all engagements he was our guiding star and hero."

14

Episode of the Cloak-and-Sword

I

ON MARCH 16, 1864, Captain Thomas Henry Hines with the blessing of Confederate Secretary of War Seddon was officially detailed for special service to Canada. From Tom Hines' viewpoint this mission was primarily designed to release Confederate prisoners of war forcibly, but from the Richmond viewpoint recovery of prisoners was only one issue of a much broader program of cloak-and-sword intrigue against the Federal Union. Although Hines was given considerable freedom of operation, he was also accountable to a special Confederate mission which was being established in Canada to conspire with the so-called Peace Democrats in the Northwestern States—the Sons of Liberty, Knights of the Golden Circle, the Copperheads.

Hines arrived in Canada late in May, and at Windsor on June 9, he met the leader of the Knights of the Golden Circle, Clement L. Vallandigham, who had been banished from Ohio by President Lincoln for making inflammatory speeches against the administration. Vallandigham, who claimed to have 185,000 followers, disclosed that the Copperheads were preparing to seize the state governments of Illinois, Indiana and Ohio. He assured Hines that his organization would be willing to co-operate with the Confederate government in a plot to release prisoners of war from Camps Douglas, Rock Island, Morton and Chase.

274

Hines was shrewd enough to detect a fundamental difference in his plans and those of the Copperheads. Hines' burning desire was to free prisoners and take them back south to continue the war; Vallandigham and his followers wanted to overthrow the Federal government and stop the war. For the time being, Hines decided to accept the aid of these dubious allies, who he secretly felt were "tarnishing the shield of the Democratic party by tagging it with the name of Copperheads."

During the following weeks, Hines busied himself with rounding up escaped Confederates in Canada and in establishing relations with Commissioner Jacob Thompson, chief of the Confederate mission to Canada. He discovered several of his old comrades of the 2nd Kentucky Cavalry in Windsor and Toronto—Lieutenants George Eastin and Ben Drake; Jack Trigg, the regimental forage master; John Ashbrook of Company E; telegrapher George Ellsworth; Bennett Young, one of Quirk's original scouts; and Henry Stone who had served under Hines as a scout on the Great Raid and had been one of the first to escape from Camp Douglas.

In letters to his family in Greencastle, Indiana, young Stone recorded the strange life of these Kentucky exiles in Canada. "I went out to the Hiron's House," he wrote upon his arrival in Windsor, "where I'm stopping now; here I found about 25 of Morgan's men, a number of whom I knew. I can board here for $2.50 to 3.00 per week. The state of my funds is $17 in money. This will last me a month anyhow. . . . Our boys register their names here as soldiers of the C. S. A. I wrote mine so in full. . . . The women all skate here; see their ankles easy. . . . I intend to study law if I can get books." Stone went on to tell of how on his first Sunday in Windsor "the Morgan men formed a company and attended Methodist church together."

They did not find life easy in Canada. Employment was almost impossible to obtain because of competition among the many refugees (who included numerous deserters from the Federal Army). Until Hines and the Confederate mission arrived with funds, they lived a hand-to-mouth existence, dependent upon money sent by relatives and friends back in the States.

All the Morgan men and a number of other Confederate fugitives cheerfully agreed to join Hines in his plot with the Copperheads.

Not being inclined to postpone action, Hines set July 4 as a tentative date for simultaneous attacks against Camps Douglas, Rock Island, Morton and Chase. As the date drew nearer, however, the Copperhead leaders asked for more time to arm and assemble their forces. The date was set back first to July 16, then to July 20. By mid-July when it became evident that the procrastinating Copperheads were nowhere near prepared, Hines called a showdown meeting in London, Ontario.

The Copperheads now proposed the last week in August as an ideal time for an uprising. During this week, they argued, the national Democratic Convention would be meeting in Chicago, and representatives of the Sons of Liberty promised to bring at least fifty thousand members into that city for a massive assault against Camp Douglas. Prisoners would be freed, armed, and used to overthrow the governments of Illinois and Indiana.

By this time Hines was growing skeptical of the Copperheads' ability to deliver on their promises. He agreed to wait until August 29, the date selected for armed revolt, but at the same time he began building up a force of his own from Confederate soldiers who escaped to Canada.

During August he acquired two valuable recruits in Toronto, Colonel St. Leger Grenfell and Captain John B. Castleman. Grenfell was delighted to be among his old comrades of the 2nd Kentucky again, but declared that he had taken an amnesty oath and could not formally join them. After leaving Richmond, the Englishman had journeyed first to Cuba, then to New York and Washington, where he had taken the oath and then had decided to delay returning to England until he had visited Canada for an excursion with some friends on Georgian Bay. When Hines asked him if he would be willing to go to Chicago, Grenfell replied that he would be pleased to accompany the party of disguised Confederates, to "go along to see how they made out." As a matter of fact, he said, he had accepted an invitation from an Englishman named Baxter at Carlyle, Illinois, to join him for the prairie-chicken shooting season, and he would be traveling through Chicago anyhow.

Whether it was coincidence or not, immediately after Castleman's arrival from Virginia, Hines was able to furnish his little army with pistols, ammunition, railroad tickets to Chicago, and one hundred dollars expense money for each man. But nowhere in the records does the name of Surgeon R. R. Goode appear; there is no mention of the Mount Sterling Farmers Bank of Kentucky.

Castleman being of equal rank was given equal responsibility by Hines. They made a strange pair of conspirators, Hines being twenty-five years old, Castleman only twenty-three. Both were mild-mannered, soft-voiced, courteous. They had come a long way in the two years since the day in Chattanooga when Castleman had sworn Hines in as a private of Company D.

Late in August, Hines gave orders to his best seventy-four men to start for Chicago. They were to travel in pairs so as not to attract attention, and each was given a slip of paper with the number of a room reservation at the Richmond House.

Castleman, Grenfell and two others made the journey on August 25, arriving on a train thronged with hundreds of delegates assembling for the Democratic Convention. One of the young Confederates who met Grenfell on the train was surprised that the Englishman was wearing a gray uniform. "Colonel," he said, "if you go in those clothes to Chicago they will arrest you; you will not live there five hours."

"No," Grenfell replied, "this is an old uniform that was worn in an English battalion I once belonged to." He smiled and added: "I have my English papers, and my gun and dog, and if they ask me what I am doing, I will say I am going hunting."

The young Confederate shook his head. He did not believe a word of it; he knew the boys were already talking of how Grenfell had volunteered to lead the assault on Camp Douglas, in a mounted charge, of course.

By Saturday evening, August 27, all the members of Hines' daring expedition had signed in at the Richmond House on the corner of Lake Street and Michigan Avenue. Above the doors of the rooms assigned to them they hung signs which read "Missouri Delegation."

Meanwhile steps were being taken to inform the prisoners at Camp Douglas to be prepared for deliverance on the night of August 29. The next move was up to the Copperheads.

2

Through the Camp Douglas grapevine, certain trusted leaders
among the Morgan prisoners learned during the week-end of August 27 the electrifying news that Captain Hines and others of their
comrades were planning to raid the stockade on Monday night. For
weeks there had been rumors of such action, but few had believed
them. Now that freedom seemed almost within their grasp, those
who knew of the plot found it almost impossible to keep the
secret.

More than a year had passed since their arrival at Douglas from
Camp Morton. After the big breakout of December, only a few
others had escaped, and the past nine months had been hard and
dreary.

All remembered well how Colonel De Land had clamped down
on them after the big escape, how severely he had punished the
men who were recaptured. The first seven of these recaptured men
were marched out before the assembled prisoners and tortured with
thumbscrews until they fainted with pain. Others were tied up by
their thumbs with their toes barely touching the ground. "I saw
men punished thus," said Private Thomas D. Henry of Company
E in a sworn statement, "until they would grow so deathly sick
that they would vomit all over themselves, their heads fall forward
and almost every sign of life become extinct; the ends of their
thumbs would burst open; a surgeon standing by would feel their
pulse and say he thought they could stand it a little longer. Sometimes he would say they had better be cut down."

After this, De Land did not remain for long as commander of
Camp Douglas. On December 16, the Union Commissary General of
Prisoners, William Hoffman, ordered him replaced by Brigadier
General William W. Orme.

The boys gave Orme credit for making an initial effort to im-
prove conditions in Camp Douglas, but the General soon appeared
to lose interest in his charges and left much of the administrative
detail to his inspector of prisoners, who in the words of Private
Henry was "a fiend named Captain Wells Sponable."

For petty offenses Sponable freely administered both physical and mental cruelties. When he discovered how important reading matter was to the prisoners, Sponable seemed to delight in depriving entire barracks of every form of literature. More than anything else the boys wanted newspapers so that they might know how the war was going, but after Sponable took charge they rarely saw one.

Raw winter weather settled down over the lake front, with nights that were bitter cold in the barracks. "The suffering of the prisoners was great in the extreme," one of them wrote. "I have seen great, stout-hearted men who had faced death in many forms weep from the intense cold."

Many days they were confined to their barracks, passing the dragging hours at playing seven-up, poker and dice, staking their food allowance or clothing and blankets. Some played checkers and chess, whittled, or slept around the clock. They washed their clothes, waited for meals, plotted escapes, or endlessly discussed the probabilities of exchange—a subject which became an obsession with most of them. Others relapsed into apathy, caring for nothing, thinking of nothing, huddling in corners, sitting for hours staring into space.

Lack of exercise, unbalanced diet, and crowded quarters inevitably led to continued sickness. In an inspection report of January 18, Surgeon Edwin D. Kittoe declared Camp Douglas "very objectionable as a depot for troops . . . The barracks and grounds in the northwest square, occupied by Morgan's men were preeminently filthy. . . . Privies removed and sinks imperfectly covered so that the filth is seeping up through the ground. When there is rain the grounds are flooded with an infusion of this poisonous matter . . . prisoners too much crowded . . . must prove a fruitful source of disease."

The epidemics predicted by Kittoe were raging two weeks later, the post surgeon reporting to Commissary General Hoffman on February 2 that of 5,750 prisoners in Douglas, 2,443 were sick. In that month the dreaded smallpox was added to the list of diseases, and by April, 1864, "had carried many to their final resting-place out on the cold cheerless prairie."

In May, Brigadier General Benjamin Sweet replaced Orme as prison commandant, and soon after Sweet's arrival, the Morgan men started a tunnel—their first in several months. "The Federals found the tunnel," Private J. M. Lynn wrote afterward, "but could not find the men who had the intolerable impudence to thus try to regain their precious liberty. The Kentuckians were the suspected parties, so the 10th Kentucky and a part of the 2nd Kentucky were ordered up near headquarters, one hundred and fifty in all, and forced to huddle up in a mass. The commander of the prison [General Sweet] came out of his office, and instructed a corporal to demand that some one step over the line and tell the names of the men who had dug the tunnel. The corporal did so, and after waiting a minute and no one moving forward, he returned to the commander, reported, received fresh orders, and came back to within ten feet of where Sergeant Beck and myself were standing and whispered to one of the armed guards near us. Instantly the guard cocked his musket, and fired into the helpless mass of prisoners. The bullet struck William Coles, killing him, and the buckshot wounded Henry Hutchins in the groin, passing through and tearing his hip frightfully. His suffering was terrible and pitiful, and he did not die till morning. . . . I would solemnly swear before any court, to the truthfulness of this account."

Yet even this did not stop efforts to escape. Camp Douglas records for August 10 note that Private Harvey Heisinger, Company E, 2nd Kentucky Cavalry, was shot while attempting to escape. In giving testimony, the sentinel who fired on Heisinger said: "Saw a prisoner crawling on his hands and knees outside the fence and under the parapet on which I was stationed. Did not halt him, but fired and hit him."

This was the situation, then, within the high board walls of Camp Douglas late in August, 1864. The prisoners had reached a point of reckless desperation where they were willing to risk all, life itself, rather than remain there. When word came from Captain Tom Hines that deliverance was at hand, it was like a reprieve from the grave, a sign from Heaven.

But the promised deliverance did not come. All day of the twenty-ninth, there was an unusual restlessness among the prisoners, a tenseness that worried the guards. When night came and the evening gun sounded, they moved unwillingly to their barracks. Many a man among the prisoners lay awake all night, listening, listening, but there were only the usual familiar sounds—the rattle of horse trolleys on Cottage Grove Avenue, the faraway hooting of trains and boats, the monotonous calls of pacing sentinels on the parapet. Tom Hines had failed them.

3

But it was not so much Captain Hines who had failed the prisoners as it was the Copperheads who had failed Hines. During the week-end of August 27, Hines and Castleman met several times with Charles Walsh, a Chicago politician and local leader of the Sons of Liberty. Walsh and his associates made grandiose promises at first, assuring Hines that thousands of Copperheads were gathering in Chicago and would be ready to strike on Monday night. As to the actual details of an armed raid against Camp Douglas, however, the Sons of Liberty were quite vague. They seemed to be willing to have Hines and his seventy-four Confederates storm the prison walls while others were somehow magically overthrowing the Illinois and Indiana state governments.

Hines rode out on a trolley car to reconnoiter Camp Douglas, and a few minutes' inspection of the bristling defenses convinced him that at least a thousand armed men would be needed to insure a successful attack.

Sunday morning he arranged a final meeting with the Copperhead leaders, stipulating that he must have a thousand men to take Camp Douglas. Walsh nodded sympathetically; he was sure that many more than a thousand would willingly join in the venture, and arms were certainly available for them in the vastness of Chicago. The problem was to bring men and arms together.

For several minutes Walsh consulted with his associates, finally offered a counterproposal to Hines' demand for a thousand men. If Hines would arrange with the Confederate government to guarantee a massive invasion of Kentucky and Missouri, then the Copperheads would guarantee an armed uprising in Illinois, Indiana and Ohio, freeing all prisoners of war in those states.

At this, Hines almost lost his temper. Such an arrangement would require months of planning and co-ordination, even if the Confederate government was willing and able to launch the invasions. He had spent two months already planning, postponing, and re-planning—with everything focused upon the date of August 29, only twenty-four hours away. To have the Copperheads now propose a plan which would delay matters indefinitely was almost too much for him to bear with equanimity.

But he restrained himself. Even if these men were only a pack of wild dreamers, their sound and fury more vocal than actual, they were his only allies for the time being. He remembered that John Castleman, just returned from a quick trip to Rock Island, had said that it would be much easier to capture the prison there than the one at Douglas.

"Give me five hundred men," Hines said to Walsh, "and we will attack and capture Rock Island."

Again the Copperheads were doubtful if five hundred men could be armed and ready by Monday night.

"Then give me two hundred!" Hines cried.

Walsh thought that might be possible. He agreed to try for five hundred, and the meeting was adjourned for a few hours while trusted messengers were sent out through the city to enlist volunteers. All afternoon Hines paced his hotel room, frustrated by these impractical visionaries forced upon him by necessity.

Late that evening when Walsh reported the results of his recruiting canvass, he told Hines that he had the promises of twenty-five men.

Tom Hines knew there was nothing more that he could do now. He gathered his little army of seventy-four in the Richmond House and informed them the game was up for the present, but that he intended to make another attempt some time in the future. He still had confidence in certain members of the Sons of Liberty in southern Illinois. Given a few weeks' time in which to drill these men in the use of arms, he believed the original plans might be carried out later in the autumn.

After selecting twenty-two men to go with him and Castleman to southern Illinois, he advised the others that he did not wish to hold them any longer; it would be too dangerous for all of them to stay together as a unit. About half the volunteers decided to return to Canada where they would be available when Hines needed them; the others, having little faith in the Copperheads, decided to try to make their ways back through the lines to the Confederacy.

A few hours later, Hines and Castleman with their reduced squadron were on an Illinois Central train bound south for the towns of Mattoon and Marshall in the southern part of the state. St. Leger Grenfell, with his gun and dog, went still farther south to Carlyle to join his English friend, Baxter, for the shooting season.

By early autumn, Hines and his boys had converted Marshall, Illinois, into a center of Copperhead activities; the town was also a sort of underground railway station for escaping Confederate prisoners. Private Henry Damon, one of Castleman's D Company troopers, who had been captured at Cynthiana in June and sent to Rock Island, escaped in September and went directly to Marshall. "To my surprise," he said, "I found comfortably established at the leading hotel, several of my comrades from whom I had parted at Cynthiana."

In the first week of November, Hines and several of the boys who had returned to Canada started traveling in small groups to Chicago. There they met the others from southern Illinois, who had come up with a number of trusted Copperheads. And either by coincidence or by plan, St. Leger Grenfell returned from his long hunting trip to Carlyle, registering with them at the Richmond House.

The night of November 7—the eve of the important Lincoln vs. McClellan election day—had been selected as the time for action. And this time—as he had not done in August—Hines had worked out a detailed plan for storming the prison. The attacking force would divide into four sections, each to gather after dark on one of the four sides of Camp Douglas. Arms would be waiting in carts and wagons for quick delivery to the released prisoners. A skyrocket would signal the moment of attack, the four separate forces moving simultaneously against the prison. At the same time other designated parties in and around Chicago would cut telegraph wires, set fire to railroad depots, and seize Federal ordnance warehouses. After that, the Copperheads could take over if they wished; Hines and the freed prisoners would be moving through Indiana, seizing horses, and possibly raiding Camp Morton on their way south.

It was an excellent plan. Practically all of those who were to be involved in it thought so. Even the Federal authorities around Chicago—who by this time knew almost as much about it as the originator himself—admired its daring.

4

The Camp Douglas inspection report of November 6 was briefly worded, almost routine: "Conduct, good, with the exception of a part of Morgan's command." On that same day the prison commandant, General Benjamin Sweet, sent a warning message to General John Cook in Springfield, informing him that Chicago "is filling up with suspicious characters, some of whom we know to be escaped prisoners, and others who were here from Canada during the Chicago convention, plotting to release the prisoners of war at Camp Douglas."

How General Sweet first learned of the raid plot is not clear from the records, but it is probable that he discovered it as early as the spring of 1864 while reading prisoners' letters. He was huddled up one cold night close to his office stove censoring letters when suddenly the heat brought invisible writing into view across one page: "The 4th of July will be a grand day for us. Old Sweet won't like it." The 4th of July, of course, was the first date set by Tom Hines for an attack on the prison. General Sweet did not know this at the time, but he was suspicious, and after that first discovery he spent many hours reading both incoming and outgoing letters.

Through the tense days of August he had observed increasing restlessness among his prisoners. Conditions were bad, he admitted to Washington. He needed more barracks for the new captives; he needed more medical officers for the older ones who were ill much of the time because of long confinement.

Early in September, after the prisoners' hopes were dashed by Tom Hines' failure to act on August 29, and after they learned of John Morgan's violent death, Sweet noted a mutinous sullenness among the Kentuckians. "The prisoners of war are more uneasy than usual," he reported. "The garrison is prepared for any trouble."

On October 16, General Joe Hooker, who had been removed for incompetence after the battle of Missionary Ridge and was then assigned to command of the district encompassing Chicago, paid a visit to Camp Douglas. Hooker and an imposing staff of colonels rolled through the gates in carriages about three o'clock in the afternoon. General Sweet greeted Fighting Joe with a thirteen-gun salute, paraded the garrison troops before him, and then escorted the distinguished visitor through the prisoners' quarters. As they passed down the line of bedraggled Kentuckians, loud hoots sounded from a section of the Morgan men, followed by cries: "Bread and meat! Give us bread and meat!"

Sweet was frozen with embarrassment; Captain Sponable's face was a mixture of horror and rage. But General Hooker ignored it all, complimented Sweet on the condition of the camp, and as he took his leave, blandly assured the newspaper men with his party that "Camp Douglas is the best prison camp in the United States."

The dust of Joe Hooker's departing carriage was scarcely settled before Captain Sponable sought his revenge upon the Morgan regiments. His first action was to stop all rations.

Within a day or so, the Kentucky boys were reaching a point of desperation. Those who had a little money purchased smuggled bread from the guards, dividing it among their comrades. Then on the evening of the third day of Sponable's starvation punishment, the camp coal wagon made deliveries in the Morgan prisoners' area. When the coal distributor entered the barracks of the 2nd Kentucky to make a delivery, a large black dog followed the man inside.

The boys in the barracks recognized the dog immediately as Captain Sponable's setter. As soon as the coal distributor left, they threw a blanket over the animal.

By the next morning Sponable missed his dog, and posted notices on the barracks bulletin boards offering ten dollars' reward for its return. Some time during the day, an anonymous wit of the 2nd Kentucky scribbled a couplet underneath the reward notice:

> For want of meat
> That dog was eat.

"Well do I remember the time and circumstance," Private H. D. Foote recalled afterward. "The dog—a fine, large, fat, black setter—followed the coal wagon into camp but did not return with it. It was, I think, more of a thrust at Captain Sponable than real hunger that caused the dog to be killed, although it was most assuredly eaten. . . . One day the dog was missing; the next day the advertisement appeared on the bulletin board, with the little epitaph. While this was being read, the dog's meat and bones were boiling in the big kettle, and it made a fine dish of stew. The next day the pit cleaner found the head and hide of the dog. Then the wrath came."

According to a letter written by Private William Christian and a later account by Private T. B. Clore, Captain Sponable acted immediately, and he seemed to have no doubts as to who the culprits were. "The 2nd Kentucky was ordered into line and marched to Captain Sponable's headquarters." An early snowstorm had blown off the lake that day, covering the ground with two or three inches of gritty snow. Sponable ordered the three hundred men into open formation, then commanded them to drop their trousers and underdrawers and sit in the snow. "One of the guards stood at the head of the line while the others stood in the rear and discovered that some of the miserable fellows had pulled their coat tails down for partial protection to their nudity. Every one that was detected was mercilessly kicked in the back with the heavy shoes of the brutal guards." Sponable kept them there for two hours.

During the six months of his command, General Sweet had come to agree with Captain Sponable that there seemed no way of suppressing devilment among the Morgan prisoners, especially the 2nd Kentucky group. There was one man among them, however, who could be used. Sweet had already used him as a petty informer, and in the first week of November the General was ready to use him as a spy. He was James T. Shanks.

Back in the early spring of 1863, when Morgan's regiments were strung out around McMinnville, Tennessee, Shanks had forced an acquaintance with St. Leger Grenfell who then introduced him to Morgan. It will be remembered that Shanks claimed to be a captain from Texas, whose company had been combined with another after suffering heavy casualties in the Stone's River fighting. Morgan accepted him at his word, and sent him out to Woodbury for picket duty with the 2nd Kentucky.

Morgan never gave James Shanks a command, and Shanks never forgave the General for this omission. During the raid across Indiana and Ohio he was attached to Hines' scouts, and Hines never liked or trusted him.

But in early November of 1864, the commandant of Camp Douglas decided that Shanks was a valuable man. General Sweet knew that Shanks was acquainted with some of the conspirators in Chicago. If he could persuade Shanks to "escape" and find the leaders, talk with them, learn their plans, then Sweet would have evidence to make arrests before the plot against Camp Douglas could be put into operation.

On November 3, Sweet summoned Shanks to his headquarters and presented his proposition. If Shanks would act as his spy and later take an oath of allegiance to the Federal government, the General would arrange for his release from prison. Shanks agreed to accept the offer.

Sweet now gave Shanks the names of suspected Confederate sympathizers in Chicago to whom he was to go for aid after his "escape" was arranged. Through these people he was to find his way to the leaders of the conspiracy.

The "escape" was cleverly contrived. One of Sweet's trusted agents was to drive the regular garbage wagon into camp on the following afternoon. Shanks in the meantime would inform his barracks mates that he was going to try to escape by hiding in the back of the wagon; he would ask them to aid him by engaging the driver in conversation while he crawled into the vehicle.

The plan worked to perfection. General Sweet himself was standing near the exit gate when the wagon was halted for guard's inspection. Sweet waved the guard aside. "Let the driver pass," he said, and the wagon rolled on through the gate.

In a few hours, James Shanks was in the home of Buckner Morris, a former judge who had once campaigned for Governor of Illinois. For some time, Judge Morris and his wife had been aiding escaped prisoners; they believed Shanks' story that he was an escaped prisoner of war, and gave him thirty dollars to help him on his way. Shanks later marked the money and passed it on to General Sweet for evidence.

From the Morris home, Shanks moved into a wider circle of Confederate sympathizers and Copperheads. By the evening of November 6 he had found his way to the Richmond House, to his surprise discovered that St. Leger Grenfell, the man who had introduced him to John Morgan, was registered there. Shanks sent up a note to Grenfell asking permission to see him.

When Grenfell received the note, he could not recall who James Shanks was. He stepped into the adjoining room and asked Tom Hines if he knew such a man. Hines remembered Shanks; he warned Grenfell not to trust him.

Although the Englishman was feeling unwell, he courteously agreed to see Shanks. "I went to his room," Shanks later testified, "and told him who I was and where I was from, told him I had just escaped from Camp Douglas, that I was under a parole of honor not to attempt escape; that I had forfeited that parole and was now in a precarious position. He expressed solicitude in my behalf. . . . He asked if the prisoners in Douglas would co-operate with any assistance from outside; I replied that they would."

But Shanks did not learn any details of the conspiracy from Grenfell. It was not until one of the young Confederates from Canada entered the room that Shanks' mission of betrayal began to look more promising. The visitor was Lieutenant John J. Bettersworth, who was using the name of Fielding. Bettersworth revealed casually that he would be leading one of the attacking parties against Camp Douglas, and from that moment Shanks clung to Bettersworth as closely as a brother.

As the evening wore on, Shanks announced that he had decided to take a room in the Richmond House, and invited Bettersworth to join him for a drink. The drink lasted until well after midnight, Shanks keeping the young Lieutenant's glass always filled. Bettersworth's tongue loosened. As he became more and more communicative, he boasted that more than a thousand armed men would be ready to make the attack on the prison camp. He also told Shanks the names of the conspiracy's leaders, enough about them to aid General Sweet considerably in his efforts to stamp out the plot and convict the plotters.

"We were to have another meeting the next morning at eight o'clock," Shanks testified. "Fielding [Bettersworth] left my room about half past one or two o'clock, and he said as he left, 'Perhaps I may return before that hour, and I will give a certain rap, so that you will admit me.' When I woke up I found I was arrested. This was the Richmond House and was about three o'clock in the morning of the 7th of November."

What Shanks had not known was that some of General Sweet's officers in plain-clothes had been following him everywhere he went. By midnight of November 6, Sweet decided that his spy had led him to enough of the leaders of the conspiracy for him to move in and make arrests, including Shanks whom he did not trust.

St. Leger Grenfell was the first to be taken. The ailing Englishman had not been able to sleep because of a malarial chill, and Sweet's executive officer found him sitting before a fire in his hotel room, drinking brandy, his dog at his side. A *Chicago Tribune* reporter described Grenfell as a "Southern aristocrat," his dog as "a bloodhound of the genuine Southern stamp."

They picked up Shanks next, but Hines and Bettersworth had disappeared and Shanks could identify none of the other Confederates registered at the Richmond House. A few hours later Sweet's patrol surrounded the homes of Buckner Morris and Charles Walsh, landing a bigger haul—three of Hines' chief lieutenants—Ben Anderson, Richard Semmes, and George Cantrill, the latter a former Morgan officer. But they still did not have the leader of the conspiracy.

They almost caught him at the home of Dr. E. W. Edwards where Hines was meeting with Colonel Vincent Marmaduke, who had brought a small group of Missouri Confederates into Chicago for the raid. While Sweet's men were banging on Edwards' door, Hines hid in a box mattress on the bed where Dr. Edwards' wife lay ill.

The patrol entered, capturing Marmaduke and searching the house thoroughly, but they did not find Tom Hines. Sweet put a guard on the house, however, and for twenty-four hours Hines was a prisoner. To arrange for Hines' escape, Dr. Edwards announced that his wife was dying, and during the following rainy afternoon friends and neighbors came in by groups of twos and threes to pay their last respects. The guards paid little attention to these harmless visitors, did not notice a slender young man who left under an umbrella with a girl at his side. An hour or so later, Tom Hines was boarding a train for Cincinnati. He had made his last try at freeing the Camp Douglas prisoners.

Regardless of whether General Sweet had made the arrests when he did, it is unlikely that Hines would have gone ahead with plans to raid the prison. The plot had leaked badly. By Sunday, November 6, too many people knew the secret.

In its late Sunday edition, the *Tribune* published a story about the arrival of sixty "butternuts" on the Chicago, Alton & St. Louis Railway. The newspaper assumed that they were guerrillas come to create a disturbance in Chicago. In its early Monday edition, the *Tribune* was predicting a raid on Camp Douglas.

As Hines and his associates always read the newspapers carefully, it seems improbable that they would have continued with their plans in the face of such widespread public knowledge of their intentions.

The man who may well have been the least guilty of the group arrested by General Sweet was the most severely punished—the romantic Englishman, St. Leger Grenfell. After a long trial lasting from January to April, 1865, the accused were sentenced to prison for varying lengths of time—all that is except Grenfell. The court could not conceal its resentment of his foreign citizenship and sentenced him "to be hung by the neck until he is dead, at such time and place as the commanding general may direct."

Had the war not ended about this time, Grenfell no doubt would have been executed. Instead his sentence was commuted by President Andrew Johnson to imprisonment for life, at hard labor, at Fort Jefferson in the Dry Tortugas.

To the very end Grenfell insisted that he was innocent, and aside from the unreliable testimony of James Shanks there is nothing in the trial record but hearsay to prove his guilt. "Had I not been arrested, I should have left for Canada by the morning train," he declared, and no one could prove he did not mean what he said.

At Fort Jefferson he was the prison gardener, and became a friend of Dr. Samuel Mudd, the physician who attended John Wilkes Booth's injured leg and was unjustly accused of participating in the Lincoln assassination plot. "A learned physician, Dr. Mudd," Grenfell noted in one of his letters, "has descended to play the fiddle for drunken soldiers to dance to or form part of a very miserable orchestra at a still more miserable theatrical performance."

For almost three years, the dauntless old cavalryman lived out his days on that moated coral island off Key West. His friends of the 2nd Kentucky, civilians again, tried to gain a pardon for him— Basil Duke, John Castleman, Tom Hines, Charlton Morgan, Henry Stone and others—but being former Confederates they had little influence with President Johnson.

On March 7, 1868, Grenfell made an almost impossible bid for freedom. With three other prisoners he attempted escape in an open boat, but soon after they put out to sea a storm arose and none of them was ever heard of again.

The survivors of the old 2nd never forgot Colonel George St. Leger Grenfell. He had taught them the fine points of the science of cavalry; he had come as close to being a genuine alligator horse as an Englishman could. "Kings, lords, and mighty warriors," one of them wrote in salutation, "have gone down to graves in the briny sea, but the blue waters never closed over a braver heart than that of St. Leger Grenfell."

5

After the November fiasco in Chicago, Tom Hines journeyed to Ohio, visited his sweetheart, Nancy Sproule, and persuaded her to join him in Covington, Kentucky, where they were married. After a hazardous honeymoon in Union-held Kentucky, Hines took his bride to Richmond where he received new orders to return to Canada for further service with the Confederate mission.

But there was little more cloak-and-sword work that Hines or any of the others could do now that would have any effect on the course of the war.

Disillusioned with the Copperheads, the Confederates in Canada engaged in a few audacious adventures on their own. Bennett Young, one of the original Quirk scouts, led a small raiding force (including some former Morgan troopers) across the border to St. Albans, Vermont, robbing the banks, and startling all of New England. The Vermonters captured Young, but could not hold him. In a border incident which almost developed into a localized war between Vermont and Canada, Lieutenant Young was taken into protective custody by Canadian soldiers, was later tried and given his freedom.

Then in late November the reckless Lieutenant Colonel Robert M. Martin, who had commanded the remnants of the 2nd Kentucky at Chickamauga, made a wild attempt to burn the city of New York. Martin had persuaded the Confederate Secretary of State, Judah Benjamin, that he could carry off this daring venture, and Benjamin had sent him to Canada to operate under the official mission.

With Lieutenant John Headley, another Morgan officer, Martin gathered a small group of the Canadian expatriates and slipped into New York. Martin's entire plan was based on the use of Greek fire, a liquid combination of sulphuric acid and other chemicals which when exposed to air would ignite. Its advantage to a saboteur was that the fire would not break out until the user had time to leave the point of sabotage. "Greek fire," one of the conspirators said afterward, "was one of the great humbugs of the war."

It certainly did not work too well for Robert Martin and his comrades. A gross of bottles containing the mixture was distributed among them, and on the night of November 25 they tried to start thirty-two fires in New York. Barnum's Museum and ten hotels were set to blazing, but the other ignitions failed.

Their efforts, nevertheless, caused considerable damage and created a great sensation for a few days, the *New York Herald* head-lining: *ATTEMPT TO BURN CITY. DISCOVERY OF A VAST REBEL PLOT. ONE OF MORGAN'S GUERRILLAS IMPLICATED.*

Lieutenant Colonel Martin and his party escaped back to Canada, but that was about the last of the cloak-and-sword adventures involving Morgan men. The so-called Northwest Conspiracy was rapidly fading away as the war moved toward its inevitable end.

6

After General Sweet demolished the Confederate plot to raid Camp Douglas on November 7, he tightened discipline in the prison. Aside from the few plotters captured, those who paid the price of failure were the objects of the raid—the prisoners.

On January 15, 1865, Captain Sponable's inspection report listed 11,700 prisoners in Camp Douglas, the largest number recorded to that date. The Morgan men had dwindled to a minority, but they were still on Sponable's black list. Life was especially miserable for the survivors of the 2nd Kentucky during the last winter of their imprisonment.

Almost every one of the several accounts written by Kentucky boys who endured that winter mentions a certain instrument of torture designed by the Captain for the Morgan prisoners. This was "Morgan's mule," a wooden frame variously described as being eight to fifteen feet tall, with a two-inch scantling set edgewise across the top. For punishment the Kentuckians were forced to mount and sit astride. "After remaining there a while, one felt as though the spinal column was being pushed out at the top of the head." Private J. M. Lynn told of "painfully straddling the sharp-edged piece of timber, with feet dangling in the air, sometimes heavily weighted." Describing a similar experience, P. H. Prince said the guards took him off "to the wooden horse called Morgan" and put him astraddle, then tied half of a coal stove to each leg and stuck bayonets in him.

"Frequently men sick in the barracks were delirious; sometimes one or two in a barracks were crazy," said Thomas Henry of Company E. "These were the cause of a whole barrack of men being mounted on the horse. . . . Sometimes the Yanks would laugh and say, I will give you a pair of spurs, which was a bucket of sand tied to each foot. I have seen men who had been left in this condition until the skin and flesh was cut nearly to the bone. Men in winter would get so cold that they would fall off. When warmed they were put back."

A form of punishment especially repugnant to these proud Kentuckians was that of being flogged. On one occasion in Tennessee, the 2nd Kentucky boys had risked courts-martial to avoid flogging a deserter; they considered such punishment too humiliating either to be given or received.

During that winter of early 1865, Captain Sponable acquired two assistant "inspectors of prisoners," one known among the Kentuckians as "Prairie Bull" McCurley, the other simply as "Billie Hell." Both these sadistic guards carried leather straps which they used unmercifully, frequently ordering the Morgan prisoners "to reach for grub," which meant to stand in line stiff-kneed and lean forward touching the ground with their finger-tips while Prairie Bull and Billie Hell applied their leather whips.

In his account of this period, T. M. Page recorded a "midnight frolic of drunken guards who dragged a score of prisoners from bed and flogged them with cartridge belts." Private Henry said the Company E men were once ordered in turn to lie naked across a barrel, the guards "using their belts which had a leaden clasp with a sharp edge; the belt would often gather wind so as to turn the clasp edgewise; every lick inflicted thus cut entirely through the skin."

Even more degrading was the punishment given a hungry prisoner caught taking a bone out of a slop barrel. J. S. Rosamond told of how he was ordered to get down on all fours and walk around the bone, growling and barking like a dog for half an hour or so, and then was forced to grovel in the dirt and gnaw at the bone.

It was the belief of the Kentuckians that if they had been guarded by soldiers with combat experience such humiliations would never have been inflicted upon them. In that winter all the guards were garrison troops, who for one reason or another—physical, moral or mental—had been ruled exempt from battle duty.

On occasions, these troops who were considered unfit to carry arms on the fighting line used their loaded weapons with deadly effect upon the unarmed prisoners. "If any one of us was heard to whisper at night," said Private Henry, "or the least ray of light was seen, the guard would fire into the barracks at once. In each barrack there was only two stoves to two hundred men, and for a stove to warm one hundred men, it was frequently red hot. When taps were sounded the fire in the stove could not be put out immediately." According to T. B. Clore of the 10th Kentucky, the guards did not need the excuse of whispers or lights to open fire. "I have known them to be passing along at the dead hour of the night and just for downright meanness fire into the barracks where we were asleep. As a protection many of us nailed a board across the head of our bunks and filled in between that and the outside boards with earth and stones."

All the guards developed loose trigger fingers when prisoners walked anywhere near the deadline, which was eighteen feet inside the fence. During one severe cold spell water hydrants froze and prisoners were forced to use snow, soon clearing all of it away up to the deadline. The veteran prisoners suffered thirst rather than risk reaching across the line, but some of the new arrivals were less cautious. "After being cooped up in the cars four or five days, they were nearly dead for water. The poor fellows would lie down close to the deadline and reach their arms through and pull the snow to them. I saw one of the guards standing twenty-five steps from a prisoner thus engaged shoot at him three times."

From this web of miseries which entangled them, this ordeal which seemed to have no ending, they were suddenly delivered in March, 1865. Yielding to pressures from Northern families with relatives in Southern prisons, Federal authorities reopened the exchange cartel.

The 2nd Kentucky boys, being among those with the longest periods of confinement, were ordered east for exchange at City Point, Virginia. "The visions of the green fields of Kentucky with its rippling waters and genial clime," one of them wrote, "were soon to be realized after nineteen months of hardships and denials."

But even though Appomattox was only a few weeks away, most of these veterans of more than three years of cavalry raids and prison life would not see the Bluegrass until they had endured one more long march. Ahead of them was Virginia in the turbulence of defeat, and then the dusty roads of the Carolinas, and a final surprising adventure in the pine forests of Georgia.

15

No More Bugles

I

IT SEEMED PROVIDENTIAL to the 2nd Kentucky boys in southwestern Virginia that Basil Duke should have been exchanged in the same week they lost John Morgan. "I hear this morning Colonel Duke is exchanged," one of them wrote from Abingdon. "If so, we are all *all right*."

Duke joined the brigade at Jonesboro, Tennessee, immediately following John Morgan's death. Colonel D. Howard Smith graciously offered to relinquish command of the 2nd Kentucky Battalion and other elements of the old Morgan regiments, and once again Duke was leading the alligator horses. There were not many of the veterans left, less than three hundred—most of them so poorly armed he wondered how they had been able to fight at all, the calibers of their rifles so varied that it was impossible to keep enough ammunition in supply.

During the two weeks they camped outside Jonesboro, he devoted most of his time to collecting weapons, supplies and equipment. Private George Mosgrove, who was serving under him at this time, described him as being nervous and impatient, "restlessly turning in his saddle, his dark eyes flashing."

General John Echols, now in active command of the department, suggested that the fragmented Morgan regiments be brought together and reorganized along new lines, a move which Duke agreed

296

would bring more efficiency to his command. In the new organization, most of the 2nd Kentucky boys ended up under their commander of the Indiana-Ohio raid, Major Thomas Webber. On official rolls they were listed as 4th Battalion, Kentucky Cavalry, but in all private communications they continued to call themselves 2nd Kentucky Cavalry.

The entire brigade was now officially Duke's Cavalry, the young commander receiving his brigadier general's commission late in September. By October he had brought his command to a strength of five hundred and seventy-eight officers and men present for duty, and was ready to march against the enemy in eastern Tennessee.

But this last autumn and winter of the Civil War was not to be a season of victories for twenty-six-year-old General Duke. In his first fight at Bull's Gap, November 13, he won the decision but lost too many men; and men lost now could not be replaced. It was a night attack, fought on foot in the mountains. "The night was cloudless," he wrote, "and the moon at its full and shedding a brilliant light. The dark lines of troops could be seen almost as clearly as by day. Their positions were distinctly marked, however, by the flashes from the rifles, coming thick and fast, making them look, as they moved along, bending and oscillating, like rolling waves of flame, throwing off fiery spray. When my brigade had moved far around upon the left, and had taken position, obliquely toward the enemy's rear, it suddenly opened. The Federal line recoiled, and closed from both flanks toward the road, in one dense mass, which looked before the fighting ceased and the rout fairly commenced, like a huge Catherine wheel spouting streams of fire."

Duke's men captured all the enemy artillery, a wagon train, and an ambulance filled with much-needed medical supplies. They also took three hundred prisoners, but the Federals' firepower, improved considerably since Duke had last faced the enemy, had riddled his brigade. Major Webber, for instance, leading twenty-eight men in one charge, had sustained fourteen casualties.

They withdrew with their wounded to the base camp at Abingdon, and began a winter of defensive operations, fighting off enemy patrols probing for weaknesses in the lines guarding the salt and lead deposits. On December 21, the Federals under General Stephen Burbridge massed their forces and broke through the Confederate

lines, wrecking the vital salt works at Saltville, demolishing buildings, kettles, machinery, pumps, wells and stores.

(That very same day General Hardee was evacuating Savannah;
Sherman had completed his march to the sea, cutting the South in
half.)

Duke's brigade, brought up as reinforcements, drove Burbridge's
cavalrymen out of Saltville and pursued them through a blinding
snowstorm all the way to the Kentucky line. Major William J.
Davis, who had been captured in Indiana after his command was
split at Twelve Mile Island, had recently been exchanged, and was
a member of the pursuing expedition. "As we ascended the steep
mountain road leading from Saltville," he wrote, "the cold intensified so as to test the greatest power of endurance. Men beat their
breasts to promote a more vigorous circulation, or, dismounting,
limped on benumbed feet beside their hobbling horses. The necks,
breasts and forelegs of the horses were covered with clinging sheets
of frozen breath or blood that had oozed from the fissures in their
swollen nostrils. Often their lips were sealed by the frost to the
steel bits, or protruded livid and rugged with icicles of blood. Soon
we met indications of the still greater suffering of our foes. Horses
dead from cold were seen along the road, frozen stiff in every
imaginable attitude; some leaned against the perpendicular cliff
on the right, with legs swollen to an enormous size and split open to
the bone from knee to hoof; some knelt with muzzles cemented to
the hard earth by blood; others lay prone but with heads upraised.
. . . These corpses actually impeded our pursuit; sometimes six or
eight lay in one heap; once I counted two hundred in one mile. . . .
You may think the sight of hundreds of horses, dead, as I have said,
horrible; what think you—you who have never seen war, but have
read of its 'pomp and pride and circumstance,' and perchance have
glorified the butchery of it—what think you of men lying on bed or
floor, some of them in the article of death, frozen, as were their
dumb beasts by the road side? The hands of some of these gallant
men were swollen and cracked with bleeding fissures a quarter of an
inch wide. Their legs, from which pantaloons had been ripped,
looked as if affected by elephantiasis; their feet, from which boots
had been cut, were a shapeless mass; legs and feet seemed red like

the shells of boiled lobsters and were split into bloody cracks like the hands."

Returning from this ordeal, the brigade settled into winter quarters at Abingdon. The men built huts against the continuing cold, but most of the time they were half-famished and half-clothed. "Many men are badly in need of clothing," Duke reported on New Year's Day of 1865, "and all are clamorous for their pay. Guns, saddles, and cartridge boxes are also needed."

In worse condition than the men were their horses. Southwestern Virginia had been stripped of fodder and grain, and as the South's transportation system had virtually collapsed no supplies could be shipped in. Duke could not bear to watch the last of his horses die of starvation; reluctantly he ordered the brigade dismounted and sent the animals overland to North Carolina. One of the men assigned to this horse detail was Sergeant Henry Stone, who had returned on a blockade runner from his Canadian exile. From Mecklenburg County, North Carolina, young Stone reported briefly: "I am now for the first time at a convalescent camp; not for the improvement of myself but for the health of my horse. Weather pleasant."

(About this same time, General Sherman, after reorganizing his army around Savannah, was starting north through the Carolinas.)

At Abingdon the icy winter dragged on through February, keeping the enemy away but making life miserable for the boys cooped up in their wooden huts. An army inspector reporting on the condition of Duke's Brigade, February 15, noted that "about one-fourth of the men need arms and one-third lack accoutrements. There were present at the date of my inspection 328 men and their discipline seemed better than that of the other commands of the department."

This favorable military comparison, however, did not mean that morale was especially high among the Kentucky boys; it merely indicated that their morale was not quite as low as that of some of the others.

For doom was in the chill winter air; no one could deny it. It was foreshadowed in the lack of arms and ammunition no longer replenished, in their rations of worm-eaten peas, rancid mess-pork, and unbolted corn meal. It showed itself in the fluttering rags they wore for uniforms, their soleless boots, the thin bedding blankets taken from horses sent southward, in the absence of the horses themselves. It could be heard in songs they sang in the huts of evenings—no more rollicking ditties of carefree cavaliers, but sad songs of lost Lorenas, of angels marching in the sky, of grief-stricken mothers and sweethearts. Basil Duke composed no more lilting poems of galloping raiders, no poems at all. The chivalry they cherished was gone with the old world of their youth, a world dying with each passing day.

Yet not one of them spoke of defeat, or dared think of it in the loneliness of the winter nights. "Two strange features characterized the temper of the Southern people in the last days of the Confederacy," Duke would recall a year or so later. "Crushed and dispirited as they were, they still seemed unable to realize the fact that the cause was utterly lost. Even when their fate stared them in the face, they could not recognize it."

In the first warm days of spring the exchanged prisoners of war began returning from Camp Douglas, pale-skinned and soft-muscled, in sharp contrast to their lean and weathered comrades. But there was something in the spirit of these returned men that was communicated to the others, a mood of desperate revenge. By the first of April, Duke's Brigade was at its highest strength, more than six hundred men—almost half of them former prisoners who had seen their last fighting during the Indiana-Ohio raid of 1863.

They arrived just in time to help stand off Federal columns moving out of east Tennessee. Although they were disappointed at having to march and fight on foot (the horses were still in North Carolina) they complained less than those who had not been in prison, and were the last to yield ground when ammunition ran out.

Duke's men held on stubbornly to their little corner of southwestern Virginia, but every day the news was bad. Sherman was already into North Carolina, and Lee's thinning lines were retreating in Virginia. After Richmond fell on April 3, the Confederacy's last hope was for Lee and Johnston to effect a junction of their forces at Danville, Virginia. As a part of this strategy, Duke's Brigade received orders to march eastward and join Lee's crippled army.

They marched out toward Roanoke—cavalrymen without horses —but with an occasional plume still thrust into a ragged slouch hat. Boots and shoes were cracked and worn through to the rocky road on which they marched, and before the first day's ending some had thrown away the worthless shells of cheap leather, walking bare-footed.

En route up the valley toward Roanoke on April 9, Duke received the news of General Lee's surrender at Appomattox. "If the light of heaven had gone out," he said, "a more utter despair and consternation would not have ensued. When the news first came, it perfectly paralyzed every one. Men looked at each other as if they had just heard a sentence of death and eternal ruin passed upon all."

During the next twenty-four hours, General Echols struggled vainly to hold the troops of his department together. Entire companies of infantrymen threw down their arms and walked away, heading for home. But most of the cavalrymen—mounted and dismounted—clung together, and at Christiansburg on April 12, Echols held a final council of war. He announced that he would take all the mounted men to North Carolina to join General Joe Johnston and continue the fighting. He would issue sixty-day furloughs to infantrymen and dismounted cavalrymen; if the war was still going on at the end of that time, these men would be recalled to duty.

Only about ten of Duke's dismounted men elected to take furloughs. With Duke's approval the others mounted themselves on mules taken from abandoned infantry wagons, determined to ride these slow-footed, barebacked animals with blind bridles and rope halters to the Mississippi River, if necessary, rather than surrender.

The march south began at four o'clock that afternoon in a torrent of April rain, four generals leading about twelve hundred men. Echols was in command, the others being Duke, George Cosby and John C. Vaughan. "The gloomy skies seemed to threaten disaster," wrote Duke. "But braver in the hour of despair than ever before, my men never faltered or murmured. The trial found them true. To command such men was the proudest honor that an officer could obtain."

2

Not all the Morgan men who had been in Northern prisons were exchanged in time to reach Duke's Brigade before the fall of Richmond. Among these were Lieutenants Winder Monroe and Leeland Hathaway, and Private Jack Messick—three young men who were about to enter upon their most exciting adventure of the war.

At the time of their capture at Buffington Island, they were with Dick Morgan's 14th Kentucky, but Monroe was one of the original members of the 2nd Kentucky, both he and Jack Messick having served with Tom Quirk's scouts. Hathaway had been transferred from the 11th Kentucky immediately before the raid.

Released in northern Virginia early in April, Monroe, Hathaway and Messick found themselves cut off from Richmond. Taking a roundabout route, they started on foot for southwestern Virginia, hoping to find Duke's command. After crossing the James River they were caught up in the stream of Lee's retreating columns. The three returning cavalrymen were shocked by the appearance of these ragged troops—their anguished yet resolute faces, their utter fatigue. "No man saw them," Hathaway noted, "except with uncovered head and reverential greetings."

At Danville where they had been told they might find Duke, they found instead another Kentuckian, General John C. Breckinridge, acting as Secretary of War. "We were worn out with our tramp of 150 miles," said Hathaway. "My boots had lost their soles and I had walked barefoot for the last fifty miles. Altogether we were in rather a sad plight. We walked into the General's office, Monroe, Messick and I. General Breckinridge rose to meet us, calling me and Winder by name."

After they learned that Duke was marching his troops south to join General Johnston's army, they told Breckinridge they would like to offer their services for this same venture. "General Breckinridge called an aide, gave him verbal orders to have our requirements met. I soon had a pair of red *leather* Confederate shoes—we all had bridles and saddles and a written order to take such horses as we could find."

The only horses apparent in all Danville were some blind coach animals, but they mounted up and started for North Carolina, exchanging the blind horses a day or so later for better ones.

For three days they rode steadily, finding no trace of Duke's outfit. Several times they sighted Federal patrols moving on the roads, but managed to elude them, dodging into bushes and woods.

"Winder Monroe told us that his grandfather, Judge Thomas Monroe * and family were at Abbeville, South Carolina, and suggested that we head for that place. We agreed to go."

On April 28, the three adventurers rode into Abbeville. It was a sunny, summery day, the air lazy and fragrant with honeysuckle, yellow jasmine and wistaria winding over the fences and galleries of the houses. After their long months of prison life and the rains and grim events of Virginia, it was like entering into Heaven.

"We found the Judge and his family as we expected very hospitable and much pleased to see Winder. They were living on the barest necessities. Not to burden them we drew the rations of musty meal and salt meat (very little of either, too) to which as soldiers we were entitled and this proved a very welcome addition to their scant larder."

Abbeville was filled with rumors that Johnston had surrendered his army to Sherman in North Carolina, but no one could be certain of anything. The boys decided to wait and see what would happen next.

Two days after their arrival in Abbeville they learned that President Jefferson Davis' wife, fleeing from Richmond, had just reached the town and was in need of assistance. "After consulting with Winder and Jack," Hathaway recorded, "I went to see her and found her very much disturbed and at a loss what to do."

Varina Howell Davis, according to young Hathaway, "was then a rather heavy dark woman about forty years old—not at all handsome or pretty, but very bright and entertaining." Her traveling party consisted of herself; her four children; her sister, Maggie Howell; two servants; and Burton N. Harrison, the President's private secretary. Harrison, who was in charge of the little caravan, did not impress the Kentucky boys with his capabilities. "Harrison was sick and utterly demoralized," Hathaway said.

Mrs. Davis was impatient to leave Abbeville and start for the Florida coast where she hoped to board a ship and take her children to safety. Her plans were quite vague; she had no exact point of de-

* Thomas Bell Monroe, a U. S. district judge of Confederate sympathies, left Lexington, Kentucky, on the same day his grandson, Winder, rode away with John Morgan for Green River in September, 1861. After the fall of Nashville, Judge Monroe took his family to South Carolina.

parture or any certain vessel in mind. She told Hathaway that nobody seemed to have authority or the discipline to give her transportation out of Abbeville.

"It is now about three o'clock," Hathaway said to her. "Can you be ready to move at sunrise tomorrow?"

"I am ready now," she replied.

"What do you want to take?" he asked.

The young Lieutenant was overwhelmed when she showed him her baggage, "a discouraging mass of every kind of household goods and other paraphernalia pertaining to her and her family in their personal and official capacities. I said, 'It is impracticable to attempt to move this mass of stuff.' She then consented to select but when the selection was made not a little was left. I insisted on taking only clothing but she was decided so I went to work with Winder and Jack. There was a Quartermaster camp near the town. We fitted out two ambulances with two mules to each and two first-class U. S. waggons with four mules to each. To each four bright true soldiers at once volunteered to drive by daylight on the morning of the 2nd of May. We began putting in the loads and promptly about sunrise we were on the road."

This strange hegira southward across Carolina and Georgia would last for eight days, and to the three Kentucky boys it was a dreamlike existence, sometimes frantic, often bewildering. As cavalrymen and prisoners of war, they had learned to be surprised at nothing, but an experience such as this was unimaginable—Morgan's alligator horses escorting the First Lady of the Confederacy on a mad flight to nowhere!

As they approached the Savannah River, they heard rumors of a smallpox epidemic, and Varina Davis began worrying because one of her children had not been vaccinated. She insisted that her escorts stop and find a physician. But in none of the sleepy little towns could a doctor be found. Mrs. Davis then asked them to make inquiries at the larger plantations. "Halting at a house near the road," Burton Harrison recorded, "Mrs. Davis had the operation performed by the planter, who got a fresh scab from the arm of a little negro called up for the purpose."

With such delays as this, and the excessive burden of luggage they were hauling, they made very slow progress. Hathaway, Monroe and Messick in turn attempted to persuade Mrs. Davis to permit them to store her goods in some plantation house along the way and start traveling lightly and rapidly both day and night. Harrison stubbornly opposed this plan, evidently considering it necessary for the wife of his chief to be surrounded by a fully equipped retinue. "We did not entirely conceal our contempt," Hathaway admitted, "for the private secretary, who was the cause of this dawdling in the face of danger."

By day the forested river bottoms were filled with bright-feathered song birds. Sweet-scented magnolias were in full bloom; grape and scuppernong vines festooned the trees. At nights mosquitoes swarmed in clouds, but Mrs. Davis was able to supply preventive netting from her adequate stores. After they moved into the pine woods, the nights were more pleasant. "This great forest of stately long-leaved pines stretched above and around us and our nights were the most delightful camping parties." Every evening before bedtime, the three boys heaped up piles of brown pine needles to soften the blanket pallets of Mrs. Davis, her sister and her children.

As a gesture of gratitude toward her soldier escorts, Mrs. Davis presented each one with a twenty-dollar gold piece, and then another gift to be shared among them—"a bottle of rare old brandy which had been sent to her by Louis Napoleon." They planned to keep the gold pieces forever, but the Napoleon brandy they considered expendable, and at night after their civilian charges were fast asleep, the trio of Kentuckians shared precious sips of the delightful liquid. Under soughing pines that towered to the stars, they pondered the wonders of chance in human destiny, and savored the French Emperor's brandy.

At Washington, Georgia, they finally persuaded Mrs. Davis to leave the heavily laden wagons in the care of friends. They dismissed the drivers, but picked up two additional members—Major Victor Maurin and Captain George Moody, who volunteered to strengthen Mrs. Davis' armed escort of three.

From Washington they headed straight south, traveling more rapidly now through an almost trackless extent of pines broken only by occasional swamps and sluggish streams. They saw no more plantation houses, but only ramshackle cabins. Food supplies ran short, and as they neared the Ocmulgee River bad weather caught up with them.

Although they were unaware of it, the pelting rains probably saved them from immediate capture, obliterating tracks of the ambulance wheels soon after they passed over the sandy roads. Union patrols were searching actively in the area, not for Varina Davis but for her husband, President Jefferson Davis, who for several days had been attempting to join his family.

On May 9, along a small creek in the pinewoods near Irwinville, President Davis and his escort overtook his wife's little cavalcade. It was an emotion-filled reunion for the President and his wife. Hathaway, Monroe and Messick stood aside, slightly awed by the presence of this fellow Kentuckian who had led the Confederacy through four years of war.

Then Monroe suddenly stared hard at one of the three colonels who had arrived with the President. He was William Preston Johnston, the officer who had sworn Winder Monroe into John Morgan's squadron at Woodsonville, Kentucky, on that long ago October day of 1861—in that time when war was all knighthood and romance, campfires in the autumn woods, dashing raids by moonlight—in a time when none dreamed of death, imprisonment, or defeat.

At that moment of recognition and remembrance, Lieutenant Monroe must have reflected again on the chance and coincidence of war; but after more than three years of it he had learned to expect the unexpected.

3

A few days before Winder Monroe and his two companions had arrived in Abbeville, South Carolina, the band of troopers for which they had been searching—Duke's Brigade—rode into Charlotte, North Carolina. Somewhere along the danger-filled Carolina roads, the trio had passed their old comrades and pushed ahead of them.

In mid-April, Charlotte was a stronghold of Confederate cavalry units which had escorted President Davis and his Cabinet from Richmond, and the arrival of Duke's troopers added to the jam of horses and men in the dusty streets. Informed that President Davis was staying at the Bates House, Duke drew his column up in front of the door. After all, Jeff Davis was an original Kentucky alligator horse, and this was the first opportunity they had had to do him honor in person since the wedding of John Morgan. They cheered and waved hats and flags until he came to the door and made them a little speech.

Davis thanked the Kentucky boys for their cordial greeting, complimented them on their gallantry as fighting men, and urged them not to despair of the Confederacy but to remain with the last organized band upholding the flag. While he was speaking, some of them dismounted and walked up on the porch steps, crowding around the President, hoping to shake his hand. As he concluded his remarks, a courier pushed through the group, handing Davis a message.

"I was standing just inside the hall door," Sergeant Will Dyer recalled afterward, "and when the President opened and read the dispatch, I noticed that he was greatly affected by it. Turning to Mr. Reagan,* who was by his side, he handed him the paper with the remark, 'This is very unfortunate, read it to the men.' " The message told of the assassination of Abraham Lincoln. For several minutes, according to Dyer, "a solemn stillness, approaching awe, settled over the crowd, then the terrible deed was discussed in whispers among the men." Abe Lincoln, they remembered, had been born a Kentucky alligator horse.

The boys of the 2nd Kentucky found several old friends in Charlotte, former regimental members who had transferred long ago to Billy Breckinridge's 9th Cavalry. Breckinridge's outfit, with three other skeleton brigades, formed the President's escort, and when Duke learned that Davis was planning to move his Cabinet farther south he went to see him and offered the services of his Kentucky cavalry to strengthen the escort force.

Davis agreed that this would be desirable, and volunteered to help the Kentuckians obtain saddles. (En route to Charlotte, Duke had picked up the brigade's horses which had wintered in Mecklenburg County, but only a few of them had saddles.)

* John H. Reagan, the Confederate Postmaster-General.

The Confederate President's inability to comprehend the full disaster which had befallen his armies is indicated by a message which he sent on April 20 to General Beauregard at Greensboro: "General Duke's brigade is here without saddles. There are none here or this side of Augusta. Send to this point 600, or as many as can be had." In late April of 1865 a Confederate general would have required supernatural powers to produce six hundred saddles.

On the day Davis sent this message, General Johnston was negotiating for surrender to Sherman, and a day or two later his Secretary of War, John C. Breckinridge, arrived in Charlotte to inform the President that all hope was gone for continuing the war. Even then, Davis refused to believe the end had come. He declared that he would go on to Alabama, join General Forrest, and if necessary fight the war from across the Mississippi.

That afternoon Breckinridge, who had served as Vice President of the United States under Buchanan and had run for President against Lincoln and Douglas, went out to Basil Duke's camp to be with old friends from Kentucky. "He seated himself at the foot of a large tree and talked for more than an hour with the men who crowded around him," Duke said. "Great curiosity was, of course, felt to learn something of the terms of the agreement with Sherman, and he answered all questions with perfect frankness." All Confederate soldiers east of the Mississippi were to surrender their arms as soon as arrangements could be completed, Breckinridge explained. The terms were honorable. They had fought bravely, but they had lost the war.

Like Jefferson Davis, however, there were still many who refused to accept the inevitability of defeat, some who felt as did one of Duke's boys who declared he would "sooner march to the Rio Grande than surrender to any Yankee."

In the last week of April, Davis issued orders to abandon Charlotte, and with Duke's Kentuckians and other units of his cavalry escort started for Abbeville. The column moved slowly down into South Carolina, through York and Union, crossing Broad River at Smith's Ford on April 29.

While on this march Duke recorded an encounter which some of his troopers had with an old lady who bitterly reproached them for taking forage from her barn. "You are a gang of thieving, rascally Kentuckians," she cried, "afraid to go home, while our boys are surrendering decently."

"Madam," one of them replied politely, "you are speaking out of your turn. South Carolina had a good deal to say in getting up this war, but we Kentuckians have contracted to close it out."

Their officers attempted to "close it out" on May 2, the day the President and his escort rode into Abbeville. On that afternoon they held the Confederacy's last council of war, with Davis presiding. Besides Generals Breckinridge and Bragg, the council consisted only of Basil Duke and the four other brigade commanders. By one of those odd coincidences of war, this last meeting of the Confederate government was held in the same town where the first secession meeting had been held five years earlier.

At the beginning of the discussion, Davis was affable, dignified, gave no sign of apprehension. He suggested that the South was suffering from unwarranted panic, that it yet had resources to continue the war, and therefore it was the duty of those who remained with arms in their hands to give an example to inspire others so that the Confederacy might be saved.

One by one, Breckinridge, Bragg, Duke, and the others reluctantly disagreed. The war was hopeless; they could not support prolonging it with useless bloodshed. Yet all agreed they would not disband their men until they had guarded the President to a place of safety.

"No," Davis cried, "I will listen to no propositions for my safety. I appeal to you for the cause of the country." For a minute or so the President lost his composure, bitterly accusing his generals of being willing to consent to the degradation of the South they had sworn to defend.

"We were silent," Duke wrote afterward, "for we could not agree with him, and respected him too much to reply. . . . When he arose to leave the room, he had lost his erect bearing, his face was pale, and he faltered so much in his step that he was compelled to lean on General Breckinridge. It was a sad sight to men who felt toward him as we did."

Resigned now to defeat, Davis' thoughts turned to the safety of his family. Determined to join them and escape from the country, he told his generals to be prepared to march at midnight for Washington, Georgia, where his family had last been reported.

The President had one more assignment for Basil Duke's Kentuckians. At ten o'clock that evening, Duke was summoned to the house where Davis and Breckinridge were staying, and was informed that his brigade had been selected to guard and transport the funds of the Confederate Treasury from Abbeville to Georgia. The Secretary of the Treasury, J. A. Trenholm, had fallen ill and could not accompany the column. Postmaster-General Reagan would act as treasurer, but Duke himself would be the responsible custodian until the money was delivered at Washington, Georgia.

It was not an assignment to Duke's liking. In the first place no one seemed to know how much treasure there was. Davis believed it consisted of about half a million dollars in gold and silver, but he had no official accounting in his possession.

Shortly before the abandonment of Richmond the treasure had been brought out by rail under guard of Captain William H. Parker and sixty midshipmen of the Confederate States Naval Academy. It was packed in sacks and boxes—double-eagle gold pieces, Mexican silver dollars, copper coins, silver bricks, gold ingots and nuggets. At Greensboro, North Carolina, Captain Parker detached two boxes of gold sovereigns, about $35,000 for expenses of the President and his Cabinet, and $39,000 to pay off General Johnston's troops.

When Parker's train reached Chester, South Carolina, he discovered the railroad was impassable beyond that point. He had to commandeer wagons, transfer his precious cargo, and haul it forty miles to Newberry where it was loaded aboard another railroad train.

On April 16, Parker brought the treasure into Abbeville, ran the boxcars containing it upon a siding, and set up a vigilant guard. He was waiting there when President Davis and the cavalry arrived on May 2, and was immensely relieved when he received orders to transfer the burden of responsibility to General Basil Duke.

It was pitch dark when Duke reported to Captain Parker with the President's transfer order. He had brought six wagons and a detail of fifty men, and without preliminaries the work of loading the treasure began.

Duke was anxious to obtain an exact statement of the sum he was to guard, but Parker had no listing whatsoever. He knew only that the bulk of the treasure was in Mexican dollars packed in nail kegs; the sacks of gold double-eagles supposedly contained five thousand dollars each; there was an undetermined number of gold ingots and some hundreds of pounds of copper cents.

"It was packed in money belts, shot bags, a few small iron chests and wooden boxes, some of them of the frailest description," Duke said afterward. "I searched through the cars by the light of a few tallow candles, and gathered up all that was shown me or that I could find. More than an hour was occupied in transferring the treasure from the cars to the wagons, and after the latter had been started off and had gotten perhaps half a mile away, Lieutenant John Cole, one of the officers of the guard, rode up to me and handed over a pine box which apparently contained between two or three thousand dollars in gold. After the rest of us had left the cars he had remained and continued the search, and in a car which we thought we had thoroughly examined he had discovered this box, stuck in a corner and covered up with a piece of brown sacking."

Although Duke had hoped to keep the nature of his cargo a secret confined to the boys of the loading detail, it was far too big a secret to conceal for long. By the time his column reached the Savannah River, the entire cavalry escort knew what was in the wagons guarded by Duke's Kentuckians.

Naturally, the boys began wondering what was going to happen to all this gold and silver. There were rumors that Jeff Davis had promised to use it to pay off all men who accompanied him to the Mississippi River, but from talk they heard among the junior officers they guessed the President had abandoned his plans to march west. Suppose the enemy overtook them before they could get the treasure out of the country; the Federals would seize all the money, give them paroles, send them home, and they would never receive their final pay.

Delegations from the ranks went to see Duke, and asked him if they could not be paid off immediately. Duke sympathized with their point of view, but passed the decision to General Breckinridge. Late on May 3, Breckinridge ordered the column halted, asked the quartermasters of each brigade to submit payrolls, and

there in the pine woods of Georgia the last armed troops of the
Confederacy lined up for their final pay.

Each of the 4,166 cavalrymen received about twenty-six dollars,
carefully counted out in gold and silver. Duke kept an exact accounting, recording $108,322.90 paid out. Before midnight his wag-
ons had been lightened by one fourth and the troopers had hard
money in their jeans pockets for the first time in many months.

Early the next afternoon when Duke halted his wagons outside
Washington, Georgia, he was pleased to learn that President Davis,
who had arrived ahead of the column, had appointed a new acting
treasurer to assume responsibility for the government funds. This
man was Captain Micajah H. Clark, former chief clerk of the Confederate executive office.

The transfer was arranged at Duke's camp about a mile outside
Washington. "Selecting the shade of a large elm tree as the 'Treasury Department,'" Micajah Clark later wrote, "I commenced my
duties as Acting Treasurer, C. S. A." His first order of business was
to count his holdings, and according to his records the amount totaled $288,022.90.

For years afterward there would be many lurid stories published
about the mystery of what happened to the Confederate treasure,
tales of buried gold in Georgia and Florida. In some of the early
stories, amounts usually were estimated at from two million to as
much as thirty million dollars in coin, bullion and gold nuggets.

As late as 1881, Captain Clark was still vainly attempting to quiet
these rumors and to deny charges that he knew more about the
treasure than he ever told. He prepared a detailed listing showing
how he disposed of the funds entrusted to his care, item by item.

Like Duke, he was eager to be rid of the treasure as quickly as
possible, handing out in a few hours large amounts to commissary
officers for purchase of rations, and to trusted officials who were
to transport the money to points where troops might be paid off before surrendering. In each case, Clark always required a signed receipt. But what happened to these "boxes of silver bullion" and
"kegs of Mexican silver dollars" after they left Clark's office under
the elm tree is not easy to determine.

The Captain's last payment before leaving Washington, Georgia,
was $86,000 in gold coin and silver bullion to "a trusted officer of

the Navy," Clark taking a receipt "for its transmission out of the Confederacy." What happened to this money is still a real mystery. Not long after Clark published his accounts in 1881, the young naval officer, William H. Parker, who escorted the treasury from Richmond to Abbeville, made a critical reply. Parker claimed that no naval officer had taken this money out of the country, and that the $86,000 had never been reported afterward. Parker also intimated that the amount which he took out of Richmond was at least $100,000 more than Clark's records showed.

One other aspect of the mystery is an official report of Major Charles M. Betts, 15th Pennsylvania Cavalry, describing the capture on May 8 of seven wagons hidden in the woods near the fork of the Appalachee and Oconee rivers, about thirty-five miles from Washington, Georgia. Major Betts discovered in these wagons four million dollars in Confederate paper money and $188,000 in coin. Whether this was a part of the treasure brought from Richmond, probably no one will ever know.

One of Duke's boys, Will Dyer, was inclined to scoff at all the furor over the mystery in later years. "There has been much written about the buried Confederate Treasure," he said, "but this is all moonshine. We got all the money there was in the treasury and the only wonder is that we got to keep it. The Yankees didn't know we had it or they would have prowled us sure." Of the $26.25 he received in final pay, he declared: "This was more money than I had seen for three years and I felt rich."

While Captain Clark was making his payments and taking his receipts on May 4, President Davis was preparing to leave Washington and continue south in hopes of overtaking his fleeing family. Aware by now that Federal cavalry patrols were in earnest pursuit of him, Davis decided to dress as a plain country farmer and travel in a covered wagon. On the insistence of his officers, however, a small military escort was formed to ride in the vicinity to insure his personal safety.

This escort consisted of Colonels William Preston Johnston, Francis R. Lubbock and John Taylor Wood, with a detail of "ten trusty men" under command of Captain Given Campbell. Captain Campbell had been with Colonel W. C. P. Breckinridge's 9th Kentucky Cavalry, but at one time he had served in the 2nd Regiment as an enlisted man. Eight of the "ten trusty men"—all carefully selected volunteers for this mission—were also from the old 2nd Kentucky.

A few hours after Davis' departure, General Breckinridge began ordering the cavalry brigades to march out in various directions from Washington. This was a scheme to divert the Federals so as to give the President time to be well on his way south before all the escort surrendered. Commanders of the different brigades were instructed not to offer battle; if confronted by Federal forces they were to surrender and take paroles.

As part of this plan, Basil Duke was ordered to march his brigade to Woodstock, Georgia, and it was there that the survivors of the 2nd Kentucky Cavalry stood their last formation on May 8, 1865.

Duke made no solemn ceremony of this disbanding of the old Morgan command. He advised the boys to return to their homes. For almost four years they had fought against heavy odds in manpower and resources, and he assured them that there was no disgrace in being released from service which they had worthily discharged. They left Woodstock in small parties, most of the Kentuckians going toward Chattanooga, a few to Augusta. The Mississippians and Texans rode off to the west.

As they came to Federal camps along the way they surrendered voluntarily, and in most cases met with no recrimination from the victors. These men who had faced each other in battle respected each other's courage. Each Confederate soldier signed a parole, a form not standardized but varying according to the issuing officer, sometimes quite brief, sometimes elaborate with a sworn statement not to bear arms against the United States, a description of the height, and the hair, eye, and complexion coloration of the parolee. Most statements included a reassuring phrase, such as, "not to be disturbed by the authorities of the United States so long as he observes this parole and obeys the laws in force where he may reside."

The disarmed Confederates treasured these fragile bits of paper above all other possessions; many would preserve them carefully to the ends of their lives. They could go home now, knowing they were free men *not to be disturbed*, losers in war, unvanquished in spirit.

4

But there were still on May 8, twelve Morgan men—eleven of them originally from the old 2nd—who were very much involved in the pursuance of their military obligations. These were Captain Given Campbell and eight of the ten troopers riding with Jefferson Davis; and Winder Monroe, Leeland Hathaway and Jack Messick who had been escorting the President's wife.

After Davis rejoined his family in the pine woods near Irwinville, the journey was temporarily delayed for a happy reunion. It was late in the day; orders were given to unhitch mules and horses for a night camp.

Hathaway and his two companions were appalled that the President had no intention of resuming travel during the night. Being veteran cavalrymen they felt that safety now lay only in rapid movement—as John Morgan had taught them on their raids—rapid movement and light equipment.

Unable to restrain himself, Hathaway made bold to approach the President and offer some polite advice. "Mr. President," he said in his slow Kentucky speech, "don't you know that the Yankees know you are traveling this course and that you are burdened with all this stuff?"

Before Davis could reply, Burton Harrison interrupted. "Not necessarily so," the secretary said coldly.

"You evidently underestimate your enemy then," Hathaway retorted, "which is always dangerous. If a regiment of Morgan's old command were in the neighborhood of such a train as this it would know to a dot everything about it."

If Davis made any comment during this conversation, Hathaway failed to record it. "I couldn't change their programme," he wrote, "and I couldn't cut loose from them situated as were Mrs. Davis and her children, so I staid—and the catastrophe came, about daylight on the morning of the 10th of May."

They bedded down that last night under tall long-needled pines, the moonlit forest quiet but for the gentle brushing of a warm spring wind in the pluming treetops. There were twenty-one men, Varina Davis and her sister, the four Davis children and two serv-

ants—all that was left of the power and glory of the Confederate
States of America. Curiously, of the twenty-one men fourteen were
Kentuckians—representatives of a state which had been divided in
loyalties.

The Yankees came at dawn, as Lee Hathaway had warned they
would, two different cavalry regiments, each unaware of the other's
presence, both eager to win credit for capturing Jeff Davis. Lieutenant Colonel Benjamin D. Pritchard's 4th Michigan arrived a few
minutes ahead of Lieutenant Colonel Henry Harnden's 1st Wisconsin, charging in and throwing a cordon around the camp.

Awakened by their approach, William Preston Johnston arose
and pulled on his boots. As he started toward the campfire he saw
eight or ten mounted men riding like ghosts out of the morning
mist. In the shadowy light he could not determine their uniforms,
but he turned back to his saddle which he had been using as a pillow, and was searching for his revolver when three men in Union
blue dashed up and ordered him to surrender. They took his
weapon and ordered him over to the campfire. A moment later a
burst of rifle fire crackled out of the forest, echoing, increasing in
rapidity. The guards hesitated a minute or so, then remounted and
rode quickly away.

Johnston hurried toward the Davis tent, some fifty yards from
the fire. The President was seated calmly on a camp stool, getting
into a pair of cavalry boots. Varina Davis was weeping; she was
both frightened and angry. She told Johnston that the intruders had
taken her husband's waterproof coat; she believed they were only
thieving guerrillas. But Johnston shook his head. "This is bad business, sir," he said to Davis, then noticing the President was shiver-
ing from cold, he turned to go and find a coat for him. The rifle fire
was continuing off to one side of the camp, but he knew now that
none of the Confederate escort was involved. They were all gathered around the campfire under guard of a Yankee captain and a
squad of dismounted troopers.

As Johnston came up to the group, he said mildly: "Captain,
your men are fighting each other over yonder." The Yankee Captain looked startled; he said he thought his men were fighting Jeff
Davis' escort.

"You have our whole camp," Johnston assured him. "I know your men are fighting each other. We have nobody on that side of the slough."

It was as Johnston said. Harnden's 1st Wisconsin had blundered into Pritchard's 4th Michigan, and for several minutes they fought among the thick pines, each believing the other was Confederate cavalry. Not until the Wisconsin troopers captured one of the Michigan men was the error discovered. Two Michigan men were already dead; several Wisconsin men severely wounded. Until long after the war there would be ill-feeling between these two regiments, each blaming the other for the error, each claiming credit for finding Jeff Davis.

The actual business of capturing the Confederate Chief of State was a simple matter, although there are almost as many versions of the affair as there were witnesses. One story has it that Davis was preparing to mount his horse and escape when a Federal soldier halted him and demanded: "Are you armed?"

"If I were armed," replied Davis, "you would not be living to ask the question."

Much was made of the costume worn by the President at the time of his capture, the Northern press publishing colorful descriptions of how he was disguised as a woman, with accompanying caricatures showing him in outlandish female garb. From all official accounts of the Federal officers present, however, it is clear that he was wearing trousers, cavalry boots, and a lady's shawl or waterproof wrapper thrown over his shoulders by his wife.

After the President and his party were taken into custody, Lieutenant Colonel Pritchard carefully recorded their names, first listing the officers and then adding the following: "Private Sanders, 2nd Kentucky Cavalry; Private Walbert, 2nd Kentucky Cavalry; Private Baker, 2nd Kentucky Cavalry; Private Smith, 2nd Kentucky Cavalry; Private Heath, 2nd Kentucky Cavalry; Private Elston, 2nd Kentucky Cavalry; Private J. W. Farley, 2nd Kentucky Cavalry."

All the captives were searched, their baggage opened and examined for arms and valuables. Monroe, Hathaway and Messick managed to conceal the precious twenty-dollar gold coins which Varina Davis had given them, but the others lost everything. Captain Given Campbell and his ten men had to surrender their last pay, more than three hundred dollars in gold. Johnston gave up fifteen hundred dollars in personal funds. In a pair of saddlebags, Pritchard's men found about three thousand dollars which had been assigned by Micajah Clark for the President's expenses in fleeing the country. Johnston vainly protested the seizure of his pair of pistols: they had been worn by his father, Albert Sidney Johnston, during the battle of Shiloh.

Lee Hathaway also lost a prized pistol, presented to him only a few hours before by the President as a token of appreciation for what the young lieutenant had done for his family. "We were then placed under heavy guard," Hathaway said, "for the melancholy march to Macon, Georgia."

On the second day of the prisoners' four-day journey to Macon, Hathaway told of being "much shocked and grieved at sight of a large streamer bearing the ominous words: $100,000 REWARD FOR THE CAPTURE OF JEFF DAVIS. This was carried aloft on a flag staff and was borne by one of a body of cavalry which came from the direction of Macon."

The legend on this banner was the first knowledge Lieutenant Colonel Pritchard and his 4th Michigan cavalrymen had of such a reward, and its immediate effect was to set in motion a number of rival claims among the men. Pritchard resolved the controversy by suggesting that the reward be distributed among all the men present at the time of Jefferson Davis' capture.

The banner's effect upon the captured Confederates was to create uneasiness among them for the President's safety. Now that it was known that Davis was worth $100,000, they feared the Yankees might shoot him to make certain he could not escape.

But their fears were groundless. In fact, when Pritchard brought his prisoners into Macon on May 13, to turn them over to Major General James H. Wilson, the latter greeted Davis by ordering his troops drawn up in double lines facing inward, and they presented arms to the Confederate President as he passed between them.

This would be the last recognition of Jefferson Davis' office, however. After the Union Army passed him on to the vindictive Secretary of War, Edwin M. Stanton, his life would become a hell of miseries and indignities.

From Macon the prisoners were taken to Augusta where they were marched aboard a gunboat, and transported to Savannah and up the coast to Hilton Head. On May 20, they were in Hampton Roads surrounded by a cordon of warships. Hathaway, Monroe and Messick were the last of the Morgan men in captivity, the others having been paroled in Georgia, and they thought surely that now they would be released. But when Jeff Davis was taken off to Fortress Monroe, the three young men were transferred to another vessel. This ship sailed north, and although they were told nothing of their destination, the boys were more confident than ever that at the end of the voyage they would be set free.

Instead, the ship docked off Fort McHenry and they were hustled ashore without ceremony and imprisoned in an old brick stable. They were locked into separate cells with heavy double oak doors, the only ventilation and light coming from a tiny slit in the outer wall. No one would tell them why they were there.

By raising their voices they could talk to one another through the walls of the adjoining cells. For several days they kept each other's spirits up by shouting encouragements back and forth; they fought bedbugs day and night; they carefully cultivated one of the friendlier guards. When they asked this guard why they were being held as prisoners, he told them frankly that he did not know, but would try to find out. The guard made inquiries, but no one at Fort McHenry seemed to know why the three young Confederates were there. When they sent the guard to bring pencil and paper so that they might write to relatives, he returned and informed them that they would not be allowed to communicate with relatives or anybody else outside.

After nearly two months of this maddening uncertainty, Hathaway decided to risk his precious twenty-dollar gold piece, the present from Varina Davis. He showed the coin to the friendly guard and told him he could have it if he would take a letter into Baltimore and mail it. When the guard agreed to do this, Hathaway tore a leaf from his Bible, and with a stub of pencil scrawled a note to his father in Kentucky. He had to rely on the guard to furnish an envelope and address it, and to make certain that this was done, Hathaway refused to release his gold coin until the guard returned with a receipt showing the letter had been mailed.

The letter reached its destination, and as soon as the boys' relatives in Kentucky learned where they were, representatives from their families journeyed to Baltimore—only to be refused admittance to Fort McHenry. Nor would the commandant give them any reason why their boys were still being held as prisoners.

Acting as spokesman for the group, Hathaway's father went directly to President Andrew Johnson in Washington and showed him the note which his son had written on the torn Bible leaf.

"What is your boy doing in Fort McHenry?" Johnson asked.

"I don't know. That's what I've been trying to learn. I've come to you for help."

"Are there charges against him?"

The elder Hathaway did not know; apparently his son did not know either. President Johnson sent him to see Secretary Stanton to find out what the charges were. Stanton seemed to be quite familiar with the names Hathaway, Monroe and Messick. They had been captured with Jeff Davis, Stanton said. He admitted there were no charges against the young men, but he declared that he eventually expected to link them directly with the assassination plot against President Lincoln. He hoped to prove that Jeff Davis had arranged the assassination, and he suspected that these three boys were involved in it. Therefore, he could not release them.

Frustrated and considerably alarmed after his interview with Stanton, Hathaway's father returned to the White House and told Andrew Johnson what he had learned. Johnson, who was already beginning to distrust Stanton, sent off a messenger to the Secretary, ordering him either to bring charges against his three prisoners or to release them. Stanton returned the messenger with a note of refusal.

In the presence of the elder Hathaway, Johnson exploded verbally. "I will show Stanton who is President!" he shouted, and wrote out an order instructing the commandant at Fort McHenry to free the prisoners Leeland Hathaway, Winder Monroe and Jack Messick.

And so it was that the last troopers of John Morgan's command —and the last representative of the 2nd Kentucky Cavalry—returned to their homes in the Bluegrass during the peaceful summer of 1865.

Others like them were still finding their different ways back to a world that looked much the same, but was not the same, and never again would be anything like the world they left in 1861 to join

John Morgan's cavalry. They were not certain how they would be received by neighbors, cousins, brothers—who had fought on the other side of the great conflict.

It was Basil Duke, their last leader, who most eloquently expressed their unspoken emotions: "There was no humiliation for these men," he wrote. "They had done their part and served faithfully, until there was no longer a cause and a country to serve. They knew not what their fate would be, and indulged in no speculation regarding it. They had been taught fortitude by the past, and, without useless repining and unmanly fear, they faced the future."

SOURCES

ALBAUGH, WILLIAM A. AND EDWARD N. SIMMONS. *Confederate Arms.* Harrisburg, Pa., 1957.

ALLEN, JAMES LANE. *The Blue-grass Region of Kentucky.* New York, 1892.

AMERICAN GUIDE SERIES. *Military History of Kentucky.* Frankfort, Ky., 1939.

Annals of the War. Philadelphia, 1879.

BEATTY, JOHN. *Memoirs of a Volunteer.* New York, 1946.

BENTLEY, W. H. *History of the 77th Illinois Volunteer Infantry.* Peoria, Ill., 1883.

BERRY, THOMAS F. *Four Years with Morgan and Forrest.* Oklahoma City, Okla., 1914.

BICKHAM, WILLIAM D. *Rosecrans' Campaign with the Fourteenth Army Corps.* Cincinnati, O., 1863.

Blackwood's Magazine, Vols. 93-97

BOWLES, JAMES W. Personal Papers, Confederate War Records, National Archives.

CALKINS, WILLIAM W. *The History of the One Hundred and Fourth Regiment of Illinois Volunteer Infantry.* Chicago, 1895.

CAMP DOUGLAS, CHICAGO. Record of Prisoners of War at Camp Douglas, Auxiliary Register No. 2, Prisoners from the Second Kentucky Cavalry, War Department Collection of Confederate Records, National Archives.

CARTER, HOWELL. *A Cavalryman's Reminiscences of the Civil War.* New Orleans, La., n.d.

CARTER, WILLIAM H. *Horses, Saddles and Bridles.* Baltimore, Md., 1906.

CASTLEMAN, JOHN B. *Active Service.* Louisville, Ky., 1917.

Century Magazine, 1891.

322

Chicago Tribune, 1863-1865.

Cincinnati Enquirer, 1863.

Cincinnati Gazette, July, 1863.

CIST, HENRY M. *The Army of the Cumberland*. New York, 1882.

Civil War History.

CLARK, THOMAS D. *A History of Kentucky*. New York, 1937.

COFFMAN, EDWARD M. "The Civil War Career of Thomas Henry Hines." Master's Thesis, University of Kentucky, Lexington, Ky., 1955.

COLEMAN, J. WINSTON, JR. *Lexington During the Civil War*. Lexington, Ky., 1938.

Confederate Veteran.

COOKE, PHILIP ST. GEORGE. *Cavalry Tactics*. New York, 1872.

COULTER, E. MERTON. *The Civil War and Readjustment in Kentucky*. Chapel Hill, N. C., 1926.

DAVIESS, MARIA T. *History of Mercer and Boyle Counties*. Harrodsburg, Ky., 1924.

DAVIS, WILLIAM J. Letters. Filson Club, Louisville, Ky.

DENISON, GEORGE T. *A History of Cavalry*. London, 1913.

DUKE, BASIL. *History of Morgan's Cavalry*. Cincinnati, O., 1867.

———. "Personal Recollections of Shiloh." Manuscript, Filson Club, Louisville, Ky.

———. *Reminiscences*. New York, 1911.

DUNKLE, J. J. (Fritz Fuzzlebug) *Prison Life During the Rebellion*. Singer's Glen, Va., 1869.

DYER, JOHN WILL. *Reminiscences; or Four Years in the Confederate Army*. Evansville, Ind., 1898.

EAST TENNESSEE HISTORICAL SOCIETY. *Publications*.

EGGLESTON, GEORGE C. *A Rebel's Recollections*. New York, 1905.

EISENSCHIML, OTTO. *The Story of Shiloh*. Chicago, 1946.

ELLSWORTH, GEORGE A. Miscellaneous folder of notes and clippings. Kentucky State Historical Society, Frankfort, Ky.

EVANS, CLEMENT A., ed. *Confederate Military History*. 10 vols. Atlanta, Ga., 1899.

FARSHLER, EARL R. *The American Saddle Horse.* Louisville, Ky., 1933.

FEDERAL WRITERS' PROJECT. *Lexington and the Bluegrass Country.* Lexington, Ky., 1938.

Filson Club History Quarterly.

FLEHARTY, S. F. *Our Regiment, a History of the 102 Illinois Infantry Volunteers.* Chicago, 1865.

FLINT, TIMOTHY. *Recollections of the Last Ten Years.* Boston, 1826.

FORD, SALLY ROCHESTER. *Raids and Romance of Morgan and His Men.* Mobile, Ala., 1863.

FREEMANTLE, SIR ARTHUR J. L. *Three Months in the Southern States.* New York, 1864.

FULLER, CLAUD E. AND RICHARD D. STEUART. *Firearms of the Confederacy.* Huntington, W. Va., 1944.

GAMMAGE, W. L. *The Camp, the Bivouac, and the Battle Field.* Selma, Ala., 1864.

Georgia Historical Quarterly.

GORGAS, JOSIAH. *Civil War Diary*, edited by Frank E. Vandiver. University of Alabama, Tuscaloosa, Ala., 1947.

HANNA, A. J. *Flight into Oblivion.* Richmond, Va., 1938.

HARDIN, BAYLESS. *Brigadier-General John Hunt Morgan of Kentucky.* 1938.

HARWELL, RICHARD B., ed. *The Confederate Reader.* New York, 1957.

HATHAWAY, LEELAND. Papers. University of Kentucky Library, Lexington, Ky.

HERR, KINCAID A. *The L & N Railroad, 1850-1942.* Louisville, Ky., n.d.

HERVEY, JOHN. *Racing in America, 1665-1865.* 2 vols. New York, 1944.

HINES, THOMAS HENRY. Papers. University of Kentucky Library, Lexington, Ky.

HOLLAND, CECIL FLETCHER. *Morgan and His Raiders.* New York, 1943.

HORAN, JAMES D. *Confederate Agent.* New York, 1954.

HORN, STANLEY F. *The Army of Tennessee.* Indianapolis, Ind., 1941.

INDIANA HISTORICAL SOCIETY. *Publications.*

Indiana Magazine of History.

JOHN, DON D. *The Great Indiana-Ohio Raid.* Louisville, Ky., n.d.

JOHNSON, ADAM RANKIN. *The Partisan Rangers of the Confederate States Army.* Louisville, Ky., 1904.

JOHNSTON, WILLIAM PRESTON. *Life of Albert Sidney Johnston.* New York, 1880.

KENTUCKY ADJUTANT GENERAL. Report, *Confederate Kentucky Volunteers, War 1861-65.* Frankfort, Ky., 1915.

KENTUCKY STATE HISTORICAL SOCIETY. *Register.*

Kentucky Statesman.

KOTT, W. T. "History of Marion County, Kentucky." Manuscript, Filson Club, Louisville, Ky.

LA BREE, BEN, ed. *The Confederate Soldier in the Civil War.* Louisville, Ky., 1897.

The Land We Love.

Lexington Herald.

Lexington Observer and Reporter.

LOGAN, MRS. INDIA W. P. *Kelion Franklin Peddicord of Quirk's Scouts, Morgan's Kentucky Cavalry, C.S.A.* New York, 1908.

LONN, ELLA. *Foreigners in the Confederacy.* Chapel Hill, N.C., 1940.

Louisville Daily Journal, 1861-1865.

MCMEEKIN, CLARK. *Old Kentucky Country.* New York, 1957.

Magazine of Western History, Vol. 4, 1886.

MAURY, D. H. *Skirmish Drill for Mounted Troops.* Richmond, Va., 1861.

MILITARY ORDER OF THE LOYAL LEGION. Ohio Commandery. *Sketches of War History, 1861-1865.* Vol. 5. Cincinnati, O., 1903.

MILLER, FRANCIS T., ed. *Photographic History of the Civil War.* 10 vols. New York, 1911.

MONROE, WINDER. Personal Papers. Confederate War Records, National Archives.

MOORE, FRANK, ed. *The Rebellion Record.* 11 vols. New York, 1864-68.

MORGAN, MRS. IRBY. *How It Was; Four Years Among the Rebels.* Nashville, Tenn., 1892.

MOSGROVE, GEORGE D. *Kentucky Cavaliers in Dixie.* Jackson, Tenn., 1957.

Munsey's Magazine, Vol. 33, 1905.

NASH, CHARLES EDWARD. *Biographical Sketches of General Pat Cleburne and General T. C. Hindman*. 1898.

New York Herald, 1863.

Ohio Archaelogical and Historical Quarterly.

Ordnance Manual for the Use of Officers of the United States Army. Philadelphia, 1861.

POLLARD, EDWARD A. *Life of Jefferson Davis, with a Secret History of the Southern Confederacy*. Philadelphia, 1869.

PLUM, WILLIAM R. *The Military Telegraph During the Civil War*. 2 vols. Chicago, 1882.

RANCK, GEORGE W. *History of Lexington, Kentucky*. Cincinnati, O., 1872.

REID, SAMUEL C., JR. *Capture and Escape of General John H. Morgan*, edited by Joseph J. Mathews. Atlanta, Ga., 1947.

REID, WHITELAW. *Ohio in the War*. Cincinnati, O., 2 vols., 1893.

Richmond Enquirer, 1864.

Richmond Whig, 1864.

RIDLEY, BROMFIELD. *Battles and Sketches of the Army of Tennessee*. Mexico, Mo., 1906.

ROSS, FITZGERALD. *A Visit to Cities and Camps of the Confederate States*, edited by Richard B. Harwell. Urbana, Ill., 1958.

SCHARF, EMILY E. *Famous Saddle Horses*. Louisville, Ky., 1932.

SENOUR, F. *Morgan and His Captors*. Cincinnati, O., 1865.

SENSING, THURMAN. *Champ Ferguson*. Nashville, Tenn., 1942.

SIMMONS, FLORA E. *A Complete Account of the John Morgan Raid through Kentucky, Indiana and Ohio, in July 1863*. Louisville, Ky., 1863.

SMITH, SYDNEY K. *Life, Army Record, and Public Services of D. Howard Smith*. Louisville, Ky., 1890.

Southern Bivouac.

SOUTHERN HISTORICAL SOCIETY. *Papers.*

Southwestern Historical Quarterly. Vol. 22, 1918-19.

STONE FAMILY PAPERS. Kentucky State Historical Society, Frankfort, Ky.

STONG, PHIL. *Horses and Americans*. New York, 1939.

SWIGGETT, HOWARD. *The Rebel Raider*. Indianapolis, Ind., 1934.

TARRANT, EASTHAM. *The Wild Riders of the First Kentucky Cavalry*. Louisville, Ky., 1894.

Tennessee Historical Quarterly.

THIELE, THOMAS FREDERICK. "The Evolution of Cavalry in the American Civil War, 1861-1863." Ph.D. Dissertation, University of Michigan, Ann Arbor, Mich., 1951.

THOMPSON, ED PORTER. *History of the First Kentucky Brigade*. Cincinnati, O., 1868.

THOMPSON, LAWRENCE. *Kentucky Tradition*. Hamden, Conn., 1956.

TIBBALS, ALMA OWENS. *A History of Pulaski County, Kentucky*. Bagdad, Ky., 1952.

U. S. COMMISSIONER OF AGRICULTURE. *Report, 1863*. Washington, D.C., 1863.

U. S. CONGRESS. 39th. 2nd sess. House of Representatives. *Message from the President of the United States in Answer to a Resolution of the House of the 19th December, Transmitting Papers Relating to the Case of George St. Leger Grenfel, Jan. 21, 1867*. (Executive Document 50) Washington, D.C., 1867.

U. S. WAR DEPARTMENT. Collection of Confederate Records, 2nd Kentucky Cavalry. Muster rolls, official correspondence and other records.

U. S. WAR DEPARTMENT. *The War of the Rebellion; a Compilation of the Official Records*. 128 vols. Washington, D.C., 1880-1901.

VALE, J. G. *Minty and the Cavalry*. Harrisburg, Pa., 1886.

WEST TENNESSEE HISTORICAL SOCIETY. *Papers*.

Wilkes' Spirit of the Times, 1863-64.

WINSTON, ROBERT W. *High Stakes and Hair Trigger, the Life of Jefferson Davis*. New York, 1930.

YOUNG, BENNETT H. *Confederate Wizards of the Saddle*. Boston, 1916.

NOTES

Abbreviations Used:

CV: Confederate Veteran

FCHQ: Filson Club History Quarterly

KSHS: Kentucky State Historical Society

OR: U.S. War Department. The War of the Rebellion, a Compilation of the Official Records

SHSP: Southern Historical Society Papers

USWD-CR: U.S. War Department. Collection of Confederate Records, National Archives.

I Kentucky Boys Are Alligator Horses

Lexington and the South in 1861: Winston Coleman, Jr., *Lexington During the Civil War;* Duke, *History,* 36-90; Holland, 29-41; Ranck, 377; Evans, IX, 32-39; Coulter, 81-137; *Kentucky Statesman,* August 10, 1858; January-September 1861.

The Lexington Rifles Enter the War: OR, Ser.I, XXX, Pt. 3, 686; Duke, *History,* 90-91; Holland, 41; Hervey, II, 247; Berry, 4-10; Allen, 38-40; Flint, 69-71; James B. McCreary, "Journal of My Soldier Life," KSHS, *Register,* XXXIII (1935), 97-117; Duke, *Reminiscences,* 32, 78, 291; Winston Coleman, Jr., "Kentucky Watering Places," FCHQ (1942), XVI, 19-20; *Lexington Observer and Reporter,* June 21, 1859.

To Green River: Castleman, 73; Allen, 201; Holland, 41-42; Duke, *Reminiscences,* 291; Berry, 11; Kentucky Adjutant General, Report, *Confederate Kentucky Volunteers, War 1861-65,* 548-94; James W. Henning, "Basil Wilson Duke," FCHQ (1940), XIV, 60-64.

II Green River Cavaliers

Scouting, Training and Horseflesh: OR, Ser.I, LII, Pt. 2, 195-97; Duke, *History,* 95-106; Berry, 29-34; Holland, 47; Denison, 362; Evans, IX,

37; William Littell, *The Statute Law of Kentucky* (Frankfort, Ky.), I, 136; Stong, 224; John B. Castleman, "The American Saddle Horse," U.S. Bureau of Animal Industry, Annual Report, XIX (1902), 62-78; Francis Morris, "Cavalry Horses in America," U.S. Commissioner of Agriculture, Report, 1863, 159-175; Allen, 24; Maury, 26-28; Kentucky Adjutant General, Report, *Confederate Kentucky Volunteers, Wai 1861-65,* 548-49; Ridley, 98-100.

Winter and Withdrawal: OR, Ser.I, VII, 12-13; Ser.II, III, 786; Nashville *Republican Banner,* December 10, 1861; Swiggett, 43; Evans, IX, 37.

Nashville to Murfreesboro: OR, Ser.I, VII, 426-30, 433-34, 904; Berry, 43; Evans, IX, 56; Duke, *History,* 112-18, 121-32; Johnson, 71; Holland, 68-70; Logan, 36.

Screening Johnston's Retreat: Evans, IX, 65; Holland, 83-88; Duke, *History,* 135-36.

III Shiloh

Burnsville to Shiloh: OR, Ser.I, X, Pt. 1, 614; LII, Pt. 1, 29; Johnston, 561-63; Duke, *History,* 138-39; Ridley, 460; Mosgrove, 61.

The Attack: Basil W. Duke, "Personal Recollection of Shiloh," Manuscript, Filson Club; Swiggett, 51; Evans, IX, 223; Johnston, 569-85; Duke, *Reminiscences,* 291, John H. Weller, "History of the Fourth Kentucky Infantry," SHSP, IX (1881), 108-15; Fitzgerald Ross, "A Visit to the Cities and Camps of the Confederate States," *Blackwood's Magazine,* XCVI (1864), 656; OR, Ser.I, X, Pt. 1, 521-22.

The Battle: Basil W. Duke, "Personal Recollection of Shiloh," Manuscript, Filson Club; OR, Ser.I, X, Pt. 1, 522, 569, 617-19, 626: Johnston, 586-606; Eisenschiml, 39-49; J. K. P. Blackburn, "'Reminiscences of the Terry Rangers," *Southwestern Historical Quarterly,* XII (1918), 55.

Rear-Guard Duty: OR, Ser.I, X, Pt. 1, 619; Duke, *History,* 154-55.

IV The Lebanon Races

Across Tennessee to Lebanon: OR, Ser.I, X, Pt. 2, 437-38, 876; LII, Pt. 2, 306-307, 309; Duke, *Reminiscences,* 300-301; Evans, IX, 83; Beatty, 102; Duke, *History,* 156-59; Fitzgerald Ross, "A Month's Visit to the Confederate Headquarters," *Blackwood's Magazine,* XCIII (1863), 8; Fitzgerald Ross, "A Visit to the Cities and Camps of the Confederate States," *Blackwood's Magazine,* XCVI (1864), 654; Berry, 66-68.

Action in Lebanon: Kentucky Adjutant General, Report, *Confederate Kentucky Volunteers, War 1861-65,* 540-56; OR, Ser.I, X, Pt. 1, 884-86; XVI, Pt. 2, 207; XXXII, Pt. 3, 256; Swiggett, 55; Duke, *History,*

160-63; Ridley, 99-100, 461; Hambleton Tapp, "Incidents in the Life of Frank Wolford," FCHQ, X (1936), 82-99; *Louisville Daily Journal*, May 14, 1862; Eastham Tarrant, *Wild Riders of the First Kentucky Cavalry;* Carl Sager, "A Boy in the Confederate Cavalry," CV, XXXVI (1928), 374-76.

Adventure in Cave City: OR, Ser.I, X, Pt. 1, 891; Holland, 103; Evans, IX, 83; Duke, *History*, 164-67.

John Castleman and Company D: USWD-CR, 2nd Kentucky Cavalry, National Archives; Castleman, 73-79; Duke, *History*, 169-70; Farshler, 163-65; Swiggett, 36; Evans, IX, 95; Scharf, 46.

St. Leger Grenfell: Milford Overley, "Old St. Leger," CV, XIII (1905), 80-81; U.S. Congress, *Case of George St. Leger Grenfel*, 598-600, 637; Duke, *History*, 180-81; A. H. Packe, Letter to the author, August 18, 1958; Lonn, 190; Duke, *Reminiscences*, 150; W. L. Chew, "Colonel St. Leger Grenfell," CV, XXXVI (1928), 446.

Affair of Major Coffey: OR, Ser.II, IV, 790, 833; Duke, *Reminiscences*, 86-90; Holland, 105, 115-16.

V RETURN TO THE BLUEGRASS

Knoxville to Celina: OR, Ser.II, IV, 877; USWD-CR, 2nd Kentucky Cavalry, National Archives; Duke, *Reminiscences*, 296; Mosgrove, 62-63, 150; Logan, 66-67.

Glasgow and Lebanon, Kentucky: USWD-CR, 2nd Kentucky Cavalry, National Archives; OR, Ser.I, XVI, Pt. 1, 767, 774-81; Ser.II, IV, 660, 915; Berry, 75; Senour, 57-59; Duke, *Reminiscences*, 152-53; Fuller and Steuart, 193, 246; Lonn, 276-77; Plum, I, 193-94, 201; CV, VIII (1900), 35-36; Duke, *History*, 179, 187; *Ordnance Manual*, 19, 75, 153; Ridley, 118.

Harrodsburg: OR, Ser.I, XVI, Pt. 1, 738; Duke, *History*, 190; Holland, 119-20; Daviess, 101-102.

Georgetown: OR, Ser.I, XVI, Pt. 1, 776; Duke, *History*, 192-94.

Adventures of Company D: Castleman, 79-91; *Lexington Herald*, July 25, 1925.

Action at Cynthiana: OR, Ser.I, XVI, Pt. 1, 756, 767, 782-83; Duke, *History*, 200-202; Paris (Kentucky) *Western Citizen*, July 22, 1862; Lonn, 190-93; Milford Overley, "Old St. Leger," CV, XIII (1905), 80-81; Berry, 81-82; Senour, 61, 70-71; Swiggett, 67.

Return to Tennessee: USWD-CR, 2nd Kentucky Cavalry, National Archives; OR, Ser.I, XVI, Pt. 1, 780-81; Duke, *History*, 25, 172-78; 204-207; 212; Fitzgerald Ross, "A Visit to the Cities and Camps of the

Confederate States," *Blackwood's Magazine*, XCVI (1864), 653, 669; XCVII (1865), 40, 162; Johnson, 455; Mosgrove, 61; Evans, IX, 91; Denison, 364; Thomas F. Thiele, "The Evolution of Cavalry in the American Civil War, 1861-1863"; Castleman, 92-93; Maury, 10-12; Mattie Wheeler, "Journal," edited by Frances L. S. Dugan, FCHQ, XXIX (1955), 124.

VI THE SPARTAN LIFE

Sparta and Prisoner Exchanges: OR, Ser.I, XX, Pt. 2, 89; Ser.II, III, 9-10, 302, 308, 551; Castleman, 93; Duke, *Reminiscences*, 128-29; 275-78; Swiggett, 69; Morgan, 59; Beatty, 134; Duke, *History*, 210; Holland, 14-15; USWD-CR, 2nd Kentucky Cavalry, National Archives.

Hartsville and Gallatin: OR, Ser.I, XVI, Pt. 1, 842-57; Holland, 136-208; Evans, IX, 33; Castleman, 93-94; Duke, *History*, 213-14, 226; L. S. Ferrell, "Morgan's Scout Childress and His Death," CV, VIII (1900), 450; Ben Drake, "Captain Quirk's Marvelous Heroism," CV, V (1897), 16-17; Plum, I, 275; Morgan, 173; Thomas F. Thiele, "The Evolution of Cavalry in the American Civil War, 1861-1863"; Duke, *Reminiscences*, 161; *Vidette*, August 16, 1862.

The Chase to Nashville: Duke, *History*, 215-17; Holland, 141, 208.

Victory over Johnson's Cavalry: OR, Ser.I, XVI, Pt. 1, 871-82; Pt. 2, 349; Evans, IX, 111; Castleman, 95-96; W. A. Kendall, "Magnanimity of General John Morgan," CV, VIII (1900), 88; *Vidette*, August 24, 1862, as reproduced in Morgan, 187-88; Logan, 114; Drake, *op. cit.*, 16-17.

Affair of the Courts-Martial: Duke, *Reminiscences*, 249-53.

VII DARK AND BLOODY GROUND

March to Lexington: Morgan, 172; Duke, *History*, 229-233; Ridley, 637; Holland, 144-46; Duke, *Reminiscences*, 292; Mattie Wheeler, "Journal," edited by Frances L. S. Dugan, FCHQ, XXIX (1955), 125-26.

Lexington Incidents: J. G. Law, Diary, SHSP, XII (1884), 542; Castleman, 127; Berry, 152; Swiggett, 74; Gammage, 47.

The 2nd Moves North: OR, Ser.I, XVI, Pt. 2, 813; Duke, *History*, 239-48.

Augusta Fight: OR, Ser.I, XVI, Pt. 1, 556-57, 895; Pt. 2, 1011-15; Lawrence Thompson, 175; Evans, IX, 3; Walter Rankins, "Morgan's Cavalry and the Home Guard at Augusta, Kentucky," FCHQ, XXVII (1953), 308-20; J. Jeffery Auer, "The Little Fight," KSHS, *Register*,

XLIX (1951), 28-34; *Louisville Daily Journal,* October 2, 1862; Senour, 73-77; McMeekin, 182-83.

Bragg Orders Retreat: OR, Ser.I, XVI, Pt. 2, 652, 915; Duke, *History,* 260-81; Coulter, 166-69; Horn, 186-89; H. V. Redfield, "Characteristics of the Armies," *Annals of the War,* 357-71.

The 2nd Returns to Lexington: OR, Ser.I, XVI, Pt. 2, 630; *Louisville Daily Journal,* October 22, 1862; Duke, *History,* 282-87; Holland, 155-56; Mattie Wheeler, *op. cit.,* 128.

Long March to Hopkinsville: USWD-CR, 2nd Kentucky Cavalry, National Archives; Duke, *History,* 287-92; Castleman, 101.

Tennessee Again: Holland, 159-60; Beatty, 135-36; Horn, 209-10.

Fiasco at Nashville: OR, Ser.I, XX, Pt. 1, 4-5; Pt. 2, 388; Duke, *History,* 296-98.

Hartsville and the New Brigade: USWD-CR, 2nd Kentucky Cavalry, National Archives; OR, Ser.I, XX, Pt. 1, 40-68; Pt. 2, 108; LII, Pt. 2, 388-89; Logan, 48-59; Ben S. Drake, "Captain Quirk's Marvelous Heroism," CV, V (1897), 16-17; U. S. Congress, *Case of George St. Leger Grenfel,* 269; Cist, 88; Young, 244.

VIII CHRISTMAS RAID

Morgan's Wedding: Leeland Hathaway Papers, University of Kentucky Library; Simmons, 78; Duke, *History,* 322; Holland, 176.

Preparations for the Christmas Raid: USWD-CR, 2nd Kentucky Cavalry, National Archives; OR, Ser.I, XX, Pt. 2, 178-79, 191, 214, 233, 462; Cist, 85; Young, 416-24; Johnson, 108; James B. McCreary, "Journal of My Soldier Life," KSHS, *Register,* XXXIII, 109-117; U. S. Congress, *Case of George St. Leger Grenfel,* 599; CV, XXIII (1915), 439.

March to Glasgow: Logan, 62; Young, 424; Berry, 107; McCreary, *op. cit.,* 109-17.

Adventures of Quirk's Scouts: John A. Wyeth, "Captain Quirk," CV, V (1897), 17; Ben S. Drake, "Marvelous Heroism of Tom Quirk," CV, V (1897), 16; Logan, 63-69; Young, 424.

Bridge at Bacon Creek: OR, Ser.I, XX, Pt. 1, 153-55; Pt. 2, 243; Plum, I, 303; Logan, 68-69; Young, 424.

Fight at Elizabethtown: OR, Ser.I, XX, Pt. 1, 153-57; McCreary, *op, cit.,* 109-117.

The Trestles at Muldraugh's Hill: OR, Ser.I, XX, Pt. 1, 153-56; Ser.II, V, 414; Henry L. Stone, Letters of December 29, 1862 and January 1, 1863, Stone Family Papers, KSHS; Logan, 72.

Wounding of Basil Duke: OR, Ser.I, XX, Pt. 1, 133-35, 139, 157; Pt. 2, 291-96; Johnson, 123, 388; Logan, 72; Drake, *op. cit.*, 16; Wyeth, *op. cit.*, 17; J. W. Cunningham, "Memories of Morgan's Christmas Raid," CV (XVII), 1909, 79-80; Young, 439; Tarrant, 180; McCreary, *op. cit.*, 109-17.

March Around Lebanon: OR, Ser.I, XX, Pt. 1, 153, 157; Johnson, 134, Logan, 72-75; McCreary, *op. cit.*, 109-17; Young, 443-44.

Lieutenant Eastin's Adventure: George B. Eastin, "The Killing of Colonel Dennis J. Halisey," SHSP, X (1882), 513-18; Castleman, 109-10; OR, Ser.I, XX, Pt. 1, 136, 144, 154, 157-58; Berry, 200; Tarrant, 180.

Return to Tennessee: OR, Ser.I, XX, Pt. 1, 157-58; Pt. 2, 243, 273, 282, 503; Logan, 75-80; McCreary, *op. cit.*, 109-17; Young, 448; *Lexington Herald*, April 21, 1907; Henry L. Stone, Letter of January 1, 1863, Stone Family Papers, KSHS.

IX Winter of Discontent

The Guerrilla Controversy: OR, Ser.I, XX, Pt. 2, 142-43, 181, 504; Bickham, 101; Johnson, 388; Fitzgerald Ross, "A Visit to the Cities and Camps of the Confederate States," *Blackwood's Magazine*, XCVII (1865), 163; Castleman, 109.

Woodbury and the Death of John Hutchinson: USWD-CR, 2nd Kentucky Cavalry, National Archives; OR, Ser.I, XXIII, Pt. 1, 18; Duke, *History*, 346-49; Castleman, 102-105; Logan, 81; Ben S. Drake, "Captain Quirk's Marvelous Heroism," CV, V (1897), 16-17; James B. Mc-Creary, "Journal of My Soldier Life," KSHS, *Register*, XXXIII (1935), 103.

Camp Life in Winter: USWD-CR, Personal Papers of James W. Bowles, National Archives; OR, Ser.I, XXIII, Pt. 2, 81; "James W. Bowles," CV, XXIX (1921), 346; McCreary, *op. cit.*, 103, 117, 192; U. S. Congress, *Case of George St. Leger Grenfel*, 35; Henry L. Stone, Letter of February 13, 1863, Stone Family Papers, KSHS; Duke, *History*, 347; Ross, *op. cit.*, XCVI (1864), 653; XCVII (1865), 45; Fuller and Steuart, 119; H. V Redfield, "Characteristics of the Armies," *Annals of the War*, 361; Bickham, 160; Morgan, 79; Mosgrove, 61-62.

Incident of the Faro Dealer: Duke, *Reminiscences*, 164, 381-82.

Springtime and Skirmishes: OR, Ser.I, XXIII, Pt. 1, 65, 214; Duke, *Reminiscences*, 274-75; Leeland Hathaway Papers, University of Kentucky Library; McCreary, *op. cit.*, 192; Castleman, 106-108; Holland, 198-201; Beatty, 182.

Morgan's Narrow Escape: OR, Ser.I, XXIII, Pt. 1, 274; Holland, 206, 212-13; Johnson, 140; Duke, *Reminiscences*, 269.

Decline of the Cavalry: OR, Ser.I, XXIII, Pt. 2, 737; Duke, *History*, 396-406; *Spirit of the Times*, August 1863; Francis Morris, "Cavalry Horses in America," U. S. Commissioner of Agriculture, Report, 1863, 159-175; S. B. Buckley, Letter, *Country Gentleman*, XXII (July 2, 1863), 12; T. T. Munford, "Reminiscences of Cavalry Operations," SHSP, XII (1884), 342-50; Fitzgerald Ross, "A Month's Visit to the Confederate Headquarters," *Blackwood's Magazine*, XCIII (1863), 17.

Planning for Something Big: USWD-CR, 2nd Kentucky Cavalry, National Archives; OR, Ser.I, XXIII, Pt. 2, 118, 622; Moore, VIII, 57; Harwell, 78; Edward M. Coffman, "The Civil War Career of Thomas H. Hines," 431; Thomas Henry Hines Papers, University of Kentucky Library; Swiggett, 121.

X THE GREAT RAID BEGINS

Preliminaries to the Invasion: USWD-CR, 2nd Kentucky Cavalry, National Archives; OR, Ser.I, XXIII, Pt. 1, 633-34, 679-81; Pt. 2, 469, 507, 622, 941-44; Duke, *History*, 406-13; James B. McCreary, "Journal of My Soldier Life," KSHS, *Register*, XXXIII (1935), 197; Logan, 114; Basil Duke, "Morgan's Raid," *Annals of the War*, 241; Young, 367; George D. Mosgrove, "Following Morgan's Plume," *New Orleans Picayune*, October 13, 1907; William E. Wilson, "Thunderbolt of the Confederacy, or King of the Horse Thieves," *Indiana Magazine of History*, LIV (1958), 121-22.

Crossing the Cumberland River: OR, Ser.I, XXIII, Pt. 1, 633-34; 679-81; Henry L. Stone, Letter of June 30, 1863, Stone Family Papers, KSHS; Holland, 226; Swiggett, 129; Smith, 57; Logan, 115; Ben S. Drake, "Captain Quirk's Marvelous Heroism," CV, V (1897), 16-17; Simmons, 5; S. P. Cunningham, in *Richmond Enquirer*, August 1, 1863; Basil Duke, "Morgan's Raid," *op. cit.*, 241; J. E. McGowan, "Morgan's Indiana and Ohio Raid," *Annals of the War*, 752; Young, 369.

Fight at Green River Bridge: OR, Ser.I, XXIII, Pt. 1, 645-47, 681-88; McCreary, *op. cit.*, 197; J. T. Tucker, "Fifty Exposed as the 'Six Hundred,'" CV, VII (1899), 364; Young, 372; Benson J. Lossing, *Pictorial History of the Civil War*, III, 92; James B. Benedict, Jr., "General John Hunt Morgan; the Great Indiana-Ohio Raid," FCHQ, XXXI (1957), 150.

Fight at Lebanon: OR, Ser.I, XXIII, Pt. 1, 647-51, 689-93; Ser.II, VI, 375; Duke, *History*, 425-28; *Central Kentuckian*, July 9, 1863; Holland, 229; Senour, 111; William J. Davis, Letter of July 22, 1863, Filson Club; *Chicago Tribune*, July 16, 1863; Logan, 119; S. P. Cunningham, *op. cit.*; Young, 367; *Marion Falcon* (Lebanon, Ky.), March 21, 1934;

W. T. Kott, "History of Marion County, Kentucky," Manuscript, Filson Club; B. G. Slaughter, "Roll of Quirk's Scouts," KSHS, *Register*, II (1904), 35-36; *Cincinnati Enquirer*, July 6, 1863.

Bardstown and Shepherdsville: OR, Ser.I, XXIII, Pt. 1, 652-54, 658-59, 691-704; Plum, II, 55-58, 110-11; Holland, 231; W. J. Davis, *op. cit.;* Johnson, 144; S. P. Cunningham, *op. cit.;* George D. Mosgrove, *op. cit.;* Basil W. Duke, "The Raid," *Century Magazine*, XLI (1891), 408.

Action at Brandenburg: OR, Ser.I, XXIII, Pt. 1, 398, 632, 640, 659, 705-10; Duke, *History*, 430-31; Louis B. Ewbank, "Morgan's Raid in Indiana," Indiana Historical Society, *Publications*, VII, No. 2, n.d., 139-156; *Cincinnati Gazette*, as quoted in Simmons, 6; Basil Duke, "Morgan's Raid," *op. cit.*, 241; *Cincinnati Enquirer*, July 10, 1863.

Crossing the Ohio River: OR, Ser.I, XXIII, Pt. 1, 659, 711-12; Duke, *History*, 432-34; Theodore F. Allen, "In Pursuit of John Morgan," Military Order of the Loyal Legion, Ohio Commandery, *Sketches of War History*, V, 223-42; Johnson, 145; Duke, *Reminiscences*, 276-77; Theodore F. Allen, "John Morgan Raid in Ohio," Ohio Archaeological and Historical Society, *Quarterly*, XVII (1908), 50-59; Ewbank, *op. cit.*, 159; *Chicago Tribune*, July 16, 1863; Logan, 126; Henry L. Stone, Letter of July 8, 1863, Stone Family Papers, KSHS; Henry L. Stone, "Morgan's Men," CV, XIV (1906), 188-92; S. P. Cunningham, *op. cit.; Cincinnati Enquirer*, July 13, 1863.

March to Corydon: OR, Ser.I, XXIII, Pt. 1, 313, 640, 659, 712-18; Arville L. Funk, "The Battle of Corydon," *Indiana Magazine of History*, LIV (1958), 131-40; Holland, 234; Johnson, 144; Ewbank, *op. cit.*, 151; Margrette Boyer, "Morgan's Raid in Indiana," *Indiana Magazine of History*, VIII (1912), 154; McCreary, *op. cit.*, 197; Logan, 101-11; 128-29; Tarrant, 187; Slaughter, *op. cit.*, 35-36; Benedict, *op. cit.*, 152; Basil W. Duke, "The Raid," *op. cit.*, 410.

March to Salem: OR, Ser.I, XXIII, Pt. 1, 659, 719-26; Ser.II, V, 363-67; *Cincinnati Enquirer*, July 11, 1863; Thomas M. Coombs, Letter, KSHS, *Register*, XLVI (1948), 398; Duke, *History*, 435-37; Allen, "In Pursuit of John Morgan," *op. cit.*, 234-35; Smith, 62; Ewbank, *op. cit.*, 158-64; Boyer, *op. cit.*, 155-56; *Indianapolis Sentinel*, July 10, 1863.

Turnabout at Vernon: OR, Ser.I, XXIII, Pt. 1, 727-35; Ewbank, *op. cit.*, 164-67; Logan, 136; Basil W. Duke, "The Raid," *op. cit.*, 410.

On to Ohio: OR, Ser.I, XXIII, Pt. 1, 659, 736-40; Duke, *History*, 438-39; Swiggett, 140; Ewbank, *op. cit.*, 169-73; Boyer, *op. cit.*, 156-58; McCreary, *op. cit.*, 197; S. P. Cunningham, *op. cit.;* Young, 380; *Cincinnati Enquirer*, July 16, 1863; *New York Tribune*, July 13, 1863.

Episode at Twelve Mile Island: OR, Ser.I, XXIII, Pt. 1, 729-41; *Corydon*

Weekly Democrat, July 14, 1863; Castleman, 100; Josiah B. Gathright narrative, in Johnson, 438; W. J. Davis, Letters, July 22, 1863 and July 28, 1864, Filson Club; Ewbank, *op. cit.*, 168.

XI Farthest Point North

Invasion of Ohio: OR, Ser.I, XXIII, Pt. 1, 741-46; John S. Still, "Blitzkrieg, 1863: Morgan's Raid and Rout," *Civil War History*, III (1957), 291-306; *Cincinnati Gazette*, July 20, 1863; Louis B. Ewbank, "Morgan's Raid in Indiana," Indiana Historical Society, *Publications*, VII, No. 2, n.d., 173-77; Margrette Boyer, "Morgan's Raid in Indiana," *Indiana Magazine of History*, VIII (1912), 156-59; James B. McCreary, "Journal of My Soldier Life," KSHS, *Register*, XXIII (1935), 199; Young, 380; William E. Wilson, "Thunderbolt of the Confederacy, or King of the Horse Thieves," *Indiana Magazine of History*, LIV (1958), 119-30.

March Around Cincinnati: OR, Ser.I, XXIII, Pt. 1, 747-55; Ser.II, V, 363-67; James B. Benedict, "General John Hunt Morgan, the Great Indiana-Ohio Raid," FCHQ, XXXI (1957), 154, 157; Whitelaw Reid, I, 144; Theodore F. Allen, "In Pursuit of John Morgan," Military Order of the Loyal Legion, Ohio Commandery, *Sketches of War History*, V, 223-42; Holland, 218; Senour, 121, 256-61; Johnson, 68, 147; Middleton Robertson, "Recollections of Morgan's Raid," *Indiana Magazine of History*, XXXIV (1938), 191; Ewbank, *op. cit.*, 173; Tarrant, 177; Henry L. Stone, "Reminiscences of Morgan's Men," *Southern Bivouac*, I (1885), 406-14; Basil W. Duke, "The Raid," *Century Magazine*, XLI, 1891, 409-10; Mary Cone, "Morgan's Raid," *Magazine of Western History*, IV (1886), 755; Logan, 140; Young, 382; Castleman, 93-94; Smith, 70; *Indianapolis Sentinel*, July 10, 1863; S. P. Cunningham, in *Richmond Enquirer*, August 1, 1863; Thomas M. Coombs, Letters, KSHS, *Register*, XL (1948), 398.

Williamsburg to Pomeroy: OR, Ser.I, XXIII, Pt. 1, 659-60, 662, 666, 755-68; Castleman, 233; Swiggett, 143-45; McCreary, *op. cit.*, 199; Logan, 141; Young, 382; George D. Mosgrove, "Following Morgan's Plume," *New Orleans Picayune*, October 13, 1907; Cone, *op. cit.*, 760; Still, *op. cit.*, 297-98; *Cincinnati Enquirer*, July 15, 1863; *Cincinnati Gazette*, July 16, 17, 18, 1863; Benedict, *op. cit.*, 155; Smith, 70; J. E. McGowan, "Morgan's Indiana and Ohio Raid," *Annals of the War*, 761.

Pomeroy to Buffington: OR, Ser.I, XXIII, Pt. 1, 656, 663, 666, 672, 769-75; Duke, *History*, 445-48; Johnson, 147; Smith, 71; McCreary, *op. cit.*,

199; Logan, 141-45; S. P. Cunningham, *op. cit.;* George D. Mosgrove, *op. cit.;* Basil W. Duke, "The Raid," *op. cit.,* 411; Cone, *op. cit.,* 761; Benedict, *op. cit.,* 157.

Fight at Buffington Island: USWD-CR, Camp Douglas, Chicago, Record of Prisoners of War, 2nd Kentucky Cavalry, National Archives; OR, Ser.I, XXIII, Pt. 1, 640-41, 657-58, 660-62, 664, 666, 669-72, 678, 776-79; Duke, *History,* 448-53; *New York Tribune,* July 24, 1863; Basil W. Duke, "The Raid," *op. cit.,* 411; Allen, *op. cit.,* 238; Johnson, 361; Smith, 72; Beatty, 223; *Cincinnati Gazette,* July 20, 1863; S. P. Cunningham, *op. cit.;* Basil Duke, "Morgan's Raid," *Annals of the War,* 255; McGowan, *op. cit.,* 761-63.

The Raid Continues: OR, Ser.I, XXIII, Pt. 1, 673-74, 677-78, 780-803; Duke, *Reminiscences,* 292-93; Duke, *History,* 453-56; Johnson, 148-49; Swiggett, 150; Smith, 78; George A. Ellsworth obituary, *Confederate Veteran,* VIII (1900), 35-36; *Cincinnati Gazette,* July 20, 23, 1863; S. P. Cunningham, *op. cit.;* Coombs, *op. cit.,* 404-09; Still, *op. cit.,* 300; Benedict, *op. cit.,* 156, 158-59.

Surrender at Farthest Point North: USWD-CR, Camp Douglas, Chicago, Record of Prisoners of War, 2nd Kentucky Cavalry, National Archives; OR, Ser.I, XXIII, Pt. 1, 637-38, 641-45, 667-69, 674-76, 804-15; Orlando B. Wilcox, "The Capture," *Century Magazine,* XLI (1891), 412-17; George W. Rue, "Celebration of the Surrender of General John H. Morgan," Ohio Archaeological and Historical Society, *Quarterly,* XX (1911), 368-75; Duke, *History,* 456-58; Swiggett, 152; Smith, 78; Tarrant, 185-87; *Cleveland Herald,* July 27, 1863; Frank Owen narrative, in Johnson, 391; Hambleton Tapp, "Incidents in the Life of Frank Wolford," FCHQ, X, 1936, 85-90.

Duke in Cincinnati: Smith, 77; *Cincinnati Gazette,* July 21, 1863; *Cleveland Herald,* July 27, 1863; *New York Post,* as reprinted in Simmons, 60-64; *Cincinnati Enquirer,* July 24, 1863.

Results of the Raid: OR, Ser.I, XXIII, Pt. 1, 815-16; Still, *op. cit.,* 304-05; William E. Wilson, *op. cit.,* 120; *Cincinnati Enquirer,* November 29, 1863; *New York Tribune,* August 8, 1863.

XII THE CAPTIVES

To Cincinnati and Camp Morton: Henry L. Stone, Letters of July 21 and August 15, 1863, Stone Family Papers, KSHS; Henry L. Stone, "Reminiscences of Morgan's Men," *Southern Bivouac,* I (1885), 406-14; Duke, *Reminiscences,* 295; Duke, *History,* 463; Thomas D. Henry,

"Treatment of Prisoners During the War Between the States," SHSP, I (1876), 276; W. Williams narrative, in Johnson, 392.

Camp Douglas: USWD-CR, Camp Douglas, Chicago, Record of Prisoners of War, 2nd Kentucky Cavalry, National Archives; OR, Ser.II, IV, 193; V, 214, 345, 400, 409; VI, 371-74, 417, 434-35, 463, 633-34, 737; Henry L. Stone, Letters of August 19, September 7, October 9 and 14, Stone Family Papers, KSHS; Henry L. Stone, "Reminiscences of Morgan's Men," *op. cit.*, 406-14; Henry L. Stone, "Morgan's Men Escape from Prison," CV, XIV (1906), 188-92; Holland, 252; Johnson, 160; Miller, VII, "Prisons and Hospitals," 68-112.

Columbus Penitentiary: OR, Ser.II, VI, 734; Thomas Henry Hines, Papers, University of Kentucky Library; Duke, *History*, 468-79; Holland, 252; Johnson, 365-66; Swiggett, 154; Smith, 82; Simmons, 64-78; James B. McCreary, "Journal of My Soldier Life," KSHS, *Register*, XXXIII (1935), 303.

Escape of Morgan and His Officers: OR, Ser.II, VI, 495-96, 588, 606, 671; Thomas Henry Hines Papers, University of Kentucky Library; Castleman, 113-18; *Cincinnati Gazette*, November 28, 1863; Holland, 271-83; Duke, *History*, 480-89; Swiggett, 167; Edward M. Coffman, "The Civil War Career of Thomas H. Hines," 49; Moore, VIII, 318-21; Thomas H. Hines, "Escape from Prison," *Southern Bivouac*, I (1885), 49, 59; Thomas H. Hines, "The Escape," *Century Magazine*, XLI (1891), 417-25; T. W. Bullitt, "More of General Morgan's Escape," *Southern Bivouac*, I (1885), 116-19.

XIII THE SURVIVORS

From the Ohio to Virginia: Johnson, 150; S. P. Cunningham in *Richmond Enquirer*, August 1, 1863; Holland, 268.

Rendezvous at Morristown: OR, Ser.I, XXX, Pt. 4, 554; Johnson, 108, 151-55; Josiah B. Gathright narrative, in Johnson, 438-46; A. C. Quisenberry, "History of Morgan's Men," KSHS, *Register*, XV (1917), 42.

Chickamauga: OR, Ser.I, XXX, Pt. 2, 20, 232, 523-30; Johnson, 156-58; Carl Sager, "A Boy in the Confederate Army," CV, XXVI (1928), 374-76; Dyer, 120; Gathright, *op. cit.*, 447-53; *Cincinnati Commercial*, September 28, 1863.

Missionary Ridge: Johnson, 147; Gathright, *op. cit.*, 456; Fitzgerald Ross, "A Visit to the Cities and Camps of the Confederate States," *Blackwood's Magazine*, XCVII (1865), 44-46; Sager, *op. cit.*, 374-76; Dyer, 135.

Gathright Meets Morgan: Gathright, *op. cit.,* 459-61; Edward M. Coffman, "The Civil War Career of Thomas H. Hines," 54.

Morgan in Richmond: OR, Ser.I, XXIII, Pt. 2, 615, 619, 621; XXXIII, 812; Holland, 265, 289-92, 304; Gorgas, 76; *Richmond Whig,* January 14, 1864.

Winter of 1863-64: OR, Ser.I, XXXII, Pt. 2, 590, 624, 658; *Richmond Dispatch,* January 13, 1864; Swiggett, 199-204; *Richmond Enquirer,* January 15, 1864; Moore, VIII, 321; Gathright, *op. cit.,* 462-65.

Morgan's New Command: USWD-CR, 2nd Kentucky Cavalry, National Archives; OR, Ser.I, XXXII, Pt. 2, 141, 602, 811-12, Pt. 3, 584, 803, 842, 855; XXXVII, Pt. 1, 41-49, 709, 740; Johnson, 158-59; Holland, 310-16; John D. Fields narrative, in Johnson, 293-94; Smith, 10, 36, 184; Fuller and Steuart, 120; Mosgrove, 97, 129, 134-36.

March Out for Kentucky: USWD-CR, 2nd Kentucky Cavalry, National Archives; OR, Ser.I, XXIX, Pt. 1, 64-65; Smith, 104; Castleman, 123; Fields, *op. cit.,* 294-95; Mosgrove, 137.

Mt. Sterling: OR, Ser.I, XXXIX, Pt. 1, 14, 19, 20-22, 44-45, 66-69; LII, Pt. 2, 472; Henry L. Stone, "Reminiscences of Morgan's Men," *Southern Bivouac,* I (1885), 406-14; Holland, 321-23; Mosgrove, 138-40.

Lexington: OR, Ser.I, XXXIX, Pt. 1, 68-69; Castleman, 124-28; Senour, 350-51; Hervey, II, 345; Mosgrove, 145-49.

Cynthiana: OR, Ser.I, XXXIX, Pt. 1, 19; G. D. Ewing, Morgan's Last Raid Into Kentucky," CV, XXI (1923), 254-56; Mosgrove, 152-63; Sager, *op. cit.,* 374-76; Smith, 110-13; Senour, 348-54, 368-70, 376-77.

Return to Abingdon: USWD-CR, 2nd Kentucky Cavalry, National Archives; OR, Ser.I, XXXVII, Pt. 2, 593, 601; XXXIX, Pt. 2, 236, 723, 736, 741; Mosgrove, 165, 166; Holland, 330; Smith, 113; Duke, *History,* 528-29; Swiggett, 234.

Affair of the Mt. Sterling Bank: OR, Ser.I, XXXIX, Pt. 1, 73-84; Pt. 2, 750; XLIII, Pt. 1, 1010-11; Castleman, 123; Holland, 334-36; Duke, *History,* 530-31; Mosgrove, 167.

Morgan's Death: OR, Ser.I, XXXIX, Pt. 1, 488-97; Smith, 126-89; Holland, 198, 337-48; *Richmond Whig,* October 1, 1864; *Richmond Dispatch,* September 11, 1864; Senour, 384-89; Mosgrove, 168-81; Ridley, 353-62; George W. Hunt, *Philadelphia Weekly Times,* May 9, 1885; Logan, 35; H. V. Redfield, "Death of Morgan," *Annals of the War,* 618; J. W. Scully, "Death of General John Morgan," SHSP, XXXI (1903), 125-28; J. J. McAfee, "General John H. Morgan, His Capture and Death," *Southern Bivouac,* I (1885), 149-56; D. Howard Smith, "The Killing of John Hunt Morgan," *Southern Bivouac,* I (1885), 447-51.

XIV EPISODE OF THE CLOAK-AND-SWORD

Captain Hines Goes to Canada: OR, Ser.I, XLV, Pt. 1, 1077-79; Ser.II, VIII, 688; Thomas Henry Hines Papers, University of Kentucky Library; Castleman, 150-60; Henry L. Stone, Letter of December 5, 1863, Stone Family Papers, KSHS; Edward M. Coffman, "Civil War Career of Thomas Henry Hines," 58-85; Obituary of George A. Ellsworth, CV, VIII (1900), 35-36; Milford Overley, "Old St. Leger," CV, XIII (1905), 80-81; U. S. Congress, *Case of George St. Leger Grenfel*, 63, 78, 82, 172, 599, 639; Horan, 71-83, 122-31.

Camp Douglas, Early 1864: USWD-CR, Camp Douglas, Chicago, Record of Prisoners of War, 2nd Kentucky Cavalry, National Archives; OR, Ser.II, VI, 778-98, 848-50, 908-09; VII, 102, 143, 187, 496, 595, 703; W. Williams narrative, in Johnson, 393-94; T. B. Clore narrative, in Johnson, 490-10; J. M. Lynn narrative, in Johnson, 411-12; Miller, VII, "Prisons and Hospitals," 114; J. William Jones, "Treatment of Prisoners During the War Between the States," SHSP, I (1876), 240; Thomas D. Henry, Deposition, SHSP, I (1876), 276-78; T. M. Page, "The Prisoners of War," CV, VIII (1900), 62-64; U. S. Congress, *op. cit.*, 161, 183.

Hines Tries Again: OR, Ser.I, XLV, Pt. 1, 1077-79; Thomas Henry Hines Papers, University of Kentucky Library; Coffman, *op. cit.*, 83; Henry G. Damon, "A Florida Boy's Experiences in Prison and Escaping," SHSP, XII (1884), 396-402; *Chicago Tribune*, October-December 1864; Castleman, 172-78; Horan, 137-47, 181-84.

Camp Douglas, Late 1864: OR, Ser.II, VII, 954-55, 1067, 1083, 1104; W. Williams, *op. cit.*, 392-93; T. B. Clore, *op. cit.*, 408-409; Thomas D. Henry, *op. cit.*, 278; H. D. Foote, "The Dog That 'Was Eat,'" CV, VIII (1900), 351; Page, *op. cit.*, 62-64; *Chicago Tribune*, October 15 and 16, 1864.

Shanks Betrays His Comrades: OR, Ser.I, XLV, Pt. 1, 1082, Ser.II, VII, 730; VIII, 502-03, 684-87, 724-25, 928; Thomas Henry Hines Papers, University of Kentucky Library; Castleman, 192-95; Horan, 125-27, 186-98; Duke, *Reminiscences,* 154; Overley, *op. cit.*, 80-81; Henry L. Stone, "Morgan's Men Escape from Prison," CV, XIV (1906), 188-92 St. Leger Grenfell, Letter to Henry L. Stone, January 13, 1868, Stone Family Papers, KSHS; *Chicago Tribune*, November 6, 7, and 8, 1864.

End of the Canadian Adventure: OR, Ser.I, XLIII, Pt. 2, 934; Ser.II, VIII, 415, 428; Horan, 166-180, 208-23; *New York Herald*, November 27, 1864.

Camp Douglas, Winter and Spring, 1864-1865: USWD-CR, Camp Douglas, Chicago, Record of Prisoners of War, 2nd Kentucky Cavalry, National Archives; OR, Ser.II, VII, 1187, 1243; VIII, 76, 337, 986; P. H. Prince, "Hardships in Camp Douglas," CV, XV (1907), 565-66; J. W. Cook, "Villainous 'Inspectors' at Camp Douglas," CV, XVI (1908), 406; J. S. Rosamond, "In Camp Douglas Prison," CV, XVI (1908), 421; W. Williams, *op. cit.*, 393-94; T. B. Clore, *op. cit.*, 409; J. M. Lynn, *op. cit.*, 411; Miller, *op. cit.*, 122; J. W. Jones, *op. cit.*, 240; T. D. Henry, *op. cit.*, 277-79; *Chicago Tribune*, October 6 and 10, December 1 and 12, 1864; Robert Ould, "The Exchange of Prisoners," *Annals of the War*, 34-38.

XV No More Bugles

Duke Returns: Henry L. Stone, Letter of August 21, 1864, Stone Family Papers, KSHS; Duke, *Reminiscences*, 368-75; OR, Ser.I, XXV, Pt. 2, 147-48.

Last Fighting in Virginia: USWD-CR, 2nd Kentucky Cavalry, National Archives; OR, Ser.I, XXXIX, Pt. 1, 889, 892-93, 897, Pt. 3, 778-820, 827; XLIII, Pt. 2, 864-66; XLV, Pt. 1, 36, 750, 813, 1208; XLIX, Pt. 1, 982, 999-1001, 1021; Pt. 2, 414; Mosgrove, 191, 197, 201, 208-09, 263; A. C. Quisenberry, "History of Morgan's Men," KSHS, *Register, XV* (1917), 42; Dyer, 276; Duke, *Reminiscences*, 191-92, 380; William J. Davis Papers, Filson Club; Henry L. Stone, Letter of March 4, 1865, Stone Family Papers, KSHS: Duke, *History*, 566-70; Evans, IX, 191.

Monroe, Hathaway, Messick and Mrs. Jefferson Davis: Winder Monroe, Personal Papers, USWD-CR, 2nd Kentucky Cavalry, National Archives; CV, IV (1896), 325; Leeland Hathaway Papers, University of Kentucky Library; Mattie Wheeler, "Journal," edited by Frances L. S. Dugan, FCHQ, XXIX (1955), 143; Ed Porter Thompson, 447; Burton N. Harrison, "The Capture of Jefferson Davis," *Century Magazine*, XXVII (1883), 130-39; Hanna, 34; James H. Wilson, "How Jefferson Davis Was Overtaken," *Annals of the War*, 562-73; W. T. Walthall, "True Story of the Capture of Jefferson Davis," SHSP, V (1878), 97-118; Winston, 240.

Duke's Brigade and President Jefferson Davis: Harrison, *op. cit.*, 136; Otis Ashmore, "Story of the Confederate Treasury," *Georgia Historical Quarterly*, II (1918), 123-36; OR, Ser.I, XLVII, Pt. 3, 816, 847; XLIX, Pt. 1, 547-551; Pt. 2, 556, 628-30; Dyer, 291-93; Duke, *History*, 570-77; M. H. Clark, "The Last Days of the Confederate Treasury and What Became of Its Specie," SHSP, IX (1881), 542-56; Winston, 240; Quisenberry, *op. cit.*, 42; Pollard, 519-22; Hanna, 5, 31-34, 190-92; William H. Parker, "The Gold and Silver in the Confederate States

Treasury," SHSP, XXI, 309; *Richmond Dispatch*, July 16, 1892; Walthall, *op. cit.*, 107-08; Wilson, *op. cit.*, 562.

Georgia to Fort McHenry to Kentucky: Leeland Hathaway Papers, University of Kentucky Library; Clark, *op. cit.*, 553; William Preston Johnston, Letter of July 14, 1877, SHSP, V (1878), 118-23; Wilson, *op. cit.*, 576; OR, Ser.I, XLIX, Pt. 1, 522-23, 535-37; FCHQ, XIV (1940), 61; Walthall, *op. cit.*, 108-16; Harrison, *op. cit.*, 144; Winston, 240; Pollard, 522; Hanna, 34; Ben Drake, "Captain Quirk's Marvelous Heroism," CV, V (1897), 16-17; Morgan, 147-50; Duke, *History*, 578.

Index

343